Have you got questions?

We've got answers:

Get Answers—Get Osborne

ANY QUESTIONS?

QUICKEN 3 FOR WINDOWS MADE EASY

*David Campbell, CPA
and Mary Campbell*

Osborne **McGraw-Hill**

Berkeley New York St. Louis San Francisco
Auckland Bogotá Hamburg London Madrid
Mexico City Milan Montreal New Delhi Panama City
Paris São Paulo Singapore Sydney
Tokyo Toronto

Osborne **McGraw-Hill**
2600 Tenth Street
Berkeley, California 94710
U.S.A.

For information on translations or book distributors outside of the U.S.A.,
please write to Osborne **McGraw-Hill** at the above address.

Quicken 3 for Windows Made Easy

1234567890 DOC 9987654

ISBN 0-07-881972-5

CONTENTS AT A GLANCE

CONTENTS

ACKNOWLEDGMENTS

We wish to thank the many individuals at Osborne/McGraw-Hill and Intuit for their help with this project. Special thanks are due to Acquisitions Editor Bill Pollock, Project Editor Claire Splan, Associate Editors Bob Myren and Emily Rader, Copy Editors Laura Sackerman and Kimberly Torgerson, and Proofreader K.D. Sullivan for helping us meet an impossible time schedule. Special thanks also go to Elizabeth Reinhardt for all her work on this book.

INTRODUCTION

Whether you are trying to manage your personal finances or those of your business, Quicken for Windows can end your financial hassles. The package contains all the features necessary to organize your finances, yet because the features are jargon-free, you can focus on your financial needs without becoming an accountant or a financial planner.

If you use the program for your personal finances, you will find that you can easily determine your financial worth or create a report with the information you need for your tax forms. You can also create budget reports or a list of all your cash, check, or credit card transactions. Everything you do will be with the benefit of menus and easy-to-use quick-key combinations. You will soon wonder how you managed your finances without Quicken.

If you are trying to manage a small business *and* deal with all the financial issues, Quicken can make the task seem manageable. Whether your business is a part-time venture or employs several people, Quicken provides all the capabilities you need to look at your profit and loss picture, analyze your cash flows, or put together a budget. Quicken's ability to handle the recording of payroll information makes it easy to monitor what you owe for federal and state income tax withholding, FICA, and other payroll-related costs such as workers' compensation and federal and state unemployment taxes. Although it is not quite the same as having an accountant on your payroll, Quicken can make an otherwise unmanageable task possible.

About This Book

Quicken 3 for Windows Made Easy is designed to help you master Quicken's features so you can apply them to your financial situation. Even if you are a complete novice with the computer, you will find that you can learn from the step-by-step exercises in each chapter. As you work through the exercises you will feel as though you have a seasoned computer pro guiding you each step of the way.

This book offers more than just instruction for using Quicken's features. The exercises throughout the book are based on the authors' personal and business transactions. Although names of the banks, suppliers, and employees as well as dollar amounts have all been changed, all of what you read is based on factual illustrations much like the ones you will need to record your own transactions.

Throughout the book we have included financial tips. When we started our business 13 years ago, we had to invest a considerable amount of time in finding answers to even the simplest questions such as federal and state agency filing requirements. We have tried to include some of this information to simplify what you are facing if your business is new.

How This Book Is Organized

This book is divided into four parts to make it easy for you to focus on Quicken basics, personal applications, or business applications. Part I, Quick Start, includes the first five chapters. This section covers all the basic skills needed to use Quicken, even if you are a new Windows user. You will find that the exercises within these chapters will make you productive with Quicken in a short period of time.

Chapter 1 provides an overview of Quicken's features. You will see examples of reports and screens that you can use for your own applications. Chapter 2 introduces the Quicken account register in which all Quicken information is recorded. In this chapter you will learn the skills needed to record your basic financial transactions. Chapter 3 teaches you how to print several Quicken reports. You are shown how to select the correct printer settings to print all the reports you will be preparing in the book. Chapter 4 illustrates how easy it is to balance your checkbook (the account register) with Quicken. The exercise actually takes you through the reconciliation steps. Chapter 5, the conclusion of Part I of the book, teaches you how to create Quicken checks. With one set of entries on a check, you can print the check and update your records.

Part II focuses on personal financial applications of Quicken. It shows you how to create accounts for checking, savings, and investments. You will learn how to determine your net worth and find the information you need to complete your tax returns in this section. Chapter 6 shows you how to set up accounts and categories for personal finances. You will learn how to enter individual transactions as well as how to memorize them and automate their entry through transaction groups. Chapter 7 introduces the concept of budgeting with Quicken and discusses the Quicken 3 for Windows graphs. You will learn how to enter your estimates by category and how to monitor actual amounts against budgeted amounts. Chapter 8 illustrates how Quicken can be used to help complete your personal tax return. The example used demonstrates how to record your tax-related financial transactions and how Quicken can be used to summarize your tax-related transactions for the entire year. Chapter 9 shows you how to determine what you are worth financially. You will learn how to keep records on stocks and other investments and how to revalue these holdings to market values. Chapter 10, the final chapter in Part II, provides a look at additional Quicken reports and the customizing options that you can add.

Part III covers business applications of Quicken. You will learn how to use the package to manage the finances of your business, including record keeping for payroll. Chapter 11 shows you how to create a chart of accounts for your business. You will also look at entering transactions for basic business expenses and revenues. Chapter 12 teaches you about payroll entries with Quicken. It not only prints your employees' paychecks, but can handle all your other payroll-related record keeping. Chapter 13 teaches you how to prepare a business budget with Quicken. You can enter the same value for each month or budget a different amount for each month. The budget reports that Quicken produces can provide an early warning of potential budget trouble spots. Chapter 14 discusses the forms you will need to file for business taxes. It also covers the income statement (the profit and loss statement) that tells you whether or not your business is profitable. Chapter 15 continues with coverage of another important financial report, as you have an opportunity to prepare a balance sheet that shows your assets, liabilities, and your equity (or investment) in the business.

Part IV includes six different appendixes. These appendixes include a glossary of financial terms, advanced Quicken options for business, a guide to all of Quicken 3's customizing options, a discussion of sharing data with other programs, and information on Quicken Companion 2 for Windows.

New Features and Improvements in Quicken 3 for Windows

There are many new features in Quicken 3 for Windows which make it easier to record your financial information. The following is a list of some of the most important improvements:

1. Transaction scheduling with the financial calendar.
2. Display capability with the financial calendar that lets you see what transactions are coming up.

3. A financial planning graph to let you make projections for the next two years.

4. Six different views of your investment portfolios to give you a better picture of your holdings.

5. Expanded loan tracking and amortization capabilities to include features such as variable rates and balloon payments.

6. QuickFill features that do much of the entry work for you.

7. A Customize window that lets you modify any report.

8. Savings goal accounts that allow you to track your progress when saving toward a specific goal.

9. A refinance calculator to help you determine if refinancing should be pursued.

10. Tax-deferred investment accounts that allow you to monitor retirement savings.

11. Coaches to help you complete tasks.

12. Automatic backup features.

Conventions Used

There are step-by-step examples for you to follow throughout the book. Every entry that you need to type is shown in boldface to make these exercises easy to follow. In addition, the names of menus, windows, and reports are shown with the same capitalization followed by Quicken.

The names of keys such as F2, Enter, and Tab are shown in keycaps. In situations where two keys must be pressed at the same time, the keycaps are joined with a hyphen, as in Ctrl-Enter. If you use the keyboard rather than the mouse to make menu selections, you will find it convenient that this book underlines the letter needed to make each selection. In the pull-down menus, this underlined letter alone is sufficient to make your selection. In the menu at the top of the screens, you will need to use the Alt key in combination with the underlined letter to activate the menu and define your selection.

In cases where there are two ways to perform the same task, we have shown you the most efficient approach. As you learn more about Quicken, you can feel free to use whichever approach you prefer.

Quicken can provide the help you need to organize your personal finances. It will enable you to establish accounts for monitoring checking and savings accounts, credits cards, and investments. You will learn how to record and organize your financial information with Quicken's easy-to-use features. You will also learn how to prepare reports for taxes, budgeting, and computing your net worth.

P A R T

1

QUICK START

CHAPTER

1

AN OVERVIEW OF QUICKEN AND YOUR COMPUTER COMPONENTS

Quicken 3 for Windows is a powerful single-entry accounting system that allows both individuals and small businesses to track their financial resources. It is an integrated system in that it accumulates the information you enter and then provides a variety of methods to group and present that information.

Quicken is as easy to use as your current manual recording methods—but it is much faster. You will be surprised at how automatic using the package can become. It can memorize and record your regular transactions or write a check for your signature. It also organizes your information for you. This chapter's overview shows you the components of the package, examples of screens used to enter data, and the output that is produced. You do not need to sit at your computer to read and understand this chapter. Later chapters, however, give step-by-step directions for using Quicken's features, and you will want to follow along.

This chapter also introduces the various components of your computer system and their relationship to Quicken. You learn how Quicken uses your computer system, disk space, memory, and keyboard. Some important mouse techniques and keys are introduced through a series of visual examples. In later chapters you'll use what you learn here to enter and review Quicken data.

Quicken Overview

Quicken will assist you in meeting all your personal and business financial planning and reporting needs.

Quicken can handle all aspects of your financial management. Everything from initial recording and maintenance of information through organizing and reporting is handled by the package. Quicken provides features for recording your financial transactions easily. You can have a direct entry made to a register that is an accounts journal or have Quicken write a check and record the information automatically. Once your information has been recorded, you can have it presented in a variety of standard and customized reports.

Quicken 3 for Windows offers many exciting features that were not present in the earlier Windows version of the product. You will find that the redesigned screen makes it easy to use Windows graphical elements as you select from an Iconbar, a buttonbar, and other screen buttons. The Windows version now provides support for the features in the current Quicken 7 for DOS and can directly read these files, making it easy to make a transition from the DOS version to the Windows version of the product.

Recording Financial Transactions

If you are tired of entering financial transactions in a handwritten journal, you will appreciate the recording abilities of Quicken. Entries are always neat—even if you have corrected several errors in the recording process—and there is no need to worry about math errors, since the package does arithmetic for you.

Accounts are the major organizational units in Quicken. Each piece of information you record affects the balance in a Quicken account. You can establish checking and savings accounts for both personal and business purposes. In addition, you can establish credit card accounts, asset accounts (stocks and real estate), and liability accounts (mortgage and other payable loans). You can also transfer funds among these accounts with the Transfer feature—for example, moving funds from savings to checking account. You can store all of your accounts, in a single file on your computer. Later, as your experience grows, you might want to create additional accounts in your Quicken file.

Quicken helps you track your investment activities.

Quicken 3 for Windows supports specialized investment accounts to allow you to track a collection of investments. You can enter information for stocks, bonds, mutual funds, and other investments. You can use features like the one shown in Figure 1-1 for updating the market price of your investments and determining your gain or loss. Quicken 3 for Windows even handles lots, to let you identify which group of shares were sold if you have purchased several lots.

Quicken can record the details of your financial transactions, both money you earn (income) and what you spend it on (expenses). Quicken can differentiate income from a number of sources, such as salary and dividend income. It also supports entry of all types of expenses, from mortgage payments to clothing purchases. If you use Quicken to record business finances, you can keep track of freight charges, payroll costs, and so on. You can also customize the package to handle additional sources of income or expenses.

The information recorded on a financial event is called a *transaction*. Purchasing an asset such as a car, or making a payment for services or goods such as groceries, is considered a transaction. In Quicken, you must record your transactions in order to have the correct balance in your accounts. This

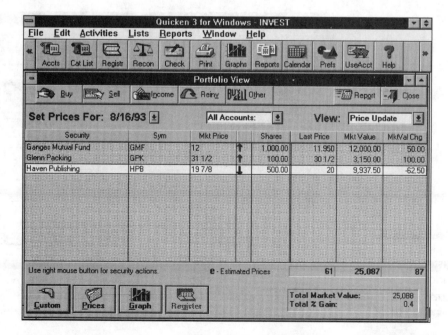

Updating the market price for your investments
Figure 1-1.

is accomplished by using a *register*, which is similar to a notebook or journal for record keeping. This serves the same purpose as your checkbook register, but with the capability of the Quicken system you can generate powerful reports that help you manage your finances. Thus, one of the major components of the system is the register that you establish for each of your accounts (checking, savings, and other assets and liabilities). Figure 1-2 provides an example of entries in the Quicken register using Quicken 3 for Windows, 1-Line Displa7y, available by clicking a button.

The account register is the center of your recording activities with Quicken.

With any checking account, reconciling the balance is tedious. Quicken reduces the time needed to reconcile the difference between the bank's balance and yours. Through the reconciliation process, you can accurately maintain the balance in your checking account and avoid the embarrassment of overdrawing your account. Quicken adjusts your register for service charges and interest earned on your checking account balance.

The ability to write and print checks is another interesting Quicken feature. Quicken is capable of automating all your check writing activities. Figure 1-3 shows a check entry form on the screen. You can acquire checking supplies from Intuit (the company that developed and markets Quicken) that allow you to write checks directly from the register and print them on your printer. While this option is particularly attractive for business activities, it can be useful for your personal checking account as well. But even if you write your checks by hand, you can still benefit from maintaining your transactions in Quicken.

Quicken register window

Figure 1-2.

Date	Num	Payee	Category	Payment		Clr	Deposit		Balance	
1/ 7/94	103	Small City Apartments	Housing	150	00	x			1,633	68
1/19/94	104	Small City Market	Groceries	43	00				1,590	68
1/25/94	105	Small City Phone Compar	Telephone	19	75				1,570	93
2/ 1/94		Service Charge	Bank Chrg	11	50	x			1,559	43
2/ 1/94		Interest Earned	Int Inc			x	1	03	1,560	46
2/ 1/94	EFT	Automatic Loan Payment	Auto:Loan	225	00	x			1,335	46
2/10/94	DEP	Dividend check	Div Income				25	00	1,360	46
2/13/94	Print	South Haven Print Suppl	Charity	58	75				1,301	71
2/13/94	Print	Holland Lumber	Home Rpair	120	00				1,181	71
2/13/94	Print	Fennville Library	Charity	100	00				1,081	71
3/ 8/94	Print	Keith Campbell	Gifts	25	00				1,056	71

Current Balance: 0.00
Ending Balance: 1,056.71

1

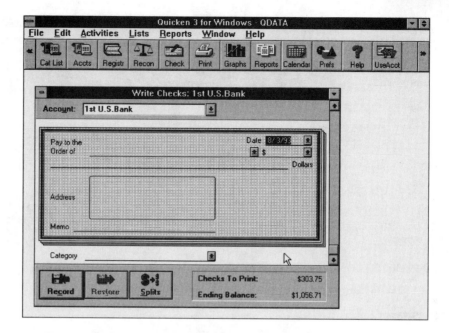

Write Checks
window
Figure 1-3.

Reports Provided by Quicken

*Quicken's
reports let
you monitor
your financial
condition
easily.*

The value of any accounting system lies in its ability to generate useful and informative reports that assist you in making financial decisions. With Quicken, you can prepare personal or home, business, and investment reports, and preview them on the screen before printing. You can choose to print an entire report after viewing it or you can print a range of pages with Quicken 3. You can access the detail behind a summary report while viewing the report with the QuickZoom feature. You can also customize a report displayed on your screen. Figure 1-4 shows an onscreen personal Cash Flow Report.

Home or Personal Reports
Besides providing you with a printout of your check register, Quicken generates other reports tailored for personal financial management. They will become valuable as the year progresses, showing how you have spent your money, as well as how much you have. You can create personal reports that summarize cash inflow and outflow, monitor your budget, summarize tax activities, and look at an overall measure of how well you are doing.

Business Reports
Quicken handles accounting transactions for businesses as well as for individuals. Because a small business has reporting needs that are different from an individual's, the package provides a separate list of standard

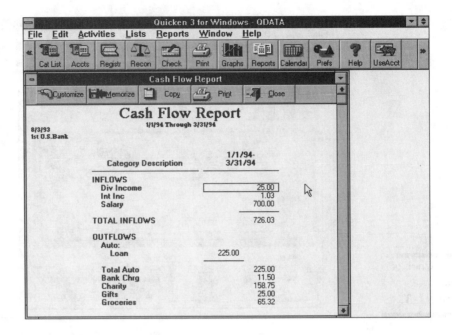

Cash Flow
Report screen
display
Figure 1-4.

business reports. Some of the business reports that you can create are a profit and loss report, an analysis of cash flow, a balance sheet, accounts payable and receivable reports, and a payroll report. Quicken also allows you to create customized reports for either home or business use.

Investment Reports

With Quicken's investment accounts, you can record and track all of your investments. The five standard investment reports provide information on portfolio value, investment performance, capital gains, investment income, and investment transactions.

Creating Graphs

Reports provide a summary or detailed record of transactions. They can be shared with others wanting to look at your financial status, but they do not provide a quick overview look at a financial situation. Graphs have always done a much better job at giving a picture of a situation with a quick look, and now Quicken 3 for Windows provides them. Quicken 3 for Windows provides four different graph types. You can further customize the appearance of these graphs by deciding what data to include. You can QuickZoom from a Quicken graph to a graph that shows more detail, and if this is still not sufficiently detailed, you can QuickZoom again to a report. You can use graphs to look at trends and other comparison information as

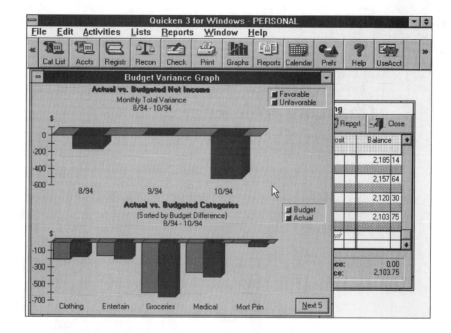

Budget
Variance
Graph
Figure 1-5.

shown in Figure 1-5, where you can see a comparison between budget and actual figures. Figure 1-6 provides another example with a Portfolio Value Trend by Security.

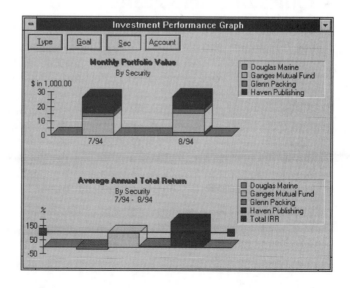

Investment
Performance
Graph
Figure 1-6.

Financial Planners

Quicken 3 for Windows provides a loan calculator and four more financial planners to let you perform what-if analysis in other areas such as retirement or college planning, investments, and refinancing.

Changing Preference Settings

Quicken provides features for customizing the package to meet your needs. This means you can make changes to fit your exact reporting requirements. It also means you can customize Quicken to work properly with the computer equipment you have selected. You can make these changes by selecting Preferences from the Iconbar, which will open a dialog box containing the icons you can choose from to make the changes you need, as shown here:

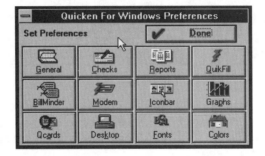

Quicken's Help Features

Quicken's onscreen help features make the package easy to use.

Onscreen help is at your fingertips. All you ever need to do is press F1 (Help) or click the Help button in the Iconbar. Quicken assesses the type of help you need and displays a superimposed help screen. Quicken's assessment of your situation is called *context-sensitive help*. Figure 1-7 shows the help screen that Quicken displays if you select the Help icon from the Investment Account Register window. The highlighted or colored text in Quicken is called *hypertext*. This text provides access to help on the highlighted topic when selected. You can select this text by moving the cursor to it with the Tab key and pressing Enter. In the section "The Keyboard, Mouse, and Screen Display" later in this chapter, you learn how to use a mouse to make selections.

If you are in another area of Quicken, the help presented might be very different. With a check on the screen, for example, Quicken assumes you need help with check writing and so provides that information. You can

1

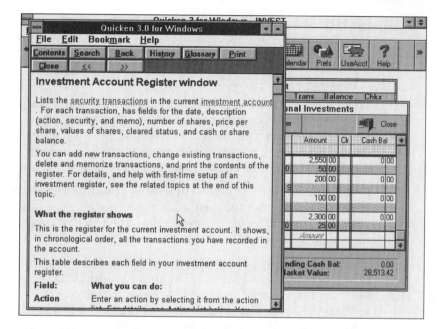

Help screen
for the
Investment
Account
Register
window
Figure 1-7.

click Contents from the Help window for direct access to the Help Index at any time. Quicken also provides tutorials to help you get started.

Quicken provides additional help through Qcards, which provide hints to walk you through the completion of some more complicated Quicken tasks like reconciling an account, creating a new account, and using the investment register. The default setting is to display Qcards for tasks on which they give guidance. To turn them off you must choose Preferences from the Edit menu and select Qcards. When the Qcards Preferences dialog box appears, you can select Qcards Off and then select OK to return to the Preferences dialog box. To complete your customization for Qcards, select the Done button.

Quicken and Your Computer System

You may have had your computer long enough to feel like a pro operating it, but if Quicken is your first computer package, read the rest of this chapter carefully. It will eliminate much of the confusion experienced by new users in attempting to figure out what is in memory, what is on disk, and exactly how their computer makes it possible for a package like Quicken to do so much work so quickly. If you are already knowledgeable about your system, you may want to skim the rest of the chapter just to see how Quicken works with the computer. It is assumed you are using Windows 3.0 or higher, and are running the DOS operating system on an IBM PC or compatible.

Memory

There are two kinds of memory in your computer: RAM and ROM. *ROM* is read-only memory—you cannot affect its contents so it's of little concern. *RAM* is random-access memory—temporary storage inside your computer. RAM contains the program you are running (for example Quicken, 1-2-3, or dBASE) and the data you are currently working with in the program.

If you lose the power to your machine, you lose the contents of RAM. This is why permanent storage media such as disks are an essential component of your computer system. If your data is saved to disk, you can always load it into memory again if it is lost in a power failure.

The amount of RAM in your system is determined by the computer you have purchased and any additional memory you may have added to the system. Memory is measured in kilobytes (K) or megabytes (MB), with 1K representing the space required to store approximately a thousand characters of information and 1MB representing the space required to store approximately one million characters. Some systems have as little as 2MB of memory, while others may have 10MB or even 32MB of memory capacity. Both Windows and Quicken require a system with at least 2MB in order to run the programs. The amount of memory you have determines the number of other Windows applications you can run and the performance of your system. A system with 4MB of RAM is required if you want to run Quicken with other programs.

The more memory you have available the better your Windows applications will operate. If enough memory is available, your applications will not need to keep swapping information in and out of memory as they operate, since everything needed by each application can remain in memory.

Disk Storage

Disk storage on your system may consist of one or more hard disks and floppy disks in either 3 1/2-inch or 5 1/4-inch sizes. Quicken requires a hard disk, with almost 5MB of available space for Quicken and limited data storage. Like RAM, disk space is measured in either K or MB.

Most hard disks provide from 20 to 120MB of storage capacity. This means you will have room for Quicken as well as other software packages such as dBASE, WordPerfect, or 1-2-3.

A letter is used to represent each drive. Typically, hard disks are called drives C and D, while floppy disk drives are designated drives A and B.

All the program files you need for Quicken are stored on your hard disk. The following illustration shows a possible configuration of the directories on a hard disk.

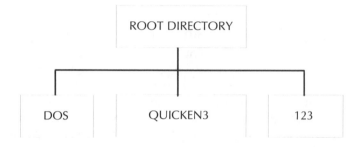

In this illustration, the root directory (main directory) would be used to contain batch files (files containing DOS instructions) on the hard disk. Separate directories are maintained for DOS, Windows, and any other program. When you install Quicken on your hard disk, it creates its own directory.

When you run Quicken for Windows, you need free space on your hard disk to store your Quicken data. You also need free space for Windows to use as temporary space as it swaps data in and out of memory. If you do not have sufficient free disk space, you will degrade the performance of Quicken and other Windows applications.

The Keyboard, Mouse, and Screen Display

Throughout this book you will be using your mouse to communicate with Quicken.

The screen and the mouse or keyboard serve as the central communication points between you and Quicken. Everything you want to tell the package must be selected with a mouse or entered through the keyboard. If you are using a keyboard, you are already familiar with many of the keys; they are used to enter data regardless of the type of program you are using. Key combinations have special meanings in Quicken; they are used to issue the commands. Even if you have used these keys in other programs, you will find that they provide different options in each program and thus are assigned to different tasks in Quicken, except for those that are standard for all Windows applications.

The mouse allows you to make selections and perform tasks without using the keyboard. You will have new terms and new ways of doing things to learn as you click, double-click, and drag with a mouse to accomplish activities. You will learn about each of these new options in this section.

Quicken uses the screen to communicate information to you. Quicken supports both monochrome monitors (one color) and monitors that can display many colors. Your screen must have a graphics card to view

Windows or Quicken for Windows. Explanation of the screen is also covered here, since it often provides information about which keys to use for various features and commands.

Keyboard Styles

Not all keyboards are alike, although virtually all of them provide every key you need to use Quicken. However, you may have to look around to find the keys you need, especially if you are getting used to a new keyboard. On all the older model PCs and compatibles, the arrow keys move the cursor (or highlight) around on your screen. These keys are located on the *numeric keypad*, at the far right side of the keyboard. They are also used to enter numbers when the Num Lock key is depressed to activate them. With Num Lock off, the arrow keys move the cursor in the direction indicated on the key top. If these keys are not set properly for your use, just press Num Lock and they assume their other function.

On newer model keyboards, called the IBM *enhanced keyboards*, there are separate arrow keys to the left of the numeric keypad that move the cursor. This allows you to leave the number lock feature on for numeric data entry and use these arrow keys to move around on the screen.

Mouse Devices

Quicken 3 for Windows supports all Microsoft-compatible mouse devices. Quicken automatically recognizes a compatible mouse and displays a mouse pointer that looks like a small arrow on the screen. As you roll the mouse over your desktop, the mouse pointer moves to different locations on your screen and sometimes changes its appearance. Your mouse device may have one, two, or three buttons on top.

Mouse Actions   A mouse button can be used to perform a variety of actions. You can *click* the button by pressing it and quickly releasing it. You can *double-click* a button by completing two clicks in rapid succession. You can *drag* with the mouse by continuing to hold down the mouse button while rolling the mouse across the desktop. Mouse actions require you to position the mouse pointer on the desired screen element before proceeding.

Left Mouse Button Tasks   The left mouse button is used for most Quicken tasks. With this button, you can accomplish the following actions:

✦ Select a command from the pull-down menus.

✦ Select an action by clicking a button in the Iconbar.

1

♦ Finalize a record by clicking on Re_cord.

♦ Select a register transaction.

♦ Display a Split Transaction dialog box by clicking the _Split button.

♦ Scroll through transactions by clicking the vertical scroll bar arrows.

♦ Page up or page down with a click to that side of the scroll box on the scroll bar.

Double-clicking is not used as often as the click action. You can use a double-click to select any item in a list. Dragging moves you to a different location in a list as you drag the scroll box vertically. Holding down the mouse button with the mouse pointer in a list or register scrolls up or down the list or register.

Menu Selections

Quicken provides pull-down menus to simplify your feature and command selections. These menus lead to all the major tasks or activities the program performs.

The menus can display either an ellipse immediately following the selection to indicate that additional information must be supplied in a dialog box, or an arrow pointing to the right to indicate that further menu selections are required. Some menu choices will display a key combination that can be used to activate the feature in lieu of making a menu selection. You can see each of these elements in the _File menu, shown here:

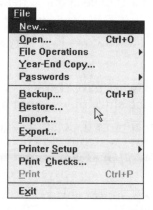

You will notice that each of the options in a menu has an underlined letter just as the menu names themselves do. You will learn to use these letters in making selections if you prefer to use the keyboard instead of the mouse.

Making Menu Selections with a Mouse

You can select a menu name by moving the mouse pointer to the desired name and pressing the left mouse button. This is referred to as clicking the menu name. The menu options will appear in a pull-down menu. You can move the mouse pointer to the desired option in this menu and click again to select it.

Making Menu Selections with the Keyboard

Working in the Windows environment encourages using the mouse, since there are many graphical elements that can be selected easily. This approach is often easier than using the keyboard for the same selections. If you are not quite ready to make the transition to the mouse, Quicken still supports the keyboard. You can select a menu by pressing the Alt key in combination with the underlined letter in the menu. This will display the options in the pull-down menu, and you can type the letter of the desired menu item to select it.

Effects of Menu Selections

Some selections result in the appearance of a *window* or *dialog box* on the screen. Windows and dialog boxes differ from menus in that there are a number of pieces of information for you to complete, as well as buttons to select. If you want to use the option already chosen (the *default*), there is no need to make a change. You can simply press Tab to accept that choice and move to the next *field*, where you will supply information. If you do not understand what is expected in a field, you can press F1 (Help) for an explanation.

Dialog boxes and windows look very similar. Here, however, are some differences:

✦ Windows always have sizing buttons in the upper-right corner. Dialog boxes do not, since they cannot be sized.

✦ When you are in a dialog box, you must complete it or cancel your request before switching to another task. You can switch between windows as often as you want using either the Windows menu or your mouse to change the active window.

✦ Dialog boxes almost always offer buttons for actions or confirmation such as Done, Save, OK, and Cancel.

QuickFill and Drop-Down Lists Saves Entry Time

Quicken's Quick Fill feature speeds up the transaction entry process and helps reduce errors.

No matter how proficient you are with the keyboard, the quickest way to enter data is to have Quicken do it for you. Quicken 3 for Windows QuickFill and drop-down list features are designed to do just that. If you are typing a check number, category, payee, security, or action, Quicken drops down a box that you can use to make a selection. If you prefer to begin typing, simply start your entry and the Quicken QuickFill feature will take effect. Quicken checks its list as soon as you type a character and displays the first match it finds. As you type additional letters, Quicken is able to refine the match. You can press Tab to accept the entry or use ↓ to advance through other matching options on the list. If you have changed the Edit Preferences options for the QuickFill feature, the drop-down list boxes may not appear for you automatically. You can press Alt-↓ to have the drop-down list box display. For the payee field, Quicken checks payees in memorized transactions, as well as the last three months of transactions. When you accept the payee, Quicken copies the entire transaction, which you can edit if you choose.

Quick Keys

Quick keys provide access to commands. You can use them throughout Quicken to speed up transaction entries in the register, check writing, and report printing. All Quick key commands are initiated by pressing the Ctrl key in combination with another key. When you pull down a menu, you see "Ctrl-" and a letter next to menu items that can be activated with a Quick key combination. The more you use the Quick keys, the easier it will be to remember the combination needed for each activity.

As you become familiar with Quicken, you will find that these keys help you reduce time spent on financial record keeping. The Quick keys are listed below if you wish to use the keyboard to activate menu options:

Quick Key	Equivalent Menu Selection
Ctrl+O	File Open
Ctrl+B	File Backup
Ctrl+P	File Print Register
Alt+Backspace	Edit Undo
Shift+Del	Edit Cut
Ctrl+Ins	Edit Copy

Quick Key	Equivalent Menu Selection
[Shift]+[Ins]	Edit Paste
[Ctrl]+[N]	Edit New Transaction
[Ctrl]+[D]	Edit Delete Transaction
[Ctrl]+[V]	Edit Void Transaction
[Ctrl]+[M]	Edit Memorize Transaction
[Ctrl]+[F]	Edit Find
[Ctrl]+[X]	Edit Go To Transfer
[Ctrl]+[W]	Activities Write Checks
[Ctrl]+[R]	Activities Use Register
[Ctrl]+[K]	Activities Financial Calendar
[Ctrl]+[H]	Activities Set Up Loans
[Ctrl]+[U]	Activities Portfolio View
[Ctrl]+[A]	Lists Account
[Ctrl]+[C]	Lists Category & Transfer
[Ctrl]+[L]	Lists Class
[Ctrl]+[T]	Lists Memorized Transactions
[Ctrl]+[J]	Lists Scheduled Transactions
[Ctrl]+[Y]	Lists Security
[F1]	Help Quicken Help

Special Keys

If you have used your computer with other Windows applications, you will find that many of the special keys work the same in Quicken as in other applications. For example, the [Esc] key is used to cancel your most recent menu selection. The [Spacebar], at the bottom of the keyboard, is used when making entries to add blank spaces. The [Backspace] key deletes the last character you typed, the character to the left of the cursor. [Del] deletes the current selection if an item is selected. It deletes the character to the right of the cursor when text is not selected and the cursor appears as a vertical bar.

The [Shift] key is used to enter capital letters and the special symbols at the top of nonletter keys. [Caps Lock] enters all letters in capitals if you press it once, but it does not affect the entry of special symbols, which always require the [Shift] key. To enter lowercase letters with [Caps Lock] on, hold down the [Shift] key. To turn [Caps Lock] off, just press it a second time.

1

The Tab key usually moves you from field to field. Pressing Shift and Tab together moves the cursor backward through the fields on the screen. Ctrl-End moves the cursor to the bottom of the display; Ctrl-Home moves you to the top of the display.

The Pg Up and Pg Dn keys move you up and down screens and menus.

Quicken uses the + and - keys on the numeric keypad to quickly increase and decrease numbers such as date and check number. When these keys are pressed once, the number increases or decreases by one. However, since the keys all repeat when held down, holding down either of these keys can rapidly effect a major change. The + and - keys perform their functions in appropriate fields whether Num Lock is on or off.

The Iconbar

The Iconbar provides a shortcut interface between you and Quicken for many of the commonly performed tasks.

The Iconbar is the band of icons that appears immediately under the menu bar in the Quicken window. It is also a useful shortcut for Quicken. You can use the Iconbar to simplify various activities you carry out in Quicken. You can use either the default Iconbar, or you can modify it to include the icons most useful to you.

When you select an icon, an action is carried out. You select an icon by pointing the mouse at the icon and clicking the left mouse button. For example, when you point the mouse at the Accts icon and click it, the Accounts List window appears in the Quicken window. Icons have both pictures and text associated with them. You can choose to display both, as is the default, or to display only the picture or the text.

You can also change the icons which appear on the Iconbar. You can create a whole new Iconbar, or modify the current one. You can use a selection of graphic images, and create text to go with them.

Buttonbars

Buttonbars are now located at the top of the register for common tasks. The investment register and the budget windows have special buttonbars with tasks related to these windows. You can click a button to have the desired action performed. Buttons can be used to copy or paste a transaction with a simple click.

The Calculator

Quicken provides two calculators which allow you to perform basic computations on the screen. You can perform computations using the mathematical operators such as + for addition, – for subtraction, * for multiplication, and / for division. Simple calculation involving two numbers or more complex formulas is possible. You can leave the Windows Calculator and return to it without losing the current calculation as long as you do not close it.

A significant feature of Calculator is its ability to compute a payment amount or other figure needed in the *current transaction entry* (the one in use) and then place, or *paste*, the result onto the screen. The following shows the calculator you get when you select Use Calculator from the Activities:

You might use the calculator to compute the total of nine invoices for $77.00 each. In this manner, one check could be written to cover all nine

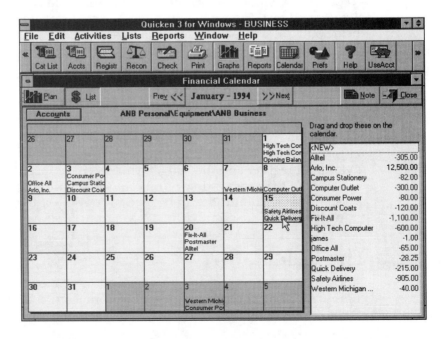

Quicken's
financial
planning
calendar
Figure 1-8.

invoices. You can also compute discounts or interest on a loan. Once Quicken computes the amount, you can use the Windows Clipboard to place the amount in the payment field. You activate the calculator by typing a + in a numeric field, such as amount.

Quicken's New Financial Calendar

Quicken 3 for Windows new financial calendar gives you a financial tool for a quick look ahead to how things are going for you financially. You can see dates with upcoming bills that must be paid as well as dates when you expect to receive a check that can be deposited. You can mark both recurring transactions and one-time payments on the calendar. You can add a note to any day and can choose to display a bar chart at the bottom for an assessment of how you are doing financially. Figure 1-8 shows a month from the financial calendar.

CHAPTER

2

MAKING REGISTER ENTRIES

If you maintain a checking account or monitor a savings account, you are already familiar with the concept of the Quicken register. The register is the backbone of the Quicken system. It allows you to maintain information on checking accounts, cash accounts, and other assets and expenses. With the register, you maintain current status information for an account so you know the precise account balance. You also keep a history of all the transactions affecting the balance. The capabilities of the Quicken register extend beyond the entries normally made in a checkbook register since they allow you to easily categorize entries as you make them. This extra capability extends the usefulness of the recorded information and facilitates report creation.

In this chapter you learn to create and maintain a single checking account register. The transactions will be similar to those you might make in a personal account. As you work with the Quicken package, you will repeatedly use the techniques you learn here.

The first thing you need to do to use this book is to turn off Quicken's Qcards, which appear by default. The Qcards provide advice on how to carry out actions in Quicken. You will not want them since you will be following the steps in this book. To prevent the Qcards from appearing, choose Preferences from the Edit menu, and then select Qcards, which opens the Qcard Preferences dialog box. Select Qcards Off, select OK, and then select Done to close the dialog box.

Maintaining a Register

Your register is your master record for all financial information.

Quicken's register works much like the manual checking account register shown in Figure 2-1. Starting with the account balance at the beginning of the period, you record each check written as a separate entry, including the date, amount, payee, and check number. You can add information to document the reason for the check. This information can be useful in the preparation of taxes or to verify that an invoice has been paid. As you enter each check, a new balance is computed. You must enter other bank charges, such as check printing fees, overdraft charges, and service fees, which are also subtracted from the account balance. You record deposits in a similar fashion. Since interest earned on an account is often automatically credited to the account, you should enter it as it appears on your monthly bank statement. (Quicken cannot compute the interest earned on your account since there is no way for the package to know the dates checks clear at your bank, and this information is needed to compute the interest earned.)

Although it is easy to record entries in a manual check register, most people at least occasionally make a mistake when computing the new balance. Recording transactions in Quicken's register eliminates this problem. It also provides many other advantages, such as categories for classifying each entry, automatic totaling of similar transactions within a category, easily created reports, and a Find feature for quickly locating specific entries.

Before entering any transactions in Quicken's register, you need to create a file and set up an account. This means assigning a name to the account and

2

RECORD ALL CHANGES OR CREDITS THAT AFFECT YOUR ACCOUNT								
NUMBER	DATE	DESCRIPTION OF TRANSACTION	PAYMENT/DEBIT	T	FEE IF ANY (-)	DEPOSIT/CREDIT (+)	BALANCE $	
	1/1 1994	Opening Balance 1st U.S. Bank				1,200 00	1,200 00 1,200 00	
100	1/4 1994	Small City Gas & Light Gas & Electric	67 50				67 50 1,132 50	
101	1/5 1994	Small City Times Paper Bill	16 50				16 50 1,116 00	
	1/7 1994	Deposit - Salary monthly pay				700 00	700 00 1,816 00	
102	1/7 1994	Small City Market Food	22 32				22 32 1,793 68	
103	1/7 1994	Small City Apartments Rent	150 00				150 00 1,643 00	
104	1/19 1994	Small City Market Food	43 00				43 00 1,600 00	
105	1/25 1994	Small City Phone Company Phone Bill	19 75				19 75 1,580 93	
	2/10 1994	Dividend Check Dividend from ABC Co.				25 00	25 00 1,605 93	

Manual entries in a checking account register
Figure 2-1.

establishing a balance. You will also want to learn a little about Quicken's built-in categories, which allow you to categorize every transaction. You may already do this with some transactions in your check register, by marking those you will need to refer back to, for instance. This activity is optional in Quicken, but using the categories allows you to create reports that are more useful.

Quicken 3 for Windows lets you use both the mouse and keyboard to move around the screen and make selections. You choose the method that seems easiest to you. In this chapter, the keyboard steps are stressed because they are not as obvious as the mouse steps. In the remainder of the book, the steps simply tell you what to do, not how to do it, so you can choose the method you prefer to use.

Establishing a File and an Account

You can have several Quicken accounts to meet your financial needs.

Establishing a file and an account is easy once you install Quicken and start it with the instructions in Appendix A. The exact procedure that you follow depends on whether you have used Quicken 3 for Windows before. If this is your first use of the package and you do not have data from an earlier release, Quicken will display some dialog boxes to help you get started with the setup. If you have data from an earlier Quicken for Windows release or from Quicken 5 or 6 for DOS, you can use that data in Quicken 3 for Windows without conversion. Quicken will locate your old files during installation and allow you to use them without change. If you have data from these earlier releases of Quicken or have used Quicken 3 for Windows before, you will not see the First Time Setup dialog box now. You will need to set up your new file and account without Quicken's help, using the instructions later in this chapter.

Regardless of which situation matches yours, you need to create a file for storing any data you enter with Quicken. When you provide a filename, Quicken adds several different filename extensions since one Quicken file actually consists of multiple files on your disk. You also need to provide an account name. Quicken can store data for various account types, and one Quicken file can hold as many as 255 accounts. You will find all the steps you need to establish a file and an account in the sections that follow.

Starting a File as a New Quicken User

Most Quicken users have only one file, but you can create a second one and save it to try out new features.

The first time you start Quicken, you are presented with the First Time Setup dialog box shown in Figure 2-2. Quicken wants you to select the type of categories that you will use to organize your financial transactions. Then Quicken leads you through the process of selecting an account type and defining the account to use. Quicken will create a file named QDATA to contain the first account that you create. When you see the First Time Setup dialog box, follow these steps:

1. Select the option button for Home and Business Categories.
2. Select OK.

   Quicken displays the Select Account Type dialog box shown in Figure 2-3.
3. Select the Bank Account option button.
4. Select OK.

   The New Account Information dialog box shown here is displayed:

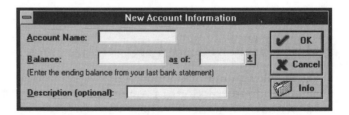

5. In the Account Name text box, type **1st U.S. Bank** to provide a name for the account, and press [Tab].
6. In the Balance text box, type **1200**, and press [Tab].
7. Type **1/1/94** and press [Tab].
8. Type **Checking account** in the Description text box, which is optional, and select OK.

2

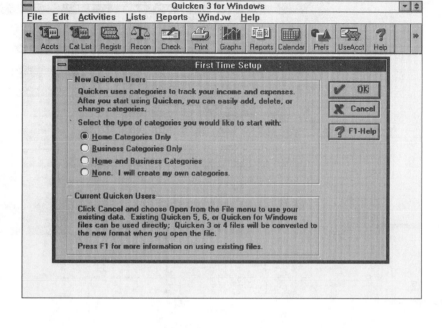

First Time
Setup dialog
box
Figure 2-2.

Quicken creates the necessary files for the 1st U.S. Bank account, storing
them in the Quicken directory, and opens the register for the account,
as shown in Figure 2-4.

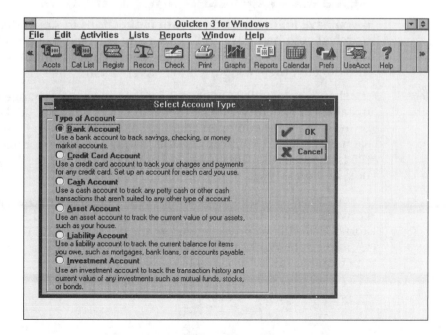

Select
Account Type
dialog box
Figure 2-3.

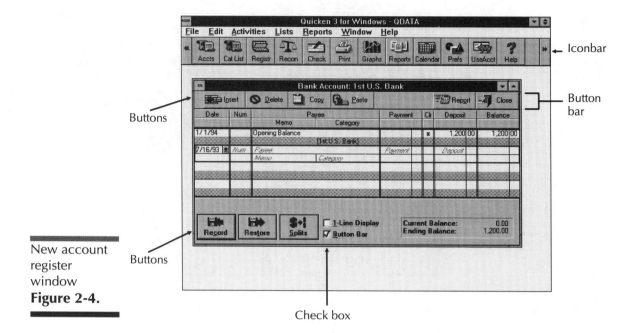

Buttons

Buttons

New account
register
window
Figure 2-4.

Iconbar

Button
bar

Check box

Using Quicken Data from Earlier Quicken Releases in Quicken 3 for Windows

If you have followed the installation directions in Appendix A, Quicken has searched your hard disk and located any Quicken 1 or 2 for Windows and DOS Quicken 5, 6, or 7 files. Since Quicken 3 for Windows can read these files directly, there is no need to convert them.

If, when you installed Quicken 3 for Windows, you changed the name of the installation directory Quicken suggested, your earlier Quicken data will not be available until you open all of the files that contain this data. To open each file, select Open from the File menu, move to the directory where the file is stored in the Directories list box, select the file in the File Name list box, and press (Enter).

If you are using a Quicken release prior to DOS Quicken 5, your files must be converted before using them with Quicken 3 for Windows. DOS Quicken 3 and 4 files will be converted automatically the first time they are opened in Quicken 3 for Windows. If you have DOS Quicken 1 or 2, contact Intuit for the required utility program to convert your data.

Creating a New File

The steps in this section tell you how to create your own Quicken 3 for Windows file. In this section you also learn how to change the location of a file. You will need to follow these steps now only if you have been using a previous version of Quicken and did not perform the first-time setup steps listed earlier. Later, when you need a new file for your own data, you should follow these same steps.

1. Select New from the File menu.
2. Select New File.
3. Use the Directories list box to specify the directory you want the file saved in.
4. Enter a name for the file in the File Name text box.

   You should select the appropriate check boxes for the category types that you want in your new file. Initially, the check boxes for both Home and Business are selected.
5. Select OK.

   The Select Account Type dialog box is displayed. You should immediately execute the steps in the next section for creating a new account since there is currently no account in the new file.

Creating a New Account

The account used for the examples in the next few chapters is called 1st U.S. Bank. In the unlikely event that this name is the same as one of your existing accounts, you need to use another name to maintain the integrity of your existing data. If you are adding an account to a file that already contains accounts, you must first choose New from the File menu and select New Account. (You can also get started by choosing Create New Account from the Activities menu.) Follow these steps if you just created a new file with the steps shown in the preceding section:

1. Select Bank Account from the Select Account Type dialog box, and select OK.

   The New Account Information dialog box is displayed.
2. Type **2nd U.S. Bank** and press Tab.
3. Type **1200** and press Tab.
4. Type **1/1/94** and press Tab.
5. Type **Checking account** for the description, and then select OK.

Establishing a File and an Account if You Have Been Using Quicken 2 for Windows

If you have been using Quicken 2 for Windows, even though you already have a file and one or more accounts set up from your earlier Quicken sessions, you will want to create a file and an account that match those used in the examples in this book. You can follow the instructions in the preceding two sections for previous Quicken users to set up a file and an account.

The Quicken Register

The Quicken register looks a lot like the paper register you use with your checkbook, but it offers much more.

Figure 2-4 shows the initial register window assuming you set up the 1st U.S. Bank account. Although you have not yet recorded any transactions, Quicken has already entered the account name, the opening balance, and the opening date. Quicken has also automatically entered an *X* in the Clr (cleared) field of the register, indicating that the balance has been reconciled and is correct. You will use this field in Chapter 4, "Reconciling Your Quicken Register," when you reconcile your entire account.

Currently there is no scroll bar at the right of the register window because there are not enough transactions to require the scroll feature. Later, after you have entered more transactions, a scroll bar will be added to the display. The scroll bar will have an arrow at the top and the bottom and a scroll box inside it. You can use a mouse with these screen elements to scroll through the register.

The highlighted area below the opening balance entry is where you will enter the first transaction. Remember that a transaction is just a record of a financial activity such as a deposit or withdrawal (a credit or a debit). The fields used, which you can see in Figure 2-4, are the same for all transactions. Table 2-1 provides a detailed description of each of these fields.

Another important element of the register display is the heavy line that appears when you enter a postdated transaction. You can see this line in Figure 2-4 above the opening balance. *Postdated transactions* are transactions with dates after the current date. In order to produce reports that match those shown in this book, you must use the transaction dates shown in the book for the examples regardless of the date at the time of your entries. You may or may not see the line that divides postdated transactions from current transactions. If the current date in your system is after January 1994 when you enter the examples, the line will not appear. Your results will be the same regardless of whether or not the postdated transaction line appears.

As you make the entries for the first transaction, notice that Quicken moves through the fields in a specific order. After entering data in a field, you press

2

Field	Contents
Date	Transaction date. You can accept the current date entry or type a new date.
Num (Number)	Check number for check transactions. For noncheck transactions, use other entries like DEP.
Payee	Payee's name for check transactions. For ATM transactions, deposits, service fees, and so on, enter a description in this field.
Payment	Payment or withdrawal amount. For deposit transactions, leave this field blank. Quicken supports entries as large as $9,999,999.99.
Clr (Cleared)	Skip this field when entering transactions. You will use it in Chapter 4 for reconciling accounts and noting checks that have cleared the bank.
Deposit	Deposit amounts. For a payment transaction, leave this field blank. The same rules for Payment apply.
Balance	A running total, or the sum of all prior transactions. Quicken computes it after you complete each transaction.
Memo	Optional descriptive information documenting the transaction.
Category	Optional entry used to assign a transaction to one of Quicken's categories. Categories are used to organize similar transactions and can facilitate reporting.

Fields in the
Register
Window
Table 2-1.

(Tab), and the cursor moves to the next field in which you can enter data. Some fields, such as Date, must have an entry in all transactions; and either the Payment or Deposit field requires an entry for the transaction to affect the balance. Other fields are optional, and you use them when they're needed. If you do not need an entry in an optional field, you just press (Tab), and the cursor moves to the next field. You can also click the desired field with the mouse. For example, you use the check number (Num) field only when writing checks, so it is an optional field.

Recording Your Transactions in the Register

When you open the register window, the highlighting is already positioned for your first transaction entry. If you have used the (↑) key to move to the opening balance entry, you need to press (Ctrl)-(End) to reposition the highlight properly. In the next sections, you enter eight sample transactions representing typical personal expenses and deposits. Don't worry if you make a mistake in recording your first transaction. Just leave the mistake in the entry and focus on the steps involved. In the second transaction, you will correct your errors. Follow these steps to complete the entries for the first transaction (use the ⊖ key, if necessary, to move the cursor to the month in the Date field):

1. Type **1/4/94** and press Tab.

Special keys let you date entries quickly.

Now that you have entered a date, you can see how Quicken dates are changed. Move the cursor back to the finalized Date field entry using Shift-Tab, and press ⊕ or ⊖ to increase or decrease the current date. A light touch to the key alters the date by one day. Holding down these keys causes a rapid date change. If you use the ⊕ or ⊖ option to change the date, you must still use Tab to move to the next field. (If you test this feature now, be sure to reenter the 1/4/94 date before proceeding.)

You can also click the drop-down list arrow to display a calendar that makes date selection easy. The current date is initially highlighted in the calendar. You can use the arrow keys to move to another date, or you can click on a different date. Also, any of the following keys can be used to change the date highlighted in the calendar and placed in the register transaction:

Key	Effect
+	Increase day by 1
−	Decrease day by 1
t	Set to current date
m	First day of month
h	Last day of month
y	First day of year
r	Last day of year

2. Type **100** and then press Tab to place the check number in the Num field.

A drop-down list box appears when the Num field is first activated. Later, you may select one of the entries in this box to fill in the Num field.

3. Type **Small City Gas & Light** and press Tab to complete the entry for Payee for this check.

Again, when you move to the Payee field, a drop-down list box appears. This feature is referred to as QuickFill. As you make entries in the Payee field, those entries will appear in this list box. Later, you will be able to select an earlier entry instead of reentering a payee name.

There is a limit of 40 characters on the Payee line for each transaction. Notice that the cursor moves to the Payment field, where Quicken expects the next entry.

4. Type **67.50** and press `Tab`.

Categories help you organize your financial data.

Since this is a check transaction, the amount should be placed in the Payment field. Notice that when you type the decimal, Quicken moves to the cents column of the Payment field. The drop-down list box arrow in this field displays a calculator if you click it. The calculator is handy when you need to compute an amount. You can click numbers and arithmetic operators to compute an amount, which is automatically placed in the field when you click =.

5. Type **Gas and Electric** and press `Tab`.

You are limited to 31 characters on the Memo line.

6. Type **U** in the Category field.

Initially Quicken displays "UIC" as its suggested match.

7. Type a **t** to continue selecting the category.

Quicken displays "Utilities." Your register window should look like the one in Figure 2-5.

If you are going to use a category, you must enter a valid Quicken option to stay within the standard category structure, or you must add a new category to Quicken's category list. The drop-down list box displays all the standard Quicken categories. You can select a category from the list box by clicking it with the mouse or by using the arrow keys to highlight the category and pressing `Enter`.

8. Select Re_c_ord to confirm the recording of the transaction, or press `Enter`.

Your screen displays an ending balance of 1,132.50. This represents the total of all transactions entered, including any transactions that may be postdated because of the relationship between the transaction date and the current date. The current balance is the account balance as of the current date. Since all the transactions are postdated based on the date when these sample screens were captured, the current balance is zero.

You have now completed your first transaction successfully. Since everyone makes mistakes in entries, you will want to learn how to correct those errors. This is easily done with Quicken.

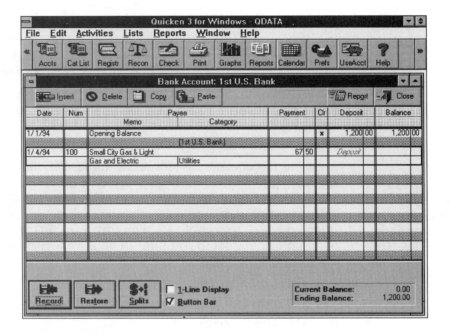

Register
window
before you
complete the
first sample
transaction
entry
Figure 2-5.

Making Revisions to the Current Transaction

One of the advantages Quicken has over manual entries is that changes can
be made easily and neatly. An incorrect amount or other error can be altered
as soon as you notice the mistake or later on. The procedure you use
depends on whether you have already recorded the transaction. Quicken's
QuickFill feature can save you time, whether you are correcting an existing
transaction or entering a new transaction.

Correcting Your Example

In this section you learn how to correct mistakes in the current transaction,
practicing the techniques covered briefly in Chapter 1, "An Overview of
Quicken and Your Computer Components." First, make the following
transaction entries:

1. Type **1/5/94** and press ⬚Tab⬚.

   Here, you must enter the date since you are entering several days'
   transactions in one session. If you enter transactions daily, you do not
   need to change the date between your transactions since each of your
   entries will be for the current day. Quicken automatically copies the
   date from the previous transaction. In the first transaction for the
   Quicken session, it uses the current date.

2. Type **110** and press Tab.

   Notice that the previous check number was 100. This check number should have been recorded as 101. In fact, if you had selected the Next Chk # option in the list box, this problem would not have occurred.

3. Move the mouse pointer to the end of the check number, and click your mouse button. Then press Backspace twice to delete the 0 and the second 1 in the number entry.

4. Type **01** to change 110 to 101, and then press Tab to finalize the entry.

5. Type **S**.

   Notice that Quicken automatically fills in the payee name from the previous transaction. This illustrates Quicken's QuickFill feature. If you were to accept QuickFill's suggestion, Quicken would complete the current transaction with the entries from the previous transaction. Quicken uses QuickFill for the Payee and Category fields as you record entries in the account register. Quicken checks the Category List for categories and looks at the payees in the last three months of transactions as it searches for an entry that matches what you type. Quicken uses the first match it finds. You can select Memorized Transactions from the Lists menu or press Ctrl-T to open the Memorized Transaction List and look through it for additional matches.

   If QuickFill is not operating for you, the option has been turned off. Check the preference setting for QuickFill. You can check it by choosing Preferences from the Edit menu and then selecting QuickFill and checking all the boxes, including Automatic Memorization of New Transactions.

6. Continue typing **malll City Times** since Quicken has not provided the match that you need.

   This entry contains an extra l. Move the mouse pointer immediately after the last *l*, and click the mouse button. Then press Backspace to delete the character before the cursor.

7. Press Tab to finalize the Payee entry.

8. Type **6.50** for the payment amount.

9. Move the mouse pointer one position to the left of the 6, and click the mouse button. Type **1**, and Quicken places a 1 in front of the 6.

10. Press Tab to move to the Memo field.

11. Type **Magazine subscription** and press Tab.

The QuickFill feature makes Quicken your assistant for completing transactions quickly.

This entry is intended to be the newspaper bill, so you need to make a change. Use Shift-Tab to reactivate the Memo field.

12. Type **Paper bill** to replace the selected entry, and press Tab.

13. Type **M** for the category.

Quicken uses the QuickFill feature and presents the Medical category. You want to use the Misc (miscellaneous) category.

14. Click Misc, and Quicken displays the Misc category designation.

If you had typed "Mi" in the Category field, Quicken would have presented Misc as the category, and you could have stopped typing and accepted it by pressing Tab.

15. Select the Record button to complete your second transaction.

Your register should look like the one in Figure 2-6.

A number of mistakes were included in this transaction, but you can see how easy it is to make corrections with Quicken.

Additional Transaction Entries

You are now somewhat familiar with recording transactions in the Quicken register. In order to test your knowledge and expand your transaction base

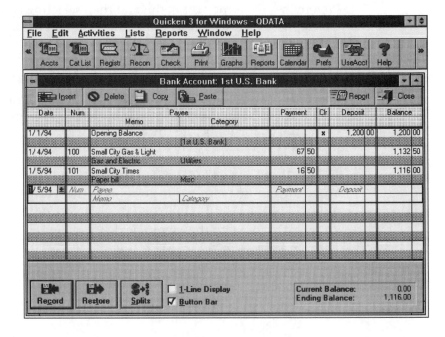

Register window after you complete the second sample transaction
Figure 2-6.

for later, enter the following additional transactions in your register, using the same procedure you used to enter the previous transaction entries. For deposit entries, leave a blank space in the Num field or select the Deposit option for Num to make Quicken expect a deposit entry. You can also select options such as ATM or Next Chk # from the drop-down list box for the Num field. You can use the QuickFill feature when entering information in the Payee or Category fields.

2

Date: **1/7/94**
Num: *Highlight the Deposit option*
Payee: **Deposit-Salary**
Deposit: **700.00**
Memo: **Monthly pay**
Category: **Salary**

Date: **1/7/94**
Num: **102** *Note that you can use Next Chk # for this entry*
Payee: **Small City Market**
Payment: **22.32**
Memo: **Food**
Category: **Groceries**

Date: **1/7/94**
Num: **103**
Payee: **Small City Apartments**
Payment: **150.00**
Memo: **Rent**
Category: **Housing**

Date: **1/19/94**
Num: **104**
Payee: **Small City Market**
Payment: **43.00**
Memo: **Food**
Category: **Groceries**

When you enter the transaction for check 104, press [Tab] after you complete the Payee field to have Quicken copy the information contained in the Payment, Memo, and Category fields from the transaction record for check 102. Then type the 43.00 payment amount, and select Record to save the new entries.

Date:	**1/25/94**
Num:	**105**
Payee:	**Small City Phone Company**
Payment:	**19.75**
Memo:	**Phone bill**
Category:	**Telephone**

Date:	**2/10/94**
Num:	*Select Deposit*
Payee:	**Dividend check**
Deposit:	**25.00**
Memo:	**Dividends check from ABC Co.**
Category:	**Div Income**

After typing and recording the entries for the last transaction, your register should resemble the one in Figure 2-7. Select Record to record the last transaction.

Viewing a Compressed Register

A compressed register view lets you see three times as many transactions on the screen.

You can switch back and forth between the standard register and a compressed register, which shows one line for each transaction and lets you see twice as many transactions on your screen. For the compressed register view, like Figure 2-8, select the 1-Line Display check box. Selecting the check box again will display the register in the original format.

Ending a Quicken Session and Beginning a New One

You do not need to finish all your work with Quicken in one session. You can end a Quicken session after entering one transaction or you can

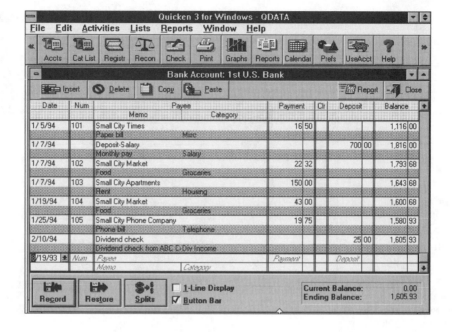

Register window after you record the entries in the last transaction **Figure 2-7.**

continue to enter transactions representing up to several months of financial activity. When you end a Quicken session, you should always use the orderly approach provided here and never turn your system off without first exiting from Quicken.

The new Automatic Backup prompt helps you remember to back up your data.

To end a Quicken session, select Exit from the File menu. All the data in your Quicken files will be saved for subsequent sessions. Quicken will even remind you about making a backup copy to another disk by displaying this Automatic Backup dialog box:

You can select Backup if you decide to back up data to another disk. If you do not want to back up right now, you can choose Exit. If you decide to

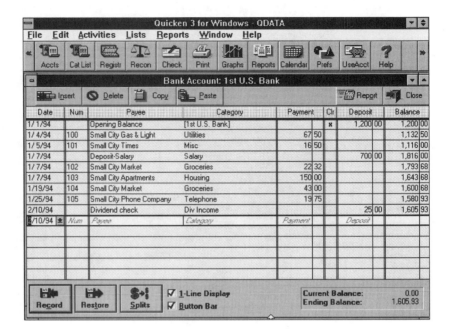

Compressed register shows one line for each transaction
Figure 2-8.

proceed with the backup, Quicken displays the Select Backup Drive dialog box shown here:

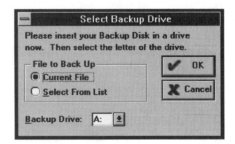

Click the drop-down arrow for the Backup Drive if you need to change it, and select OK.

To reenter Quicken, start the program from the Windows Program Manager, as you learned in Chapter 1.

REMEMBER: Quicken automatically enters the current date in the Date field for the first transaction in a session.

Remember that when you work through the examples in this book, you will specify dates that are unlikely to agree with the current date. This approach allows you to create reports identical to the ones that are shown in this book. If you are now reentering Quicken, use 2/10/94 as the next date in the register.

Reviewing Register Entries

Reviewing transaction entries in the Quicken register is as easy as flipping through the pages of a manual register, and it's more versatile. You can scroll through the register to see all the recorded transactions, or you can use the Find feature to search for a specific transaction. You can also focus on transactions for a specific time period by using the Find feature from the Edit menu with the Search field set to Date.

Scrolling Through the Register

You can use the mouse to scroll through the register quickly.

You can use the mouse to scroll through the register once you have entered enough transactions for a scroll bar to appear. The following mouse actions will help you locate the place you want to be quickly:

✦ Click the vertical scroll bar arrows to scroll to the next transaction or the previous transaction.

✦ Point to one of the vertical scroll bar arrows and hold down the mouse button to move quickly through the transactions.

✦ Click above or below the scroll box to move up or down one page of transactions.

✦ Drag the scroll box up or down in the scroll bar to move to a different location.

If you prefer to use the keyboard to move in the register, you can put some of the keys introduced in Chapter 1 to work. You can probably guess the effects some of the keys will have from their names. The ⬆ and ⬇ keys move the highlighting up or down a transaction. Quicken scrolls information off the screen to show additional transactions. Once a transaction is highlighted, you can use the ➡ and ⬅ keys to move across the current field. Tab moves to the next field, and Shift-Tab moves to the previous field. The Pg Up and Pg Dn keys move up and down one screen at a time.

The Home key moves the cursor to the beginning of the current field. If you press Home twice, Quicken moves to the beginning of the transaction. When you press Ctrl-Home, Quicken moves the cursor to the top of the register.

The (End) key moves the cursor to the end of the current field. If you press (End) twice, Quicken moves to the end of the transaction. When you press (Ctrl)-(End), Quicken moves the cursor to the last transaction in the register.

Pressing (Ctrl)-(Pg Up) moves the highlight to the beginning of the current month. Pressing it again moves the highlight to the beginning of the previous month. Pressing (Ctrl)-(Pg Dn) moves the highlight to the last transaction in the current month; pressing it a second time will move it to the end of the next month. As you enter more transactions, the value of knowing quick ways to move will be more apparent.

Using the Find Feature

The Find feature can locate a transaction that you want to check instantly.

Quicken's Find feature allows you to locate a specific transaction easily. You can find a transaction by entering a minimal amount of information from the transaction in a special Find window. Choose Find from the Edit menu, or activate the Find window by using the Quick Key (Ctrl)-(F). The menus display the Quick Key sequences, such as (Ctrl)-(F) for Find.

Quicken can search forward or backward through the register entries for an exact match to the information you enter for a field. You can also use Quicken's wildcard feature to locate a transaction with only part of the information from a field. After looking at the examples in the next two sections, refer to the rules for finding entries in Table 2-2.

Finding Matching Entries

To look for a transaction that exactly matches data, all you need to do is fill in some data in the window. Quicken will search for entries in the Payee, Category/Class, Date, Check Number, Amount, Memo, and Cleared Status fields. You do not need to worry about the capitalization of your data entry since Quicken is not case sensitive. When you enter the data for your first Find operation, the Find text box will be blank. For subsequent Find

Locating Transactions
Table 2-2.

Entry	Quicken Finds
electric	electric, Electric, ELECTRIC, electric power, Electric Company, Consumer Power Electric, new electric
~electric	groceries, gas—anything but electric
e..c	electric, eccentric
s?n	sun, sin, son—any single letter between an *s* and an *n*
..	ice, fire, and anything else except blanks
~..	all transactions with a blank in that field

2

operations, Quicken will supply the data you entered in the previous Find operation. You can edit the data in the text box, type over what's there, or clear the entire text box and begin again with blank fields. For example, to locate a specific check number in the 1st U.S. Bank register you developed earlier, complete the following steps:

1. Move to the first transaction in the register using the scrollbar, or by pressing Ctrl-Home.

   Starting at the beginning of the register lets you conduct a complete forward search through the data. (Quicken also supports a backward search to allow you to locate entries above the currently highlighted transaction.)

2. Select Find from the Edit menu to display the Find dialog box shown here:

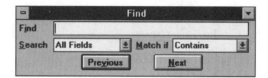

3. Type **103** in the Find text box.
4. Select the Search text box.

You can search all fields or a specific field with the Find feature.

5. Highlight Check Number in the Search drop-down list box, and press Tab.
6. Select Next to find the next matching transaction.

   When Quicken reaches the end of the register, it will ask you about starting from the beginning. When Quicken is not able to find any matches, it displays an appropriate message.

7. You can double-click the box in the upper-left corner of the Find dialog box to close it.

Quicken started the search with the current transaction and proceeded toward the bottom of the register, attempting to find matching transactions. In this example, Quicken tried to find transactions that have 103 in the Num field. You can search for only one criteria at a time. In addition to narrowing the search by selecting a field to search in the Search drop-down list box, you can select how the criteria is matched in the Match if drop-down list box. You can specify that Quicken find a match if the transaction contains the text in the Find text box, begins with it, ends with it, exactly matches it or is greater than, greater than or equal to, less than, or less than or equal to its value.

The more transactions in the register, the more useful Quicken's Find capability becomes. For instance, you might want to find all the transactions involving a specific payee or all the transactions on a certain date. Visually scanning through hundreds of transactions could take a long time, and you could miss a matching transaction. Quicken makes no mistakes and finds the matching transactions quickly.

You can search from the current transaction toward the beginning or the end of the register.

You can speed up the search process by bypassing the Edit menu and using the Quick Keys for your Find selections. Let's perform a second Find operation—one that begins the search with the current transaction and searches back toward the first entry in the register. To use the Quick keys to do this, follow these steps:

1. Press ⌈Ctrl⌉-⌈F⌉ to open the Find window. (This approach replaces opening the Edit menu and selecting Find.)

2. Type **100** in the Find text box, and press ⌈Tab⌉.

3. Click the arrow for the Search drop-down list box, and select Check Number.

4. Select Previous to search backward through the entries and highlight the transaction with 100 in the Check Number field.

5. Close the Find window by double-clicking the box in the upper-left corner of the Find window.

If you were searching for an option that might have the same entry in multiple records and you wanted to continue performing the search to see other transactions that might match your entry, you could continue to search by repeatedly selecting Previous or Next after completing the selections in the Find window.

TIP: After entering transactions for months of entries, you will find it hard simply to backtrack to transactions for a specific date. One way to find those transactions is to set the Search field to Date and enter a date in the Find text box. This will move you quickly to the appropriate section of the register and make it easy to locate those old transactions.

Key Word Search

You can enter a less-than-exact match and still locate the desired transactions if you search the Payee, Category, or Memo field and select a match other than Exact from the Match if drop-down list box. To look for an exact match, you must select Exact.

1. Choose Find from the Edit menu to display the Find window.

2. Type **Small** in the F̲ind text box, and press Tab.
3. Select Payee in the S̲earch drop-down list box.
4. Select Starts With from the M̲atch if drop-down list box.
5. Select N̲ext to search from the current location toward the end of the register. Quicken highlights the next entry for *Small City Times*.

If you continue to search with N̲ext, Quicken moves through the transaction list, highlighting each entry starting with "Small". After you have found all matching transactions, selecting N̲ext again causes Quicken to display a message asking if you want to continue checking from the beginning of the register. Double-click the upper-left corner of the Find dialog box when you want to close it.

Revising Transactions

You have already learned how to make revisions to transactions in the check register as you are recording a transaction, but sometimes you may need to make changes to previously recorded transactions. It is important to note that although Quicken allows you to modify previously recorded transactions, you cannot change the balance amount without entering another transaction. This protects you from unauthorized changes in the register account balances. By forcing you to enter another transaction, Quicken is able to maintain a log of any changes to an account balance.

You may also find it necessary to void a previously written check, deposit, or any other adjustment to an account. Voiding removes the effect of the original transaction from the account balance, although it maintains the history of the original transaction and shows it as voided. To remove all trace of the original transaction, you must use Quicken's D̲elete Transaction command. You can use either Quick Keys or selections from Quicken's E̲dit menu to void and delete transactions. You can reinstate a voided transaction by clicking the Rest̲ore button before finalizing the transaction. After recording a voided transaction, you need to delete the entire transaction and re-create it to restore it to a nonvoided status.

Changing a Previous Transaction

You must use the following steps when changing a previously recorded transaction:

1. Move to the desired transaction.
2. Use the same techniques discussed in the "Making Revisions to the Current Transaction" section of this chapter.

Quicken does not allow you to change the balance amount directly. You need to enter another transaction to make an adjustment. Another option is to void or delete the original transaction and enter a new transaction.

Voiding a Transaction

Voiding a transaction is usually a better approach than deleting it as it maintains an audit trail for you.

When you void a transaction, you undo the financial effect of the transaction. Using the Void operation creates an automatic audit trail (or record) of all transactions against an account, including those that have already been voided. Let's try the Void option with check number 100. Follow these steps:

1. Move to check number 100.

2. Choose Void Transaction from the Edit menu, or press Ctrl-V. The word "VOID" is entered in front of the payee name, as shown in Figure 2-9.

3. Press Enter to record the modification to the transaction.

If you change your mind and do not want to void the transaction, you can select Restore instead of recording the changes.

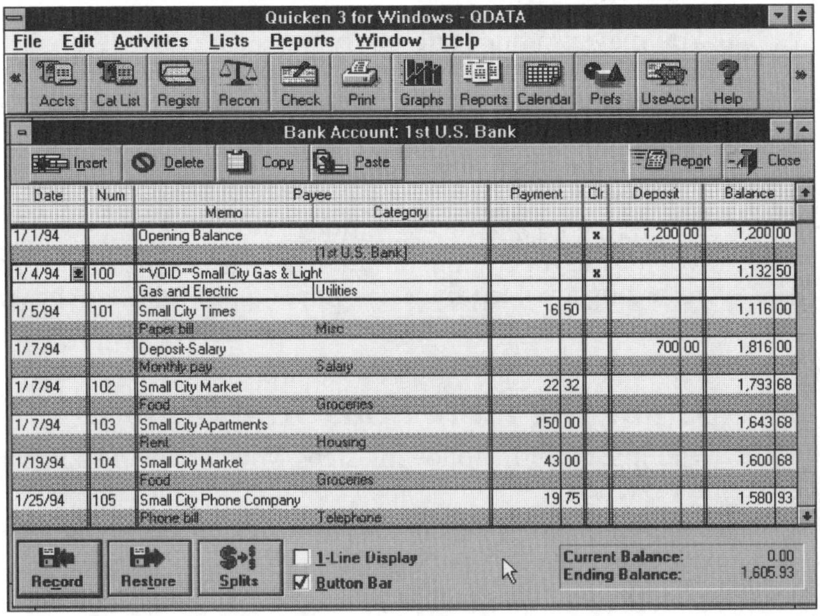

Voided transaction
Figure 2-9.

Deleting a Transaction

You can delete a transaction by pressing Ctrl-D, selecting Delete transaction from the Edit menu, or selecting the Delete button. Try this now by deleting the voided transaction for check number 100.

1. Move to the voided transaction for check number 100.
2. Choose Delete Transaction from the Edit menu, select Delete, or press Ctrl-D. Quicken displays the Delete the Current Transaction? window.
3. Select Yes to confirm the deletion.

Reinstating a Transaction

There is no "undo" key to eliminate the effect of deleting a transaction; you must reenter the transaction. For practice, reinstate the transaction for check number 100 with these steps:

To reinstate a transaction deleted in error, you must retype it.

1. Press Ctrl-End to move to the end of the register.
2. Type **1/4/94**, and press Tab to set the date to 1/4/94.
3. Type **100**, and press Tab to supply the check number in the Num field.
4. Type **Small City Gas & Light**, and press Tab to complete the entry for the payee for this check.
5. Type **67.50** and press Tab.
6. Type **Gas and Electric** and press Tab.
7. Type **Utilities:Gas & Electric**, or use QuickFill to select it, then select Record to complete the transaction. The transaction is reentered into the register.

You can see from this example that you expended a considerable amount of effort to rerecord this transaction. Avoid unnecessary work by confirming a void or deletion before you complete it.

CHAPTER

3

QUICKEN REPORTS

In Chapter 2, "Making Register Entries," you discovered how easy it is to enter transactions in the Quicken system. In this chapter, you find out about another major benefit of using Quicken—the ability to generate reports. Reports present your data in an organized format that makes it easy to analyze. With Quicken 3 for Windows, the Reports menu allows you to customize a report while viewing it and to zoom in for a close-up look at details. You can use Quicken to produce a quick printout of the register or more complex reports that analyze and summarize data. Some of these reports, such as the Cash Flow report and the Itemized Categories report, would require a significant amount of work if they were compiled manually. This chapter focuses on the basic reports and some customizing options. More complex reports are covered in later chapters.

Quicken, like other Windows products, uses the Windows printer drivers to print. While Windows handles most aspects of printing, you change the settings for printing from within Quicken. This chapter teaches you to change the basic print settings if Quicken does not create acceptable output with the default Windows settings.

Printing the Check Register

Although it is convenient to enter transactions on the screen, a printout of your entries is often easier to review and is much more portable than a computer screen. Try printing the register first without changing the print settings. If your output is very different from the sample shown in this chapter, try customizing your print settings, and then print the register again. You will find instructions for customizing the settings at the end of this chapter. To print your register, follow these steps with the register you want to print onscreen:

1. Select Print Register from the File menu, or click on the Print icon in the Iconbar. Quicken displays the Print Register dialog box:

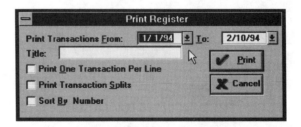

TIP: Pressing Ctrl-P opens the Print Register dialog box directly, without going through the File menu.

2. Type **1/1/94** in the Print Transactions From field.

This entry selects the first transaction to be printed, by date. Another way to select the date is to click the drop-down arrow or press Alt-↓, which displays a calendar like this:

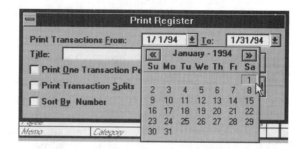

You can click on the arrows at the top of the calendar or you can press ↑ or ↓ to move to a new month. To move to the correct date, you can click on the date, or you can use ← or → to move to the date and then press Enter. Since you already know the precise dates used in the examples in this book, however, it should be easier just to type them. The calendar is available for all date fields in Quicken 3 for Windows.

Printing your check register at regular intervals provides a paper backup of your Quicken accounts.

3. Type **1/31/94** in the To field.

    This entry establishes the last transaction to be printed. The dates supplied in steps 2 and 3 are inclusive; that is, Quicken will print all register transactions with dates from 1/1/94 through 1/31/94.

4. Type **January Transactions** in the Title field.

    This customizes the title of the check register. If you do not make an entry in this field, Quicken uses the default title "Check Register" for the report heading. Your heading can be up to 26 characters long.

5. Clear the Print One Transaction Per Line check box, if necessary.

    The Print One Transaction Per Line check box is blank by default; this causes Quicken to use three lines to print each transaction. If you want to have more transactions printed on each page, select this check box so it is filled with an *X*. This causes Quicken to print the document using only one line per transaction by abbreviating the information printed.

6. Clear the Print Transaction Splits check box, if necessary.

    You can ignore transaction splits for the time being. This type of transaction is introduced in Chapter 6, "Expanding the Scope of Financial Entries." For now, leave the check box cleared to print your reports properly.

7. Clear the Sort by Number check box, if necessary.

The Sort By Number check box is also clear by default, causing Quicken to print the register in order by date and then by check number. If you wanted to first sort by check number and then by date, you would select this check box.

8. Select Print. The Print Report dialog box opens, as shown in Figure 3-1.

    You use the Print Report dialog box to select where you are printing to and what you want included in your printed document.

9. Select the Printer button, if necessary.

    There are five options for where to print your report, and Printer is the default option. You can choose to print to a printer, to an ASCII file, to an ASCII file that has delimiters to separate your data, to a .PRN file like those created with Lotus 1-2-3, or to the screen. You choose a destination by selecting the appropriate button under Print to. As a rule, you will want to print to your printer, but you may want to print to a file so that you can use the copy of your register in another program. You can print to the screen to preview how your register will look when printed, and then you can select Print to go ahead and print to your printer.

10. Select Printer, if necessary.

11. If you have a color printer, you can select the Print in color check box to have your register print using colors.

12. Clear the Print in draft mode button, if necessary.

    Draft mode printouts print faster than final quality printouts, but they will not look as good because they are printed using lower resolution.

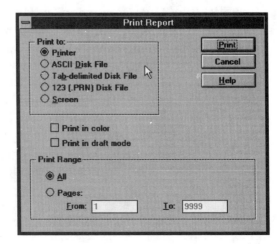

Print Report
dialog box
Figure 3-1.

13. If you know the pages you want to print, select the Pages button and enter the first and last page to print in the From and To boxes.

14. Select Print.

    Once you have completed the Print Report dialog box, Quicken is ready to print the check register for the period you defined. Make sure your printer is turned on and ready to print before selecting Print.

Your printed register should look like Figure 3-2. Notice that the date at the top-left corner of your report is the current date, regardless of the month for which you are printing transactions.

3

```
                          January Transactions
1st U.S.Bank                                                  Page 1
07/22/94
Date_ Num_           Transaction_         Payment_ C_ Deposit_   Balance
01/01        Opening Balance                       x  1,200.00  1,200.00
/1994 memo:
      cat:  [1st U.S.Bank]


01/04 100    Small City Gas & Light        67.50              1,132.50
/1994 memo: Gas and Electric
      cat:  Utilities:Gas & Electric


01/05 101    Small City Times              16.50              1,116.00
/1994 memo: Paper bill
      cat:  Misc


01/07 DEP    Deposit-Salary                          700.00   1,816.00
/1994 memo: Monthly pay
      cat:  Salary


01/07 102    Small City Market             22.32              1,793.68
/1994 memo: Food
      cat:  Groceries


01/07 103    Small City Apartments        150.00              1,643.68
/1994 memo: Rent
      cat:  Housing


01/19 104    Small City Market             43.00              1,600.68
/1994 memo: Food
      cat:  Groceries


01/25 105    Small City Phone Company      19.75              1,580.93
/1994 memo: Phone bill
      cat:  Telephone
```

1st U.S. Bank checking account register printout
Figure 3-2.

Printing the Cash Flow Report

Quicken's Cash Flow report compares the money you have received during a specified time period with the money you have spent. Quicken provides this information for each category you used in the register. The Cash Flow report combines transactions from your Bank, Cash, and Credit Card accounts. (Cash and Credit Card accounts are discussed in Chapter 6.) Preparing the Cash Flow report for the transactions you recorded in the 1st U.S. Bank account in Chapter 2 involves the following steps:

1. Select <u>H</u>ome from the <u>R</u>eports menu, or click the Reports icon in the Iconbar and select the <u>H</u>ome button from the Create Report dialog box.

   The <u>R</u>eports menu and the Create Report dialog box offer several families of report types, such as home, business, investment, and memorized reports. You can select the type of report you want.

2. Select Cash <u>F</u>low.

3. Type **1/1/94** in the <u>f</u>rom field.

   Quicken automatically places January 1 of the current year in this space. It may be easier to change this date by typing a new date or by pressing ⊞ or ⊟ , depending on the current date in your system.

4. Type **1/31/94** in the <u>t</u>o field.

   You can enter dates in the <u>f</u>rom and <u>t</u>o text boxes, or you can select one of the options from the drop-down list box in front of the date text boxes. Whether you used the menu or the icon method in step 1, the Create Report dialog box now looks like Figure 3-3.

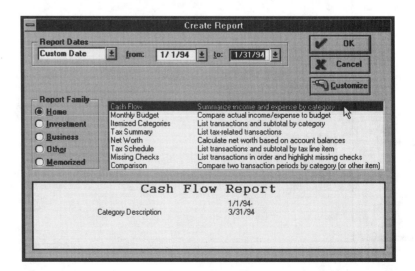

Create Report
dialog box
Figure 3-3.

5. Select <u>C</u>ustomize.

6. Type **Cash Flow Report** - and your name in the Title box under Report Layout.

   If you do not make an entry for the report title, Quicken uses the default title for the report. The default title of this report is "Cash Flow Report." Your report title can be up to 39 characters long. If you don't see the Title field, make sure the Report Layout button is selected under Customize. Each button under Customize accesses different customization options for your report.

7. Select OK, and the Cash Flow report appears on your screen.

3

TIP: If your report window is very small, you will be able to see only a part of the report. You can use your mouse to drag the window border and make the window containing the report larger. In some types of reports, the fields Category, Memo, and Payee appear. If your report window is narrow, these fields will be truncated; only the first few letters will show. Making the report window wider displays the entire entries in these fields.

Notice that the Cash Flow report has inflows and outflows listed by category.

8. Click on the outflow for groceries, or move the highlight to it using the arrow keys.

9. Click on the outflow for groceries again, or press Ctrl-Z or Enter to use Quicken's QuickZoom feature. QuickZoom shows you the transactions that make up the 65.32 shown for groceries, as you can see in Figure 3-4.

10. Click <u>C</u>lose in the report's buttonbar or press Esc to return to the Cash Flow report.

    You can continue to examine the details for any of the entries by using the QuickZoom feature. When you're done, print the report.

11. Select the Pri<u>n</u>t button on the buttonbar in the Cash Flow Report window.

    Quicken displays the Print Report dialog box. You need to select where you are printing the report. The default is to print to the default Windows printer.

NOTE: Ctrl-P is the Quick key for printing.

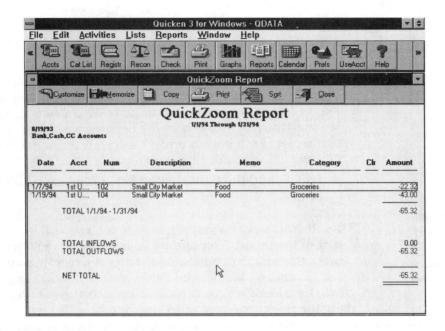

Using
Quicken's
QuickZoom
feature
Figure 3-4.

12. Select Print to select the Printer default option. The report shown in Figure 3-5 is printed.

You can have Quicken send the Cash Flow report to the default printer, to a disk as an ASCII file, or to a disk as a 1-2-3 file. If you need to customize any of the printer settings, select Cancel and use the Printer Setup command from the File menu to change the printer settings.

13. To close the report, press [Esc] or select Close.

Memorizing a Report

If you find that you frequently create a single type of report, you may want to be able to re-create it quickly. To do this, you need to memorize the report when you create it.

1. Select the Memorize button from the report window's buttonbar. The Memorize Report dialog box appears:

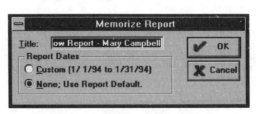

2. Enter the title you want to be regularly assigned to the report in the Title field.

3. Select the Custom option button if you want to repeatedly create the report with the same range of dates. If you prefer to print the report using the current default dates, select None.

4. Select OK to memorize the report.

Memorizing frequently used reports saves time.

Later, when you want to quickly re-create the report, select Memorized from the Reports menu, highlight the report title in the dialog box, select Use, and select OK to recall the report. You can also select the Reports icon to open the Create Report dialog box, select the Memorized button, highlight the report name, and select OK. Because the report you just created was quite simple, these procedures do not save you many steps. However, your reports will become more complicated and more customized as you gain experience

3

```
            Cash  Flow  Report  -  Mary  Campbell
                     1/1/94 Through 1/31/94
     7/22/94                                           Page 1
     1st U.S.Bank

                                        01/01/1994-
                  Category Description   01/31/1994


          INFLOWS
            Salary                           700.00


          TOTAL INFLOWS                      700.00


          OUTFLOWS
            Groceries                         65.32
            Housing                          150.00
            Misc                              16.50
            Telephone                         19.75
            Utilities:
              Gas & Electric       67.50


            Total Utilities                   67.50


          TOTAL OUTFLOWS                      319.07


          OVERALL TOTAL                       380.93
```

Standard Cash Flow report **Figure 3-5.**

with Quicken, and re-creating them will be equally complicated. Memorized reports save you a great deal of time when you're working with these more advanced report styles.

Printing the Itemized Categories Report

The Itemized Categories report lists and summarizes all the transactions for each category used in the register during a specific time period. Although here you will use this report to work with only the information in the 1st U.S. Bank checking account, the report is much more sophisticated than it might appear. It can summarize information from your Bank, Cash, and Credit Card accounts and, unlike the Cash Flow report, it incorporates category information from Asset and Liability accounts, which you will establish in Chapter 6, "Expanding the Scope of Financial Entries."

The Itemized Categories report gathers all the transactions affecting each category together for your review.

You can print an Itemized Categories report by following these steps:

1. Select Home from the Reports menu, or select the Reports icon from the Iconbar and select Home from the Create Report dialog box.

2. Select Itemized Categories.

3. Type **1/1/94** in the from field.

   Quicken automatically places in this field either January 1 of the current year or the date of the last report you created. You can change the date by using ⊞ and ⊟, instead of typing in a new date.

4. Type **1/31/94** in the to field.

   This tells Quicken to create a report of itemized categories through the end of January.

5. Select OK.

   The Itemized Categories report appears on the screen. You can scroll down the report by using the scroll bar or ⊡.

6. Select the Print button, or press Ctrl-P.

   This opens the Print Report window on your screen.

7. Select Print to print the Itemized Categories report.

   You have the same options here that you have with the Cash Flow report. You can choose to print to a printer, create an ASCII file with or without delimiters, create a 1-2-3 file, or print to the screen. Use the Printer option button, which is the default. Note that the report is two pages long. The top of page 1 of the Itemized Categories report is shown in Figure 3-6.

8. To close the report, press Esc or select Close.

```
                 Itemized Category Report
                    1/1/94 Through 1/31/94
7/22/94                                              Page 1
1st U.S.Bank

     Date       Num       Description      Memo      Category     Clr      Amount


                INCOME/EXPENSE
                  INCOME
                     Salary

1/7/94      DEP        Deposit-Salary    Monthly pay   Salary             700.00

                  Total ...                                               700.00

                TOTAL INCOME                                              700.00


                EXPENSES
                  Groceries

1/7/94      102       Small City Market  Food          Groceries         -22.32
1/19/94     104       Small City Market  Food          Groceries         -43.00

                  Total ...                                               -65.32

                  Housing

1/7/94      103       Small City Apart... Rent         Housing          -150.00

                  Total ...                                             -150.00

                  Misc

1/5/94      101       Small City Times   Paper bill    Misc             -16.50

                  Total ...                                             -16.50

                  Telephone

1/25/94     105       Small City Phone... Phone bill   Telephone        -19.75

                  Total ...                                             -19.75

                  Utilit...


                     Gas & ...

1/4/94      100       Small City Gas &... Gas and Electric  Utilities:Gas & ...  -67.50

                  Total ...                                             -67.50

                Total ...                                               -67.50
```

Standard
Itemized
Categories
report
Figure 3-6.

Customizing Reports

When printing the Cash Flow and Itemized Categories reports, you have many customization options available. These customization options are the same ones used to create custom reports, which are discussed in later chapters.

There are many customizing options you can select to provide reports that meet your specific needs.

You can access the customization options from the Create Report window by selecting Customize, as you did to add a custom title to the Cash Flow report. You can also access this dialog box from the report window by selecting the Customize button from the buttonbar. Remember that once you open the customization dialog box, you can access help on each of the options by pressing F1.

There are six major categories of customization changes you can make. You can select each set of customization options in the Customize Report dialog box by selecting an option button under Customize on the left side of the dialog box. Depending on which option button you select, different options appear on the right side of the dialog box. The options made available by each of these option buttons are shown and explained in Tables 3-1 through 3-6. There are a lot of options you can change for each type of report. For the most part, these options are the same for all types of reports. However, some of them vary depending on the type of report, simply because some options make no sense for a particular report type.

There is no reason for you to be concerned with most of these report customization options at first. For most of Quicken's predefined reports, you will want to change only one or two options that are appropriate to that type of report. Only later, when you create custom reports, will you really need to know about all these selections.

Although the customization options for the reports require a little time to learn, the result can be a dramatic difference in the appearance and content of your reports. Since the Cash Flow and Itemized Categories reports share several layout features, you may find some of the same options useful in both reports. Don't change these options unless the changed report will be more useful to you than the unchanged one. You can change the labeling information on a report as well as the basic organization of the entries.

Changing Column Headings

Quicken lets you change the column headings on reports. You can print a report for the standard monthly time period, or you can change it to one week, two weeks, half a month, a quarter, half a year, or one year. You make

Option	Effect on Report
Title	Sets the title to appear at the top of the report
Row	Sets whether rows display information by category, class, payee, or account name (Summary reports only)
Column	Sets whether columns display totals for periods of time, categories, classes, payees, or accounts (Summary, Budget, and Account Balance reports only)
Subtotal by	Sets whether transactions are grouped by time period, category, class, payee, account, or tax schedule with totals displayed for each group (Transaction reports only)
Interval	Displays a column for total account balances for a time period
Sort by	Sets how transactions are sorted in the report (Transaction reports only)
Cents in Amounts	Sets whether cents or only dollar amounts are shown in reports
Totals Only	Sets whether individual transactions or only totals for sets of transactions are shown
Memo	Sets whether the transaction memos are shown in the report (Transaction reports only)
Category	Sets whether categories are shown in the report (Transaction reports only)
Split Transaction Detail	Sets whether the details of split transactions or only the totals of the transactions are shown (Transaction reports only)

Report
Customization
Report Layout
Options
Table 3-1.

To Include:	Select:
Specific accounts	Individual accounts in the list by clicking or highlighting and pressing [Spacebar]
Types of accounts	Account type button (Bank, Cash, Credit Card, Investment, Asset, or Liability)
All or no accounts	Mark All to toggle between all or none

Report
Customization
Accounts
Options
Table 3-2.

Option	Effect on Report
Amounts	Includes all transactions or only those that are equal to, greater than, or less than the amount you specify
Include Unrealized Gains	Generates transactions for changes in the prices of securities (unrealized gains/ losses) (Transaction reports only)
Include Unrealized Gains	Includes income or inflows for unrealized gains (Summary reports only)
Tax-related Transactions Only	Includes only transactions categorized with tax-related categories
Transaction types	Includes all transactions or only one type (deposits, unprinted checks, or payments)
Status	Sets whether transactions are included that have not cleared, are marked by you as cleared, or have been cleared during reconciliation

Report Customization Transactions Options
Table 3-3.

Option	Effect on Report
Transfers	Includes all transfers, excludes all transfers, or excludes transfers between accounts included in the report
Subcategories	Displays subcategories and subclasses beneath their parent categories or classes, hides all subcategories and subclasses, or displays subcategories or subclasses with parent categories or classes beneath them
Categories	Includes all categories, regardless of use, includes only categories used or with assigned budget amounts, or includes only categories with assigned budget amounts (Budget reports only)

Report Customization Show Row Options
Table 3-4.

To Include:	Select:
A specific category	Categories, then the category in the list
A specific class	Classes, then the class in the list
All or no categories	Categories, then Mark All to toggle between all and none
All or no classes	Classes, then Mark All to toggle between all and none

Report Customization Categories/ Classes Options
Table 3-5.

Field	Includes
Payee Contains	Transactions that have the entered text in the Payee field
Category Contains	Transactions that have the entered text in the Category field
Class Contains	Transactions that have the entered text in the Class field
Memo Contains	Transactions that have the entered text in the Memo field

Report
Customization
Matching
Options
Table 3-6.

3

this change by selecting Customize from the Report buttonbar, and then selecting Report Layout. Simply select the time period you want to use from the Column drop-down list box:

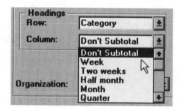

Figure 3-7 shows a report created with half-month time periods used as the column headings.

Follow these steps to create a Cash Flow report that shows biweekly time periods:

1. Select Home from the Reports menu, or click on the Reports button and select Home from the Create Report dialog box.
2. Select Cash Flow.
3. Type **1/1/94** in the from field.

    You can skip steps 3 and 4 if you used this same time period for your last report.
4. Type **1/31/94** in the to field.

    If you selected OK at this point, Quicken would create the report without customization.
5. Select Customize.
6. Move to the Columns field, and open the drop-down list box by clicking on the drop-down arrow or pressing [Alt]-[↓].

7. Select Half month from the drop-down list box.

8. Select the Accounts option button, which is underneath Customize at the left side of the dialog box.

   Notice how the options available on the right side of the dialog box change.

9. Select 1st U.S. Bank to mark the account to be included in this report in the event you have created other accounts.

10. Select OK to create the report.

Quicken displays the completed report on the screen. Figure 3-7 shows the result of the preceding steps.

Changing Row Headings

The Customize Report dialog box also allows you to change the row headings shown in a report. Instead of categories as row headings, as in Figure 3-7, one of

```
                    Cash Flow Report
                   1/1/94 Through 1/31/94

   7/22/94                                              Page 1
   1st U.S.Bank
                              01/01/1994-      01/16/1994-
         Category Description  01/15/1994      01/31/1994


   INFLOWS
      Salary                      700.00            0.00

   TOTAL INFLOWS                  700.00            0.00


   OUTFLOWS
      Groceries                    22.32           43.00
      Housing                     150.00            0.00
      Misc                         16.50            0.00
      Telephone                     0.00           19.75
      Utilities:
         Gas & Electric            67.50            0.00

      Total Utilities              67.50            0.00

   TOTAL OUTFLOWS                 256.32           62.75


   OVERALL TOTAL                  443.68          -62.75
```

Biweekly report for cash flow
Figure 3-7.

```
                        Cash Flow Report
                      1/1/94 Through 1/31/94
    7/22/94                                              Page 1
    1st U.S.Bank

                                            01/01/1994-
                            Payee           01/31/1994

        Deposit-Salary                          700.00
        Small City Apartments                  -150.00
        Small City Gas & Light                  -67.50
        Small City Market                       -65.32
        Small City Phone Company                -19.75
        Small City Times                        -16.50

        OVERALL TOTAL                           380.93
```

Using payee
names as row
headings
Figure 3-8.

your options is to show payees in this location. Figure 3-8 shows the report created after changing the Row drop-down list box to Payee and the Column drop-down list box back to the default Don't Subtotal.

You can make these customization changes by using the buttonbar at the top of the report window. To change the row headings, select Customize, and then select the Report Layout button under Customize, if necessary. Move to the Row box in the Customize Report dialog box, and select Payee from the drop-down list box. To change the column headings, move to the Column box in the Customize Report dialog box, which is under the Row box, and select Don't Subtotal from the drop-down list box.

Changing Other Report Layout Options

There are many other customization options you can choose. Some of these options let you select the organization of your report or determine how transfers are handled. The Report Layout options for the Itemized Categories report include a few more items under Show at the right side of the dialog box than for the Cash Flow report. More items appear because there are more things you may want to show or not show in this report: the Itemized Categories report shows complete transactions, whereas the Cash Flow report shows a summary of transactions. The Report Layout options for the Itemized Categories report are shown on the following illustration.

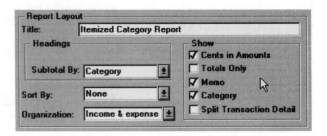

The Organization drop-down list box lets you change from the default organization, which shows separate totals for income and expenses, to an organization that shows information on a cash flow basis.

The items under Show at the right side of the dialog box let you specify the combination of totals, memos, and categories to be shown on the report. You can also elect to show the details of split transactions. Split transactions are discussed in Chapter 6, "Expanding the Scope of Financial Entries." Notice that you have the option of showing cents in the report form. The default setting for this option is to display cents.

Setting Row Contents

When you select Show Rows under Customize in the Customize Report dialog box, you find options that let you determine which row contacts are shown in your report. The Show Rows options look like this:

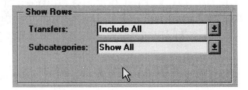

The Transfers drop-down list box allows you to define how you want your reports to handle transfers between accounts. For example, when Quicken transfers cash from your check register to your savings register, do you want these transfers included or excluded from the individual reports? Transfers are covered in detail in Chapter 10, "Creating Custom Reports."

The Subcategories drop-down list box lets you define how you want your reports to display the contents of subcategories. You can choose to show all subcategories, to hide all of them, to only show totals for the parent categories, or to reverse the display of categories and subcategories so that the report is divided by subcategories rather than by categories.

Filtering Reports

Filters let you select the data to be shown in a report. You should read the overview that follows and then do the exercise at the end of this section for practice using filters.

You can use filters to confine your report to entries that have specified text in the Payee, Memo, Category, or Class field. This allows you to create a report for all entries relating to utilities or groceries, for example. You can use a standard report form to display a report for a specific payee, such as Small City Times, or you can display a report for all records that contain "Small". To establish filters based on Payee, Memo, Category, or Class field matches, select Matching under Customize in the Customize Report dialog box.

3

If you want to further narrow searches, you can use special characters. You can enter = to specify an exact match, .. to specify any text, ~ to specify anything but the following text, or **?** to substitute for any one character.

The Matching options in the Customize Report dialog box for an Itemized Categories report are shown here:

If the dialog box contains the word "Small" in the Payee Contains text box, then processing this request would create a report of all the records with a Payee entry containing "Small." You can modify the printed report further by limiting the report to transactions that have specified text in any combination of the Payee, Memo, Category, and Class fields.

You can filter reports to search for specific payees, categories, classes, or memo contents.

Another way to filter a report is to determine which transactions to include based on their amount, type, or status. To set this type of filter, select Transactions under Customize. You can designate whether to include transactions below, below and equal to, equal to, above, or above and equal to a designated amount by selecting an option from the Amounts drop-down list box and then, in the following field, entering a value to be used to compare to the transaction amounts. You can limit which transactions are included based on their type by selecting Payments, Deposits, Unprinted Checks, or All Transactions from the Transaction Types drop-down list box.

Use these options to create a Cash Flow report for all the transactions that begin with "Small" in the Payee field. Complete the following steps:

1. Select Home from the Reports menu, or click on the Reports icon in the Iconbar and select Home from the Create Report dialog box.
2. Select Cash Flow.
3. Enter **1/1/94** in the from field and **1/31/94** in the to field.
4. Select Customize.
5. Type a new title in the Title field. If this field is not displayed, select Report Layout under Customize to display it.
6. Select Matching under Customize.
7. Type **Small** in the Payee Contains text box, and select OK to create the report.

   Since the report shows categories for the row headings, you cannot tell if the correct information is displayed. To correct this problem, you can customize the report so that Quicken lists the payee names as the row headings. You can use the buttonbar at the top of the report to make your changes.

8. Select Customize from the report window's buttonbar.
9. Select Report Layout under Customize, if necessary.
10. Select Payee from the Row drop-down list box, and then select OK to return to the report.
11. Press [Esc] to close the report window.

Working with Category Totals

You can create an Itemized Categories report that shows only the totals for each category. To create a total report for the January transactions, follow these steps:

1. Select Home from the Reports menu, or click on the Reports button and then select Home from the Create Report dialog box.
2. Select Itemized Categories.
3. Type **1/1/94** in the from field and **1/31/94** in the to field, if they contain different entries.
4. Select Report Layout from beneath Customize, if necessary.
5. Select the Totals Only check box under Show at the right side of the dialog box.
6. Select OK to create the report.

Changing Printer Settings

As mentioned previously, like other Windows products, Quicken 3 for Windows uses the Windows printer drivers when printing. A printer driver is a file containing all the information specific to your printer that is needed to print a document on that printer. When you print a document from Quicken, it is read into a special temporary file. Then the Windows Print Manager program sends the information to the printer while you continue working with Quicken, so you don't lose much time to the printing process.

Within Quicken, you can select which printer to use, how the paper is fed to the printer, and which of the available fonts to use for the body and the headings of your report. You can also use Quicken to activate the Windows dialog box that sets the defaults for some of the features your printer has available. When you make these changes, the defaults change, not only for Quicken, but for all Windows applications.

The following examples illustrate making setting changes to an HP LaserJet III printer. Some of the options you see will be quite different if you are using another type of printer. If you are using a different printer, you will be unable to make identical choices, but you may be able to make parallel ones, depending on the features that your printer supports.

You can follow these steps to change the print settings:

1. Select Printer Setup from the File menu.
2. Select Report/Graphs Printing Setup. The Report Printer Setup dialog box appears, as shown in Figure 3-9.
3. Select the printer you want to use from the Printer drop-down list box.

   This list includes all the printers currently installed in Windows. If you want to use an uninstalled printer, you need to use the Windows Control Panel to install that printer. For more details, consult your Windows manual.
4. Enter the margins you want to use for your report in the Left, Right, Top, and Bottom text boxes under Margins. Margins are the spaces between the edges of the paper and the printed text. By default, all margins are set to .5 inch.
5. From the Paper Feed drop-down list box, select how the paper is fed into the printer. You should leave this set to the default, Auto-detect, unless Quicken is not printing properly on the paper.
6. Select Head Font to change the font used to print the headings of your report. The Report Default Headline Font dialog box opens, as shown in Figure 3-10.

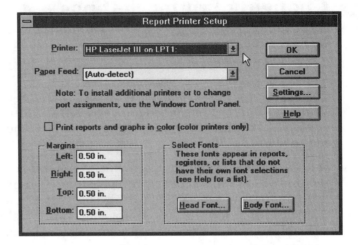

Report Printer
Setup dialog
box
Figure 3-9.

Select a font in the <u>F</u>ont list box, a style in the Font St<u>y</u>le list box, and a size in the <u>S</u>ize list box. Then select OK to return to the Report Printer Setup dialog box.

7. Select <u>B</u>ody Font to change the font used to print the body of your report. A dialog box opens that looks just like the Report Default Headline Font dialog box shown previously and is used in the same fashion.

8. To make changes to the printer's default settings, select <u>S</u>ettings. A Setup dialog box opens, similar to the one shown in Figure 3-11.

The options available in this dialog box depend on the features that your printer supports, so your printer probably will not have identical options. When you are finished setting these options, select OK. Remember that these settings are now the default for all Windows applications, not just for Quicken.

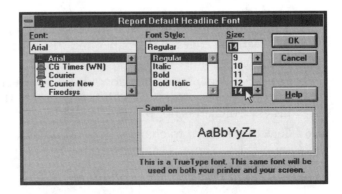

Report Default
Headline Font
dialog box
Figure 3-10.

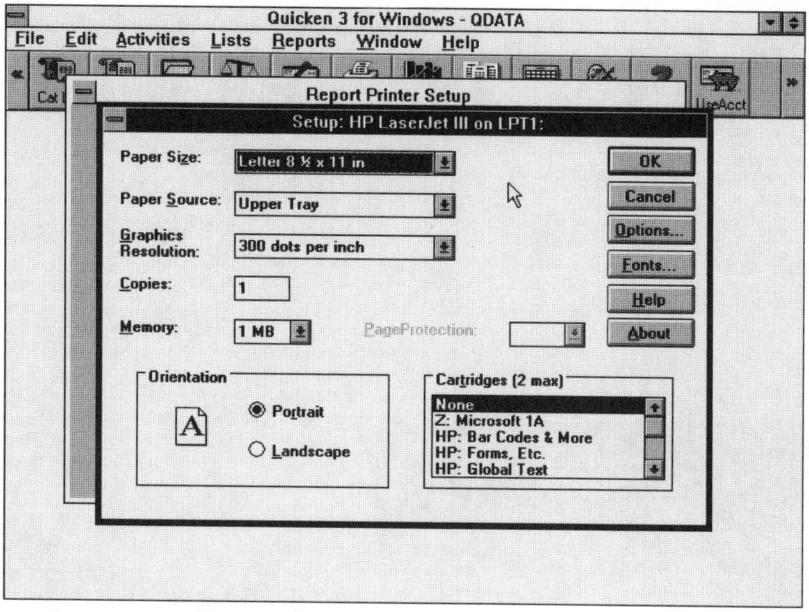

3

Setup dialog
box for
printing
Figure 3-11.

CHAPTER

RECONCILING YOUR QUICKEN REGISTER

Reconciling your account is the process of comparing your entries with those of the bank. This allows you to determine whether discrepancies between the bank's record of your balance and your record are due to errors or timing differences. Timing differences occur because your balance includes transactions up to the present date, but your bank statement was compiled before transactions you have recorded cleared the bank. These timing differences must be reconciled to ensure neither

Monthly bank statement reconciliations should be part of your personal financial planning program.

you nor the bank has made an error. If you are serious about monitoring your financial activities, a monthly reconciliation of your checking accounts, both personal and business, should be considered a necessary step in your financial record keeping.

In addition to timing differences, there may be transactions not recorded in your register or errors in the amount entries. With manual check registers, you can also make addition and subtraction errors when you record checks and deposits. This is one type of error you do not need to worry about with Quicken since its calculations are always perfect if you record the amount correctly.

Another cause of differences is transactions the bank has recorded on your bank statement that you haven't entered in your register. For example, you may have automatic monthly withdrawals for house or automobile payments or savings transfers to another bank account or mutual fund. In addition, you may have a bank service charge for maintaining your checking account or printing checks, or you may have earned interest. These differences are addressed in detail throughout this chapter.

In this chapter you look at how reconciliation works and walk through a reconciliation exercise. The last part of the chapter deals with problems that can occur and the methods for getting your account to agree with your bank's records. This part of the chapter does not require entries since it is designed to show potential problems rather than show how to make additional corrections to your entries.

Quicken's Reconciliation Process

Quicken reduces the frustration of the monthly reconciliation process by providing a systematic approach to reconciling your checking accounts. Since the process includes more steps than the exercises you have completed so far, looking at some overview information first will help you place each of the steps in perspective to the overall objective of the process.

A Few Key Points

There are three points to remember when using the Quicken reconciliation system. First, Quicken reconciles only one checking account at a time, so you have to reconcile each of your personal and business accounts separately.

Second, you should make it a habit to reconcile your checking accounts on a monthly basis. You can easily monitor your checking balances once you begin a monthly routine of reconciling your accounts, but attempting to reconcile six months of statements at one sitting is a frustrating experience, even with Quicken.

Third, before beginning the formal Quicken reconciliation process, examine your bank statement for any unusual entries, such as check numbers that are out of the range of numbers you expected to find on the statement. (If you find checks 501 and 502 listed as cleared, and all the other cleared checks are numbered in the 900s, the bank might have charged another customer's checks against your account.) This examination provides an indication of what to look for during the reconciliation process.

An Overview of the Process

Quicken leads you through the reconciliation process.

When you begin reconciliation, Quicken asks for information from your current bank statement, such as the opening and ending dollar balances, service charges, and any interest earned on your account. (Quicken records these transactions in the check register and marks them as cleared since the bank has already processed these items.)

4

Once you have entered this preparatory information, Quicken presents a summary screen for marking cleared items. All the transactions you recorded in the account, as well as the service charge and interest-earned transactions, are shown on this screen.

Quicken maintains a running total of your balance as you proceed through the reconciliation process. Each debit or credit is applied to the opening balance total as it is marked cleared. You can determine the difference between the cleared balance amount and the bank statement balance at any time. Your objective at the end of the reconciliation process is a difference of zero.

The first step is to check the amounts of your Quicken entries against the amounts listed on the bank statement. Where there are discrepancies, you can switch to your Quicken register and check the entries. You may find incorrect amounts recorded in the Quicken register or incorrect amounts recorded by your bank. You may also find that you forgot to record a check or a deposit. You can create or change register entries from the register window.

Once you have finished with an entry, you mark the transaction as cleared. After resolving any differences between your balance and the bank's, you can print the reconciliation reports. A check mark is used in the cleared column until Quicken confirms an entry. Then Quicken replaces it with an X, as you will see as this lesson proceeds.

Preparing the Printer for Reconciliation

Before you begin reconciliation, you should check your printer settings. This is important because at the end of the reconciliation process, you are given an opportunity to print reconciliation reports. You can't change printer settings after Quicken presents you with the Print Reconciliation Report window; it's too late. If you attempt to make a change by pressing (Esc), the dialog box is closed, and you have to start over. However, you don't need to complete the detailed reconciliation procedure again.

Select Printer Setup from the File menu to check your printer settings now. Then you will be ready to start the reconciliation example.

A Sample Reconciliation

From reading about the objectives of the reconciliation process, you should understand its concept. Actually doing a reconciliation will fit the pieces together. The following exercise uses a sample bank statement and the entries you made to the 1st U.S. Bank register in Chapter 2, "Making Register Entries."

1. Select Use Register from the Activities menu, or click the Register icon in the Iconbar. This step is necessary only if your register does not appear in the Quicken window.

   You should be in the 1st U.S. Bank register, which contains the entries you made in Chapter 2.

2. Select Reconcile from the Activities menu or click the Recon icon in the Iconbar to start Quicken's reconciliation system.

   You see the Reconcile Bank Statement dialog box:

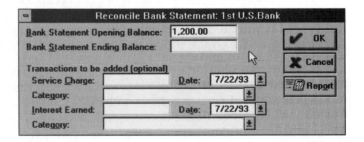

   Figure 4-1 is a copy of your first bank statement from 1st U.S. Bank; you will use it to respond to Quicken's prompts for information.

   The first time you reconcile an account, Quicken enters the opening balance shown in the register. Since you are reconciling your account with the first monthly bank statement, this should be the balance on your screen.

3. Enter **1398.21** in the Bank Statement Ending Balance text box.

4. Enter **11.50** in the Service Charge text box.

   You must enter all the service charges and similar charges in a lump sum. In this case, the bank has charged you a monthly service charge and a check printing charge that total 11.50 (3.50 + 8.00). Although it is

4

	1st U.S. Bank P.O. Box 123 Small City, USA	DATE 2/10/94 PAGE 1 OF 1

Mary Campbell
P.O. Box ABC
Small City, USA

DATE	DESCRIPTION	AMOUNT	BALANCE
1-1	Deposit	1,200.00	1,200.00
1-6	100 check	77.50-	1,122.50
1-7	Deposit	700.00	1,822.50
1-11	101 check	16.50-	1,806.00
1-12	103 check	150.00-	1,656.00
1-20	102 check	22.32-	1,633.68
2-1	Loan payment deduction	225.00-	1,408.68
2-1	Service charge	11.50-	1,397.18
2-1	Interest	1.03	1,398.21

Date	Check No.	Amount
1-6	# 100	77.50-
1-11	# 101	16.50-
1-20	# 102	22.32-
1-12	# 103	150.00-

STATEMENT

Bank
Statement for
the 1st U.S.
Bank account
Figure 4-1.

easy enough to add these two numbers in your head, if you need to compute a more complex addition, you can always call up the Quicken Calculator by selecting Use Calculator from the Activities menu. To add numbers using the calculator, you type the first number, press ⊕, type the next number, and so on.

5. Enter **2/1/94** in the Date text box as the date for the bank charge.

   Remember that the dates in the examples are used so that your reports and data will exactly match what is in this book. You can use the calendar to select this date.

6. Enter **Bank Chrg** in the Category text box.

   Entering a category is optional; however, to take full advantage of Quicken's reporting features, you should use a category for all transactions. You can ensure that the category is entered correctly by starting to type it and then letting QuickFill complete the entry, or by selecting the entry from the drop-down list.

> You can use Quicken's calculator during the reconciliation process to handle any calculation.

7. Enter **1.03** in the Interest Earned text box.

8. Enter **2/1/94** in the Date text box.

9. Enter **Int Inc** in the Category text box.

10. Select OK.

    The Reconcile Bank Account window shown in Figure 4-2 appears. Here you mark cleared items. The payments and checks are on the left side of the window and the credits are on the right because many bank statements divide transactions by whether they add money to your account or remove it. The window shows totals at the bottom. You will find all your register entries and the new service charge and interest transactions in this window. The new transactions have a check mark in the Clr column to indicate that they are cleared. The cleared balance shown at the bottom of the window is your opening balance of 1200.00 modified by the two new transactions. Quicken also monitors the difference between this cleared total and the bank statement balance.

    Note that Quicken enters an X in the Clr column and an * in the Clr field of your check register as shown in Figure 4-3.

11. Press ⊕ once, and the entry for check number 100 is highlighted. Since the bank statement entry and this summary entry do not agree, select Edit to move to the register window.

    The register window looks like Figure 4-3. Check to be certain that check number 100 is highlighted in the 1st U.S. Bank register. If you looked at your canceled check for this transaction, you would see that it was for **77.50** and that it cleared the bank for that amount. Since the register entry is wrong, you must make a correction.

12. Move to the Payment field, type **77.50**, and select Record or press Enter.

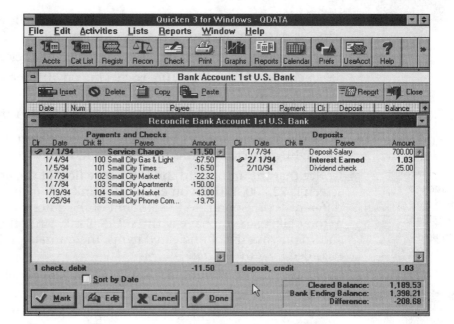

Reconcile
Bank Account
window
Figure 4-2.

4

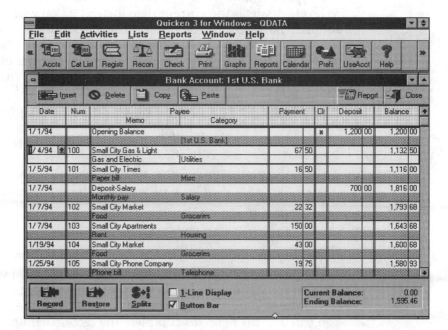

Check register
window
Figure 4-3.

13. Return to the Reconcile Bank Account window by clicking on the window or selecting it from the Windows menu.

14. Select the newly corrected transaction to mark it as cleared.

15. Select checks 101 through 103 by clicking on 101, moving to 103, and clicking 103 while pressing down the `Shift` key.

    Quicken adds check marks to the Clr column for 101 through 103.

When the
Difference
field shows
no amount
remaining, your
reconciliation
is complete.

16. Mark the deposit on 1/7/94 as cleared by clicking on it or by moving the highlight to it with the arrow keys and then pressing `Spacebar`.

    Notice that the amount in the Difference field at the bottom of the screen is 225.00. When you check the bank statement, you see that this difference corresponds to the amount of the automatic deduction for an automobile loan you have with 1st U.S. Bank. Since this amount is not shown on your list of uncleared items, the transaction is not yet recorded in your register.

17. Move to the register window by clicking on it or by selecting it from the Windows menu.

18. Move to the end of the register by using the scroll bar or by pressing `Ctrl`-`End`.

19. Enter **2/1/94** in the Date column.

    You enter the date 2/1/94 in the Date column so that the transaction will be recorded on the same date that the bank deducted the amount from your account. When you reconcile your own accounts, you can record the date as the current date instead if you wish. Since this is an automatic deduction, you don't use a check number. You can select EFT (which stand for Electronic Funds Transfer) from the Num field's drop-down list box, indicating an automatic transfer of funds. This is not required, but it makes identifying this type of transaction easier in your reports.

20. Type **Automatic Loan Payment** in the Payee field.

21. Type **225** in the Payment field.

22. Type **Auto payment** in the Memo field.

23. Enter Auto:Loan in the category field by using the drop-down list box. If you use the drop-down list box, you don't have to type the category name.

24. Select Record to record the transaction.

25. Return to the Reconcile Bank Account window.

26. Select the new transaction in the Payments and Checks list.

    The Difference field indicates that you have balanced your checking account for this month because it shows an amount of 0.00. Figure 4-4 shows the Reconcile Bank Account window with the account balanced. You can use this figure to complete the reconciliation.

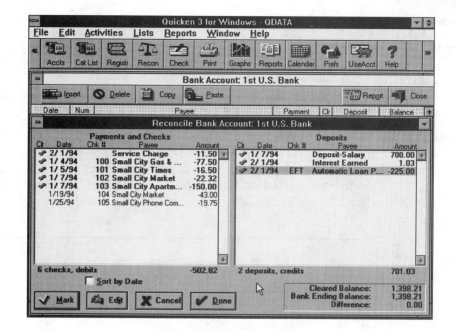

The new entry
reconciles the
account
Figure 4-4.

27. Select Done, and the Reconciliation Complete dialog box appears.

28. Select Yes from this dialog box. The Reconciliation Report Setup
window appears:

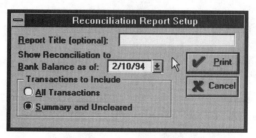

You must complete this window to print the reconciliation reports.

29. Type **2/10/94** in the Show Reconciliation to Bank Balance as of text box.

This changes the reconciliation date to conform to the example date.

30. Select All Transactions.

31. Select Print.

32. Select Printer in the Print Report dialog box, if necessary, and then
select Print.

You have now completed the reconciliation process, and Quicken is printing
your reconciliation reports.

NOTE: If the automobile referred to in the reports is used for business, the interest on loan payments for it is tax deductible (with certain limitations).

Quicken's Reconciliation Reports

Since you selected Quicken's <u>A</u>ll Transactions option, you have received four reconciliation reports: Reconciliation Summary, Cleared Transaction Detail, Uncleared Transaction Detail up to 2/10/94, and Uncleared Transaction Detail after 2/10/94. Three of these reports are shown in Figures 4-5 through 4-7. Note

```
                         Reconciliation Report
      1st U.S. Bank                                          Page 1
      07/22/94
                           Reconciliation Summary




         BANK STATEMENT -- CLEARED TRANSACTIONS:


             Previous Balance:                              1,200.00


                 Checks and Payments      6   Items          -502.82
                 Deposits and Oth...      2   Items           701.03


             Ending Balance of Bank Statement:              1,398.21



         YOUR RECORDS -- UNCLEARED TRANSACTIONS:


             Cleared Balance:                               1,398.21


                 Checks and Payments      2   Items           -62.75
                 Deposits and Oth...      1   Item             25.00



             Register Balance as of 02/10/1994:            1,360.46
                 Checks and Payments      0   Items             0.00
                 Deposits and Oth...      0   Items             0.00



             Register Ending Balance:                       1,360.46
```

Reconciliation
Summary
report
Figure 4-5.

```
                         Reconciliation Report
   1st U.S. Bank                                          Page 2
   07/22/94
                         Cleared Transaction Detail


   Date    Num      Payee            Memo         Category      Clr Amount

   Clr Checks and Payments

   1/ 4/94 100   Small City Ga... Gas and Elec... Utilities:Gas &  x    -77.50
   1/ 5/94 101   Small City Times Paper bill      Misc             x    -16.50
   1/ 7/94 102   Small City Ma... Food            Groceries        x    -22.32
   1/ 7/94 103   Small City Ap... Rent            Housing          x   -150.00
   2/ 1/94       Service Charge                   Bank Chrg        x    -11.50
   2/ 1/94 EFT   Automatic Loa... Auto payment    Auto:Loan        x   -225.00

   Total Clr Checks and Payments                          6  Items-502.82



   Clr Deposits and Other Credits

   1/ 7/94 DEP  Deposit-Salary   Monthly pay      Salary           x    700.00
   2/ 1/94      Interest Earned                   Int Inc          x      1.03

   Total Clr Deposits and Other Credits                   2  Items 701.03




   Total Clr Transactions                                 8  Items 198.21
```

Cleared
Transaction
Detail report
Figure 4-6.

that the spacing in these figures may differ from that in your printed reports
because you are probably using a different printer.

NOTE: Remember that the dates on these reconciliation reports will vary
depending on when they are created. The dates in the upper-left corner
of your document will not match those shown here. However, if you enter
the dates of the transactions and the reports as given in this book, your
reports should match those shown in all other particulars.

The Reconciliation Summary report, shown in Figure 4-5, lists the beginning
balance of 1,200.00 and summarizes the activity the bank reported for your
account during the reconciliation period in the section labeled "BANK

```
                    Reconciliation Report
   1st U.S. Bank                                    Page 3
   07/22/94
                Uncleared Transaction Detail up to 02/10/1994


    Date   Num      Payee         Memo      Category     Clr Amount


   Uncleared Checks and Payments

    1/19/94 104  Small City Ma... Food      Groceries        -43.00
    1/25/94 105  Small City Ph... Phone bill Telephone        -19.75


   Total Uncleared Checks and Payments         2  Items -62.75



   Uncleared Deposits and Other Credits

    2/10/94 DEP  Dividend check   Dividend che... Div Income    25.00

   Total Uncleared Deposits and Other Credits   1  Item  25.00



   Total Uncleared Transactions                 3  Items -37.75
```

Uncleared
Transaction
Detail Up to
2/10/94 report
Figure 4-7.

STATEMENT — CLEARED TRANSACTIONS." The first part of the section headed "YOUR RECORDS — UNCLEARED TRANSACTIONS" summarizes the difference between your register balance at the date of the reconciliation—2/10/94—and the bank's balance. In this case, there are two checks written and one deposit made to your account that were not shown on the bank statement. The report shows any checks and deposits recorded since the reconciliation date. In your sample reconciliation, no transactions were entered after 2/10/94, so the register balance at that date is also the register ending balance.

The Cleared Transaction Detail report, shown in Figure 4-6, contains two sections: "Clr Checks and Payments" and "Clr Deposits and Other Credits." The items they contain were part of the reconciliation process. Notice that this report provides detail for the "CLEARED TRANSACTIONS" section of the Reconciliation Summary report.

The Uncleared Transaction Detail up to 2/10/94 report, shown in Figure 4-7 contains the sections "Uncleared Checks and Payments" and "Uncleared

Deposits and Other Credits," which provide the details of uncleared transactions included in your register up to the date of the reconciliation. This report provides detail for the "UNCLEARED TRANSACTIONS" section of the Reconciliation Summary report.

The Uncleared Transaction Detail after 2/10/94 report (not shown) provides detail for those transactions recorded in the check register that have a later date than the reconciliation report. In this example no transactions dated after the reconciliation date were recorded, as you can see in the final section of the Reconciliation Summary report.

These four reports are all printed automatically when you select Quicken's All Transactions option. If you had selected Quicken's Summary and Uncleared option, which is the default option, you would have received only the Reconciliation Summary report and the Uncleared Transaction Detail up to 2/10/94 report.

4

Additional Reconciliation Issues and Features

The reconciliation procedures discussed so far provide a foundation for using Quicken to reconcile your accounts. This section covers some additional issues that may prove useful in balancing your accounts in the future.

Updating Your Opening Balance

Although you can wait to begin reconciling your bank accounts, you should begin as soon as you start using Quicken.

The importance of maintaining a regular reconciliation schedule has already been noted, and you should balance your checking account before you begin to use Quicken to record your transactions. However, there may be times when the opening balance Quicken enters in the Reconcile Bank Statement window differs from the opening balance shown in the check register.

This can happen in three situations. First, when you reconcile a Quicken register for the first time, there may be a discrepancy due to timing differences. Second, there may be a difference if you start Quicken at a point other than the beginning of the year and then try to add transactions from earlier in the year. Third, balances may differ if you use the reconciliation feature *after* recording Quicken transactions for several periods.

First-Time Reconciliations

If you open a new account and begin to use Quicken immediately, there will not be a discrepancy, but a discrepancy will occur if you do not enter the first transaction or two in Quicken. For example, suppose you open an account on 12/31/93 for 1300.00 and immediately write a check for a 1993 expenditure of 100.00. Then you decide to start your Quicken register on 1/1/94, when the balance in your manual register is 1200.00. The bank statement would show the opening balance as 1300.00. In order to reconcile the difference between the bank statement and the Quicken register balance on 1/1/94, you can do one of two things.

The first alternative is to switch to the check register while performing the reconciliation procedures, enter the 100.00 check, correct the opening balance to reflect the beginning bank balance of 1300.00, and proceed with the reconciliation process, without any opening balance difference.

The second option is to have Quicken enter an adjustment in the reconciliation to correct for the difference between the check register's and the bank statement's beginning balances, after marking all of the cleared transactions and accounting for other differences in the ending balances. When Quicken enters the opening balance as 1200.00 and you change it to agree with the bank statement's 1300.00, Quicken displays a Create Opening Balance Adjustment dialog box, which provides a written description of the nature of the problem and offers to make an adjustment:

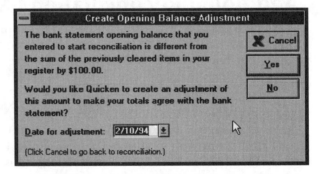

Quicken displays this dialog box after you select Done from the Reconcile Bank Account window. Quicken also adds an Opening Bal Difference field to the bottom of the Reconcile Bank Account window and places a –100.00 balance in it.

If you want to search for the problem on your own, select Cancel to return to the Reconcile Bank Account window. If you want to have Quicken make a correction, follow these steps:

1. Enter a date in the Date for adjustment text box.

2. Select Yes.

   Quicken reconciles the opening balances by making an adjustment to the check register for the 100.00 transaction. The Adjust Balance dialog box appears.

3. If you want Quicken to make an adjustment for you, select Adjust Balance.

The Reconciliation Complete:Balance Adjusted dialog box appears after Quicken makes an adjustment for the difference.

4. Select <u>Y</u>es to have Quicken display the Reconciliation Report Setup dialog box.

   You can now complete the reconciliation report printing process. Note that if you select Cancel in any of these dialog boxes, you will be returned to the reconciliation process.

Adding Previous Transactions to Quicken

You most likely purchased Quicken at a point other than the beginning of your personal or business financial reporting year. In this case, you probably started recording your transactions when you purchased Quicken and entered your checking account balance at that time as your opening balance. This discussion assumes that you have been preparing reconciliations using Quicken and now want to go back and record all your previous transactions for the current year in Quicken. Obviously, your bank balance and the Quicken balance will not agree after the transactions have been added.

Follow these steps:

1. Since you are going to be adding to your Quicken register, be sure you have the latest printout of your Quicken register. If you don't, print your check register now, before you enter any additional transactions. This gives you a record of your transactions to date, which is important should you later need to reconstruct them.

2. Go to your Quicken register window and change the amounts in the Date and Deposit fields of the Opening Balance transaction to correspond to the bank statement that you used at the beginning of the year.

NOTE: The importance of saving your bank statements is apparent. Old statements are not important only for the reconstruction of your Quicken system but also in the event you are audited by the Internal Revenue Service. It takes only one IRS audit for you to realize the importance of maintaining a complete and accurate history of your financial transactions.

3. Using your manual records and past bank statements, enter the previous transactions in your Quicken register. Remember to enter bank service charges and automatic payment deductions in case you have not previously entered them in your register, but only used them during reconciliation.

4. When you have completed the updating process, compare your ending check register balance with the printed copy you made in step 1. This is

important because if they do not balance, you have made an error in entering your transactions. If this is the case, determine whether the difference is an opening account balance difference or an error. (Your options for fixing discrepancies between opening balances are described earlier in this chapter in the section "First-Time Reconciliations.")

5. The next time you reconcile your Quicken account (assuming you have reconciled the account before), type the opening balance on the latest bank statement over that provided by Quicken in the Reconcile Bank Statement window.

6. Before completing the new reconciliation, go to the check register and type **X** in the Clr column for all transactions that have cleared in previous months.

7. Reconcile the current month's transaction. (Go to the section "A Sample Reconciliation" if you need help.)

First-Time Reconciliation for Existing Users

Although you may have been using Quicken for some time, you may not have used the Reconciliation feature before. If you are in this situation, the recommended process for reconciling your account is as follows:

1. Begin with the first bank statement that applies to your Quicken account, and reconcile each of the past bank statements as if you were reconciling your account upon receipt of each of the statements.

2. Follow this process for each subsequent statement until you have caught up to the current bank statement.

Correcting Errors

Hopefully there will not be many times when you need Quicken to correct errors during the reconciliation process. However, there may be times when you can't find the amount displayed in the Difference field on your reconciliation screen, and rather than searching further for your error, you want to have Quicken make an adjustment to balance your register with your bank statement.

This situation could have occurred in the 1st U.S. Bank reconciliation process described in the section "Quicken's Reconciliation Process." In that section you made an adjustment of 10.00 to check number 100 in order to correct your recording error, but if you had been careless you might have missed the error when comparing your bank statement with your check register. In this case, the Difference field in your Reconcile Bank Account window would show a 10.00 difference after clearing all items. If you can't find an error, you can perform the following steps to have Quicken make an adjustment.

CAUTION: This process could have a serious impact on your future reports and check register; don't take this approach to the reconciliation difference lightly.

1. In the Reconcile Bank Account window, select <u>D</u>one. The Adjust Balance dialog box appears, and the amount of the difference is indicated.

   At this point you can still return to the register and check for the difference by selecting Cancel.

2. Select OK.

   You have told Quicken that you do not want to search any longer for the difference and that you want an adjustment to be made. The adjustment will be dated the current date and will be recorded as "Balance Adjustment." If you had selected Cancel, Quicken would have returned you to the Reconcile Bank Account window, and you could have continued to search for the difference.

3. Select OK. The Reconciliation Report Setup window appears. Now you can complete the window as described in the "A Sample Reconciliation" section of this chapter.

4

CHAPTER

5

WRITING AND PRINTING CHECKS

In addition to recording the checks you write in Quicken's register, you can enter check writing information on your screen and have Quicken print the checks for you. Although this requires you to order preprinted checks that conform to Quicken's check layout, it means that you can enter a transaction once—in the Write Checks window— and Quicken will print your check and record the register entry.

You can order Quicken checks in five different styles, and checks for both tractor-feed printers and laser printers are available. Regardless of the check style, there is no problem with acceptance by banks, credit unions, or savings and loans since the required account numbers and check numbers are preprinted on the checks.

The available check styles include standard 8 1/2- by 3 1/2-inch checks, voucher-style checks that have a 3 1/2-inch tear-off stub, and 2 5/6- by 6-inch wallet-style checks with a tear-off stub. You can order all these check types for traditional printers, and you can order the regular or voucher checks for laser printers, directly from Intuit.

To print out a check order form, you choose Order Supplies from the Activities menu and select OK. As you can see on the order form, Quicken also sells window envelopes to fit the checks and can add a company logo to your checks.

Even if you are not certain whether you want to order check stock, you can still try the exercises in this chapter. You may be so pleased with the ease of entry and the professional appearance of the checks that you decide to order checks to start entering your own transactions. You will definitely not want to print your own checks without the special check stock, since banks will not cancel (or stop) payments on checks that don't have a preprinted account number.

Using CheckFree with Quicken allows you to pay bills electronically.

You can also enter transactions in Quicken for transmission to the CheckFree payment processing service via a modem. Your Quicken register entries are updated after transmission, and the CheckFree processing center handles the payment for you. This chapter provides some information on this service, since you might want to consider it as a next step in the total automation of your financial transactions.

Writing Checks

Writing a check in Quicken is as easy as writing a check in your checkbook. Although a Quicken check has a few more fields, most of these are optional and are designed to provide better records of your expense transactions. All you really need to do is fill in the blanks on a Quicken check form.

Entering the Basic Information

To activate the check writing features, select Write Checks from the Activities menu, or select the Check icon on the Iconbar. The exercise presented here is designed to be entered after the reconciliation example in

Chapter 4, "Reconciling Your Quicken Register," but it can actually be entered at any time.

Figure 5-1 shows a blank Quicken check form on the screen. The only field that has been completed is the Date field; by default, the current date is placed on the first check. On checks after the first, the date matches the last check written. For this exercise, you change the dates on all the checks written to match the dates on the sample transactions. When an electronic payment check box appears, you will need to clear it if you plan to mail out checks yourself. You should already be familiar with most of the other fields on the Write Checks window from the entries you made in Quicken's register. However, the Address field was not part of the register entries. It is added to the check for use with window envelopes. When the check is printed, all you have to do is insert it in a window envelope and mail it; the recipient's address shows through the window.

As many as three monetary amounts may appear in the bottom-right corner of the window. The Checks to Print field shows the total dollar amount of any checks written but not yet printed. This field is not displayed until you fill in the first check and record the transaction.

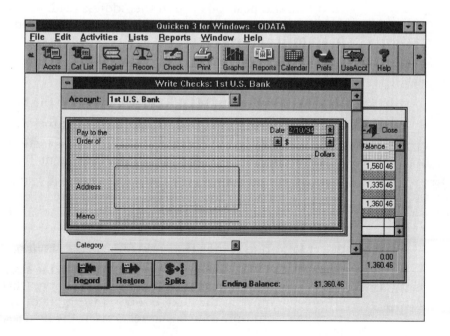

Blank Write
Checks
window
Figure 5-1.

The Current Balance field appears if you write checks with dates after the current date, called *postdated checks*. Postdated checks do not affect the current balance, but they alter the ending balance. They are written to record future payments. All of the checks shown in this book are postdated because the dates they are assigned are after the dates this book is being written. They may or may not be postdated for you as you enter them, depending on when you are reading this book. The Ending Balance field shows the balance in the account after all the checks written have been deducted.

If you are using the keyboard to enter checks, you can use `Tab` and `Shift`-`Tab` to move from field to field on the check form. When you are finished entering the check information, select Record to record the transaction.

Follow these instructions to enter the information for your first check:

1. Type **2/13/94** in the Date field.

   You can use `+` or `-` to change the date, or you can use the drop-down calendar to select a date.

2. Type **South Haven Print Supply** in the Pay to the Order of field.

3. Type **58.75** in the amounts field under the date.

   Quicken supports amounts as large as $9,999,999.99. Notice that when you complete the amount entry, Quicken spells out the amount on the next line and positions you in the Address field. Although this entire field is optional, entering the address here allows you to mail the check in a window envelope.

4. To copy the payee name, type ' and press `Enter`.

5. Type **919 Superior Avenue**, and press `Enter`.

6. Type **South Haven, MI 49090**, and move to the Memo field.

7. Type **Printing Brochure - PTA Dinner** in the Memo field.

8. Enter **Charity** in the Category field since you are donating the cost of this printing job by paying the bill for the Parent-Teacher Association.

   Remember that you can use Quicken's QuickFill feature by typing **Ch** to make the Charity category appear on your screen, or you can use the drop-down list box. No matter which approach you choose, your screen looks like the one in Figure 5-2.

9. Select Record to complete and record the transaction.

   You can enter as many checks as you want in one session. Use the preceding procedure to enter another transaction. Check each field before you move to the next, but don't worry if you make a mistake or two; you learn how to make corrections in the next section. Enter this check now:

Writing a check with Quicken is easier than using your checkbook.

Date:	**2/13/94**
Payee:	**Holland Lumber**
Payment:	**120.00**
Address:	**Holland Lumber** **2314 E. 8th Street** **Holland, MI 49094**
Memo:	**Deck repair**
Category:	**Home Rpair**

3

Remember that you can select Home Rpair from the drop-down category list, or you can use QuickFill.

When you have finished, select Record to record the transaction. Although Quicken moves you to the next check, you can use the scroll bar or press [Pg Up] to see the check you've just completed, which is shown in Figure 5-3.

Reviewing Checks and Making Corrections

You can make corrections to a check before or after completing the transaction. Although it is easiest to make them before completion, the most important

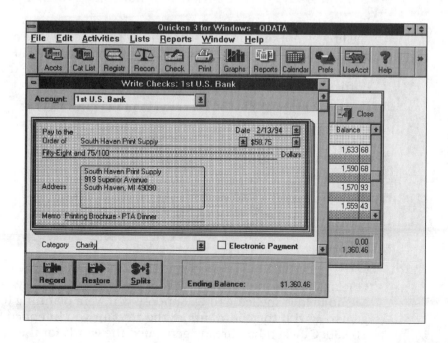

Entering the
first check
transaction
Figure 5-2.

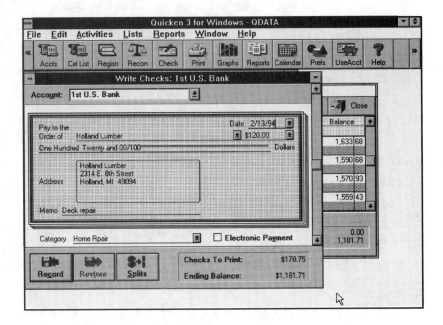

Entering a check for Holland Lumber
Figure 5-3.

thing is catching the error before printing the check. To prevent problems, you will always want to review your transactions before printing.

Enter one more transaction exactly as shown in Figure 5-4, including the spelling error (func) in the Memo field. Then you'll take a look at making the required corrections. Press (Pg Dn) to move to a new check form if you are still looking at the check for Holland Lumber, and make the following entries without recording the transaction. (Do not correct the misspelling.)

Date:	**2/13/94**
Payee:	**Fennville Library**
Payment:	**10.00**
Address:	**Fennville Library** **110 Main Street** **Fennville, MI 49459**
Memo:	**Building func contribution**
Category:	**Charity**

One mistake in the entries in Figure 5-4 is obvious. The word "fund" in the Memo field is spelled wrong. Suppose you were planning to be a little more generous with the contribution; the amount you intended to enter was 100.00. Quicken has already generated the words for the amount entry, but

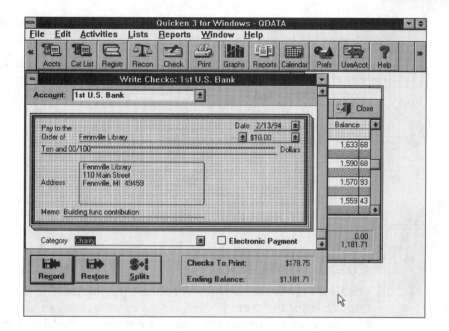

Entering a
check with
errors
Figure 5-4.

it changes the words if you change the amount. Since the transaction has
not been recorded yet, all you need to do is move back to the fields and
make corrections. Follow these instructions:

1. Move to the amount field by clicking it with the mouse or pressing
    Shift - Tab .

2. Position the cursor immediately after the 1 in the amount field.

3. Type another **0**.

    The amount now reads "100.00."

4. Move to the Memo field.

5. Delete the *c* in "func," and then type **d**.

    The corrected check is for $100.00 and has "Building fund contribution"
    in the Memo field.

6. Select Record to record the transaction.

You can browse through the other transactions by using the scroll bar or by
pressing Pg Up and Pg Dn to move from check to check. Pressing Home three
times takes you to the first check, and pressing End three times takes you to
the last check, which is a blank check form for the next transaction. You can
make any changes you want to a check, but you should record it by selecting
Record before using Pg Up or Pg Dn to move to a new check, or you will be

prompted to confirm that you want to update the transaction. Quicken updates the balances if you change the entry in an amount field.

To delete an entire transaction, you can select Delete Transaction from the Edit menu or press Ctrl-D, and then confirm the deletion. Since the checks have not been printed, there is no problem in deleting an incorrect transaction. After printing, you must void the entry in the register rather than deleting the check since you will need a record of the disposition of each check number.

If you are curious about how these entries look in the register, you can select the Registr icon from the Iconbar or press Ctrl-R. You see the checks you have written in the register with "Print" in the Num field. Figure 5-5 shows several entries made from the Write Checks window.

Postdating Checks

Postdated checks are written for future payments. The date on a postdated check is after the current date; if you enter a check on September 10 for a December 24 payment, the check is postdated. Postdated entries are allowed to permit you to schedule future expenses and write the check entry while you are thinking of it. It is not necessary to print postdated checks when you print checks. Quicken displays both a current and an ending balance for your account.

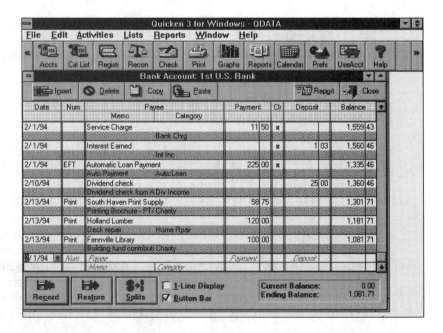

Check transactions in the register with "Print" for check numbers
Figure 5-5.

Depending on when you are entering the February 1994 checks in these examples, Quicken may be classifying the entries as postdated. The only difference when postdated checks are recorded is that you have the option to print only checks before a certain date.

Return to the Write Checks window by selecting Write Checks from the Activities menu or selecting the Check icon, and complete these entries to write a check for an upcoming birthday:

Date:	**3/8/94**
Payee:	**Keith Campbell**
Payment:	**25.00**
Memo:	**Birthday gift**
Category:	**Gifts**

Note that the Address field was deliberately left blank since this is a personal check that will not be mailed. What makes this check different from the others you have entered is that although the current date is supposedly 2/13/94, the check is written for 3/8/94 (later than the current date). Select Record to finalize the transaction.

Now that you have written a few checks, you should try printing a few. You should use plain paper even if you have check stock since these are just practice examples.

Putting Earlier Tactics to Work

Even though you are working with the Write Checks window, many of the special features you learned to use in earlier chapters still work. You can use the Calculator if you need to total a few invoices or perform another computation for the check amount. All you have to do is move to the amount field, then select the drop-down arrow, or select Use Calculator from the Activities menu.

The Find option also works. You can select Find from the Activities menu or you can press Ctrl-F to invoke this feature. (See Chapter 2, "Making Register Entries," for more information about the Find option.)

Printing Checks

Printing checks is easy. The only difficult part of the process is lining up the paper in your printer, but after the first few times even this will seem easy, especially since Quicken has built some helps into the system for you.

You can print some or all of your checks immediately after writing them, or you can defer the printing process to a later session. Some people wait until

Quicken lets you print checks when you record the transaction or wait until another session.

a check is due to print it, and others elect to print all their checks immediately after they are written.

Check Stock Options

Quicken checks come in three sizes: regular checks, wallet checks, and voucher checks. Figure 5-6 shows a sample wallet check. The voucher design is shown in Figure 5-7. All styles are personalized and can be printed with a logo. The account number, financial institution number, and check number are printed on each check. Special numbers are added to the edges of checks for tractor-feed printers to assist in the alignment process.

Setting Up a Check Printer

The first step in printing checks is to set up the check printer. When you set up the check printer, you select the printer to use, how the paper is fed to the printer, and the orientation of partial pages of checks. You can also select the font used to print the checks. Finally, you can select other printer settings that depend on what printer you are using.

1. Select Printer Setup from the File menu.

2. Select Check Printer Setup from the cascading menu. The Check Printer Setup dialog box opens, as shown here:

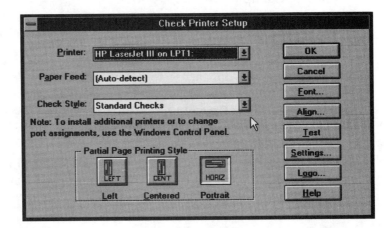

3. In the Printer drop-down list box, select the printer you want to use to print your checks.

4. Do not change the Paper Feed default, Auto-detect. This option causes Quicken to check your printer to determine if it feeds paper contin-uously like a tractor feeder or if it is page oriented like a laser printer.

You can force Quicken to assume your printer uses a specific type of paper feed by selecting one of the other options.

5. Select the style of check you are using from the Check Style drop-down list box. You can choose wallet, standard, or voucher checks.

6. Select one of the options under Partial Page Printing Style to tell Quicken how the page will be oriented if you are printing on a page that has already been used. If you are using a tractor-feed printer, the only option is Portrait.

7. To change the font used to print your checks, select the Font button and make your selections from the Check Printer Font dialog box. When you are finished making your selections, choose OK to return to the Check Printer Setup dialog box.

8. To add a logo to your checks, select Logo; then select File, and enter the name of the graphic image file that contains the logo. Quicken can use .BMP files, such as those created by Windows' Paintbrush program.

9. To change other settings specific to your printer, select Settings. The contents of the resulting dialog box depend on the printer you have selected. One of the options is always the height, or size, of the paper you are using. You must select the size of the checks you are printing. When you have finished making your selections, select OK to return to the Check Printer Setup dialog box.

   Remember that changing printer settings affects the Windows default settings for that printer. Make sure that you reinstate your original settings after you print your checks.

10. Select OK to save your Check Printer settings.

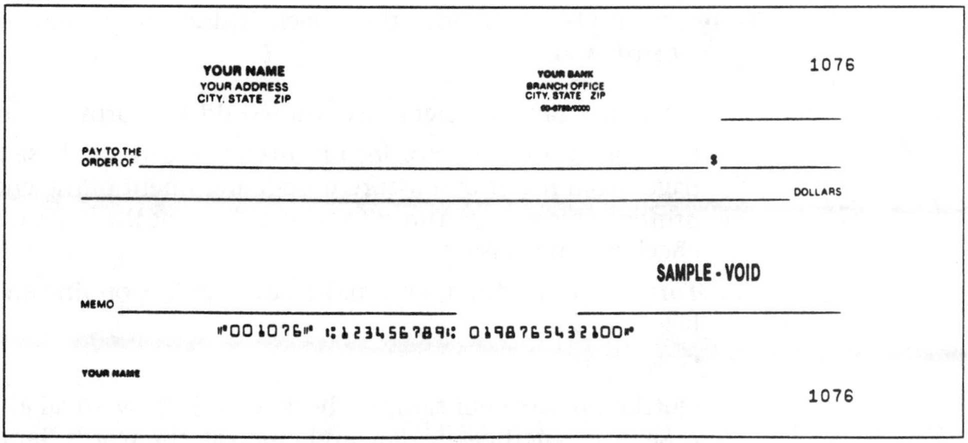

Sample wallet check
Figure 5-6.

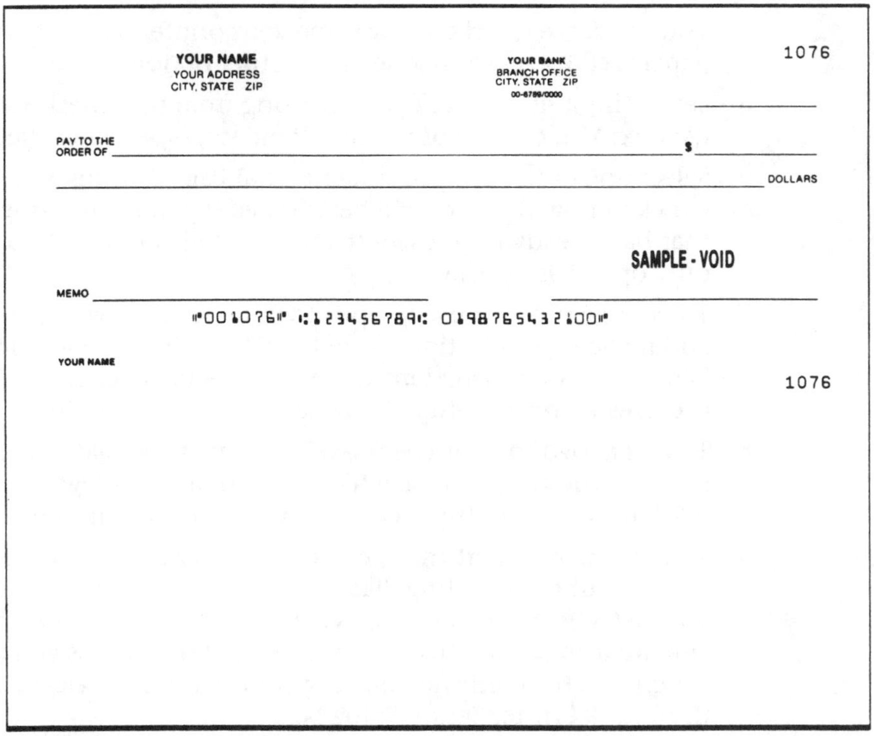

Sample
voucher check
Figure 5-7.

Printing a Sample to Line Up Checks

Before printing your first check, print a sample to test the alignment.

As part of setting up the check printer, you should print a sample check to test the alignment of the checks in the printer. You can then adjust the printer's alignment, if necessary. This will ensure perfect alignment of the preprinted check forms with the information you plan to print. This procedure is basically the same for tractor-feed printers and laser printers.

To test a sample check, open the Check Printer Setup dialog box and follow these instructions:

1. Insert the sample checks as you would any printer paper.

    If you are using a tractor-feed printer, you can purchase forms leader pages from Intuit that assure proper alignment of the checks in the printer. This way you won't waste a check at the beginning of each check writing session.

2. Turn on your printer, and make sure that it is on line and ready to begin printing.

3. Select <u>T</u>est.

    Quicken prints your sample check. Check the vertical alignment by observing whether the date and amount, the words "Jane Doe" (for the

Pay to the Order of field), and the phrase "For Services Rendered" (for the Memo field) are printed just above the lines on the sample check.

NOTE: Do not move the check up or down in the printer after printing the sample; Quicken does this automatically.

3

4. If your sample check did not align properly, continue with the following steps. Look at Table 5-1, and make the appropriate corrections.

5. Select <u>A</u>lign. The Check Printer Alignment dialog box opens, as shown in Figure 5-8.

6. You want to make the check shown in the Check Printer Alignment dialog box look like the misaligned check you have printed by dragging the text of the check with the mouse.

   If you are not using a mouse or if you want to make very small alignment changes, you can enter measurements in the <u>H</u>oriz and <u>V</u>ert text boxes to tell Quicken how much to move the text in that direction.

Print Problem	Correction Suggestion
Print lines are too close	The printer is probably set for eight lines to the inch. Change to six.
Print lines wrap, and the date and amount are too far to the right	The font selected is too large. Change to 12-point type.
Print does not extend across the check, and the date and amount print too far to the left	The font selected is too small (perhaps compressed print). Change to 12-point type, and turn off compressed print if necessary.
Print does not align with the lines on the check	The checks are not aligned properly in the printer. Reposition them by following the instructions in this chapter.
Print seems to be the correct size but is too far to the right or left	Reposition the checks from right to left.
Printer is spewing paper or producing illegible print	The wrong printer has probably been selected. Check the selection in the printer list.
Printer does not print	The printer is probably not turned on, not on line, or not chosen in the printer list; or the cable may be loose.

Correcting
Printer Errors
Table 5-1.

Changes you enter in these text boxes are not shown on the check in the dialog box.

NOTE: On most tractor-feed printers, the feeds that guide the paper are movable. If you move yours often, perhaps for using different sizes of paper, make sure that you note where they are positioned when you print your sample check, or you will have to print test checks and reset the alignment each time you print checks.

7. Select <u>T</u>est again to print another sample check. If your check is still misaligned, try steps 5 and 6 again, repeating them until the check is correctly aligned.

8. Select OK when your sample check is properly aligned.

You are now ready to print your checks.

NOTE: If you are using a tractor-feed printer, you will want to align a specific object on the check stock with some part of the printer, like the top of the tractor feeds, and note that alignment somewhere. This will prevent you from having to test your check alignment and adjust it each time you print checks because you will be able to vertically align the check stock on these markers.

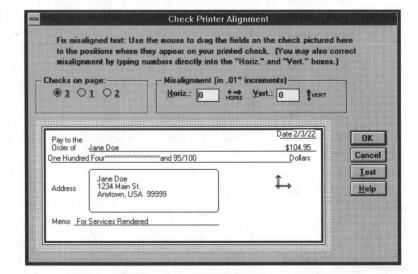

Check Printer
Alignment
dialog box
Figure 5-8.

Selecting Checks to Print

When you are ready to print checks, you need to tell Quicken the printer
you want to use, the check style you have selected, the checks to print, and
the first check number. The instructions that follow assume that you have
already checked the alignment for your check stock when setting up your
check printer.

1. Select File, and then select Print Checks.

   Another option is to press Ctrl-P rather than opening the File menu.
   The Select Checks to Print dialog box appears.

2. Type **1001** in the First Check Number text box, and press Tab.

   You must always make sure that this check number agrees with the
   number of the first check placed in the printer. Double-check this entry
   since Quicken uses it to complete the register entry for the check
   transaction. When Quicken prints the check, it replaces "Print" in the
   Num field with the actual check number.

3. Select the Selected checks option button to print only certain checks.

4. Select Choose to select the checks to be printed. The Select Checks to
   Print dialog box opens, as shown in Figure 5-9. Checks that will be
   printed have "Print" in the rightmost field. To add or remove the word
   "Print," double-click on the check, or highlight the check and select
   Mark. Select OK when you have finished marking the checks to print.

5. Select Print to open the Print Checks dialog box shown here:

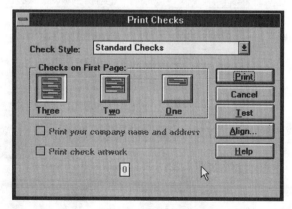

6. Select the style of check you are using from the Check Style drop-down
   list box.

   Since you have already printed samples, there is no need to print
   additional ones now. In subsequent sessions, you might want to select
   Sample to print a sample and check its alignment before proceeding.

3

7. If you are using a page-oriented printer, such as a laser printer, and some of the checks on the first page you are using have already been used, select the option under Checks on First Page to tell Quicken how many checks on that page are usable.

8. Select <u>P</u>rint to print your checks.

9. Quicken responds with a Did checks print OK? dialog box.

Review the checks printed, and check for errors in printing. If you used preprinted check forms, your checks might look something like the ones in Figure 5-10.

If there are no errors, select OK to close the check printing dialog boxes and to return to the Write Checks window. Select the Registr icon or select Use <u>R</u>egister from the <u>A</u>ctivities menu to look at the register entries with the check numbers inserted. If there are problems with the checks, follow the directions in the next section.

Correcting Mistakes

Quicken allows you to reprint checks that have been printed incorrectly. Since you are using prenumbered checks, new numbers will have to be assigned to the reprinted checks as Quicken prints them. Before starting again, make sure that you correct any feed problems with the printer.

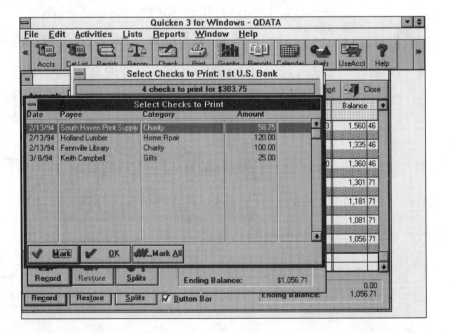

Selecting the checks to print

Figure 5-9.

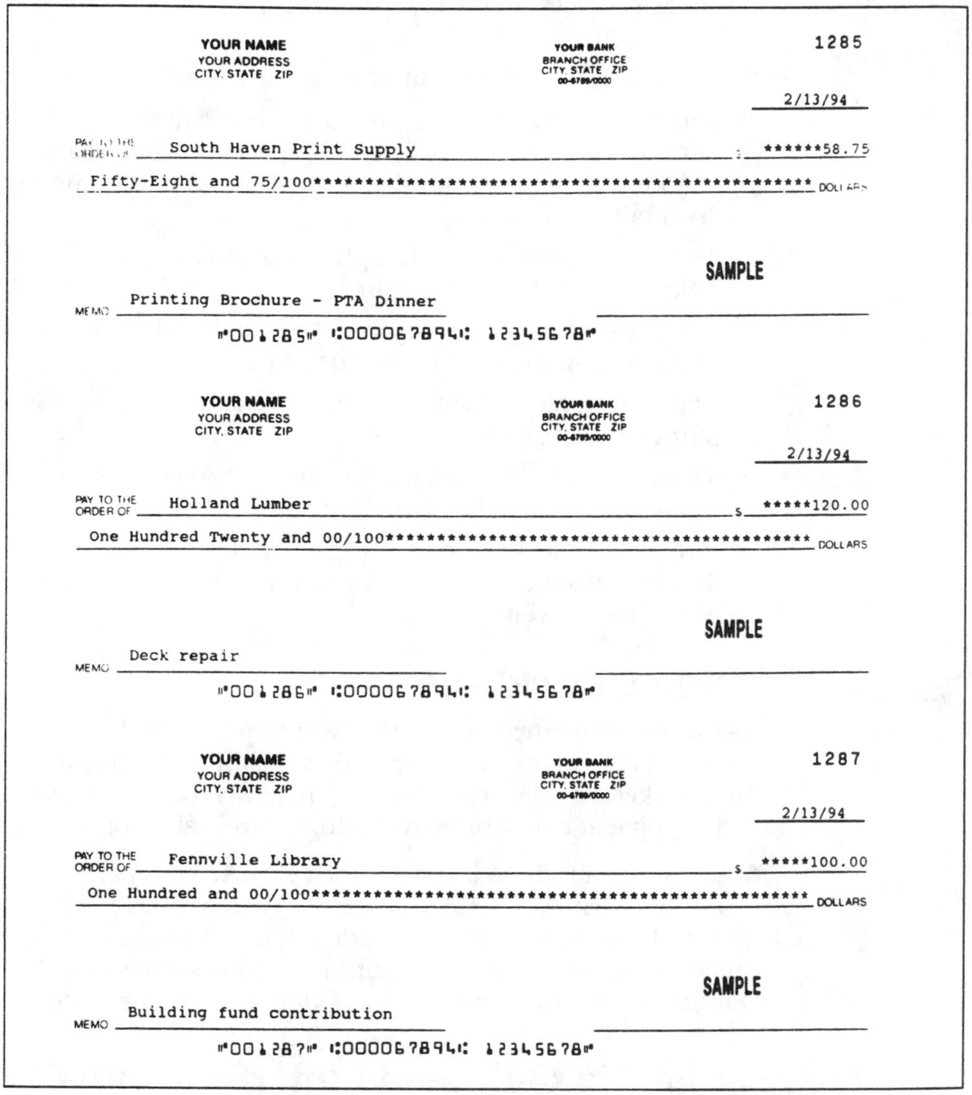
YOUR NAME
YOUR ADDRESS
CITY, STATE ZIP

YOUR BANK
BRANCH OFFICE
CITY, STATE ZIP
00-6789/0000

1285

2/13/94

PAY TO THE ORDER OF South Haven Print Supply $ ******58.75

Fifty-Eight and 75/100** DOLLARS

SAMPLE

MEMO Printing Brochure - PTA Dinner

⑈001285⑈ ⑆000067894⑆ 12345678⑈

YOUR NAME
YOUR ADDRESS
CITY, STATE ZIP

YOUR BANK
BRANCH OFFICE
CITY, STATE ZIP
00-6789/0000

1286

2/13/94

PAY TO THE ORDER OF Holland Lumber $ *****120.00

One Hundred Twenty and 00/100** DOLLARS

SAMPLE

MEMO Deck repair

⑈001286⑈ ⑆000067894⑆ 12345678⑈

YOUR NAME
YOUR ADDRESS
CITY, STATE ZIP

YOUR BANK
BRANCH OFFICE
CITY, STATE ZIP
00-6789/0000

1287

2/13/94

PAY TO THE ORDER OF Fennville Library $ *****100.00

One Hundred and 00/100*** DOLLARS

SAMPLE

MEMO Building fund contribution

⑈001287⑈ ⑆000067894⑆ 12345678⑈

Standard check sample printout
Figure 5-10.

If you find yourself frequently correcting printer jams and having to reprint checks, you may want to print checks in smaller batches or set your printer to wait after each page.

Complete the following steps to restart and finish your printing batch:

1. Since you did not select OK when you finished printing checks, Quicken is still waiting for you to identify the first incorrectly printed check so that it can reprint any checks that didn't print or that printed

incorrectly. Type the check number of the first check you want to reprint, and select OK.

2. The Select Checks to Print dialog box appears.

   The Check Number text box now shows the next available check number. Check the first Check Number text box against the number of the next check in your printer. Type a new check number in the Check Number text box, if appropriate.

3. Select the Selected Checks option button and then Choose to open the Select Checks to Print window.

4. Select the checks to be reprinted by double-clicking on them, or by highlighting them and selecting Mark.

5. Select Print to confirm the beginning check number for this batch. The Print Checks dialog box opens.

6. Check that the settings for the checks to be printed are correct, and then select Print.

7. When the checks stop printing, select OK to indicate that all the checks have printed correctly. If they haven't all printed correctly, repeat the steps described in this section.

Using CheckFree

CheckFree eliminates the need for you to print checks. After you enter data into Quicken, you can electronically transmit the information to CheckFree. The CheckFree service handles the payments for you by printing and mailing a paper check or by initiating a direct electronic transfer.

Although the ability to interface with CheckFree is part of Quicken, you must subscribe to the service before you can use it. To subscribe, complete the CheckFree Service Form included in the Quicken package or contact CheckFree at (614) 899-7500. Currently, CheckFree's monthly charge is $9.00, which entitles you to 20 transactions without an additional charge.

Setting Up Quicken to Interface with CheckFree

To use CheckFree with Quicken, you must set up your modem so that you can use Quicken's electronic payment capability. Next you change your account settings to set up the bank account specified on the CheckFree Service Form. You will then be ready to compile an electronic payee list and write electronic checks.

Modem Settings

To set up your modem so that you can establish a link between your computer and your bank via the telephone line, click on the Pref icon in the

Iconbar, or select P̲references from the E̲dit menu and then select M̲odem. The Modem Preferences dialog box, shown here, is displayed:

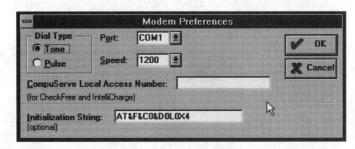

3

You can accept the defaults for the modem speed and the computer port to which the modem is attached, or you can change them to match your modem and computer setup.

You must enter the phone number supplied by CheckFree when you sign up with the service for transmission. When you enter the phone number, type a comma if your phone system requires a pause. For example, if you must dial an 8 or a 9 to get an outside line, type a comma after the 8 or 9 to allow a pause so that the connection with the outside line can be established. Check your modem's documentation for the appropriate initialization string to enter in the I̲nitialization String text box. An initialization string may not be required with your modem, but you will have to check its documentation to be sure. Now you can edit the settings for the current account to use it with CheckFree, as discussed next.

Account Settings

You can modify the account settings for any bank account for use with CheckFree, provided that you supply the bank information to CheckFree on the CheckFree Service Form. To set up an account for use with CheckFree, choose Chec̲kFree from the A̲ctivities menu, and then select S̲etup. Quicken presents an Electronic Payment Setup dialog box with your current account listed, like the one shown here:

Highlight the name of the account you wish to enable electronic trans-
missions for, and select Setup. Select the Electronic Payments Account
Settings check box on the next dialog box to enable payments, and then
complete the form shown next for your account:

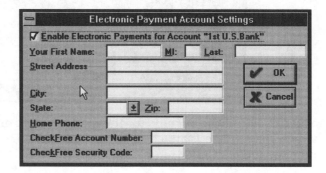

CheckFree supplies you with the number for the last text box on this form.
After you select OK, you are ready to enter electronic payees or enter either
check or register transactions and transmit them.

Compiling an Electronic Payee List

You cannot write electronic checks for regular payees. Instead, you must
compile an electronic payee list which includes information that the
CheckFree service needs. To do this, follow these steps:

1. Select CheckFree from the Activities menu, then select Electronic Payee
    List to open the Electronic Payee List window.

2. Select New to add a new payee to this list, opening the Choose Type of
    Electronic Payee dialog box.

3. Select either the Normal Payee or the Fixed, Recurring Payee option
    button, depending on whether or not you plan to send many checks to
    this payee. Then select OK.

4. In the Set Up Electronic Payee dialog box, enter the payee's name,
    address, telephone number, and your account number with that payee,
    then select OK.

You can now create electronic checks for the payee you have added to the
list. This information is sent along with the check to the CheckFree service
for their use.

Writing Electronic Checks

You can write both electronic payments and regular checks during the same Quicken session.

The procedure for writing electronic checks is almost identical to that for creating checks that you print, which is covered earlier in this chapter. Your check displays "Electronic Payment" if you have electronic payments set for the current account. You can toggle to a paper check any time you need to by clearing the Electronic Payment check box that appears in the Write Checks window. Quicken automatically postdates the payment date by five working days to allow for transmission of the payment to the payee. The Pay To field must contain the name of an electronic payee. If your entry does not match an existing payee, Quicken allows you to add it. Once you are finished with your entries, select OK.

3

Quicken lists your electronic checks in the register. The Num field contains "XMIT" before transmission and "EPMT" after transmission. You can enter these electronic payments directly in the register rather than using the Write Checks window, if you prefer.

Transmitting Electronic Payments

You can transmit electronic payments from the Write Checks window or the register. Select CheckFree from the Activities menu, and then select Transmit to display the Transmit Payments window. You can preview your transmission by selecting Preview, or you can select Transmit to start the transmission process.

TIPS

PC AND WINDOWS TIPS

Whether Quicken is the first program you have used on your system or is one of many, you will want to look through the PC and Windows tips in this section. Even if your primary interest is in Quicken, you may be able to learn a little bit more about your computer and Windows if you read a few of these tips each day.

1. Buy unformatted disks and format them yourself to save money.

2. Always create a label for your disks before you store data on them.

3. Write-protect disks that contain backup copies of data.

4. Wrist pads may help avoid carpal tunnel syndrome especially when using notebook computers regularly.

5. Consider buying a keyboard membrane to protect the keyboard from food and beverages if you insist on eating while working at the computer.

6. Always keep disks in boxes to protect them from dust and spills.

7. If you spill something into your keyboard, save your file immediately, then turn your keyboard upside down and shake it gently. Contact your computer store for additional options, which will depend on the type of keyboard and the liquid spilled.

8. Use static spray on carpets or install an anti-static carpet near the computer, especially in cold, low-humidity climates.

9. Avoid placing disks near obvious magnetic fields, as well as the not-so-obvious ones such as television sets, vacuum cleaners, and conveyor belts at airports.

10. Consider propping your monitor up on a monitor stand or even a small box if the height is better for reading screen information.

11. If your printer tells you that your toner cartridge is low, pull it out and shake the cartridge gently from side to side before reinserting it. You will get several hundred pages more. We usually do this once or twice before recycling the cartridge.

12. Look for a reliable supplier who can refill toner cartridges or re-ink ribbons.

13. Don't leave disks in a hot car or car trunk. Your data is likely to become unreadable.

14. Establish a directory structure for your PC that models your manual filing system.

15. Keep the environment around your PC dust free. If it is not, you should consider having your PC cleaned at your computer store. Simply cleaning a PC can fix apparent malfunctions.

16. Keep your PC away from windows. Heat, sunlight, and moisture can damage it. Also, a system in the window is more likely to attract the attention of a burglar.

17. Before setting up the entire system, position the PC monitor and check the glare on the screen. Reflected light from outside, or hallway lights, can make it difficult to read the display.

18. If you cannot avoid glare, buy an anti-glare screen or screen cover. The best way to reduce glare is to use indirect lighting. The best way to produce indirect lighting is to use a strong, direct, overhead light source.

19. Secure your system with wire cables to the floor or wall, if you cannot restrict access to the system after hours.

20. Make sure you are using a comfortable chair if you sit at the computer for hours. Some users prefer the backless computer chairs.

21. Create a regularly scheduled backup plan and assign responsibility for meeting it.

22. Backup important files that are being updated regularly after each major update, even if this is twice a day.

23. Consider joining a computer users' group to learn more about PCs.

24. Place a blank disk in each disk drive when traveling with a computer; this will serve as a replacement for the cardboard that was in the drive when you first received it.

25. Use surge protectors to keep your PC from being damaged by a sudden surge in your power line. Universal power sources can be used to give you time to save data if your power goes out.

26. If you find you need more memory or disk space, see if you can add it to your existing unit instead of upgrading to a new computer. You can greatly enhance your computer by adding on memory, another or larger hard disk, or features such as internal modems, usually at less cost than buying a new system. On the other hand, if you have a model that is more than a couple of years old, its clock speed may be so slow that upgrading it would not be a good idea.

27. If your desk tends to be cluttered, use a trackball instead of a mouse. Unlike a mouse, trackballs are not actually moved around on the desk; instead, you move the ball itself.

28. Use a screen saver program to provide security for your work. A screen saver takes control of your screen and hides it by displaying an image whenever you haven't touched the keyboard or mouse for awhile. Some screen savers let you assign a password that must be entered before the screen will clear.

29. Consider buying a power strip into which you can plug all of your computer's elements. You can use the power switch to turn your entire system on at once. Many power strips are also surge suppressors.

30. If you have more than one computer, but only one printer, use a printer switch box that lets you switch which computer has access to the printer at any one time. This makes it easier to share one printer.

31. You can create very professional looking documents by using special paper. Paper that is preprinted with a design can make even the simplest document look professionally prepared, enhancing your image when presenting business or financial papers.

32. Avoid storing vital files only on your computer. A very important backup is to have hard copies or printouts filed appropriately, especially for personal files that you may not have off-site backups for. Circumstances which can destroy your computer files may not destroy your printouts. For example, keep a printout of financial data in a fire-proof safe box so that it can't get destroyed as easily.

33. If you find you are frequently short of hard-disk space, try the following solutions. You may simply need to delete old files regularly. You can start saving data files on floppy disks instead of your hard drive. Consider getting a disk compression utility that squeezes files into smaller spaces on your disk, or zipping old files with a file compression program and expanding them only when they are needed. Keep all of your Windows temporary files in one directory and delete them regularly.

34. Invest in a high-resolution monitor when you first get your system. Even programs that use lower resolutions will look better on high-resolution systems. More recent programs that require higher resolutions may be unreadable on a low-resolution monitor.

35. Computer-based fax boards are a great solution for faxing documents. You can use these boards to fax a document directly from your computer, without printing it out. When the fax is printed by the recipient, your document is much more readable, since there will be no scanning errors.

36. Make sure your computer is 100 percent DOS, Windows, and IBM compatible. Some aren't. Programs written to run under DOS may not run correctly if the system is not completely compatible.

37. Make sure cables are securely attached to their connectors. If you simply attach them, but don't secure them, they may fall out, or you may experience errors because information can get lost when the connections are loose.

38. Make sure you know your disk drive capacities and buy disks that match. Disk drives cannot read disks formatted to a greater capacity. Attempting to format a disk to a higher capacity than your disk drive is designed for means that any information you try to save on that disk is going to be gibberish.

39. Remember to clean your mouse ball and keyboard occasionally, using compressed air or a special vacuum. Many mice can be opened so that you can remove the ball from the bottom, and clean it separately.

40. Never spray cleaners directly on your computer or computer screen. You can spray cleaner on a cloth and wipe the monitor screen or keyboard to insure that moisture does not damage your computer.

41. Write-protect disks that contain important data so they cannot be formatted accidentally. To do this, cover the notch on a 5 1/4-inch disk or slide the tab on a 3 1/2-inch disk toward the outside edge to expose the hole beneath it.

42. Use the DOS ATTRIB command to make important files that you will not need to update read-only. An entry of ATTRIB MYFILE +R at the DOS prompt will make MYFILE read-only.

43. Establish a naming standard for all of your files. Although you will probably not be creating new Quicken files, you may create data for other programs. These naming standards are essential to being able to keep data organized and to use the features of DOS which allow you to select more than one file at a time. For example, if you write a monthly budget report with your word processing program, you might want to use a name such as BGT94JAN and follow this pattern throughout the year rather than entering the next months as FEB94BGT, 94MARBGT, and BUDG0494. Although any of these other entries would have been fine if used as the pattern for the entire year, mixing them will cause problems.

44. Create a batch file for backing up your data to make the task easier.

45. When you have multiple files on a disk, you may not be able to use every byte on that disk for data storage, since space is allocated by *allocation units*. These vary in size by disk but the smallest allocation unit in common use today is 1,024 bytes. A file that contains one character will require this minimum space allocation on the disk.

46. When naming files, avoid the use of special characters other than the underscore (_). Also, do not use spaces in filenames.

47. If a file is larger than the capacity of your disk, use BACKUP (or MSBACKUP in DOS 6) to make a copy of the file.

48. Knowing some commonly used filename extensions will make it easier to determine what your files contain. Check this list:

.ASC	ASCII file
.BAK	Backup file
.BAT	Batch file
.COM	Program file
.EXE	Program file
.SYS	System file
.TXT	Text file

49. You cannot restore backup data with COPY. Only the RESTORE command can read data written with BACKUP.

50. Run a defragmentation program if you begin to get sluggish performance from your hard disk. Norton Utilities Speed Disk is one option.

51. You can delete commands like FDISK and FORMAT from computers that are accessed by many people to prevent accidental or planned use of these programs to eliminate data on a hard disk.

52. In Windows, remove the highlight from selected text by clicking somewhere else on your screen.

53. Reduce a window to an icon by clicking the Minimize button or by selecting Minimize from the control box menu that appears when you click the upper-left box in the window.

54. You can double-click the Program Manager control menu box to display the Exit Windows dialog box.

55. You can cascade open windows to display an edge of each in order to move between them with a quick click. To cascade document windows, select Cascade from the application's Windows menu. To cascade application windows, select Cascade from the Active Task List.

56. If you want to see more of each open window than cascading allows, tile the windows to make a floor tile pattern by selecting Tile from the Active Task Manager for application windows, or Tile from the Windows menu from an application.

57. To open the control menu for a document window, click on the control menu button at the left edge of the title bar, or press Alt-—.

58. To open a control menu for an application window press Alt-Spacebar.

59. Windows provides several extra programs such as games and accessories. When you have time you will want to explore these extras which include everything from a drawing application to a word processing application.

60. Reset the date and time on your computer from within Windows by opening the Control Panel, usually found in the Main program group, then selecting the Date/Time icon.

61. Get a closeup look at the Windows print queue by double-clicking the Print Manager icon. When are finished, minimize the Print Manager again using the Minimize button or Minimize from the control menu. Don't exit the Print Manager until all of your printing is done.

62. Later versions of DOS give better Windows performance, with a major improvement realized with DOS 5 and 6.

63. You can set up Windows to start automatically when you turn your computer on by including WIN as the last line in your AUTOEXEC.BAT file, thus avoiding the DOS prompt.

64. Program items included in the Start Up program group are loaded automatically when you start Windows. You can include the program items you want loaded all the time to make getting started easier.

65. Program items can be either programs or documents. For example, if you keep track of your work hours in a spreadsheet, create a program item for that document. Windows will automatically load the program with that spreadsheet, if you have associated the spreadsheet extension with the spreadsheet.

66. Organize your program groups so your most frequently used program items are together.

67. You can change the colors of your display by starting the Windows Control Panel, then selecting the Colors icon. If you use dark background colors, you will reduce the radiation emitted by your monitor and help reduce eyestrain.

68. You can start Windows so the File Manager comes up instead of the Program Manager. You can start programs in the File Manager by double-clicking on them in the directory listings. To change this setting in Windows 3.1, you open the file SYSTEM.INI using Notepad, and change the line that reads **shell=progman.exe** to read **shell=winfile.exe**.

69. You can associate various file extensions with their related programs. For example, you could associate the extension .QDT with Quicken 3 for Windows. You can open associated programs either by selecting a program item or double-clicking on them in the File Manager.

70. You can maximize a program window so it takes up the whole screen, or a document window so it fills the space in the application window by clicking on the Maximize button at the upper-right end of the title bar, or by opening the window's control menu and selecting Maximize.

71. There are two ways to do virtually everything in Windows, the keyboard way and the mouse way. Use the method you are most comfortable with. The mouse is usually the easier method for new users, but it's usually slower as well.

72. You can switch the mouse buttons to make using it left-handed easier. To switch them, open the Control Panel, select the Mouse icon, and select the Swap Left/Right Button check box, then OK.

73. You can change how quickly you need to click the mouse to have Windows recognize a double-click. The faster the setting, the closer

together the clicks have to be. You change this setting in the Mouse dialog box in the Windows Control Panel.

74. You can change how quickly the mouse pointer reacts when you move the mouse. Change this setting using the Mouse dialog box in the Windows Control Panel.

75. All Windows programs print using the Windows Print Manager, which lets you continue working in Windows applications while your documents print. When you move to a window in which you are running a DOS-based program, your printing will stop, because the DOS-based program is not set up to let the Print Manager continue printing in the background.

76. All Windows programs use the same printer drivers, which are the files containing the information that lets your computer talk to your printer. Make sure that you install your printer in Windows with default settings, so that each program can alter settings as needed, such as changing to printing in landscape mode, without changing the basic printer driver file.

77. Windows allocates memory among the open applications. You can change settings to allocate memory differently using the Control Panel's 386 Enhanced dialog box. You cannot do this if you are running Windows on a 286-based computer.

78. Windows running on a 386 or higher computer uses virtual memory, in which it treats part of your hard disk as a part of memory by storing some information on the disk. The file it stores this information in is called a swap file. You can change the type and size of the swap file from the 386 Enhanced dialog box in the Control Panel.

79. Swap files can be temporary or permanent. Temporary swap files are added when necessary and deleted when you exit Windows. You can set a maximum size for your temporary swap file. These files are slower and less efficient than permanent swap files. Permanent swap files always take the same amount of space on your hard disk and are never deleted. However, they are much faster.

80. Windows comes with a number of icons you can use for program items that do not have their own. Some icons are part of the PROGMAN.EXE file. Others are included in the MORICONS.DLL file. MORICONS.DLL includes many icons for popular DOS-based applications.

81. Watch the mouse pointer change shapes to know when you can perform certain actions. For example, you will know when the mouse pointer is in the correct position to size a window when it becomes an arrow.

82. In all Windows applications, you press [Alt] and the underlined or boldfaced letter in menu or dialog box elements to activate that feature. These letters are called *mnemonics*.

83. Different symbols in menus of Windows applications tell you different things. Menu items without anything after them activate commands. Menu items followed by arrows open submenus that offer further menu selections. Menu items followed by an ellipsis open dialog boxes.

84. Different dialog box elements do different things. You can type entries in text boxes, and select items from list boxes. Click an arrow button after what looks like a normal text box, and a list box is displayed. You can also press [Alt]-[↓].

85. Arrange cables so they are out of the way—tripping over them causes as much harm to the cables as it does to your ego.

86. Unplug computers during storms.

87. A quick way to make more professional looking documents is to buy a fonts package. Several font packages are available for Windows and you can use these new fonts in most Windows applications.

88. Use the File Manager in Windows instead of the DOS prompt to arrange, copy, and delete files. The File Manager will prompt you for the information it needs and you can use the mouse.

89. Add your favorite DOS programs as program items to the Program Manager. You can use Windows Setup in the Main application group and then select Setup Applications in the Options menu to have Windows find installed applications on your hard drive, including DOS programs that are not Windows applications.

90. If Windows' performance is sluggish, close applications you are not using.

91. If you think your system has locked up, leave it alone for a few minutes. Your computer may be unresponsive simply because it requires so much memory to carry out another task, such as loading a program, that it has none left to respond to you.

92. If you get a general format error, don't panic. Windows will stop an application if it is trying to do something it is not allowed. Depending on the error message you see, you can start the application again, or you may want to first leave Windows then restart it, or leave Windows and reboot your computer.

93. Don't quit applications just by turning your system off. When you leave an application or Windows, Windows performs several housekeeping tasks. Exiting the application as designed by the program will also alert you if you need to save your data. If you turn the computer off to close

T
I
P
S

the application, the housekeeping is not done. Also, you may see a message that Windows' swap file is corrupt.

94. Use the automatic save features in applications that have them when you want to be sure that you do not lose the changes you are making. Some applications have this feature and others do not.

95. Remember that there are several Windows key combinations that work the same in most applications. These include F1 for help, F10 or Alt for the menu, and Alt-F4 to close the Windows application.

96. If you are just starting to use the computer, you may want to use the mouse. A mouse lets you select items by pointing at them and pressing a mouse button.

97. Use different icons for applications. For example, if you add several non-Windows applications as program items to run from Windows, make sure that they have different icons. The different icons help you select the right application you want.

98. Learn one application at a time and at your own pace. You probably will not use every Windows accessory or program you have on your computer. Remember that it is important that you use the computer to make other tasks easier for *you*. You do not have to learn a lot to make a computer useful; you only have to learn what you need to complete the tasks you want to finish.

99. Unless you are short on disk space, make the Windows' swap file a permanent file that is as large as possible.

100. If you have problems running an application, you may need to change your PATH command. This is a command in your AUTOEXEC.BAT file that DOS, Windows, and other applications use when you tell the computer to run a program that is not in the current directory. Most applications that require their directory be included in the PATH command will modify the file for you when you install the application. If that is not the case, you may need to add the directory yourself.

101. When you have a problem with your computer, take a deep breath, calm down, and try to work through the problem step by step. When you are rushed, you can forget the most obvious things, such as you can't start your favorite Window's packages without starting Windows first, or that printing requires that you first remember to turn the printer on. Just remind yourself that, intimidating as it seems, your computer is essentially an over-grown Nintendo game.

PART

2

HOME
APPLICATIONS

CHAPTER

6

EXPANDING THE SCOPE OF FINANCIAL ENTRIES

The last five chapters have aimed to give you a quick start in using Quicken's features. The basics you learned in those chapters will help you better manage your checking account transactions. For some individuals, this knowledge is sufficient. Others will want to increase their ability to take full advantage of Quicken's capabilities. Even if you think you learned all the tasks you need in the first few chapters, read the first two sections in this chapter. These sections will teach you about Quicken files and setting up an account separate from the one you used for the practice exercises. Then, if you feel you know enough to meet your needs, stop reading at the end of the section titled "Quicken Files" and enter some of your own transactions.

Even personal finances can be too complex to be handled with a single account. In one household, there may be transactions for both individual and joint checking accounts, credit card accounts, and savings accounts. Quicken allows you to set up these different accounts within one Quicken file, which enables you to include information from multiple accounts in reports.

Accounts alone are not always enough to organize transactions logically. You may find you need to change the categories to assign to your transactions; you may even want to establish main categories with subcategories beneath them. You used categories earlier to identify transactions as utilities expense or salary income. Using subcategories, you might create several groupings under the utilities expense for electricity, water, and gas.

Classes are another way of organizing your transactions to provide a different perspective from categories. You might think of classes as answering the "who," "what," "when," or "where" of a transaction. For example, you could assign a transaction to the clothing category and then set up and assign it to a class for the family member purchasing the clothing.

In this chapter, you will also learn how to assign transactions to more than one account—for example, how to transfer funds between accounts.

All of the these features in this "Home Applications" section are presented assuming that you are recording transactions for your personal finance. If you are interested in using Quicken to record both personal and business transactions, read the chapters in this section (Chapters 6 through 10) first. When you get to Chapter 11, you learn how to set up Quicken for your business. You can then select a category structure and create accounts that will allow you to manage both business and personal transactions.

The material in these chapters builds on the procedures you have already mastered. Feel free to adapt the entries provided to match your actual financial transactions. For example, you may want to change the dollar amount of transactions, the categories to which they are assigned, and the transaction dates shown.

Again, be aware of the dates for the transaction entries in these chapters. As you know, the date of the transaction entry, relative to the current date, determines whether a transaction is postdated. The current date triggers the reminder to process groups of transactions you want to enter on a certain date. Using your current date for transaction entries may cause this not to occur. Also, creating reports that match the examples in this book will be difficult unless you use the dates presented for the transaction. The varied dates used permit the creation of more illustrative reports.

Before you start with the examples in this chapter, check the memorization setting for the QuickFill feature. To do this, select Preferences from the Edit menu, then select QuickFill. Select the Automatic Memorization of New Transactions check box if it is cleared. You will want this feature turned on for the entries you are going to make in the new Quicken file so that you can carry out the examples for memorized transactions and scheduled transaction groups later in the chapter.

Quicken Files

One Quicken file can contain many accounts. Once you start recording your own data, you will probably keep all of your accounts in one file.

When you first started working in Chapter 2, Quicken created several files on your disk to manage your accounts and the information within them. Since all the files have the same filename, QDATA, but different filename extensions, this book will refer to them collectively as a file. When you copy a Quicken data file, all of these files must be copied.

6

You worked with only one account in QDATA, but you can use multiple accounts within a file. You might use one account for a savings account and a different one for checking. You can also have accounts for credit cards, cash, assets, and liabilities, although most individuals do not have financial situations that warrant more than a few accounts.

You could continue to enter the transactions from this chapter in the 1st U.S. Bank account in the QDATA file, or you could set up a new account in the QDATA file. However, if you adapted the chapter entries to meet your own financial situation, your new data would be intermingled with the practice transactions from the last few chapters. To avoid this, you will need to establish a file for the practice transactions. In this section, you will learn how to set up new transactions that are stored separately from the existing entries. You will also learn how to create a backup copy of a file to safeguard the data you enter.

Adding a New File

You already have the QDATA file for all the transactions entered as explained in the first section of this book. Now you will set up a new file and create accounts within it. Later, if you wish, you can delete the QDATA file to free the space it occupies on your disk.

The file will be called PERSONAL. Initially, it will contain a checking account called Cardinal Bank. This account is similar to the 1st U.S. Bank checking account you created in QDATA. Since it is in a new file, a different name is used. Other appropriate names might be BUSINESS CHECKING and JOINT CHECKING, depending on the type of account. Naturally, if you have more than one account at Cardinal Bank, they cannot all be named Cardinal Bank. In the section "Creating a New Savings Account" later in this chapter, you will add the account Cardinal Saving to the PERSONAL file.

Follow these steps to set up the new file and to add the first account to it:

1. Select New from the File menu.

   Quicken displays the dialog box shown here:

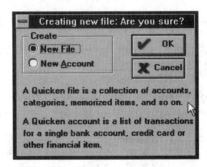

2. Select the New File option button and select OK.

   Quicken presents a dialog box for creating a file.

3. Type **PERSONAL** as the name for the file in the File Name text box.

4. Check the directory shown in the Directories list box and make changes if a change is required.

5. Clear the Business check box under Predefined categories. This will restrict your categories to Home categories when Quicken presents the Categories & Transfers dialog box.

6. Select OK to complete the creation of the new file.

   Quicken creates several files for each filename by adding different filename extensions to the name you provide. This means you must provide a valid filename of no more than eight characters. Do not include spaces or special symbols in your entries for filenames.

   Quicken displays the Select Account Type dialog box shown in Figure 6-1.

7. Select Bank Account for the account type and select OK.

8. Type **Cardinal Bank** in the Account Name text box.

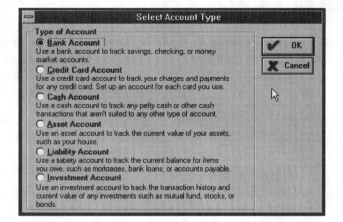

Select
Account Type
dialog box
Figure 6-1.

9. Type **2500** in the Balance text box.

10. Type **7/13/94** in the as of text box, or use the drop-down calendar to select this date.

11. Type **Personal Checking** in the Description text box.

12. Select OK.

Quicken displays the register for the Cardinal Bank account in the Personal file.

Changing the Active File

The result of the last exercise was the creation of a second file. You can work in either file at any time and select any account within a file. To change from the current file, PERSONAL, to QDATA, follow these steps:

1. Select Open from the File menu.

2. Select QDATA in the File Name list box and select OK.

The QDATA file is now active. The register and check writing window show the 1st U.S. Bank account as active. Change the file back to PERSONAL and activate the account for Cardinal Bank by following the same steps.

TIP: As a shortcut, you can press Ctrl-O to open the Open Quicken File dialog box rather than making selections from the menu.

6

Backing Up a File

On a regular basis, you will want to create backup copies of the data managed by Quicken. This allows you to recover all your entries in the event of a disk failure, since you will be able to use your copy to restore all the entries. You need a blank formatted disk to record the backup information the first time. Subsequent backups can be made on this disk without reformatting it. You can create a formatted disk with the Windows File Manager by using the Format Disk command from the Disk menu.

Creating Backup Files

Quicken has a backup command that allows you to safeguard the investment you have made in entering your data. You can back up all your account files. Follow these steps to back up the current file:

1. Select Backup from the File menu.
2. Select Current File.
3. Place your blank, formatted disk in drive A, then select A in the Backup Drive drop-down list box.
4. Select OK.
5. Select OK to acknowledge the completion of the backup when Quicken displays the successful backup message.

With backups, if you ever lose your hard disk, you can recreate your data directory and then select the Restore command from the File menu to copy your backup files to the directory. You can also copy Quicken data files from one floppy drive to another as a quick means of backup if you do not have a hard disk.

Customizing Categories

When you set up the new PERSONAL file, you selected Home categories as the standard categories option. This selection provides access to the more than 40 category choices displayed in Table 6-1. You can see that some categories are listed as expenses and others as income; some of them even have subcategories. Any subcategories that you create later will also be shown in this column. The last column in the table shows which categories are tax related.

Category	Type	Tax Related
Bonus	Income	Yes
Canada Pen	Income	Yes
Div Income	Income	Yes
Gift Received	Income	Yes
Int Inc	Income	Yes
Invest Inc	Income	Yes
Old Age Pension	Income	Yes
Other Inc	Income	Yes
Salary	Income	Yes
Auto	Expense	No
Fuel	Subcategory	No
Loan	Subcategory	No
Service	Subcategory	No
Bank Chrg	Expense	No
Charity	Expense	Yes
Childcare	Expense	Depends on income bracket
Christmas	Expense	No
Clothing	Expense	No
Dining	Expense	No
Dues	Expense	No
Education	Expense	No
Entertain	Expense	No
Gifts	Expense	No
Groceries	Expense	No
GST	Expense	Yes
Home Rpair	Expense	No
Household	Expense	No

6

Standard
Categories
Table 6-1.

Category	Type	Tax Related
Housing	Expense	No
Insurance	Expense	No
Int Exp	Expense	Yes
Invest Exp	Expense	Yes
Medical	Expense	Yes
Doctor	Subcategory	Yes
Medicine	Subcategory	Yes
Misc	Expense	No
Mort Int	Expense	Yes
Other Exp	Expense	Yes
PST	Expense	Yes
Recreation	Expense	No
RRSP	Expense	No
Subscriptions	Expense	No
Supplies	Expense	No
Tax	Expense	Yes
Fed	Subcategory	Yes
Medicare	Subcategory	Yes
Other	Subcategory	Yes
Prop	Subcategory	Yes
Soc Sec	Subcategory	Yes
State	Subcategory	Yes
Telephone	Expense	No
UIC (Unemploy Ins)	Expense	Yes
Utilities	Expense	No
Gas & Electric	Subcategory	No
Water	Subcategory	No

Standard
Categories
(*continued*)
Table 6-1.

Editing the Existing Category List

You can change the name of any existing category, change its classification as income, expense, or subcategory, or change its tax-related status. To modify a category, follow these steps:

1. Display the category list by selecting Category & Transfer from the Lists menu or selecting the Cat List icon from the Iconbar.
2. Highlight the category you want to change.
3. Select Edit to edit the information for the category.
4. Change the entries you wish to alter using the Edit Category dialog box, shown here:

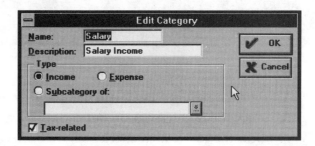

5. Select OK to complete the changes.

If you change the name of the category, Quicken will automatically change it in any transactions that have already been assigned to that category.

Adding Categories

You can also add your own categories to provide additional options specific to your needs. For example, if you have just set up housekeeping, buying furniture might be a major budget category. Since you would otherwise have to lump these purchases with others in the Household category, you might want to add Furniture as a category option. Typing **Furniture** in the category field when you enter your first furniture transaction automatically makes it a category option. When Quicken does not find the category in the existing list, it displays a window in which you can create the category.

However, if you have a number of categories to add, it is simpler to add them before starting to enter data. To use this approach for adding the Furniture category, follow these steps:

6

1. Open the Category & Transfer List by selecting Category & Transfer from the Lists menu or selecting the Cat List icon from the Iconbar.

2. Select New.

   Quicken will allow you to enter a new category by using the Set Up Category dialog box, shown here, which contains entries for a new Furniture category that you could add to your Category list:

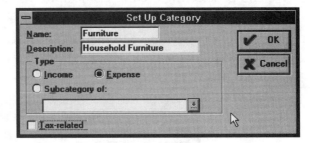

3. Type **Furniture** in the Name text box.

4. Type **Household Furniture** in the Description text box.

5. Select the Expense option button.

6. Clear the Tax-related check box, then select OK to complete the entry.

Categories will be added as transactions are entered for the remaining examples in this chapter. Feel free to customize the categories as you enter them.

NOTE: Later you will learn how to add categories and subcategories to customize your account list. You can also delete them if they offer more detail than you want. In the examples in this book, the subcategories under Medicine have been deleted to provide one category for all medical expenses.

Requiring Categories in All Transactions

Another customization option Quicken offers is a reminder to place a category entry in a transaction before it is recorded. If you attempt to record a transaction without a category, Quicken will not complete the transaction until you confirm that you want to enter it without a category. The default for Quicken 3 for Windows is to have this option activated.

If this option has been turned off, you will want to change it back. To require the entry of categories, select Preferences from the Edit menu, then select General. Select the Warn Before Recording Uncategorized Transactions check box and select OK to finalize the settings change. To have Quicken not warn you about uncategorized transactions, you would have cleared this check box. The next time you attempt to record a transaction without a category, Quicken will stop to confirm your choice before saving.

Using Subcategories

Now that you have set up your file and new account and have customized your categories, you are ready to enter some transactions. Since you are already proficient at basic transaction entry from earlier chapters, you will want to look at some additional ways of modifying accounts as you make entries.

One option is to create categories that are subcategories of an existing category. For instance, rather than continuing to allocate all your utility bills to the Utilities category, you could create more specific subcategories under Utilities that let you allocate expenses to electricity, water, or gas. You could add the subcategories just as you added the new category for furniture. You can also create them when you are entering transactions and realize that the existing categories do not provide the breakdown you would like.

6

Entering a New Subcategory

When you enter both a category and a subcategory for a transaction, you type the category name, followed by a colon (:) and then the subcategory name. It is important that the category be specified first and the subcategory second.

You will enter utility bills as the first entries in the new account. Follow these steps to complete the entries for the gas and electric bills, creating a subcategory under Utilities for each:

1. With the next blank transaction in the register highlighted, enter **7/25/94** as the date for the first transaction. Type **101** as the check number.

2. Type **Consumer Power** in the payee field. Enter **35.45** as the payment amount. Type **Electric Bill** in the Memo field. Type **Utilities:Electric** in the Category field.

3. Select Record to record the transaction.

   Quicken prompts you to create the category by displaying the Set Up Category dialog box.

4. Type **Electric Utilities** in the Description text box.

Although this description is optional, it is a good idea to enter one so your reports will be informative. Your dialog box now looks like this:

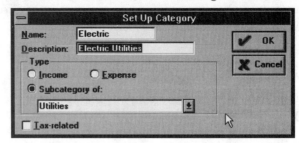

Please note that the Name text box was already filled in, and the new category is already marked as a subcategory of Utilities, based on the entry you made in the Category field.

5. Select OK to complete the settings and record the transaction.

Completing the Utility Subcategories

To create a subcategory for the gas bill, enter the following information in each of the fields shown.

Date: 7/25/94
Num: 102
Payee: West Michigan Gas
Payment: 17.85
Memo: Gas Bill

Do not record the transaction. With the cursor in the Category field, follow these steps:

1. Select the Cat List icon from the Iconbar or select Category & Transfer from the Lists menu to display the Category & Transfer List window.
2. Move to Utilities: Gas & Electric.
3. Select Edit to edit the current category.
4. Change the Name text box in the Edit Category dialog box to Gas.
5. Change the Description text box to Gas Utilities.
6. Select OK and Use to use the category.
7. Select Record to finalize the transaction entry.

You still need to enter the telephone bill, but since Quicken already defines Telephone as a Home category, you cannot consider Telephone as a subcategory of Utilities. However, you could edit the Telephone category and change it from an expense to a subcategory. For now, leave it as a separate category and put the following entries in the transaction fields.

Date:	7/30/94
Num:	103
Payee:	Alltel
Payment:	86.00
Memo:	Telephone Bill
Category:	Telephone

Splitting Transactions

Split transactions are transactions that affect more than one category. You can decide how the transaction affects each of the categories involved. If you split an expense transaction, you are saying that portions of the transaction should be considered as expenses in two different categories. For example, a check written at a supermarket may cover more than just groceries. You might purchase a $25.00 plant as a gift at the same time you purchase your groceries. Recording the entire amount of the check as groceries would not accurately reflect the purpose of the check. Quicken allows you to record the $25.00 amount as a gift purchase and the remainder for groceries. In fact, after allocating the $25.00 to gifts, it even tells you the remaining balance that needs to be allocated to other categories. You could also enter a transaction in which you cashed a check and use the split transaction capability to account for your spending. As an example of splitting transactions, enter the following transaction for check number 100.

6

Date:	7/20/94
Num:	100
Payee:	Cash
Payment:	100.00
Memo:	Groceries & Misc

Do not record the transaction. With the cursor in the Category field, follow these steps:

1. Select Splits.
2. Type **Groceries**, the name of the first category you want to use in the Category field.

You can stop typing as soon as QuickFill provides a match.

3. Type **Groceries & Market** in the Memo field.

4. Type **75** in the Amount field.

5. Type **Misc** as the category for the next line.

6. Type **Drug & Hardware Store** in the Memo field.

   At the bottom of the dialog box, Quicken displays 25.00, the remainder of the total transaction amount you entered in the Payment field, in the Amount field of the next line, as shown here:

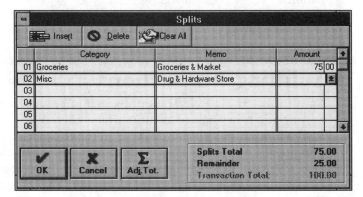

7. Select OK and assign the 25.00 amount on the second line to the Misc category.

   The category appears as —Splits—.

8. Select Record to record the transaction.

NOTE: Instead of entering the amount being assigned to each category in the Amount field of the Split Transaction dialog box, you can enter a percentage. Quicken will use this percentage to calculate the exact amount, using the total amount you already entered in the Payment or Deposit field in the Register.

There are many other times when you might elect to use split transactions. Assigning part of a mortgage payment to interest and the balance to principal is a good example. Credit card purchases can also be handled in this fashion if you elect not to set up a special credit card account. Normally, the split transaction approach is a better alternative if you pay your bills in full each month.

Notice that up to the point when you enter the category, there is no difference between a split transaction entry and any other entry in the register. Complete the following entries to add another split transaction for a credit card payment:

1. Enter **8/3/94** as the date.
2. Enter **105** as the check number.
3. Type **Easy Credit Card** in the Payee field.
4. Type **450** for the payment amount entry.
5. Type **July 25th Statement** in the Memo field.
6. In the Category field, select <u>S</u>plits.

    Quicken displays the Split Transaction window with up to six category fields displayed. You can assign as many as 30 split categories.

7. Display the drop-down list box showing the available categories and select Clothing.
8. Type **Blue Blouse** in the Memo field.
9. Type **50** in the Amount field.

    Quicken allocates the first $50.00 of credit card expense to Clothing and shows the $400.00 balance at the bottom of the dialog box.

10. Complete the remaining entries shown here to detail how the credit card expenses were distributed:

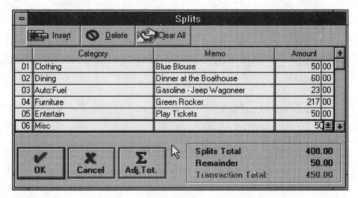

    When you select OK for final processing, you will see —Splits— in the Category field.

11. Select Re<u>c</u>ord to record the transaction.

Using Multiple Accounts

Quicken makes it easy to create multiple accounts. Since here all the accounts will be created in the same file, you can choose to have separate

6

reports for each account or one report that shows them all. You will have an account register for each account that you create.

Types of Accounts

Savings accounts, investment accounts, cash accounts, and credit card accounts are all possible additional accounts. Savings accounts and investment accounts should definitely be kept separate from your checking account, since you will want to monitor both the growth and balance in these accounts

The need for cash and credit card accounts varies by individual. If you pay the majority of your expenses in cash and need a detailed record of your expenditures, a cash account is a good idea. With credit cards, if your purchases are at a reasonable level and you pay the balance in full each month, the extra time required to maintain a separate account may not be warranted. Neither cash nor credit card accounts have been used in the sample files in this book. If you decide you need them, you can use the same procedures to create them that you used to create the savings account. The section "Using a Separate Credit Card Account" near the end of the chapter provides additional information about maintaining a separate credit card account.

Creating a New Savings Account

If you want to transfer funds from your checking account to a savings account, you must have a savings account set up. Follow these steps to create the new account:

1. Select Create New Account from the Activities menu.
2. Select OK to accept the Bank Account account type.
3. Type **Cardinal Saving** in the Account Name text box.

    You cannot call this account Cardinal Savings, with the final "s" because Quicken only allows 15 characters in an account name.
4. Type **500** in the Balance text box.
5. Enter **7/15/94** in the as of text box. Remember, you can use the drop-down calendar to select the date rather than typing it.
6. Type **Savings account** in the Description text box.
7. Select OK.

    Quicken will open the Cardinal Saving register.
8. Return to the Cardinal Bank register by clicking the window with the mouse or selecting it from the Window menu.

NOTE: If you would like to include further information about this account, including the bank name and address, the account number, or the rate of interest you receive on the account, select Info in the New Account Information dialog box, opening the Additional Account Information dialog box.

Transferring Funds to a Different Account

It is easy to transfer funds from one account to another as long as both accounts are established. You might transfer a fixed amount to savings each month to cover long-range savings plans or to cover large, fixed expenses that are due annually or semi-annually. Follow these steps to make a transfer from the checking account to the savings account:

1. Complete these entries in the Cardinal Bank register for the transaction fields down to Category:

Date:	8/5/94
Num:	Select TXFR from the drop-down list.
Payee:	Cardinal Savings
Payment:	200.00
Memo:	Transfer to savings

2. In the Category field, use the drop-down list box, or the QuickFill feature to enter Cardinal Saving as the category.

3. Select Record to confirm the transaction.

You will notice brackets around the account name in the Category field of the register, indicating that this is actually an account, which you can use as a category. Quicken has automatically created the parallel transaction in the other account, as you will see if you switch to the Cardinal Saving register. Quicken will also delete both transactions when you delete either of them.

Memorized Transactions

Many of your financial transactions are going to repeat. You pay your rent or mortgage payments each month. Likewise, utility bills and credit card payments are paid at about the same time each month. Cash inflows in the form of paychecks are also regularly scheduled. Other payments such as groceries also repeat, but probably not on the same dates each month.

Quicken can memorize transactions that are entered from the register or check writing window. Once memorized, these transactions can be used

6

to generate similar transactions. Amounts and dates may change, and you can edit these fields without having to reenter the payee, memo, and category information.

Memorizing a Register Entry

Memorized transactions can be recalled for later use, printed, changed, and deleted. All transactions are memorized if the Automatic Memorization of New Transactions check box in the QuickFill Preferences dialog box is selected, rather than cleared. To select this check box, you select Preferences from the Edit menu, then select QuickFill. The examples in this chapter assume that this check box is selected, so that all of the transactions you have entered are memorized. To try using memorized transactions, you will need to add a few more transactions to the account register to complete the entries for August. Add these transactions to your register:

Date:	8/1/94
Num:	Select DEP from the drop-down list.
Payee:	Payroll deposit
Deposit	1585.99
Memo:	August 1 paycheck
Category:	Salary

Date:	8/2/94
Num:	104
Payee:	Great Lakes Savings & Loan
Payment:	350.00
Memo:	August Payment
Category:	Mort Pay

NOTE: Mort Pay is a new category to add, since you do not have the information required to split the transaction between the existing interest and principal categories in the Home category list. Use Entire Mortgage Payment as the description when you add the category.

Date:	8/4/94
Num:	106
Payee:	Maureks
Payment:	60.00
Memo:	Groceries
Category:	Groceries

Date:	8/6/94
Num:	107
Payee:	Orthodontics, Inc.
Payment:	100.00
Memo:	Monthly Orthodontics Payment
Category:	Medical

Date:	8/15/94
Num:	108
Payee:	Meijer
Payment:	65.00
Memo:	Groceries
Category:	Groceries

6

Quicken will memorize split transactions in the same way as any other transactions. You should carefully review the split transactions for information that changes each month. For example, the entry for the credit card payment is likely to be split across several categories if you are entering the detail in the check register rather than in a separate credit card account. You will want to edit both the categories into which the main transaction is split and the amounts.

You can select Memorized Transaction from the List menu or press Ctrl-T to display the Memorized Transaction List; your list should match this:

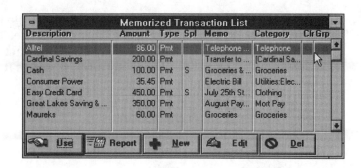

If you want to print the list once it is displayed, select Print List from the File menu, or select the Print icon from the Iconbar. To remove the list from the screen, press Esc. To enter a new transaction, select New.

Memorizing Transactions Manually

If your automatic memorization feature is turned off, you can memorize a transaction before or after it is recorded in the register or check. First, fill out all the fields for the register or check transaction that you want to memorize. You can either record the transaction or immediately memorize it. Select Memorized Transaction from the Edit menu. When Quicken displays a dialog box warning you that the transaction is about to be memorized, select OK.

Changing and Deleting Memorized Transactions

Quicken allows you to change a memorized transaction in the Memorized Transaction List by activating the list and then selecting Edit to edit the highlighted transaction.

To delete a memorized transaction, you must activate the transaction list, select the transaction you want to delete, and select Del. A warning message will appear asking you to confirm the deletion. When you select OK, the transaction is no longer memorized.

Follow these steps to delete some transactions from your Memorized Transaction List.

1. Activate the Memorized Transaction List by selecting Memorized Transaction from the Lists menu.
2. Highlight the third transaction, with the description "Cash."
3. Select Del.
4. Select OK to confirm that you do want to delete the transaction from the Memorized Transaction List.
5. Repeat these steps to delete the transactions with the descriptions "Maureks" and "Meijer".

These three transactions are not regular ones. While the categories of the last two will probably remain the same whenever a check is made out to them, the amount will change each time. Deleting transactions you are not going to use from the Memorized Transaction List makes it easier to access the ones that you will use.

Using Memorized Transactions

To recall a memorized transaction and place it in the register, move to the next blank transaction in the register (unless you want the recalled transaction to replace a transaction already on the screen). Open the Memorized Transaction List dialog box by selecting Memorized Transaction from the Lists menu. Use the arrow keys to highlight the transaction you want to add to the register and then select Use. The selected transaction appears in the register with the date of the last transaction you entered, not the date of the transaction you memorized. You can edit the transaction in the register and select Record when you are ready to record the entry.

Memorizing a Check

If you write checks with Quicken, you will want to memorize checks rather than register entries.

Checks written in the check writing window are memorized the same way that transactions entered in the register are. Memorized check and register transactions for the same account will appear in the same Memorized Transaction List and can be edited, deleted, or recalled from either the check writing or register window.

As you use Quicken more, you may find that only a few of your transactions really need to be memorized. By changing the default settings, you can keep transactions from being automatically memorized. Once you do this, you will have to memorize manually each transaction that you want memorized.

6

Working with Scheduled Transactions

Although you can recall memorized transactions individually as a way to reenter similar transactions, a better method can be to have Quicken automatically schedule and enter transactions for you. Quicken 3 for Windows can schedule individual transactions or groups of transactions. You can use the Financial Calendar to schedule individual transactions whether or not they are memorized, or you can schedule groups of memorized transactions using the Scheduled Transaction List.

You can use Quicken's Financial Calendar to either prompt you to enter scheduled transactions or even to enter the transactions for you at the scheduled time. You can use this automation to save you the time of entering regularly scheduled transactions. You can also use the Scheduled Transaction List to create scheduled transaction groups, which are groups of transactions scheduled to occur together.

Scheduling with the Financial Calendar

The Financial Calendar provides the easiest method for quickly scheduling repeated transactions. There are other uses for the Financial Calendar, which also shows when each of the transactions entered in your register occurred. The Financial Calendar can also be used for tracking your future obligations.

Scheduling Transactions

You can schedule any transaction you have entered in the Financial Calendar, whether or not it is memorized. You can schedule a transaction that will occur only a specified number of times, or you can set the transaction to recur indefinitely.

You can display the Financial Calendar by selecting Financial Calendar from the Activities menu, or by selecting the Calendar icon from the Iconbar. Your Financial Calendar should look like Figure 6-2.

NOTE: The Financial Calendar initially shows the calendar for the current date. Since it is unlikely that you will be using this book during the dates given for the transactions, you will probably have to change the calendar shown by selecting the Prev or Next buttons at the top of the calendar to move to July of 1994.

At the right side of the window, Quicken displays a list of the transactions you have entered. You can quickly schedule a transaction by dragging one of these transactions to a day on the Calendar with the mouse. When you release the mouse button, Quicken displays the Set Up Scheduled

Your Financial
Calendar
Figure 6-2.

	Financial Calendar						
Plan	List	Prev ◄◄	**July – 1994**	►►Next		Note	Close
Accounts		Cardinal Saving\Cardinal Bank					Drag and drop these on the calendar.
Sun	Mon	Tue	Wed	Thur	Fri	Sat	
26	27	28	29	30	1	2	<NEW>
							Alltel -86.00
3	4	5	6	7	8	9	Cardinal Savings -200.00
							Cash -100.00
							Consumer Power -35.45
10	11	12	13	14	15	16	Easy Credit Card -450.00
			Opening Balan		Opening Balan		Great Lakes Saving... -350.00
							Maureks -135.00
17	18	19	20	21	22	23	Meijer -93.20
							Orthodontics, Inc -100.00
			Cash				Payroll deposit 1,585.99
24	25	26	27	28	29	30	West Michigan Gas ... -17.85
	West Michigan Consumer Po					Alltel	
31	1	2	3	4	5	6	
	Payroll deposit	Great Lakes S	Easy Credit Ca	Maureks	Cardinal Savin	Orthodontics,	

Transaction dialog box. For example, to schedule the regular deposit of paychecks, follow these steps:

1. Display the Financial Calendar by selecting Financial Calendar from the Activities menu or the Calendar icon from the Iconbar.
2. Select Prev or Next to display the calendar for August of 1994.
3. Drag the transaction described as Payroll deposit from the list box on the right side of the window to September 1, at the bottom of the calendar. This Set Up Scheduled Transaction dialog box appears:

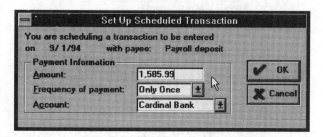

4. Enter Month in the Frequency of payment text box using QuickFill or the drop-down list box.
5. Select OK. When you see the message about the scheduled transaction, select OK again.

   If you look at this transaction in the Calendar, you will note that it is the first transaction that does not have an asterisk before it. When the transaction is entered in your register, the asterisk will appear.

Quicken will prompt you about entering the scheduled transaction the first time you start Quicken 3 for Windows after the scheduled date for the transaction.

Editing Scheduled Transactions
You can easily edit your scheduled transactions. For example, you can edit the payroll transaction you just scheduled so that it does not enter the transaction without prompting you first. To edit a scheduled transaction, follow these steps:

1. Click on the day the transaction is scheduled for, in this case, 9/1/94. Quicken will display the dialog box shown here:

6

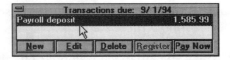

2. Select Edit, opening the Edit Scheduled Transaction dialog box
   shown here:

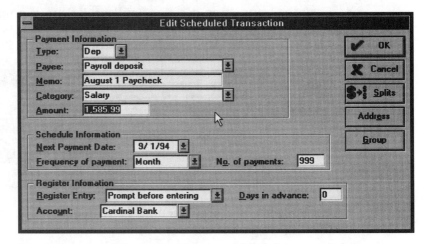

3. Delete the contents of the Memo text box. You will want to edit your
   transaction every month and enter a new memo, or simply ignore
   the memo.

4. Select Enter w/o prompting in the Register Entry drop-down list box.
   Now Quicken will enter your payroll deposit without prompting you
   about it.

5. Select OK.

You may edit your transaction again when you receive a raise, or if you
decide you want it entered in the register a few days before it will actually be
there. This is useful as a reminder about bills you need to pay.

Paying a Scheduled Transaction Early

You may want to register a transaction as being paid early, either because
you are going out of town or because you decided to pay the bill before the
due date. To do this, click on the day containing the scheduled transaction,
then select Pay Now.

 Quicken will prompt you to review the details of the transaction. When you
select Enter, the transaction is entered in the register.

Scheduling Transaction Groups

Quicken 3 for Windows can schedule both individual transactions as described earlier or groups of transactions. If you have several memorized transactions that occur at the same time, a scheduled transaction group lets you focus on other tasks while Quicken remembers to enter the transactions you need. Quicken will record the entire group for you with or without prompting you about its entries depending on how you define the scheduled transaction.

Defining a Scheduled Transaction Group

Quicken allows you to set up as many as 12 scheduled transaction groups. Defining a group is easy, but it requires several steps after memorizing all the transactions that will be placed in the group. You will need to describe the group. Finally, you will need to assign specific memorized transactions to the group. Although expense transactions are frequently used to create groups, you can also include an entry for a direct deposit payroll check that is deposited at the same time each month.

6

For your first transaction group, which you will title Utilities, you will group the gas and electric transactions that occur near the end of each month. Follow these steps to create the transaction group:

1. Select Scheduled Transactions from the Lists menu.
2. Select New.

Quicken displays a dialog box in which you define the group. Figure 6-3 shows this dialog box with the entries you will make in the next steps.

3. Enter **8/25/94** in the Next Payment Date text box. Remember you can use the drop-down calendar to select this date.
4. Select Month in the Frequency of payment text box.
5. Make sure that the No. of payments box is still set to 999, which causes Quicken to continue entering these transactions indefinitely.
6. Make sure that the Register Entry text box still shows "Prompt before entering," so that Quicken prompts you about the transactions before entering them in your account.
7. Enter Cardinal Bank in the Account text box as the account these transactions are going to be entered into.
8. Select Group.

   The Set Up Transaction Group window shown in Figure 6-4 is displayed.

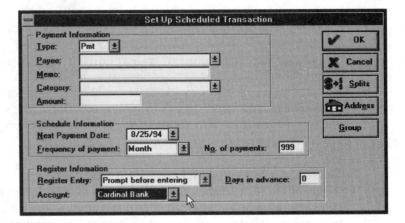

Set Up
Scheduled
Transaction
dialog box
Figure 6-3.

NOTE: If you are prompted about a category, simply select <u>Y</u>es to continue without entering one. You do not want to enter a category for a group of transactions, since each transaction uses a different category.

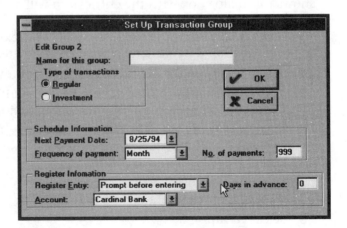

Set Up
Transaction
Group
dialog box
Figure 6-4.

9. Type **Utilities** as the name for the group and select OK.

10. In the Assign Transactions to Group dialog box, double-click Consumer Power or highlight it with the arrow keys and select <u>M</u>ark to assign the transaction to the Utilities group.

The numeral 1 appears in the Grp column, which indicates that the transaction is now a part of the Utilities group.

11. Select the Western Michigan Gas and Alltel transactions by double-clicking them or highlighting them and selecting <u>M</u>ark.

Quicken marks these transactions as part of the Utilities group, as shown in Figure 6-5.

12. Select <u>D</u>one to indicate you are finished selecting transactions.

You may want to define other scheduled transaction groups to include payroll, loan payments, and anything else that you might pay at the beginning of the month. You can enter individual scheduled transactions for transactions that occur on a specific date each month using the Financial Calendar or the Scheduled Transaction List, as described above. You do not need to define additional scheduled groups or transactions in order to complete the remaining exercises in this section.

6

You can also create transaction groups that generate checks for you. These groups contain transactions that are memorized from the check writing

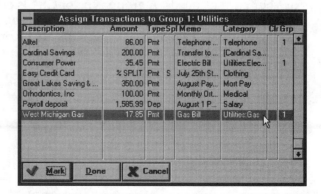

Assign
Transactions
to Group
dialog box
Figure 6-5.

window. The procedure is the same as that just shown. You can identify these transactions in the Assign Transactions window by the Chk entry in the Type field.

Changing a Scheduled Transaction Group

You can edit a transaction group at any time by selecting Scheduled Transactions from the Lists menu. Highlight the group and select Edit. As you proceed through the normal group definition procedure, you can change the description of the transaction group and how frequently it is supposed to be entered in the register, and you can select additional transactions for inclusion in the group.

To delete a scheduled transaction group, select Scheduled Transactions from the Lists menu and highlight the group you want to delete. Then select Del. When Quicken warns you that you are about to delete the group, select OK. Quicken eliminates the group but does not delete the memorized transactions that are part of it. It also does not affect any transactions recorded in the register by earlier executions of the scheduled group.

If you want to alter a transaction that is part of the transaction group, you will need to alter the memorized transaction. This means you have to open the Memorized Transaction List, highlight the transaction and select Edit, then edit the options for the transaction.

Recording a Transaction Group

Once you have defined a scheduled transaction group, you can forget about it and Quicken will handle the entries. If you want to record the group early for some reason, you do not need to wait for Quicken. You can select it and record it yourself. Since you can memorize entries for either the register or the check writing window, make sure you have the group correctly defined for your current needs. A group type of Chk is created in the check writing window and can be recorded in either the account register or the check writing window. Payment (Pmt) groups are recorded in the account register and can only be used to record account register entries.

To execute a transaction group from the account register, complete the following steps:

1. Select Scheduled Transactions from the Lists menu.
2. Highlight the Utilities group.
3. Select Pay Now.

Quicken displays the Enter Scheduled Transaction dialog box that looks like this:

If you were actually planning to pay these bills early, you would enter the current date in the Date in register text box, so that the register showed the date you actually recorded the transaction. In this case, you are not going to do this.

4. Select Enter to enter.

Enter the new transactions with a date of 8/25/94, as shown here:

8/15/94	108	Meijer		65	00					2,621	69
		Groceries	Groceries								
8/25/94	Sched	Alltel		86	00					2,535	69
		Telephone Bill	Telephone								
8/25/94	Sched	Consumer Power		35	45					2,500	24
		Electric Bill	Utilities:Electric								
8/25/94	Sched	West Michigan Gas		17	85					2,482	39
		Gas Bill	Utilities:Gas								

Modify the Utilities transaction group entries just recorded and add the last transaction for Meijer to complete the August transactions for your account register. (Remember to record each transaction after the modifications have been made.) Then enter these transactions:

Num:	109
Payee:	Alltel
Payment:	23.00

Num:	110
Payee:	Consumer Power
Payment:	30.75

Num:	111
Payee:	West Michigan Gas
Payment:	19.25

6

Record the final transaction for the month of August as follows:

Date:	8/27/94
Num:	112
Payee:	Meijer
Payment:	93.20
Memo:	Food
Category:	Groceries

Notice that Quicken's QuickFill feature completed the entire transaction for you when you typed **Meijer**. You only needed to change the memo and payment amount. The last few transactions entered and modified should now look like this:

8/25/94	109	Alltel		23	00				2,598	69
		Telephone Bill	Telephone							
8/25/94	110	Consumer Power		30	75				2,567	94
		Electric Bill	Utilities:Electric							
8/25/94	111	West Michigan Gas		19	75				2,548	19
		Gas Bill	Utilities:Gas							
8/27/94	112	Meijer		93	20				2,454	99
		Food	Groceries							

Responding to Quicken Reminders to Record a Scheduled Group

If you have chosen to be prompted before a scheduled group is recorded, Quicken displays a dialog box that asks you if you want to enter the scheduled group when that day arrives, unless you have chosen to have entries made without prompting. The prompt will either appear in Windows when you load it or when you start Quicken. Hard disk users who have the default setting for Billminder still set at Yes will see a message when they open Windows reminding them to pay postdated checks or to record transaction groups. If you do not have a hard disk or if you have turned Billminder off, the prompt will not appear until you start Quicken.

Using Classes

You have used categories as one way of distinguishing transactions entered in Quicken. Since categories are either income, expense, or a subcategory, these groupings generally define the transaction to which they are assigned. Also, the status of a category as tax related or not affects the transactions to which it is assigned. Specific category names and descriptions provide more information about the transactions to which they are assigned. They explain what kind of income or expense a specific transaction represents. You can tell at a glance which costs are for utilities and which are for entertainment.

In summary reports, you might see totals of all the transactions contained in a category.

Classes allow you to "slice the transaction pie" in a different way. Classes recategorize to show where, to whom, or for what time period the transactions apply. It is important not to think of classes as a replacement for categories; they do not affect category assignments. Classes provide a different view or perspective of your data.

For example, you might use classes if you have both a year-round home and a vacation cottage. One set of utility expenses is for the year-round residence, and another is for the vacation cottage utility expenses. If you define and then assign classes to the transactions, they will still have categories representing utility expenses, but you will also have class assignments that let you know how much you have spent for utilities in each of your houses.

Since the expenses for a number of family members can be maintained in one checking account, you might want to use classes for those expenses that you would like to review by family member. You can use this approach for clothing expenses and automobile expenses if your family members drive separate cars. Another method for automobile expenses is to assign classes for each of the vehicles you own. You can then look at what you have spent on a specific vehicle at the end of the year and make an informed decision regarding replacement or continued maintenance.

Quicken does not provide a standard list of classes. As with categories, you can set up what you need before you start making entries, or you can add the classes you need as you enter transactions. Once you have assigned a class to a transaction, you enter it in the Category field by placing it after your category name (if one exists) and any subcategories. You always type a slash (/) before entering the class name, as in Utilities: Electric/Cottage.

To create a class before entering a transaction, you can select Class from the Lists menu or press [Ctrl]-[L] to open the Class List window, as shown here:

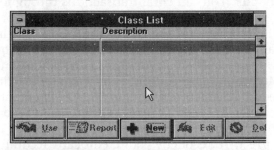

Select <u>N</u>ew to create a new entry. Quicken displays the Set Up Class dialog box, shown here,

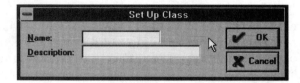

where you can enter the name and description of a class. Each new class is added to the Class List dialog box. To create a class as you enter a transaction, simply type the category and any subcategories, followed by a slash and the class name you want to use, and select Re<u>c</u>ord. The following is an example of a class entry for "Jim" that could be used if you wanted to separately categorize personal expenses for each individual in the household:

8/12/94	Beach Shop		54	00			2,632	69
	New sweater	Clothing/Jim						

If Jim were not an existing class, Quicken would display the Set Up Class dialog box and you could create it. You will find more detailed examples of class entries in later chapters.

Using a Separate Credit Card Account

If you charge a large number of your purchases and do not pay your credit card bill in full each month, a separate account for each of your credit cards is the best approach. It will enable you to better monitor your individual payments throughout the year. Also, your reports will show the full detail for all credit card transactions, just as your checking account register shows the details of each check written.

You will need to set up accounts for each card by using the procedure followed when you created the account for Cardinal Saving earlier in the chapter. You can enter transactions throughout the month as you charge items to each of your credit card accounts, or you can wait until you receive the statements at the end of the month. Figure 6-6 shows how your credit card account appears on the screen. You record transaction information in the same fashion as you record checkbook entries designating the Payee, Memo, and Category fields for each transaction. The Charge field is used to record transaction amounts and the Payment entry is recorded as part of the reconciliation process. You should use a reconciliation procedure similar to the one you used for your checking account to verify that the charges are correct. To reconcile your credit card account and pay your bill, select Pay <u>C</u>redit Card Bill from the <u>A</u>ctivities menu with the credit card register active.

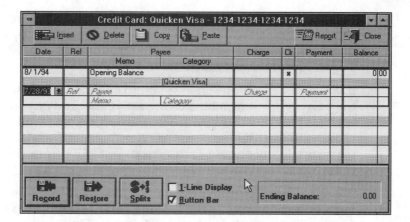

Example of
how a credit
card account
appears
Figure 6-6.

You can use Quicken's transfer features to transfer funds between your
checking account and credit card accounts. If you have overdraft protection,
you can also create a transaction to record the overdraft charges to your
credit card and checking accounts.

A new feature added to Quicken lets Quicken record all credit card
transactions for you. IntelliCharge is your own Quicken Visa card that
provides this new option. You can receive your IntelliCharge transactions
on diskette or modem each month. With this feature, you select Get
IntelliCharge Data from the Activities menu and your data is read into
your credit card account. Even the categories are completed for you as
the data is recorded. You can reconcile your account and decide on the
payment amount.

Adding Passwords

To add passwords, select Passwords from the File menu. Quicken presents
the following submenu:

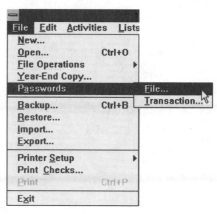

This menu allows you to decide if you want to password-protect a file by using a main password, or only existing transactions by using a transaction password. Although you can add protection with a password at both levels, you will need to select each individually.

If you select File, Quicken asks you to enter a password. Once you select OK, the password will be added to the active file, and anyone wishing to work with that file must supply it. The transaction password is used to prevent changes to existing transactions prior to a specified date, without the password. If you choose Transaction, you will be presented with a window that requires you to enter both a password and a date.

If you want to change a password or remove it in a subsequent session, you must be able to provide the existing password. Quicken will then provide a Change Password dialog box for the entry of the old and new passwords. After completing the entries and selecting OK, the new password is in effect.

CHAPTER

7

QUICKEN AS A BUDGETING TOOL

A budget is usually thought of as a constraint on your spending. But that is not what budgets are designed to be. Instead, a budget is a financial plan that shows your projected income and expenses so that you can plan your expenses within the limits of your income. Although a budget may sometimes cause you to deny yourself a purchase, this denial will supply the funds for expenses you have given greater priority.

Given the same income, five families would prepare five different budget plans. One family might budget to save enough for a down payment on a new house. Another family might construct its budget so that they could afford a new car. A third family might enjoy eating out and traveling, and budget accordingly. Within the constraints of your income, the choice is yours.

A budget is your financial plan. It is meant to guide you as you confront financial decisions.

If a budget is meant to facilitate getting what you want, why do so many people procrastinate in putting together a budget? It may be because budgeting takes time or because it forces you to make decisions, or perhaps the reason is simply that most people are not sure where to begin. One thing is certain: budgeting is an important component of every successful financial plan. You should create a budget even if you have already successfully built a financial nest egg. It will allow you to protect your investment and ensure that your spending meets both your short- and long-range goals.

Quicken is ideally suited for maintaining your budget information. The program guides you through the budget development process; you need only specify categories and make simple entries to record budgeted amounts in these categories. After a modest initial investment of time, Quicken generates reports you can use to monitor your progress toward your financial goals. You don't need to wait until the end of the budget period to record your progress. You can enter your expenses daily and check the status of your actual and budgeted amounts at any time you wish.

In this chapter you prepare budget entries for several months. You use scheduled transaction groups from Chapter 6, "Expanding the Scope of Financial Entries," to expedite the entry process and provide a sufficient number of transactions so that you can get a sense of what Quicken can do. After making your entries, you see how Quicken's standard reports can help you keep expenses in line with your budget, and you take a quick look at the insights graphs can provide.

Quicken's Budgeting Process

Quicken allows you to enter projected income and expense levels for any category. You can enter the same projection for each month of the year, or you can change the amount allocated for each month. Quicken matches your planned expenses with your actual expense entries and displays the results in a Monthly Budget report. There is one entry point for budget information, but Quicken combines actual entries from all your Bank, Cash, and Credit Card accounts in the current file. Although Quicken can take much of the work out of entering and managing your budget, it cannot prepare a budget without your projections. If you have never prepared a budget before, you should take a look at a few budget planning considerations, which are shown in the special "Budget Planning" section of this chapter. Once you have put together a plan, it's time to record your decisions in Quicken.

Specifying Budget Amounts

In this section, you enter budget amounts for the transaction categories you entered in the Cardinal Bank account register in Chapter 6. Later, when you create your own budget, you will need to expand the budget entries to include all the categories of income and expenses you want to monitor.

Consider a few points before you complete the budget entries:

◆ By default, Quicken includes categories and subcategories in budget reports if it finds budgeted amounts in the categories and subcategories. You can change this default setting so that Quicken's Monthly Budget report includes all categories found in the Category & Transfer List, or so that it includes all categories that have either budgeted or actual amounts assigned to them.

◆ It doesn't matter what period of time you define as the reporting period. (Although the default reporting period is monthly, you can make your reporting period quarterly or biannually, for example.)

◆ All the categories you have available in your Category List are shown in the Budget window. This includes Quicken's predefined personal Category List as well as any new categories you have added.

◆ You can assign budget amounts to subcategories as well as to categories.

To set up the budget, follow these steps from the register window:

1. Select Set Up Budgets from the Activities menu.

   Quicken opens the Set Up Budgets window, as shown in Figure 7-1. Notice that the window contains rows and columns. Normally, you would enter realistic amounts that matched your budget plan in this window. In this exercise, you enter budget amounts provided for you. You also learn to use the window's buttonbar to help you complete your entries.

2. Move to the Salary category in the Jan column by using the mouse or ⊡.

3. Type **1585.99**, and move to another row or column.

   Quicken rounds your entry to 1586 and displays it in the Salary category, the Total Inflows row at the bottom of the window, and the Totals column at the right side of the window.

4. Move back to the Salary entry for January, and select Edit from the Set Up Budget window's buttonbar.

5. Select Fill Row Right, and then select Yes to copy the salary across, as shown in Figure 7-2.

Budget Planning

You must begin the budgeting process before you start making budget entries in Quicken. Start with an analysis of expected income. If your income flow is irregular, estimate on the low side. Remember to use only the net amount received from each income source. Also, do not include projected salary increases until they are confirmed.

The next step is analyzing projected expenses. First, budget for debt repayment and other essentials such as medical insurance premiums. In addition to monthly items such as mortgage and car loan payments, consider irregular expenses that are paid only once or twice a year. Tuition, property taxes, insurance premiums, children's and personal allowances, and church pledges are examples of irregular expenses.

Project your expenses for medical, pharmacy, and dental bills for one year. Compute the required yearly expenses, and save toward these major expenses so that the entire amount does not need to come from a single month's check.

The next type of expense you should plan into your budget is savings. If you wait until you cover food, entertainment, and all the other day-to-day expenses, it's easy to find that nothing is left to save. You should plan to write yourself a check for at least five percent of your net pay for savings when you pay your other bills.

The last type of expense you must budget for is day-to-day expenses such as food, personal care, home repairs, gasoline, car maintenance, furniture, recreation, and gifts.

Naturally, if your totals for expenses exceed your income projections, you must reassess your budget before entering projected amounts in Quicken.

During the first few months of budgeting, err on the side of too much detail. At the end of the month, you will need to know exactly how your money was spent. You can then make realistic adjustments between expense categories to ensure that your budget stays in balance.

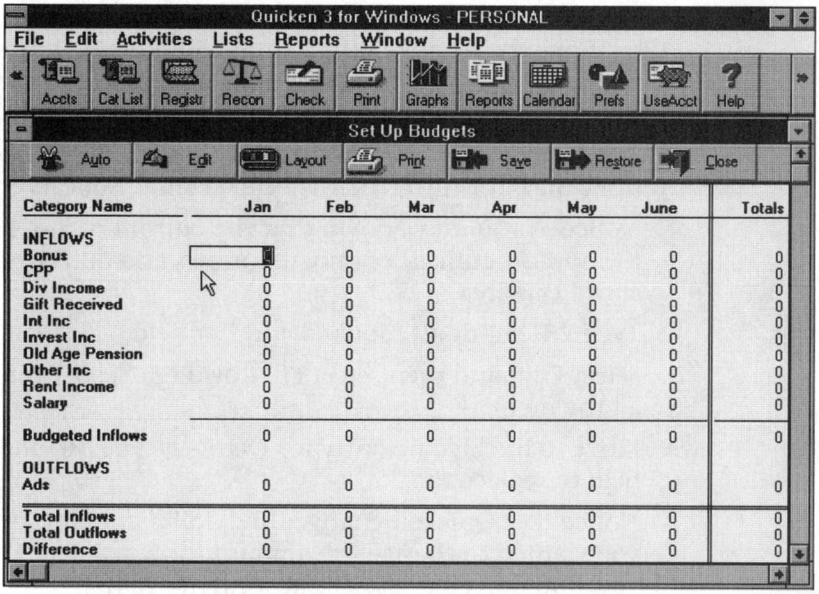

Set Up
Budgets
window
Figure 7-1.

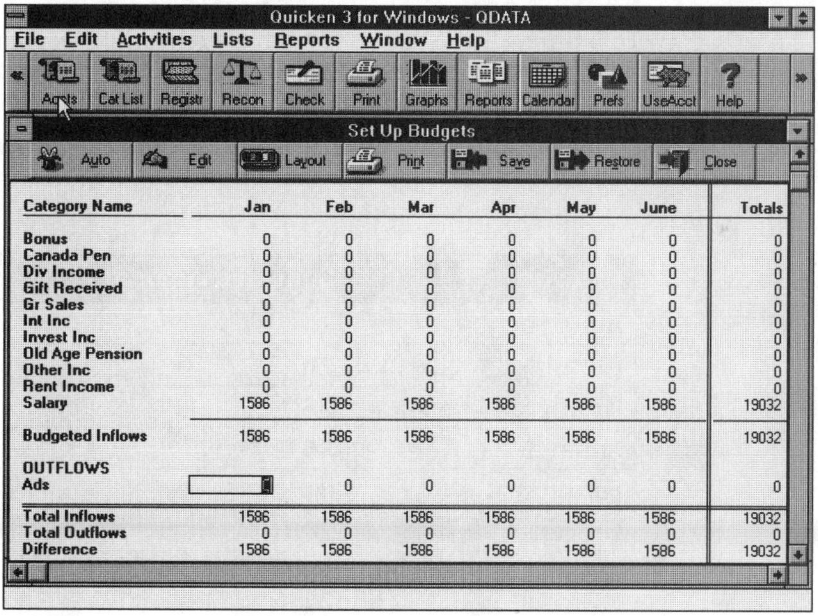

Set Up
Budgets
window after
Fill <u>R</u>ow Right
is used for
salary
Figure 7-2.

7

You must move back to the entry because you finalized the salary entry by moving elsewhere. You can use Fill Row Right immediately after typing an entry if you haven't yet finalized the entry.

6. Highlight the January entry for the Electric subcategory under Utilities. If the subcategories are not currently displayed, select the Layout button from the buttonbar, then select the Show Subcats check box and OK.

   Notice as you move down that the bottom part of the screen continues to show a summary of budget inflows and outflows; the scrolling occurs above this area.

7. Type **25**, but don't move to another field.

8. Select Edit, and then select Fill Row Right and Yes to copy 25 across for all the months.

9. Move to the Electric entry for October, type **30**, and move to another field to replace the 25.

   Notice that Quicken changed the dollar amount for only one month. If you wanted to change the amount for November and December as well, you would need to use Fill Row Right again.

10. Move back to the October entry, select Edit, select Fill Row Right, and select Yes.

    This time, all the values for subsequent months change to 30. You might make this type of change because new power rates are expected or because you have installed a number of new outside lights.

11. Using the following information, move to the January column and complete the budgeted amounts for the categories in that column.

Category	Budgeted Amount
Auto: Fuel	30
Clothing	70
Dining	55
Entertain	55
Furniture	0
Groceries	200
Medical	120
Misc	75
Mort Pay	350
Telephone	30
Utilities: Gas	20

12. To enter a budgeted amount of 200 as a transfer to the Cardinal Saving account each month, start by selecting La̲yout from the buttonbar, then selecting the Show T̲ransfers check box and OK.

    Quicken adds the transfer account categories to the categories shown.

13. Move to the [Cardinal Saving] January entry at the bottom of the Outflow section, type **200**, and then select E̲dit, Fill R̲ow Right, and Y̲es to copy 200 across for all the months.

    In the early stages, it generally takes several months to develop sound estimates for all your expenditure categories. For example, this illustration shows a desired transfer to savings of $200.00 per month. You anticipate that your excess cash inflows at the end of the month will be $200.00, and you plan to transfer the excess to savings. If you find that your outflows actually exceed your inflows, however, you'll need to transfer money from savings. Once you have established your spending patterns and monitored your inflows and outflows, you may find that excess inflows occur during parts of the year and excess outflows during others, such as during the holiday season. You can use your Quicken budget to plan for these seasonal needs and anticipate the transfer of funds between your savings and checking accounts. As a rule, you should transfer any excess cash to savings at the end of each month.

14. Select La̲yout, clear the Show T̲ransfers check box and select OK to toggle the transfer categories off again so that you don't see them. The entries you make into subcategories are not lost when they are hidden, they are simply shown as part of the category.

15. Select E̲dit, and then select Fill C̲olumns and Y̲es to copy the values across from January to all the other months, as shown in Figure 7-3. This changes the figure for Utilities: Electric in Oct-Dec back to 25. When you use Fill C̲olumns, you cannot copy across selectively; if you want varying amounts for different months, you need to customize the entries after using Fill C̲olumns.

16. For the Furniture category, enter **185.00** for October and **250.00** for December.

17. Select the C̲lose button from the Set Up Budget window's buttonbar.

18. Select Y̲es when Quicken asks you to confirm that you want to save the budget.

7

Creating a Monthly Budget Report

Now that you have completed your initial budget entries, you will want to prepare a monthly budget summary to compare your budgeted amounts to

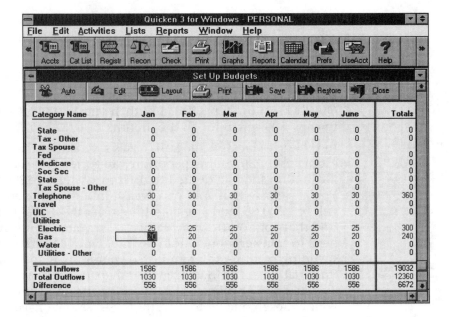

Some of the
budget
outflows after
Fill Columns
is used
Figure 7-3.

the actual amounts. To create a Monthly Budget report like the one shown
in Figure 7-4, follow these steps:

1. Select Home from the Reports menu.
2. Select Monthly Budget.
3. Enter **8/1/94** in the from text box.
4. Enter **8/31/94** in the to text box.
5. Select OK.
6. Select Customize, clear the Cents in Amount check box, and select OK.
7. Select the Print button, and then select Print to print the report.

NOTE: The reports shown in this chapter probably look different from
yours. Before these reports were created, the report printer setup was
changed to use different fonts. You can change the appearance of your
reports by changing your report printer setup.

Analyzing the Monthly Budget Report

Notice when you print the Monthly Budget report that it's dated for the
one-month period you defined. Also notice that Quicken combines all the
Bank, Cash, and Credit Card accounts in the actual and budgeted figures of

```
              Monthly Budget Report
               8/1/94 Through 8/31/94
7/28/94                                           Page 1
PERSONAL-Bank,Cash,CC Accounts
                           08/01/94       -        08/31/94
       Category Description  Actual     Budget       Diff
      ---------------------  ----------  ----------  --------

       INFLOWS
        Salary                 1,586      1,586        -0
                             ----------  ----------  --------
       TOTAL INFLOWS           1,586      1,586        -0

       OUTFLOWS
        Auto:
          Fuel                    23         30         -7
                             ----------  ----------  --------
          Total Auto              23         30         -7
        Clothing                  50         70        -20
        Dining                    60         55          5
        Entertain                 50         55         -5
        Furniture                217          0        217
        Groceries                218        200         18
        Medical                  100        120        -20
        Misc                      50         75        -25
        Mort Pay                 350        350          0
        Telephone                 23         30         -7
        Utilities:
          Electric                31         25          6
          Gas                     19         20         -1
                             ----------  ---------   -------
          Total Utilities         50         45          5
                             ----------  ---------   -------
       TOTAL OUTFLOWS          1,191      1,030        161

                             ----------  ----------  --------
       OVERALL TOTAL            395        556        -161
                             ==========  ==========  ========
```

Monthly
Budget report
for all accounts
Figure 7-4.

7

the Monthly Budget report. This means that as you scroll down the report, you don't see the $200 transfer to Cardinal Saving. Quicken views all your accounts as a single unit for budget report purposes, and it considers the transfer to have a net effect of zero since it is within the system. In the next section, you see how you can change the report to show this transfer since a transfer of $200 to savings can be a significant event from a budgeting perspective, and consequently, something you might want to show on a report.

In Figure 7-4, you can see by the negative value for the overall total difference that you were over your budget for the period by $161. When Quicken compares your budgeted versus actual expenditures for each category, if your actual expenditure exceeds the budgeted amount, a *positive* number is shown in the Diff column of the report. If the actual expenditure is less than the budgeted amount, a *negative* number appears in that column. When you read the report, you can quickly see whether you met your budget objectives for each category. As already noted, in this report your total actual outflows exceed your total budgeted outflows (1,191 – 1,030 = 161).

On closer examination, you can see that the unexpected expenditure for furniture during the month was not budgeted. The Monthly Budget report shows all your budgeted categories and the amount you were over or under budget in each. This category-by-category breakdown is the heart of budget analysis and pinpoints areas for further scrutiny.

Modifying the Monthly Budget Report

Since a budget is just a plan, you can make modifications as the need arises.

As mentioned previously, you may want to modify the Monthly Budget report to cover only the current account, Cardinal Bank. This change will allow you to see the transfer to your savings account on the report. Follow these steps to modify the Monthly Budget report:

1. Select Customize from the report window's buttonbar. The Customize Report dialog box opens.
2. Select Month from the Column drop-down list box to tell Quicken you want a monthly report prepared.
3. Select Accounts, and then unmark everything except the Cardinal Bank account.
4. Select OK, and the modified report appears. Notice that Quicken used only the Cardinal Bank checking account to prepare this report and that the transfer to savings shows in the outflow section.
5. Select the Print button from the window's buttonbar, and then select Print to print the Monthly Budget report.

Quicken displays your new Monthly Budget report for the file PERSONAL and the account Cardinal Bank on the screen and then prints it. The report looks like Figure 7-5. Notice that the transfer to Cardinal Saving is shown in your report but that your results haven't changed. The upper-left corner of your report shows that the report is for the Cardinal Bank account only. If you take another look at Figure 7-4, you'll see that that Monthly Budget report included the Bank, Cash, and CC (credit card) accounts. Unless you have chosen otherwise, Quicken lists these three account types, even if such accounts have not been established.

```
                    Monthly Budget Report
                     8/1/94 Through 8/31/94
    7/28/94                                              Page 1
    PERSONAL-Cardinal Bank

                              08/01/94      -       08/31/94
         Category Description   Actual     Budget      Diff
    --------------------------  --------  ----------  ---------

    INFLOWS
      Salary                     1,586      1,586       -0
      FROM Cardinal Saving           0          0        0
                               ---------  ----------  ---------
    TOTAL INFLOWS                1,586      1,586       -0

    OUTFLOWS
      Auto:
        Fuel                        23         30       -7
                               ---------  ----------  ---------
        Total Auto                  23         30       -7
      Clothing                      50         70      -20
      Dining                        60         55        5
      Entertain                     50         55       -5
      Furniture                    217          0      217
      Groceries                    218        200       18
      Medical                      100        120      -20
      Misc                          50         75      -25
      Mort Pay                     350        350        0
      Telephone                     23         30       -7
      Utilities:
        Electric                    31         25        6
        Gas                         19         20       -1
                               ---------  ----------  ---------
        Total Utilities             50         45        5
      TO Cardinal Saving           200        200        0
                               ---------  ----------  ---------
    TOTAL OUTFLOWS               1,391      1,230      161
                               ---------  ----------  ---------
    OVERALL TOTAL                  195        356     -161
                               =========  ==========  =========
```

Monthly
Budget report
for the
Cardinal Bank
account
Figure 7-5.

Tying the Monthly Budget Report to Other Quicken Reports

You have completed the basic steps in preparing your Monthly Budget
report. Now let's see how this report relates to the reports you prepared in
Chapter 3, "Quicken Reports." Figures 7-6 and 7-7 show a Cash Flow report

and a portion of an Itemized Categories report for the Cardinal Bank account. Since the example Monthly Budget report is based on only one month, the Cash Flow report (shown in Figure 7-6) and the Actual column in the Monthly Budget report (shown in Figure 7-5) contain the same inflows and outflows. Normally, the budget summary would cover information for a longer period of time (such as a quarter or a year) and you would prepare a Cash Flow report for each of the months included in the Monthly Budget report. Be sure you think through your reporting requirements instead of just printing all the reports.

```
                     Cash Flow Report
                   8/1/94 Through 8/31/94
 7/28/94                                          Page 1
 PERSONAL-Cardinal Bank
                                          08/01/94-
               Category Description       08/31/94
 --------------------------------   ---------------------

 INFLOWS
   Salary                                   1,585.99
                                          ------------

 TOTAL INFLOWS                              1,585.99

 OUTFLOWS
   Auto:
     Fuel                         23.00
                                --------
   Total Auto                                  23.00
   Clothing                                    50.00
   Dining                                      60.00
   Entertain                                   50.00
   Furniture                                  217.00
   Groceries                                  218.20
   Medical                                    100.00
   Misc                                        50.00
   Mort Pay                                   350.00
   Telephone                                   23.00
   Utilities:
     Electric                     30.75
     Gas                          19.25
                                ----------
   Total Utilities                            50.00
   TO Cardinal Saving                        200.00
                                          -----------
 TOTAL OUTFLOWS                             1,391.20

                                          -----------
 OVERALL TOTAL                                194.79
                                          ===========
```

Cash Flow report for the budget period **Figure 7-6.**

You might be wondering why the Cash Flow report shows a positive $194.79 net cash inflow while the Monthly Budget report indicates that you were over budget by $161.00. This occurs because the Cash Flow report looks only at actual cash inflows and outflows. The Monthly Budget report, on the other hand, examines what you want to spend and what you actually spent. Looking at the Budget column of Figure 7-5, you can see that there would

```
              EXPENSES
                Auto:
                -------

                  Fuel
                  ------
 8/3/94    105    Easy Credit Card    Gasoline - Jeep Wago...    x     -23.00
                                                                       --------
                  Total ...                                            -23.00
                                                                       --------
                Total ...                                              -23.00

                  Clothing
                  ----------
 8/3/94    105    Easy Credit Card    Blue Blouse                x     -50.00
                                                                       --------
                  Total ...                                            -50.00

                  Dining
                  --------
 8/3/94    105    Easy Credit Card    Dinner at the Boathouse    x     -60.00
                                                                       --------
                  Total ...                                            -60.00

                  Entertain
                  -----------
 8/3/94    105    Easy Credit Card    Play Tickets               x     -50.00
                                                                       --------
                  Total ...                                            -50.00

                  Furniture
                  -----------
 8/3/94    105    Easy Credit Card    Green Rocker               x    -217.00
                                                                       --------
                  Total ...                                           -217.00

                  Groceries
                  -----------
 8/4/94    106    Maureks              Groceries                 x     -60.00
 8/15/94   108    Meijer               Groceries                 x     -65.00
 8/27/94   112    Meijer               Food                      x     -93.20
                                                                       --------
                  Total ...                                           -218.20
```

Partial Itemized Categories report for the budget period **Figure 7-7.**

have been an additional $356.00 to transfer to savings if you had met your budget objectives.

Figure 7-7 provides detailed information for selected categories. Notice that the Easy Credit Card split transaction dialog box provides details for each of the categories you used when you recorded the credit card payment. Also notice that the Groceries category is printed by check number and provides details for the "Groceries" amount in the Budget and Cash Flow reports. When you're looking at Budget and Cash Flow reports that cover a longer period of time, the Itemized Categories report can provide useful insights into your spending patterns by showing where you spent and the frequency of expenditures by category. This information can help you analyze the changes you might want to make in your spending patterns.

Creating a Quarterly Report

The reports presented so far in this chapter give you an overview of the budgeting process by looking at expenditures for one month. You would need to extend your examination over a longer period of time to tell if the over-budget situation in August was unusual or if it is part of a trend that should be remedied.

To extend the time period covered by the Monthly Budget report, you will need to add transactions for other months. Fortunately, you can use the transaction groups discussed in Chapter 6, "Expanding the Scope of Financial Entries," to make the task easy. As you add more information to the reports, you will also learn how to create wide reports with Quicken.

Additional Transactions

To create a more realistic budget, you will extend the actual budget amounts for several months by creating new register transactions. This also gives you an opportunity to practice techniques you learned in earlier chapters, such as recalling memorized transactions and making changes to split transactions. Remember that you will use the transactions recorded in Chapter 6. Figure 7-8 shows the check register entries you will make to expand your data for this chapter. To record the first transaction in the Cardinal Bank account register, follow these steps:

1. Select Memorized Transactions from the Lists menu to display the list of memorized transactions.

    In Chapter 6, you deleted some of the memorized transactions. Unless you have altered your settings again, Quicken is still set to memorize all transactions.

You can group smaller expenses into the miscellaneous category, but any expense that needs to be monitored closely should be shown separately. Also, consider what percentage of your total budget a category represents when making this decision.

2. Move to the transaction you want to recall, Cardinal Saving, and select Use.

3. Make any changes necessary to reflect the transaction you want to record. In this case, change the date to 9/1/94 and the amount to 194.79, and select Record.

As mentioned earlier, excess cash in any month should be transferred to savings. This helps prevent impulsive buying if you are saving for larger outflows in later months of the year. But remember that when you plan your budget, you can build in varying monthly savings rather than setting a minimum amount and transferring any excess inflow or outflow at the end of each month.

4. Complete the example by entering all the information in your register exactly as shown in Figure 7-8.

You will primarily be recalling memorized transactions, scheduled transactions and transaction groups, and split transactions throughout the recording process. The only transactions that are not memorized or scheduled are the grocery checks.

You use the Split Transaction windows to enter the Easy Credit Card transactions for check numbers 114 and 122. Notice that the Furniture category is not used in check 114, but it is part of the credit card transaction for check 122. All the information you need to record these two transactions is included in Figure 7-8.

5. After entering the last transaction in Figure 7-8, select Home from the Reports menu.

6. Select Monthly Budget.

7. Type **8/1/94** in the from text box.

8. Type **10/31/94** in the to text box.

9. Select Customize.

10. Select Month in the Column drop-down list box under Report Layout, if necessary.

11. Clear the Cents in Amounts check box under Show.

12. Select the Account option button, and then unmark all accounts except Cardinal Bank.

13. Select OK, and the Monthly Budget report appears.

Wide Reports

The quarterly Monthly Budget report you just generated is wider than can be displayed in a window and may be difficult to comprehend until you understand its structure. In this section, you explore the quarterly report and become more familiar with Quicken results.

```
                       Check Register
        Cardinal Bank                              Page 1
        07/30/94
        Date  Num       Transaction    Payment  C  Deposit   Balance
        ----  ---    ------------------ --------  -- -------- --------


        09/01 TXFR  Cardinal Savings     194.79           2,260.70
        /1994 memo: Transfer to savings
              cat:  [Cardinal Saving]


        09/01 DEP   Payroll deposit             1,585.99 3,846.69
        /1994 memo: September Paycheck
              cat:  Salary


        09/01 114   Easy Credit Card     233.00           3,613.69
        /1994 SPLIT August 25th Statement
              cat:  Clothing


                    Clothing             50.00
                    Red Blouse
                    Dining               60.00
                    Dinner at the Boathouse
                    Auto:Fuel            23.00
                    Gasoline - Jeep Wagoneer
                    Entertain            50.00
                    Play Tickets
                    Misc                 50.00


        09/02 113   Great Lakes Saving & Loan 350.00      3,263.69
        /1994 memo: September Payment
              cat:  Mort Pay


        09/03 115   Maureks              85.00            3,178.69
        /1994 memo: Food
              cat:  Groceries


        09/08 TXFR  Cardinal Savings     200.00           2,978.69
        /1994 memo: Transfer to savings
              cat:  [Cardinal Saving]


        09/08 116   Orthodontics, Inc    170.00           2,808.69
        /1994 memo: Monthly Orthodontics Payment
              cat:  Medical


        09/20 117   Maureks              95.00            2,713.69
        /1994 memo: Food
              cat:  Groceries


        09/25 118   Alltel               29.00            2,684.69
        /1994 memo: Telephone Bill
              cat:  Telephone


        09/25 119   Consumer Power       43.56            2,641.13
        /1994 memo: Electric Bill
              cat:  Utilities:Electric
```

Additional
account
register entries
Figure 7-8.

Check Register

```
Cardinal Bank                                              Page 2
07/30/94


Date  Num         Transaction      Payment   C   Deposit   Balance
----  ---    ------------------    ---------  --  --------  --------
09/25 120    West Michigan Gas        19.29                 2,621.84
/1994 memo: Gas Bill
      cat:  Utilities:Gas


10/01 TXFR   Cardinal Savings        166.35                 2,455.49
/1994 memo: Transfer to savings
      cat:  [Cardinal Saving]


10/01 Dep    Payroll deposit                   1,585.99   4,041.48
/1994 memo: October Paycheck
      cat:  Salary


10/02 121    Great Lakes Saving & Loan 350.00              3,691.48
/1994 memo: August Payment
      cat:  Mort Pay


10/04 122    Easy Credit Card        957.00                2,734.48
/1994 SPLIT September 25th Statement
      cat:  Clothing


             Clothing            75.00
             White Dress
             Dining              45.00
             Dinner at the Boathouse
             Auto:Fuel           37.00
             Gasoline - Jeep Wagoneer
             Furniture          550.00
             Table and chairs
             Entertain          100.00
             Play Tickets
             Misc               150.00

10/05 123    Maureks                 115.00                2,619.48
/1994 memo: Food
      cat:  Groceries


10/05 TXFR   Cardinal Savings        200.00                2,419.48
/1994 memo: Transfer to savings
      cat:  [Cardinal Saving]


10/08 124    Orthodontics, Inc       100.00                2,319.48
/1994 memo: Monthly Orthodontics Payment
      cat:  Medical


10/19 125    Maureks                 135.00                2,184.48
/1994 memo: Food
      cat:  Groceries
```

Additional
account
register entries
(*continued*)
Figure 7-8.

7

```
                        Check Register

        Cardinal Bank                                    Page 3
        07/30/94


        Date   Num        Transaction      Payment   C   Deposit   Balance
        ----   ---    ------------------    --------- --  --------  --------
        10/25  126    Alltel                  27.50                 2,156.98
        /1994  memo:  Telephone Bill
               cat:   Telephone

        10/25  127    Consumer Power           37.34                2,119.64
        /1994  memo:  Electric Bill
               cat:   Utilities:Electric
```

Additional account register entries (*continued*)
Figure 7-8.

The steps listed here will help you become familiar with the quarterly Monthly Budget report:

1. Use the scroll bars, the arrow keys, (Pg Up), (Pg Dn), (Home), and (End) to become familiar with the appearance of the quarterly Monthly Budget report.

   It's easy to move around the report. Pressing (Home) returns you to the top-left corner of the wide-screen report. (End) takes you to the bottom-right corner of the report. (Pg Up) moves you up one screen, and (Pg Dn) moves you down one screen.

2. It is recommended that you use a small font and landscape orientation when printing wide reports, if your printer supports these options. Doing so significantly increases the amount of information that can be printed on a page.

   When you print wide-screen reports, Quicken numbers the pages so that you can easily follow the flow of the report.

Using the Quarterly Monthly Budget Report

The steps for preparing and printing the quarterly Monthly Budget report will become familiar with a little practice. The real issue is how to use the information. Let's look at the quarterly Monthly Budget report and discuss some of its findings.

Move to the lower-right side of the quarterly Monthly Budget report. The report shows that you spent $1,041.00 more than you had budgeted for the quarter. You can see that part of the explanation for the actual outflows exceeding the inflows is due to $361.00 being transferred to savings. Most of us would not view that as poor results. On the other hand, if you move up in the report, you can see that you have spent $582.00 more on furniture than you had budgeted. This may be because sale prices justified deviating from the budget, but it could also be compulsive buying that can't be afforded over the long run. If you find yourself over budget, the special section entitled "Dealing with an Over-Budget Situation" provides some suggestions for improving the situation.

Dealing with an Over-Budget Situation

Expenses cannot continue to outpace income indefinitely. The extent of the budget overage and the availability of financial reserves to cover it dictate the seriousness of the problem and how quickly and drastically cuts must be made to reverse the situation. Although the causes of an over-budget situation are numerous, the following strategies can help correct the problem:

✦ If existing debt is the problem, consider a consolidation loan—especially if the interest rate is lower than existing installment interest charges. Then don't use credit until the consolidated loan is paid in full.

✦ If day-to-day variable expenses are causing the overrun, begin keeping detailed records of all cash expenditures. Look closely at what you are spending for eating out, entertainment, and impulse purchases of clothing, gifts, and other nonessential items.

✦ Locate warehouse, discount, thrift, and used clothing stores in your area, and shop for items you need at these locations. Garage sales, flea markets, and the classified ads can sometimes provide what you need at a fraction of the retail cost.

✦ Be certain that you are allocating each family member an allowance for discretionary spending and that each is adhering to that amount.

✦ If you cannot find a way to lower expenses any further, consider a freelance or part-time job until your financial situation improves. Many creative people supplement their regular incomes with a small-business venture.

✦ Plan ahead for major expenses such as car insurance, property taxes, and so on by splitting the cost over 12 months and transferring each month's portion to savings until it is time to pay the bill. If you have saved for the expense, you can transfer the amount saved to your checking account the month of the anticipated expenditure.

7

Figure 7-9 shows the budget summary for the period 8/1/94 through 10/31/94. It was produced by requesting a Monthly Budget report using Half Year for the column headings. The Cents in Amounts check box in the Customize Report dialog box was cleared to toggle off the display of cents. Remember that the information Quicken used in the Budget column came

```
                   Monthly Budget Report
                      8/1/94 Through 10/31/94

    7/28/94                                                    Page 1
    PERSONAL-Cardinal Bank

                                     08/01/94        -        10/31/94

         Category Description        Actual        Budget        Diff
    ------------------------------  -----------   -----------   --------

    INFLOWS
      Salary                           4,758         4,758          -0
      FROM Cardinal Saving                 0             0          -0
                                    ------------   ----------   --------
    TOTAL INFLOWS                      4,758         4,758           0

    OUTFLOWS
      Auto:
        Fuel                             83            90           -7
                                    ------------   ----------   ---------
      Total Auto                         83            90           -7

      Clothing                          175           210          -35
      Dining                            165           165            0
      Entertain                         200           165           35
      Furniture                         767           185          582
      Groceries                         648           600           48
      Medical                           370           360           10
      Misc                              250           225           25
      Mort Pay                        1,050         1,050            0
      Telephone                          80            90          -10

      Utilities:
        Electric                        112            75           37
        Gas                              55            60           -5
                                    ------------   --------     ----------

      Total Utilities                  167           135           32
      TO Cardinal Saving               961           600          361
                                    ------------   --------     ----------

      TOTAL OUTFLOWS                  4,916         3,875        1,041

                                    ------------   --------     ----------
    OVERALL TOTAL                      -158           883       -1,041
                                    ==========    =========    ==========
```

Three-month
Monthly
Budget report
Figure 7-9.

from the budgeted amounts you established earlier in this chapter. The information in the Actual column is summarized from the account register entries recorded in your Cardinal Bank checking account. You could also request a Cash Flow report by month for the budget period and examine the monthly outflow patterns. You might want to print out itemized category information for some categories during the period for a more detailed analysis of expenditures.

Graph Options

Quicken's graphs let you take a quick look at your budget picture.

You can use Quicken to create graphs that help you monitor your budget. Quicken provides different graph options under the Graphs selection on the Reports menu. Both the Income and Expense selection and the Budget Variance selection that appear on the submenu provide tools for monitoring your budget.

You may be interested in taking a look at the composition of your expenditures to help you to identify areas of major costs and see if any of them can be reduced. To display a graph showing expense composition on your screen, follow these steps:

1. Select the Graphs icon in the Iconbar, or select Graphs from the Reports menu.
2. Select Income and Expense from the dialog box or menu.
3. Type **8/94** in the From text box.
4. Type **10/94** in the To text box.
5. Select Create.

   Quicken displays the graph shown in Figure 7-10. The window actually displays two graphs. The first one, the bar graph at the top of the window, shows you the comparison between inflow and outflow each month. The pie graph at the bottom of the window displays what percentage of the outflow each category constituted. If you click on Next 10 at the bottom of the window, you see a pie graph displaying the next ten categories.

You can use a graph to focus on the details for budget categories as well. You might want to look at categories that are either under or over budget, for example. To see a bar chart that displays the actual versus budgeted amounts for categories that are under budget, follow these steps:

1. Select the Graphs icon from the Iconbar, or select Graphs from the Reports menu.
2. Select Budget Variance from the dialog box or menu.

7

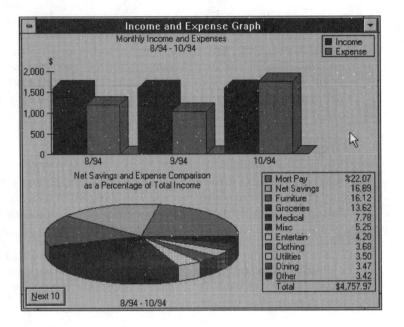

Expense
Composition
graph
Figure 7-10.

3. Type **8/94** in the From text box.

4. Type **10/94** in the To text box.

5. Select Create.

The graph shown in Figure 7-11 is displayed on your screen.

You should feel free to experiment with the other graph types. None of your selections will affect register entries, so you don't have to worry about making mistakes.

Forecasting Your Budget

You were introduced to the Financial Calendar in Chapter 6, as a way to schedule transactions. All your transactions are noted in the calendar. The calendar is also useful for forecasting how well you are complying with your budget and how your financial planning is progressing. Follow these steps to view a graph presented by the Financial Calendar that you can use to help with your financial planning.

1. Select the Calendar icon from the Iconbar, or select Financial Calendar from the Activities menu. The Calendar window opens.

2. Since you are not going to be scheduling transactions with the calendar, select List from the window's buttonbar.

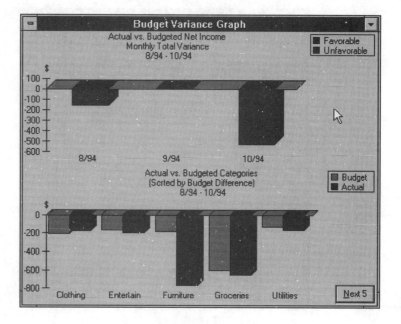

Expense
Categories
Under Budget
graph
Figure 7-11.

The list of transactions at the right side of the window disappears, and
the calendar expands to fill the extra space.

3. Click on Next or Prev in the buttonbar to display the calendar for 8/94.

4. Select Plan from the buttonbar. The window should now look like
   Figure 7-12.

   The graph shows the accumulated account balances for all your
   accounts on each day of the month. The graph uses your actual
   transactions, scheduled transactions, and transaction groups to
   calculate these balances.

5. Select the Accounts button and the Select Accounts to Include dialog
   box appears. You can double-click on the accounts, or you can
   highlight them and select Mark to change whether they are marked
   with Include in the last column. Unmark everything except Cardinal
   Bank, and select OK.

6. Select Dates and the Graph View dialog box appears.

7. Select Three Months. Then select OK to return to the Calendar window,
   which should look like Figure 7-13.

   Note that the general trend of your balance over these three months is
   slightly down. Most of this is probably because you have been
   transferring excess funds into your savings account each month.

7

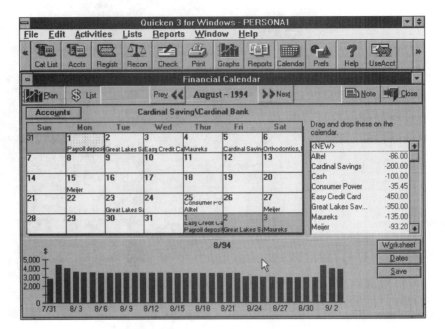

Financial
planning
graphs for all
accounts
Figure 7-12.

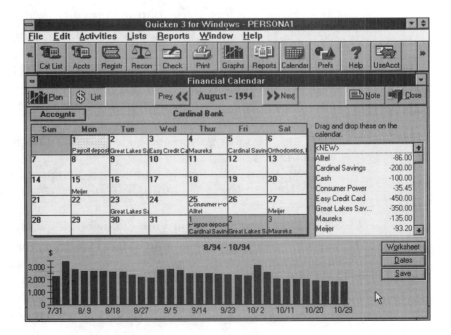

Financial
planning
graph for
Cardinal Bank
account
Figure 7-13.

8. Select Accounts, unmark Cardinal Bank, and include the Cardinal Savings account only. After you select OK, your graph looks like this:

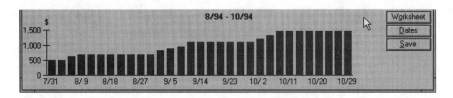

Notice that the balance of your savings account is steadily increasing. You may want to compare this increase to your planned savings increase, to see if you are matching your budget.

9. Click on the bar for 9/5. The actual total balance on that date is displayed in a small box.

You can use the Financial Calendar's planning graph to help you predict how well you are meeting your budget. Since it includes your current transactions, your scheduled transactions, and the amounts you budgeted to predict your future expenditures, you can also move ahead into future months and consider the planning information it provides.

7

CHAPTER

8

USING QUICKEN TO ORGANIZE TAX INFORMATION

Quicken's contribution to your financial planning and monitoring goes beyond recording transactions. You have already used Quicken to handle your budget entries and reports. Quicken can also help you with your tax preparation. Although using Quicken probably won't make tax preparation fun, it can reduce the tax-time crunch by organizing your tax information throughout the year. If you plan your categories and classes correctly and you faithfully complete all your entries, the hard part is done. You will then be able to use Quicken's summaries to provide the entries for specific lines on tax forms.

In this chapter, you see how Quicken can help you at tax time. After looking at a few ideas for organizing tax information, you'll modify the account register prepared in Chapters 6 and 7 to better show your tax-related information. You'll prepare tax summary information as a report. You'll also look at Quicken's features that allow you to assign categories to lines within tax schedules. This allows Quicken to better organize your tax information.

NOTE: Keep in mind that Quicken reports are not sufficient documentation of tax-deductible expenses. See the special section "Essential Tax Documentation" for a list of some of the forms you might need to substantiate expense claims to the IRS in an audit.

Quicken Tax Overview

The organization Quicken offers will make tax time much easier for you.

This chapter focuses on how Quicken can help you prepare your tax returns. You can use Quicken's categories and classes to categorize data for your taxes. Categories are defined as tax related or not and can be assigned to tax schedules. You can change the tax-related status and tax schedule assignment of any of the existing categories by editing the current category in the category list. You can also define the tax-related status for any new category as you enter it.

Quicken can be used to collect information for specific line items on tax forms such as Form 1040, Schedule A (itemized deductions), Schedule B (dividends and interest), and Schedule E (royalties and rents). Figures 8-1 and 8-2 show two of these forms. Defining and using classes for your transactions allows you to collect useful details about your financial transactions. Assigning tax schedules and lines to categories allows Quicken to accumulate the information you need for a particular line on a tax form.

In fact, once you become familiar with Quicken, you can use it to accumulate the exact information you need to prepare your taxes. For example, you may decide to tag specific tax information by setting up classes for transactions that are tax related and specific to a particular tax form. At the end of the year, you can have Quicken print the transactions that you need for a particular line. In your own Quicken system, you may want to identify the specific forms associated with these items. For example, "Tax Fed/1040" indicates a class for transactions affecting Form 1040. Another

The Tax Form Library, 518 W. Main St., Louisville, Ky., 40202, (502) 589-7466

Form **1040** Department of the Treasury—Internal Revenue Service
U.S. Individual Income Tax Return (T) 19**92**

For the year Jan. 1–Dec. 31, 1992, or other tax year beginning _____ , 1992, ending _____ , 19 ___ OMB No. 1545-0074

IRS Use Only—Do not write or staple in this space.

Label
(See instructions on page 10.)
Use the IRS label. Otherwise, please print or type.

Your first name and initial | Last name | Your social security number

If a joint return, spouse's first name and initial | Last name | Spouse's social security number

Home address (number and street). If you have a P.O. box, see page 10. | Apt. no.

City, town or post office, state, and ZIP code. If you have a foreign address, see page 10.

For Privacy Act and Paperwork Reduction Act Notice, see page 4.

Presidential Election Campaign (See page 10.)
Do you want $1 to go to this fund? . . . . Yes □ No □
If a joint return, does your spouse want $1 to go to this fund? . Yes □ No □

Note: Checking "Yes" will not change your tax or reduce your refund.

Filing Status (See page 10.)
Check only one box.

1 □ Single
2 □ Married filing joint return (even if only one had income)
3 □ Married filing separate return. Enter spouse's social security no. above and full name here. ▶ _____
4 □ Head of household (with qualifying person). (See page 11.) If the qualifying person is a child but not your dependent, enter this child's name here. ▶ _____
5 □ Qualifying widow(er) with dependent child (year spouse died ▶ 19 ___). (See page 11.)

Exemptions (See page 11.)

6a □ Yourself. If your parent (or someone else) can claim you as a dependent on his or her tax return, do not check box 6a. But be sure to check the box on line 33b on page 2
b □ Spouse
c Dependents:

(1) Name (first, initial, and last name)	(2) Check if under age 1	(3) If age 1 or older, dependent's social security number	(4) Dependent's relationship to you	(5) No. of months lived in your home in 1992

If more than six dependents, see page 12.

No. of boxes checked on 6a and 6b
No. of your children on 6c who:
• lived with you
• didn't live with you due to divorce or separation (see page 13)
No. of other dependents on 6c
Add numbers entered on lines above ▶

d If your child didn't live with you but is claimed as your dependent under a pre-1985 agreement, check here ▶ □
e Total number of exemptions claimed

Income

Attach Copy B of your Forms W-2, W-2G, and 1099-R here.

If you did not get a W-2, see page 9.

Attach check or money order on top of any Forms W-2, W-2G, or 1099-R.

7 Wages, salaries, tips, etc. Attach Form(s) W-2 . . . . | 7
8a Taxable interest income. Attach Schedule B if over $400 . . . . | 8a
b Tax-exempt interest income (see page 15). DON'T include on line 8a | 8b
9 Dividend income. Attach Schedule B if over $400 . . . . | 9
10 Taxable refunds, credits, or offsets of state and local income taxes from worksheet on page 16 | 10
11 Alimony received . . . . | 11
12 Business income or (loss). Attach Schedule C or C-EZ . . . . . | 12
13 Capital gain or (loss). Attach Schedule D . . . . | 13
14 Capital gain distributions not reported on line 13 (see page 15) . . | 14
15 Other gains or (losses). Attach Form 4797 . . . . | 15
16a Total IRA distributions . 16a ___ | b Taxable amount (see page 16) | 16b
17a Total pensions and annuities 17a ___ | b Taxable amount (see page 16) | 17b
18 Rents, royalties, partnerships, estates, trusts, etc. Attach Schedule E | 18
19 Farm income or (loss). Attach Schedule F . . . . | 19
20 Unemployment compensation (see page 17) . . . . | 20
21a Social security benefits 21a ___ | b Taxable amount (see page 17) | 21b
22 Other income. List type and amount—see page 18 . . . . | 22
23 Add the amounts in the far right column for lines 7 through 22. This is your total income ▶ | 23

Adjustments to Income (See page 18.)

24a Your IRA deduction from applicable worksheet on page 19 or 20 | 24a
b Spouse's IRA deduction from applicable worksheet on page 19 or 20 | 24b
25 One-half of self-employment tax (see page 20) . . . . | 25
26 Self-employed health insurance deduction (see page 20) . | 26
27 Keogh retirement plan and self-employed SEP deduction . | 27
28 Penalty on early withdrawal of savings . . . . | 28
29 Alimony paid. Recipient's SSN ▶ ___ | 29
30 Add lines 24a through 29. These are your total adjustments . . . . . . ▶ | 30

Adjusted Gross Income

31 Subtract line 30 from line 23. This is your adjusted gross income. If this amount is less than $22,370 and a child lived with you, see page EIC-1 to find out if you can claim the "Earned Income Credit" on line 56 . . . . ▶ | 31

Cat. No. 11320B

Form **1040** (1992)

Federal Form 1040

Figure 8-1.

8

SCHEDULES A&B
(Form 1040)

Department of the Treasury
Internal Revenue Service   (L)

Schedule A—Itemized Deductions

(Schedule B is on back)

▶ Attach to Form 1040. ▶ See Instructions for Schedules A and B (Form 1040).

OMB No. 1545-0074

19**92**

Attachment
Sequence No. 07

Name(s) shown on Form 1040 | Your social security number

Medical and Dental Expenses	**Caution:** *Do not include expenses reimbursed or paid by others.*		
	1	Medical and dental expenses (see page A-1)	1
	2	Enter amount from Form 1040, line 32. ⌊ 2 ⌋	
	3	Multiply line 2 above by 7.5% (.075)	3
	4	Subtract line 3 from line 1. If zero or less, enter -0-. . . . . . ▶	4
Taxes You Paid (See page A-1.)	5	State and local income taxes	5
	6	Real estate taxes (see page A-2)	6
	7	Other taxes. List—include personal property taxes · ▶	7
	8	Add lines 5 through 7 . . . . ▶	8
Interest You Paid (See page A-2.) **Note:** Personal interest is not deductible.	9a	Home mortgage interest and points reported to you on Form 1098	9a
	b	Home mortgage interest not reported to you on Form 1098. If paid to an individual, show that person's name and address. ▶	
		....	9b
	10	Points not reported to you on Form 1098. See page A-3 for special rules	10
	11	Investment interest. If required, attach Form 4952. (See page A-3.)	11
	12	Add lines 9a through 11 . . . . ▶	12
Gifts to Charity (See page A-3.)	**Caution:** *If you made a charitable contribution and received a benefit in return, see page A-3.*		
	13	Contributions by cash or check	13
	14	Other than by cash or check. If over $500, you **MUST** attach Form 8283	14
	15	Carryover from prior year	15
	16	Add lines 13 through 15 . . . . ▶	16
Casualty and Theft Losses	17	Casualty or theft loss(es). Attach Form 4684. (See page A-4.) . . . . . ▶	17
Moving Expenses	18	Moving expenses. Attach Form 3903 or 3903F. (See page A-4.). . . . . . ▶	18
Job Expenses and Most Other Miscellaneous Deductions (See page A-5 for expenses to deduct here.)	19	Unreimbursed employee expenses—job travel, union dues, job education, etc. If required, you **MUST** attach Form 2106. (See page A-4.) ▶	19
	20	Other expenses—investment, tax preparation, safe deposit box, etc. List type and amount ▶	20
	21	Add lines 19 and 20	21
	22	Enter amount from Form 1040, line 32. ⌊ 22 ⌋	
	23	Multiply line 22 above by 2% (.02)	23
	24	Subtract line 23 from line 21. If zero or less, enter -0- . . . . . . ▶	24
Other Miscellaneous Deductions	25	Other—from list on page A-5. List type and amount ▶ .... ▶	25
Total Itemized Deductions	26	Is the amount on Form 1040, line 32, more than $105,250 (more than $52,625 if married filing separately)?	
		• **NO.** Your deduction is not limited. Add lines 4, 8, 12, 16, 17, 18, 24, and 25. ⎫ ⎬ ▶	26
		• **YES.** Your deduction may be limited. See page A-5 for the amount to enter. ⎭	
		Caution: *Be sure to enter on Form 1040, line 34, the **LARGER** of the amount on line 26 above or your standard deduction.*	

For Paperwork Reduction Act Notice, see Form 1040 Instructions.   Cat. No. 12614K   Schedule A (Form 1040) 1992

Schedule A for
itemized
deductions
Figure 8-2.

approach is to create a class that represents a line item on a specific form. For example, "Mort Int/A—9A" is very specific. The class entry "A—9A" indicates Schedule A, line 9A—mortgage interest paid to financial institutions. You could then have Quicken generate the tax-related information by tax form or line item and use these totals to complete your taxes.

Essential Tax Documentation

The entries in your Quicken register will not convince the IRS that you incurred expenses as indicated. You need documentation of each expense to substantiate your deductions in the event of an audit. Although you may be able to convince the IRS to accept estimates for some categories based on other evidence, the following are some ideas of the optimal proof you will want to be able to present:

Expense Claimed	Proof
Dependents other than minor children	Receipts for individuals' support. Records of the individuals' income and support from others
Interest	Creditor statements of interest paid
Investments	Purchase receipts and brokerage firms' confirmation receipts
Medical and dental care	Canceled checks with receipts indicating the individual treated
Medical insurance	Pay stubs showing deductions or other paid receipts
Moving expenses	Itemized receipts and proof of employment for 12 months in your previous job
Pharmacy/drugs	Itemized receipts and canceled checks
Real estate taxes	Receipts for taxes paid. Settlement papers for real estate transactions in the current year
Unreimbursed business expenses	Itemized receipts, canceled checks, and mileage logs

8

In this chapter, you create tax-related categories for federal income tax withholdings and state income tax withholdings. You also establish a category for local income tax withholdings. You split entries for mortgage payments into mortgage interest and payments against the principal. Also, you modify some of the transactions from earlier chapters to provide the additional tax information that you need here.

In later chapters, you combine Quicken's personal tax-related reports with business reports. These two types of reports combined are a powerful tax-monitoring and planning tool.

Planning to Use Quicken for Taxes

There is no one correct way to record tax information in Quicken. The best method is to tailor your transaction entries to the information that is required on your tax forms. This is a good approach even if you have an accountant prepare your return. If you organize your tax information, your accountant won't have to—and you'll pay less for tax preparation as a result.

Start the planning process with the forms you filed last year. This may be just the Form 1040 that everyone files, or it may include a number of schedules. Although the forms change a little from year to year and you may not need to file exactly the same forms every year, last year's forms make a good starting place. Form 1040, part of which is shown in Figure 8-1, is the basic tax form used by individuals. Schedule A, shown in Figure 8-2, is used for itemized deductions.

You can choose from three methods to have Quicken accumulate information for the various tax forms and schedules that you need to prepare at the end of the year. The first method is to use category assignments to identify tax-related information and to produce a tax summary at the end of the year that contains all the tax-related category entries. This is the simplest method, but it provides the least detail.

You need to use the tax schedules option if you want to get the most use out of Quicken's tax support features.

In Quicken for Windows, you also have the option of assigning each category and subcategory to a particular line of a tax schedule. Before you can do this, you need to change a preferences setting. Select Preferences from the Edit menu, or select the Prefs icon from the Iconbar and then select General. Make sure the Use Tax Schedules with Categories check box is selected—select it if necessary. Select OK and Done.

To assign a category to a tax schedule, display the category list by selecting the Cat List icon or selecting Category & Transfer from the Lists menu, highlight the category for which you want to make a tax schedule assignment, and select Edit to edit the category. When the Edit Category dialog box appears, you can select the Tax-related check box and then select a line of a tax schedule or form from the Form drop-down list box. The lines of the forms are given names rather than numbers to make your selection easier. If you use these methods, you can produce a tax schedule report that lists all tax-related entries by line within schedules.

Classes provide another option for organizing the tax information you need.

The third option for categorizing tax data is to use a class assignment. Class assignments provide a way to further organize categories and subcategories. You can assign multiple classes to your existing categories and subcategories. You make these assignments as you enter transactions by typing / followed by the class name after a category or subcategory. Although this is more work than using Quicken's tax schedule assignments, it can provide the greatest level of detail within your existing category structure.

If you have unreimbursed business expenses that exceed a certain percentage of your income, you might want to set up a class for Form 2106, which is used exclusively for these expenses, or you might want to set up a category for these expenses and assign this category to tax schedule 2106 with Quicken's Tax Schedule feature. If you own and manage rental properties, you must use Schedule E to monitor income and expenses for these properties. With Quicken, you can classify the income and expense transactions for Schedule E.

If you have Form 2106 expenses, you won't know until the end of the year if you have enough expenses to deduct them. With the class code approach, you use a class called 2106 for unreimbursed business expense transactions, and you check the total at year-end. Travel and entertainment expenses, meals, and professional association dues and subscriptions should all be assigned this class code to ensure that you collect them all. If you use the tax schedule assignment method, you need to set up a new category for unreimbursed business expenses and assign this category to tax schedule Form 2106.

8

Keep an eye out for the timing of expense recognition. *Expense recognition* determines which tax year expenses at the beginning or end of the year affect. This is a particular problem for items that are charged since the IRS recognizes an expense as occurring the day you charge it rather than the day you pay for it. Unreimbursed air travel charged in December 1993 and paid by check in January 1994 is counted in 1993 totals since you incur the liability for payment the day you charge the tickets. A separate Quicken account for credit purchases makes these necessary year-end adjustments easier than when you just keep track of credit card payments from your checkbook.

If you decide to use classes rather than tax schedule assignments to categorize tax information, you might decide your class codes should indicate more than the number of the tax form where the information is used. If you look at the forms shown in Figures 8-1 and 8-2, you will find that each of the lines where information can be entered is numbered. For example, line 7 of your 1040 is "Wages, salaries, tips, etc.," which you can probably fill in with the total from the Salary category if you have only one source of income. But when you set up Quicken categories for income from several sources, you might want to assign a class called 1040—7 to each income transaction so that you can display a total of all the entries for this class. Likewise, you can set up classes for other line items, such as A—6 for real estate tax and A—13 for cash contributions. You could also set up 1040—21a for Social Security benefits and 1040—9 for dividend income, but if you decide to use classes, establish a class for only those lines that you are likely to use.

REMEMBER: When entering a class, you must enter the category, a slash (/), and then the class.

Classes are almost a requirement for rental property management since the same types of expenses and incomes are repeated for each property. You might use the street address or apartment number to distinguish the transactions generated by different properties. You can use the Splits feature if one transaction covers expenses or income for more than one property.

Most of your entries will focus on the current tax year, but you might sometimes need longer-term tax-related information. When you sell assets such as a house or stock holdings, information must be accumulated over the time you own the asset. Maintaining information on these assets in separate accounts is the best approach. Separate accounts can make it much easier to calculate the profit on the sale of the asset. For example, if you purchase a house for $100,000 and sell it five years later for $150,000, it might seem that the profit is $50,000. However, if you accurately record improvements such as a new deck and a fireplace, these amounts can be added to the cost of the asset since they are items that added value to the asset. When the $35,000 cost of these improvements is added to the price of the house, the profit is $15,000 for tax purposes. Take a look at the sample transaction in the next section and the tax reports before making your final decisions about classes and categories for your tax information. Depending on the complexity of your tax situation, simple category assignments might be sufficient.

Recording Detailed Tax Information

In Chapter 7, "Quicken as a Budgeting Tool," you recorded detailed transaction information in the account register for your Cardinal Bank checking account. Scroll through these transactions and notice how the monthly paycheck and mortgage payment transactions were treated. For the paycheck, you entered the amount of the check after deductions for items such as FICA, federal withholdings, medical insurance, and state withholdings. For the monthly mortgage payment, you established a tax-related category called Mort Pay and used that for the entire payment. However, Quicken can provide much better tax-related information in both these areas. If you want Quicken to accumulate tax schedule information for you, you'll want to make some changes. The following sections show you how.

Gross Earnings and Salary Deductions

Highlight the first payroll transaction you recorded in your Cardinal Bank personal account register. The amount of the net deposit was $1585.99—you didn't record any of the tax-related information for deductions. The entry you made then is adequate for maintaining a correct check register. It is also adequate for budgeting purposes since you only need to match cash inflows and outflows, and the net amount of the payroll check represents the inflow for the period. However, for tax purposes, more information is needed. If you complete the following entry, you will be able to monitor the amounts on your pay stub. You will also be able to verify the accuracy of your Form W-2 at the end of the year.

To expand the payroll transaction, you need some additional information. Your gross earnings for the pay period were $2000.00. The deduction withheld for FICA taxes was $124.00, Medicare was $29.00, medical insurance was $42.01, federal taxes were $130.00, state taxes were $80.00, and local taxes were $9.00.

8

The following steps illustrate how you can use Quicken's Splits feature to capture all the information related to the tax aspects of your paycheck and still show the net deposit of $1585.99 to the checking account.

1. With the first payroll entry highlighted, select Splits, and the Splits dialog box appears on your screen.
2. Leave Salary as the category.
3. Type **Gross Wages Earned** in the Memo field.
4. Type **2000.00** in the Amount field.

   These modifications set your Salary category as your gross earnings for the period. When you record your paycheck this way, Quicken can accumulate your year-to-date gross earnings. After recording this portion of the transaction, you are left with –414.01 in the Remainder field. This is Quicken's way of telling you there is currently a negative difference between the amount of the net deposit and the gross wages recorded. This difference equals the amount of the withholdings from your paycheck that you will record in the remaining steps.

5. Enter **Tax:Soc Sec** as the category.

6. Type **FICA Withholding** in the Memo field.

7. Type **–124.00** in the Amount field.

   Quicken records the information in the Splits dialog box and leaves a balance of –290.01 in the Remainder field. This category is predefined as tax related in Quicken, even though FICA withholdings are not ordinarily tax deductible on your Form 1040. Quicken works this way because you should monitor the amount of your FICA withholdings if you change jobs during the year. Since there is a limit on the amount of earnings taxed for Social Security, switching jobs can cause you to pay more than you owe; the second employer will not know the amount that was withheld by the first. You can include excess FICA payments on your Form 1040 with other withholding amounts (on line 58). If you earn less than the upper limit, you won't use this category when you prepare your taxes.

8. Enter **Tax:Medicare** as the category.

9. Type **Medicare Withholding** in the Memo field.

10. Type **–29.00** in the Amount field.

11. Enter **Medical** as the category.

12. Type **Health Insurance** in the Memo field.

13. Type **–42.01** in the Amount field.

14. Enter **Tax:Fed** as the category.

15. Type **Federal Income Tax** in the Memo field.

16. Type **–130.00** in the Amount field.

17. Enter **Tax:State** as the category.

18. Type **State Income Tax** in the Memo field.

19. Type **–80.00** in the Amount field.

20. Enter **Tax:Local** as the category.

    When you try to move to the next field, Quicken displays the Set Up Category dialog box. To set up the category, follow these steps:

21. Type **Local Tax** in the Description text box.

22. Select the Tax-related check box.

23. Select OK.

24. Type **Local Income Tax** in the Memo field.

25. Type **–9.00** in the Amount field.

You see the dialog box shown next. Notice that there is no balance left to explain in the Splits dialog box.

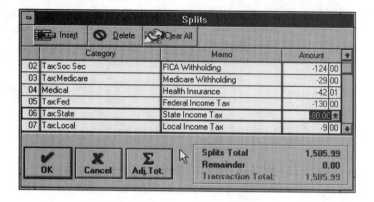

26. Select OK, and Quicken returns you to the register window.
27. Select Record to tell Quicken to accept the changed transaction.

After you complete this process, all the information in the Splits dialog box is recorded in your accounts. Your reports will show gross earnings for tax purposes at $2000.00, with tax-related deductions for FICA, Medicare, medical insurance, and federal, state, and local taxes.

Mortgage Principal and Interest

The mortgage payment transaction recorded in Chapter 6 is fine for recording changes to your checking account balance or monitoring budgeted expenses. However, it doesn't capture the tax-related aspects of the transaction. Although you identified the transaction as tax related, the mortgage principal and interest were not isolated. You would not be able to tell how much to list on your tax return as interest expense. Perhaps your bank will provide you with a statement that lists this information at the end of the year. In some cases, the bank even divides your previous month's payment among principal, interest, and escrow on the current month's bill. However, if you purchased your home from a private individual, you won't receive this information. You can have Quicken calculate it for you since accurate records are necessary to take the mortgage interest expense as a tax deduction. Quicken will continue to assist you by organizing it in the recording process.

On your screen, highlight the first Great Lakes Savings & Loan mortgage payment of $350.00 on 8/2/94, which you recorded in Chapter 6. Using Quicken's Splits feature, you will modify the record of this transaction to distribute the payment between principal and interest. For the steps outlined here, it is assumed that you know which payment number you are making and that you pay your insurance and taxes directly to the insurer and local taxing unit with checks recorded separately in your register. If the financial institution has established an escrow account for these payments, you can easily add that amount to this transaction, assuming that you have defined a tax-related category called Escrow.

The following steps show you how to create a loan amortization schedule and track your mortgage principal and interest payments:

1. With the first mortgage payment entry highlighted, select Activities, select Financial Planners, and then select Loan.
2. Type **39999** in the Loan Amount text box.
3. Type **9.519** in the Annual Interest Rate text box.
4. Type **25** in the Number of Years text box.
5. Type **12** in the Periods Per Year text box.
6. Select Schedule to view the schedule.

    The following illustration shows the top part of the schedule:

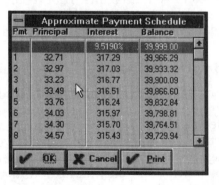

Pmt	Principal	Interest	Balance
		9.5190%	39,999.00
1	32.71	317.29	39,966.29
2	32.97	317.03	39,933.32
3	33.23	316.77	39,900.09
4	33.49	316.51	39,866.60
5	33.76	316.24	39,832.84
6	34.03	315.97	39,798.81
7	34.30	315.70	39,764.51
8	34.57	315.43	39,729.94

Approximate Payment Schedule

    You can print it out for future reference by selecting Print. Since you are about to make your fifty-third payment, look down the schedule for payment 53 to get the numbers you need.

7. Select Cancel and Close to return to the register.
8. Make certain your Great Lakes Savings & Loan transaction for August is highlighted.
9. Select Splits, and the Splits dialog box appears.

10. Enter **Mort Prin** in the category field.

    Since you do not have the Mort Prin category in your Category List, add it by following the steps listed in the section "Adding Categories" in Chapter 6. Use Mortgage Principal Exp as the description for this category, and make the category not tax related.

11. Type **Principal Part of Payment** for the memo.

12. Type **49.33** to record the portion of the transaction related to principal.

13. Enter **Mort Int** in the second category field.

14. Type **Interest Part of Payment** for the memo.

15. Type **300.67** as the amount. You see the dialog box shown here:

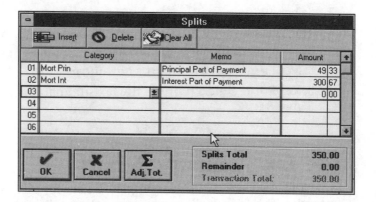

16. Select OK, and Quicken returns you to the highlighted mortgage payment transaction in your register.

17. Select Record to record the new split transaction information.

After you record these two transactions, you can see the benefits of having Quicken organize the information. You should now rememorize this transaction for monthly recording purposes. In the next section, you take a look at the tax information you have entered into your Quicken system.

Printing Quicken's Tax Reports

You can use Quicken's tax reports to get the detailed information you need to prepare your taxes. In this section you examine reports generated by using the information from the Cardinal Bank account register for the first month

8

(8/1/94 through 8/31/94). Follow these steps to generate Quicken's Tax Summary report:

1. From the account register, select the Reports icon; then select the Home option button and select Tax Summary from the list box, or select Home from the Reports menu and then select Tax Summary.
2. Enter **8/1/94** in the from text box.
3. Enter **8/31/94** in the to text box.
4. Select Customize.
5. Select the Accounts option button.
6. Clear the marks for all accounts except Cardinal Bank.
7. Select OK.

   The Tax Summary report appears on your screen. You can use the arrow keys to move through the report.
8. Select Print from the report's buttonbar.
9. Select Print. Quicken prints the tax summary by category, as shown in Figure 8-3.

The Tax Summary Report

By default, Quicken prints the complete details for each of the tax-related categories. This format allows you to use the totals generated at the end of the tax year for entry on your tax returns. The totals generated in Figure 8-3 would be used on the following lines of your personal income tax form for 1993:

Income/Expense Category	Tax Return Location
Total Salary Income	Form 1040, line 7
Total Federal Tax	Form 1040, line 54
Total Medical & Dental	Schedule A, line 1
Total Mortgage Interest Exp	Schedule A, line 9a
Total State Tax	Schedule A, line 5
Total Local Tax	Schedule A, line 5

These totals also provide an excellent summary and could prove useful in the event of an IRS tax audit inquiry.

```
                        Tax Summary Report
                       8/1/94 Through 8/31/94
7/30/94                                                        Page 1
PERSONAL-Cardinal Bank


 Date     Num     Description        Memo            Category   Clr    Amount
 -----    -------  ----------------   ------------------  ------------   ---   --------

          INCOME/EXPENSE
            INCOME
              Salary

8/1/94    DEP    Payroll deposit   Gross Wages Earned  Salary          2,000.00

                 Total ...                                             2,000.00

                 TOTAL INCOME                                          2,000.00


            EXPENSES
              Medical

8/1/94    DEP    Payroll deposit   Health Insurance    Medical           -42.01
8/6/94    107    Orthodontics, Inc  Monthly Orthodon... Medical         -100.00

                 Total ...                                              -142.01

              Tax:


                Fed

8/1/94    DEP    Payroll deposit   Federal Income Tax  Tax:Fed          -130.00

                 Total Fed                                              -130.00

                Local

8/1/94    DEP    Payroll deposit   Local Income Tax    Tax:Local          -9.00

                 Total ...                                                -9.00

                Medicare
```

8

Partial Tax Summary Report for the Cardinal Bank checking account Figure 8-3.

```
                        Tax Summary Report
                      8/1/94 Through 8/31/94
7/30/94                                                        Page 2
PERSONAL-Cardinal Bank


Date      Num     Description        Memo            Category    Clr   Amount
-----     -------  ----------------   ------------------  ------------  ---   --------


8/1/94    DEP     Payroll deposit    Medicare Withhol... Tax:Medicare       -29.00

                  Total ...                                                 -29.00

                  Soc Sec

8/1/94    DEP     Payroll deposit    FICA Withholding    Tax:Soc Sec       -124.00

                  Total ...                                                -124.00

                  State

8/1/94    DEP     Payroll deposit    State Income Tax    Tax:State          -80.00

                  Total ...                                                 -80.00


                  Total Tax                                                -372.00

              TOTAL EXPENSES                                               -514.01


              TOTAL INCOME/EXPENSE                                        1,485.99
```

Partial Tax
Summary
Report for the
Cardinal Bank
checking
accoun*t (cont.)*
Figure 8-3.

As you will see in Chapter 10, "Creating Custom Reports," all Quicken reports can be customized for many different report formats (reports that cover months, quarters, half years, and so on). In Chapter 7, you compared a report prepared for a single account, Cardinal Bank, to a report prepared for all accounts. The report for all accounts used the Bank checking accounts, the Cash accounts, and the Credit Card accounts from the PERSONAL file.

Here, Figure 8-3 shows a report that was prepared for a single account, Cardinal Bank. Figure 8-4 shows a Tax Summary report that includes all the accounts in the PERSONAL file. Note that the second column from the left (Acct) shows the source of the tax-related transaction. In this report, all the

```
                        Tax Summary Report
                      8/1/94 Through 8/31/94
7/30/94                                                        Page 1

PERSONAL-Bank,Cash,CC Accounts


Date      Acct     Num    Description        Memo         Category  Clr  Amount
----      ----     ---    -----------        ----         --------  ---  ------

          INCOME/EXPENSE
            INCOME
              Salary

8/1/94   Card... DEP     Payroll deposit    Gross Wages Earned  Salary    2,000.00

            Total...                                                      2,000.00

          TOTAL INCOME                                                    2,000.00



            EXPENSES
              Medical

8/1/94   Card... DEP     Payroll deposit    Health Insurance    Medical     -42.01
8/6/94   Card... 107     Orthodontics, Inc  Monthly Orthodon... Medical    -100.00

            Total...                                                        -142.01

            Tax:


              Fed

8/1/94   Card... DEP     Payroll deposit    Federal Income Tax Tax:Fed     -130.00

            Total...                                                        -130.00

            Local

8/1/94   Card... DEP     Payroll deposit    Local Income Tax    Tax:Local    -9.00

            Total...                                                          -9.00

            Medi...
```

Tax Summary
Report for
PERSONAL
file accounts
Figure 8-4.

8

```
                      Tax Summary Report
                    8/1/94 Through 8/31/94
 7/30/94                                                       Page 2
 PERSONAL-Bank,Cash,CC Accounts


 Date      Acct    Num   Description       Memo          Category   Clr  Amount
 ----      ----    ---   -----------       ----          --------   ---  ------

 8/1/94  Card... DEP   Payroll deposit   Medicare Withhol... Tax:Medicare -29.00

                 Total...                                                 -29.00

                 Soc Sec

 8/1/94  Card... DEP   Payroll deposit   FICA Withholding   Tax:Soc Sec -124.00

                 Total...                                                -124.00

                 State

 8/1/94  Card... DEP   Payroll deposit   State Income Tax    Tax:State   -80.00

                 Total...                                                 -80.00

                 Total...                                                -372.00

              TOTAL EXPENSES                                             -514.01


           TOTAL INCOME/EXPENSE                                        1,485.99
```

Tax Summary
Report for
PERSONAL
file accounts
(*cont.*)
Figure 8-4.

sources are from the Cardinal Bank account, but you can see how, in a more
complex situation, this type of report would be useful in tracking the source
of a tax-related transaction. For year-end tax purposes, a report of all your
accounts provides an overview by category that integrates the various
accounts. When you prepare your taxes, you should select the report format
best suited to your needs.

NOTE: The Tax Summary and Tax Schedule reports shown in this
chapter show transactions from 8/1/94 through 8/31/94 because those
are the only transactions you have entered. Normally, when you create a
tax-related report, you use transactions from the entire reporting period,
which is usually a year.

Another report format is shown in Figure 8-5. In this case, Quicken was instructed to print only the Medical category. This information was included in the report shown in Figure 8-3, but you can see that filtered reports become useful as you increase the number of recorded transactions and want details on particular items. The procedures for generating this type of report are covered in Chapter 10, "Creating Custom Reports."

A final point to note about all Quicken reports is that the date the report was prepared is displayed in the upper-left corner of the report. When you use a Quicken report to make your financial decisions, always check the report date to ensure you are using the most recent report.

The Tax Schedule Report

If you choose to assign categories to tax schedules and lines, you will want to create a Tax Schedule report. This report provides useful information only if you have edited your categories and assigned them to the schedules and forms where you want the income and expenses they represent to appear. Figure 8-6 shows a section of a Tax Schedule report that displays Schedule A medical expenses. These expenses are the same as those you saw in Figure 8-5, where a filter was used to create a Tax Summary report; however, you

8

```
                          Tax Summary Report
                         8/1/94 Through 8/31/94
7/30/94                                                         Page 1
PERSONAL-Bank,Cash,CC Accounts


Date    Acct   Num   Description        Memo            Category  Clr  Amount
----    ----   ---   -----------        ----            --------  ---  ------

        INCOME/EXPENSE
          EXPENSES
            Medical

8/1/94  Card... DEP  Payroll deposit    Health Insurance  Medical    -42.01
8/6/94  Card... 107  Orthodontics, Inc  Monthly Orthodont... Medical -100.00

               Total...                                             -142.01

          TOTAL EXPENSES                                            -142.01


        TOTAL INCOME/EXPENSE                                        -142.01
```

A sample Tax Summary Report showing a specific category
Figure 8-5.

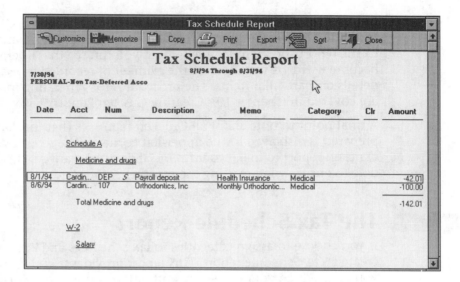

Schedule A
medical
expenses in a
Tax Schedule
Report
Figure 8-6.

would have to print many filtered Tax Summary reports to get the same
information contained in one Tax Schedule report.

To produce the Tax Schedule report, first check that medical expenses are
assigned to the "Medicine and drugs" line of Schedule A. (They will be by
default after you select the Use Tax Schedules with Categories check box as
described earlier in this chapter.) Then select Home from the Reports menu
and then select Tax Schedule; or select the Reports icon, select the Home
option button, and select Tax Schedule from the list box. Select OK to accept
the default title and time period for the report, or change the title and time
period and then select OK.

CHAPTER

9

MANAGING YOUR INVESTMENTS AND DETERMINING YOUR NET WORTH

In previous chapters, you used Quicken as a tool for financial planning and monitoring. Many of the activities were simply repetitive steps; you applied the same techniques repeatedly to record transactions. These activities were procedural—they did not require analysis before entry, and each transaction followed exactly the same steps. Although such activities are an important part of managing your finances, they do not provide the total picture.

Basic Concepts of Financial Management

You probably have financial goals you would like to meet, such as buying a new car, purchasing a house, or retiring at the age of 60. Whatever your goals are, you will need a certain level of financial resources to meet them. You might try to accumulate the necessary resources by making deposits to a savings account or by aquiring investments such as stocks and bonds. In this chapter, you learn to measure how successful you have been in your financial management activities.

One important measure of your financial status is your net worth. *Net worth* is a measurement of the difference between your total assets and your total liabilities at a given time. When you look at your net worth over a period of time, you can tell how well you have managed your resources and obligations. The process of preparing a statement of net worth differs from the procedural activities of earlier chapters. To estimate your net worth, you must make judgments estimating the worth of items you purchased earlier. Some investments, such as stocks, have a clearly defined market value because they are publicly traded. Other investments, such as land or real estate, require a more subjective evaluation.

Net worth is a financial measure that you can use to assess your financial condition at a point in time.

You must look at more than just the assets you own to determine your net worth. Although you may live in a $300,000 house, it's likely that the bank owns more of it than you do. For net worth purposes, you must determine what your remaining financial obligation is on the house. If you still have a mortgage of $270,000, your net worth in the property is $30,000. The following equation is a simplified formula for determining net worth:

Financial resources – Financial obligations = Net worth

As you can see, your net worth describes your financial position after you consider all your financial holdings and deduct all your financial obligations. In accounting terms, your financial resources are things of value that you hold (*assets*). Your assets may include checking, savings, and money market accounts. These are examples of *liquid assets*—they can be readily converted into cash. Stocks, bonds, real estate holdings, and retirement funds (Individual Retirement Accounts (IRAs) and Keogh plans) are other examples of investments you might hold. These assets are not as liquid as those in the previous group because their cash value depends on the market at the time you try to sell them. Your residence, vacation property, antiques, and other items of this nature are classified as *personal assets*. These assets are the least liquid because antique and real estate values can decline, and it may take considerable time to convert these assets to cash.

The other part of the net worth equation is your financial obligations. Financial obligations include credit card balances and other short-term loans such as those for automobiles. In addition, you must consider long-term loans for the purchase of a residence, vacation property, or other real estate.

Net worth is the measure most people focus on when monitoring the success of their financial planning activities. The key point to remember is that net worth increases when your financial resources increase—through savings, compounding interest on an investment, appreciation, and reducing the amount of your financial obligations. Take a look at the special section, "Effects of Compounding Interest on $100 Invested Monthly for 20 Years," in this chapter to see the effects of compounding interest on an investment and the rapid rate at which even a small investment can grow.

Financial obligations are not necessarily a sign of poor financial management. If you borrow money and invest it so that it returns more than you are paying to use it, you have *leveraged* your resources. Of course, there is more risk in this avenue of financial planning. Don't take on more risk than you can handle—either financially or emotionally.

After completing this chapter, you will be able to begin monitoring your financial condition. In accounting terms, you can look at the bottom line. The *bottom line* in personal financial management is your net worth if you value your assets realistically. How you manage your financial assets and related obligations determines your net worth.

9

You should assess your financial condition at least once a year.

If you set an annual goal of increasing your net worth by a certain percentage, you can use Quicken to help you record your financial activities and monitor your success. For example, if you start using Quicken in January and you record your assets and obligations throughout the year, you can contrast your financial condition at the beginning and end of the year and compare the results with your goals. As a result of this comparison, you might decide to change your strategy in some areas of your financial plan. For instance, you might decide to switch from directly managing your portfolio of stocks to using a mutual fund with its professional managers, or you might decide to shift some assets from real estate to liquid assets that can be converted to cash more quickly.

Effects of Compounding Interest on $100 Invested Monthly for 20 Years

Cash Value after	6% Return	8% Return	10% Return
1 year	$ 1,234	$ 1,245	$ 1,257
2 years	$ 2,543	$ 2,593	$ 2,645
3 years	$ 3,934	$ 4,054	$ 4,178
4 years	$ 5,410	$ 5,635	$ 5,872
5 years	$ 6,977	$ 7,348	$ 7,744
10 years	$16,388	$18,295	$20,484
15 years	$29,082	$34,604	$41,447
20 years	$46,204	$58,902	$75,737

Establishing Accounts for This Chapter

In earlier chapters, you used bank accounts in a file called PERSONAL to record all your transactions. In this chapter, you learn about Quicken's other account types. These accounts are ideally suited for recording information about assets you own, debts you have incurred, and investments. You establish a file called INVEST for the examples in this chapter. This makes it easy to obtain the report results shown in this chapter even if you did not complete the examples in earlier chapters. This new file will be established for illustration purposes only. In fact, for your own financial planning, you will probably record all your activities in a single file. That way, Quicken will have access to all your personal information when preparing your reports and assessing your net worth.

Adding a New File

You have already used the following process in the "Adding a New File" section of Chapter 6, "Expanding the Scope of Financial Entries." In the new file, INVEST, you establish six new accounts to use throughout this chapter. Follow these steps to set up the new file:

1. Select New from the File menu.
2. Select New File, and select OK.
3. Type **INVEST** as the name of the file.

Quicken creates four files, with four different filename extensions, from the filename you enter. You must provide a valid filename of no more than eight characters. Do not include spaces or special symbols.

4. Make sure the selected directory is the one in which you normally store your data files.

5. Clear the Business check box to restrict your categories to home categories, and select OK.

   Quicken displays a Select Account Type dialog box, as shown in Figure 9-1.

6. Select the Investment Account option button, and select OK to establish the account as an Investment account.

   Quicken presents a New Account Information dialog box.

7. Type **Investments** in the Account Name text box.

8. When you want to establish an account for a single mutual fund, select the Account contains a single mutual fund check box. When you want to establish a tax-deferred account, select Tax-Deferred Account-IRA, 401 (K), etc. For tax-deferred accounts, you should assign tax schedules to the money you put into the account, and that you take out, using the Transfers In and Transfers Out drop-down list boxes.

   For example, if your account is a Keogh plan, you select Form 1040: Keogh Deduction from the Transfers In drop-down list box to assign any transfers into this acount to this line of the 1040 tax form. You will also want to assign withdrawls from this account to the appropriate line of a tax form for creating tax reports. To do this, select 1099R: Pension Total dist-taxable from the Transfers Out drop-down list box.

9. Type **Personal Investments** in the Description (Optional) text box, and select OK.

9

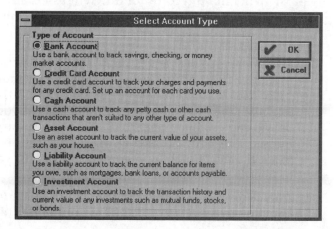

Select
Account Type
dialog box
Figure 9-1.

10. Quicken asks whether you want to add an icon to have access to the Portfolio View window from your buttonbar. In this example, select <u>N</u>o at this prompt.

Quicken may display a warning message to inform you of the advanced nature of Investment accounts. Press ⌶Enter⌷ to exit this warning. Because Investment accounts are always established with a zero balance, you will not be asked to supply a beginning balance or date, as you are when you create other types of accounts.

11. Establish the five remaining accounts as shown in the Account List illustrated here:

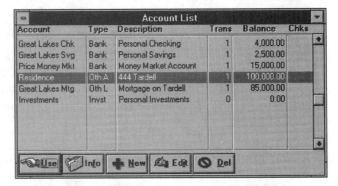

Be sure to enter the correct account type and balance. Use 8/1/94 as the date when entering your beginning balance for each account. When you establish your Liability account, select Cancel to cancel Quicken's Set Up Amortization Loan dialog box and clear the View Loan dialog box if it appears.

The three new types of accounts you have just established are used to separately maintain records for different assets and liabilities. A little background on when to use each account type will help you make selections when you start recording your own information.

✦ *Investment accounts*   Investment accounts are tailored to investments that have fluctuating prices, such as stocks, mutual funds, bonds, Individual Retirement Accounts (IRAs) and 401(K) plans. You can establish an Investment account for each of your investment holdings, or you can establish one Investment account to parallel your transactions with a brokerage firm. In addition to recording information in special fields such as Shares and Amounts, you can use these accounts to track a cash balance in an account.

✦ *Asset accounts*   Asset accounts are appropriate for investments that have a stable price, such as CDs or Treasury bills. This type of account is also the most appropriate selection for assets that don't have a share price—for example, real estate holdings.

✦ *Liability accounts* You use Liability accounts to record debts. A mortgage on a property and a car loan are examples of obligations that decrease your net worth and should be recorded in a Liability account.

Establishing the Initial Balance in Your Investment Account

Investment accounts are always established with an initial balance of zero. To transfer existing holdings to an Investment account, you transfer the shares in at cost. You can establish a complete list of securities before you begin, or you can add the information for each security as you enter the information that establishes its cost. To activate the Investments account and record the securities, follow these steps:

1. Open the Account List by selecting the Accts icon from the Iconbar. If you are in the Account List window already, go to step 2.

2. Highlight Investments, and select Use.

   Quicken presents the Investments register. Notice that the fields differ from the bank account registers you have used previously. The Investments register is tailored to investments that have a share price.

   You can type an action from those listed in Table 9-1, or you can use the buttonbar to display the appropriate action dialog box. When you use the buttonbar buttons listed in the first column of the table, only the Other button actually displays the actions shown. The other buttons all present dialog boxes and code the action in your register entry automatically. If you are working directly in the register, you can use a drop-down list to directly select the actions in the second column of this table.

3. Select the Other button.

   ShrsIn is highlighted, as shown here:

ShrsIn	Add shares to Acct
ShrsOut	Remove shares from Acct
MargInt	Margin Interest expense
MiscExp	Miscellaneous expense
Reminder	Reminder transaction
RtrnCap	Return of capital
StkSplit	Stock split
XIn	Transfer cash in
XOut	Transfer cash out

4. Select ShrsIn. The Add Shares to Account dialog box appears.

Buttonbar	Action	Description
Buy	Buy	Used to buy a security with cash from an Investment account
	BuyX	Used to buy a security with cash from another account
Income	Div	Used to record cash dividends in an Investment account
	DivX	Used to transfer cash dividends to another account
	IntInc	Used to record interest income in an Investment account
	CGLong	Used to record cash received from long-term capital gains distribution
	CGLongX	Used to transfer cash received from long-term capital gains distribution to another account
	CGShort	Used to record cash received from short-term capital gains distribution
	CGShortX	Used to transfer cash received from short-term capital gains distribution
	MiscInc	Used to record cash received from miscellaneous income sources to another account
Other	ShrsIn	Used to transfer shares into an Investment account
	ShrsOut	Used to transfer shares out of an account
	MargInt	Used to pay a margin loan from a Cash account
	MiscExp	Used to pay miscellaneous expenses from a Cash account
	Reminder	Used with the Billminder feature to notify you of a pending event
	RtrnCap	Used to recognize cash from the return of capital
	StkSplit	Used to change the number of shares resulting from a stock split
	XIn	Used to transfer cash into an Investment account
	XOut	Used to transfer cash out of an Investment account

Investment
Actions
Table 9-1.

Buttonbar	Action	Description
Reinvest	ReinvDiv	Used to reinvest dividends in additional shares
	ReinvInt	Used to reinvest interest in additional shares
	ReinvLg	Used to reinvest long-term capital gains distribution
	ReinvSh	Used to reinvest short-term capital gains distribution
Sell	Sell	Used when you sell a security and leave the proceeds in an Investment account
	SellX	Used to transfer the proceeds of a sale to another account

Investment Actions (*cont.*)
Table 9-1.

5. Enter **10/10/88** in the Date text box.

6. Type **Haven Publishing** in the Security text box, and press Tab to leave the text box.

   Quicken displays a Set Up Security dialog box. When the dialog box is completed for this example, it looks like this:

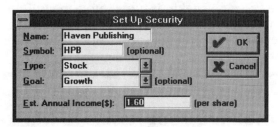

   You can use Ctrl-Y at any time from the Investments register to open and update the entire Security list at once.

7. Type **HPB** in the Symbol text box.

8. Select Stock from the Type drop-down list box.

9. Select Growth from the Goal drop-down list box.

10. Enter **1.60** in the Est. Annual Income($) text box, and select OK.

11. Type **500** in the Number of Shares text box, and press Tab.

12. Type **20** in the Price per Share text box, and press Tab to leave this text box and tell Quicken to calculate the contents of the Total Cost Basis text box.

13. Type **Initial Cost** in the Memo text box.

14. Select OK to record the transaction.

9

Repeat the process for Ganges Mutual Fund and Glenn Packing, using the entries shown in Figure 9-2. Figure 9-3 shows a view of the same transactions in the Portfolio View window. You can obtain this view by selecting Port View from the Investments register. You can record all your investment transactions in this window if you like. When the Set Up Securities dialog box appears for the new securities, repeat steps 7, 8, 9, and 10 with the following information:

	Ganges Mutual Fund	Glenn Packing
Symbol	GMF	GPK
Type	Mutual fund	Stock
Goal	Growth	Income
Est. Income	.40	1.00

Although you now have your stock holdings entered at cost, you must perform an additional step to establish a current market value for your holdings.

NOTE: You can use the mouse in the Portfolio View window to display a list of special security actions. If you move the mouse pointer to any of the first three fields, it turns into a magnifying glass with a Z inside it. When you click the field with the right mouse button, you will be able to choose New security, Edit Security, Delete Security, or Quick Report from the pop-up list box.

Revaluing Your Assets to Market Value

When using Quicken to determine your net worth, you must assign values to your investments, liabilities, and assets. This means that you need to exercise some judgment in evaluating asset worth. Don't be intimidated; it's not as complex as it might seem. The easiest assets to evaluate are your checking, savings, and money market accounts. You know what your cash balance is in each of these accounts, so you can easily determine their value at any time. After you complete your monthly reconciliation, you have the current value of your accounts. If you own stocks and bonds, you can generally determine their current value by looking in the financial section of your local newspaper. If you own stock in a closely held corporation, you will have to use other sources for valuation—for example, recent sales of similar companies in that industry or your area. If your assets are land holdings, you can ask a realtor familiar with the local area about the approximate value of your lot or other property holdings, or you might be able to use recent sale prices of similar properties in your area.

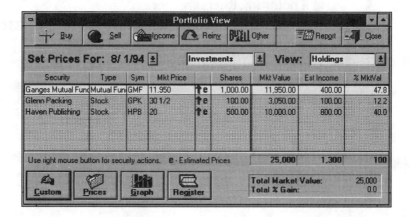

Initial
investment
transactions in
the
Investments
register
Figure 9-2.

Valuing your residence presents similar problems. You know what you paid
for the property, and with Quicken you can accumulate the additional cost
incurred in improving it. It's more difficult to know what value to place on
the property when you prepare your Net Worth report. Once again, try to
determine the sale prices of properties in your area, and consider how your
house compared in price with neighboring properties when you bought it.
This will provide a basis for comparison in the future. However, remember
that improvements you made to your house may increase the value of your

9

Initial
investment
transactions in
the Portfolio
View window
Figure 9-3.

home relative to others in the area. For example, adding a new bath and renovating the kitchen may significantly enhance the value of your home over time.

The amount you owe, or the associated liability, on your home should be easy to track. You receive annual statements from the financial institutions from which you have borrowed money for your residence and any home improvements. These statements indicate the remaining financial obligation you have on the house and should be used for net worth valuation purposes.

Use prudent judgment when determining values for your assets. A conservative but not very useful approach would be to say that any assets whose values you cannot determine from external sources should be valued at what you paid for them. Accountants call this *historical cost*. For your own planning and monitoring, this is not a realistic approach to determining your net worth. Try to determine fair value, or what you think your home could be sold for today, by taking into consideration current national and local economic conditions, and use reasonable values. Those familiar with the local market will certainly have some knowledge of the value of homes in your area. Inflating the value of your properties does not help you accurately assess your net worth.

Follow these steps to enter the current value of your stocks:

1. From the Investments register, select Port View, and select Price Update from the View drop-down list.

   Your next step is to establish the date for which you want to enter the market values: 7/31/94.

2. Press Ctrl-G, enter **7/31/94**, and select OK.

   You can also select 7/31/94 from the drop-down calendar in the Set Prices For field. You can enter new market prices for any of the investments, or you can use the + and - keys to change them by 1/8th of a point in either direction.

3. With Ganges Mutual Fund highlighted, type **13.210** in the Mkt Price field, and press ⬇.

4. With Glenn Packing highlighted, press - four times to change the market price to 30, and press ⬇.

5. With Haven Publishing highlighted, type **22**, and press ⬆.

   Figure 9-4 shows the Portfolio View window after you have entered the new prices. Notice that Quicken shows arrows that indicate whether the new price is higher or lower than the previous price.

6. Select Register to return to the Investments register.

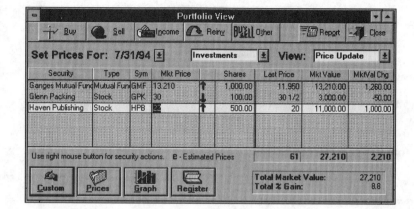

Updated prices in the Portfolio View window
Figure 9-4.

Viewing Portfolio Information at a Glance

Later you will see how to use Quicken to prepare reports from the Investment Report menu. However, if you're like most investors, you'll want to take a quick look at your investments without preparing the formal reports. You can get a quick glance at your Investment account from the Portfolio View window by using the View drop-down list. This list gives you several options for viewing your Investment account data: Holdings (the default setting for the Portfolio View window), Performance, Valuation, Custom 1, and Custom 2.

The Holdings view shows the percentage of your total account balance that each element in your portfolio represents. You also see the estimated income expected for each security based on past payouts for the security, and the latest market price for each security.

The Performance view shows the return on investment for each of your account holdings, both in dollar values and as a percentage. This view also displays the amount invested in each security.

The Valuation view compares the current market value of each of your holdings with the amount you have invested in each security. The total shows the market value of your holdings at the most recent date at which you updated your valuations.

The preset Custom 1 view illustrated in Figure 9-5 shows the percentage gain or loss on each security in your portfolio, as well as the average cost, the number of shares held, and the latest market price entered for each security. In the DOS version of Quicken, this view is called the Portfolio Summary view.

In addition to using these preset views of your portfolio, you can create customized views. Figure 9-6 shows Quicken's Customize Portfolio Summary

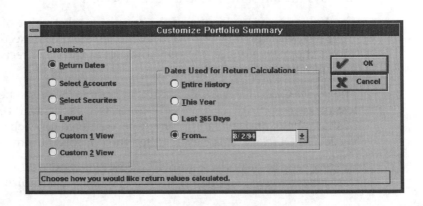

Preset
Portfolio View
column
headings for
the Custom 1
view
Figure 9-5.

dialog box, which lists the following customization options: Return Dates, Select Accounts, Select Securities, Layout, Custom 1 View, and Custom 2 View.

The Return Dates option lets you select the period for which you want Quicken to compute your portfolio's returns. The default setting is Entire History, which shows information recorded throughout the entire history of your Investment account. You can also select This Year, Last 365 Days, or From.... The last selection allows you to specify a day from which you want your return computed.

The Select Accounts option lets you select the accounts you want to include, and the Select Securities option allows you to select the securities you want to display.

The Layout option is preset to display the name of each security and its ticker symbol. The other options you can choose are Name Only, Name/Type, and Name/Type/Symbol.

The Custom 1 View and Custom 2 View options allow you to select from 17 column heading options for the last 3 columns of your Portfolio View

Customize
Portfolio
Summary
window for
the Return
Dates selection
Figure 9-6.

window. The preset views for both custom settings are Avg. Cost in Column 1, % Gain/Loss in Column 2, and Mkt. Value in Column 3. You can assign a custom name to your reports in the View Nme field.

Using Prodigy's Quote Track to Update Security Prices

You can use Prodigy to help update your investment reports in a timely and efficient manner.

The manual method of updating security prices works fine when you have only a few stocks. If your portfolio is large, it can take quite a time commitment to keep your stock values up to date. Because Quicken accepts stock prices for securities with standard symbols, you might want to download prices from a service such as Prodigy.

If you are a Prodigy member, you can download prices for your stocks from the Prodigy system into an ASCII file. You need to perform a few tasks within both Quicken and Prodigy to import this data, but the time savings over manual updates is worth it if you have several stocks to track. These are the basic tasks you need to perform:

1. Check your Quicken investment file to make sure that all the securities for which you want to import data have symbols assigned. (Quicken matches data by symbol.)
2. Create a Prodigy Quote Track list for the securities you want to monitor.
3. Within Prodigy, set up a report. You should specify closing prices and a comma-delimited file format.
4. Print the results to a file. The file you have created will be in ASCII format which you can then use in Quicken.
5. From the Quicken Portfolio View window, select Import Prices from the File menu.
6. Supply the name of the file you created in Prodigy. Include the complete path for the file (for example, D:\PRODIGY\QTRACK25.CSV).
7. Press Tab.
8. Specify a date unless you want to use the current date.
9. Select OK to begin importing the data into the Quicken file.

9

NOTE: There are other stock price services you can use. As long as the service creates an ASCII file for you with one symbol, price, and date on each line of the file and uses either comma or space delimiters, you will be able to import its data.

Your First Net Worth Report

When you completed the steps in the previous section, you recorded balances in all the accounts in your INVEST file. At this point, you can determine your net worth. Remember that your net worth is determined by the following formula:

Financial resources – Financial obligations = Net worth

Follow these steps to print your first Net Worth report:

1. Return to the Investments account register and select Home from the Reports menu. Then select Net Worth.

   The Create Report dialog box appears.

2. Type **8/1/94** in the Report Balance as of text box, and select OK.

   The Net Worth report appears on your screen.

3. Select Print. The Print Report dialog box appears.

4. Select Printer, and then select Print. Your printer prints the report shown in Figure 9-7. (Again, the spacing in your report may differ from that shown in the figure because of adjustments made to fit the material onto these pages.)

Notice that the Net Worth report is presented for a specific date—in this example, 8/1/94. The report presents your assets and liabilities at this date and gives you a base point against which to make future comparisons. As you can see, your net worth on 8/1/94 is $63,710.00. At the end of this chapter, you prepare another Net Worth report and compare how your net worth has changed.

The Impact of Investments and Mortgage Payments on Net Worth

In this section, you record various transactions in the INVEST file to demonstrate the effects of certain types of transactions on your net worth. You will see how Quicken can monitor your mortgage balance as part of your monthly record-keeping in your checking account. You will also see how you can record a transaction only once and trace the financial impact on both your checking and your investment account registers.

```
                        Net Worth Report
                     (Includes unrealized gains)
                          As of 8/1/94

  8/2/94                                                    Page 1
  INVEST-All Accounts

                                                  8/1/1994
                            Acct                   Balance
  -------------------------------------------   ----------------

  ASSETS
    Cash and Bank Accounts
      Great Lakes Chk                                 4,000.00
      Great Lakes Svg                                 2,500.00
      Price Money Mkt                                15,000.00
                                                 ----------------
    Total Cash and Bank Accounts                     21,500.00


    Other Assets
      Residence                                     100,000.00
                                                 ----------------
    Total Other Assets                              100,000.00


    Investments
      Investments                                    27,210.00
                                                 ----------------
    Total Investments                                27,210.00


                                                 ----------------
  TOTAL ASSETS                                      148,710.00

  LIABILITIES
    Other Liabilities
      Great Lakes Mtg                                85,000.00
                                                 ----------------
    Total Other Liabilities                          85,000.00


                                                 ----------------
  TOTAL LIABILITIES                                  85,000.00

                                                 ================
  OVERALL TOTAL                                      63,710.00
```

Net Worth
report for
8/1/94
Figure 9-7.

9

Additional Stock Transactions

When you prepared your Net Worth report, you were in the Investments
account. You will now record the acquisition of some additional stock,

dividends, dividends reinvested, and the sale of stock. The following steps demonstrate how easy it is to record transactions with Quicken for Windows' Investment accounts.

1. Go to the Investments account register, if you are not already there.
2. Move to the last entry.
3. Select Buy from the buttonbar.
4. Type **8/2/94** in the Date text box.
5. Type **Douglas Marine** in the Security text box, and press Tab.
   Because this security is not in the Security list, it must be added.
6. Type **DGM** in the Symbol text box.
7. Select Stock in the Type text box.
8. Select Growth in the Goal text box.
9. Type **.30** in the Est. Annual Income($) text box.
10. Select OK to finalize the Security list entries.
11. Type **100** in the Number of Shares text box, and press Tab.
12. Type **25** in the Price text box, and press Tab to have Quicken calculate the content of the Total of Sales text box.
13. Type **50** in the Commission/Fee text box, and press Tab to have Quicken adjust the content of the Total of Sales text box.
14. Select [Price Money Mkt] from the Transfer Acct drop-down list box.
    The transfer amount is automatically computed as the price of the stock plus the commission.
15. Type **Buy 100 Douglas Marine**.
16. Select OK to finalize the entry.

The next transactions record dividends and transfer them to another account or reinvest them in shares of the stock. Rather than transferring funds in and out for each transaction, you can choose to leave a cash balance in your brokerage account. Quicken allows you to mirror almost any investment situation. To record the dividend transaction, follow these steps:

1. Select Income. The completed Record Income dialog box for this example is shown in Figure 9-8.
2. Type **8/10/94** in the Date text box.
3. Select Haven Publishing from the drop-down list in the Security text box.
4. Type **200** in the Dividend text box, and press Tab until the Total text box is filled.

5. Select [Great Lakes Svg] from the drop-down list in the Transfer Account text box.

6. Type **Div @ .40 per share** in the Memo text box.

7. Select OK to finalize the transaction.

The next transaction also recognizes a dividend distribution. These dividends are reinvested in shares purchased at the current market price. Follow these steps to record the transaction:

1. Select Reinv from the buttonbar.

2. Type **8/15/94** in the Date text box.

3. Select Ganges Mutual Fund from the Security drop-down list box.

   Another option is to type **G**, and Quicken will complete the name for you using the QuickFill feature. You have seen QuickFill at work in entries you made in earlier chapters. Quicken tries to match the characters that you type for the Payee, Category, Security, and Action fields to entries in existing lists. If you want to use the Glenn Packing security, you must select it from the drop-down list box.

4. Type **100** in the Dividend Dollar Amount text box, and press Tab.

   Quicken supplies the number of shares, if you enter the price and the amount of the dividend that you are reinvesting.

5. Type **7.531** in the Dividend Number Shares text box, and press Tab.

6. Type **Dividend Reinvestment** in the Memo text box.

7. Select OK.

9

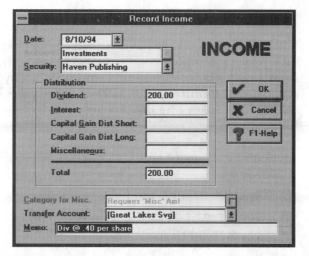

Record Income dialog box
Figure 9-8.

To record the sale of stock with the transfer of proceeds to another account, follow these steps:

1. Select Sell from the buttonbar.

2. Type **8/25/94** in the Date text box.

3. Select Haven Publishing from the drop-down list in the Security text box.

4. Type **100** in the Number of Shares text box, and press Tab.

    If you select Lots, Quicken presents a Specific Identification of Shares dialog box that allows you to select specific shares from various acquisition dates for the security being sold. You designate the specific shares that are being sold in this situation. This allows you to assign the cost of the shares that are being sold when gain or loss is being determined on this sale for tax purposes. In this example, all the shares were purchased at one time, so you let Quicken do the work for you. Unless you make a selection, Quicken uses the first-in-first-out selection method. That method assumes that the oldest shares of this stock are being sold first. The shares will be sold in order, beginning with the oldest shares held, until the number of shares sold in this sale transaction is reached.

5. Type **23 1/4** in the Price text box, and press Tab.

6. Type **25** in the Commission/Fee text box, and press Tab.

7. Select [Price Money Mkt] from the Transfer Account drop-down list box.

8. Type **Sell 100 Haven Publishing** in the Memo text box.

9. Select OK.

Your register entries look like the ones in Figure 9-9.

A Mortgage Payment Transaction

You recorded mortgage payments in earlier chapters, but here you will see how you can monitor your principal balance when you make your payment. In this example, you make your monthly payment from your checking account and monitor the impact of the payment on your principal balance in the Great Lakes Mtg liability account. Follow these steps to record this transaction:

1. Enter the Great Lakes Chk register, move to the Date field, and type **8/5/94**.

2. Type **100** in the Num field.

3. Type **Great Lakes Bank** in the Payee field.

4. Type **875.00** in the Payment field.

5. Select Splits. The Splits dialog box appears on the screen. When you finish entering information into this dialog box, it will look like the one shown here:

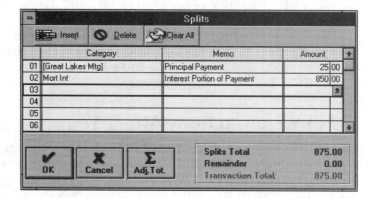

6. Select [Great Lakes Mtg] from the drop-down list box.

7. Type **Principal Payment** in the Memo field, type **25.00** in the Amount field, and press Tab.

   You have recorded the first part of the transaction.

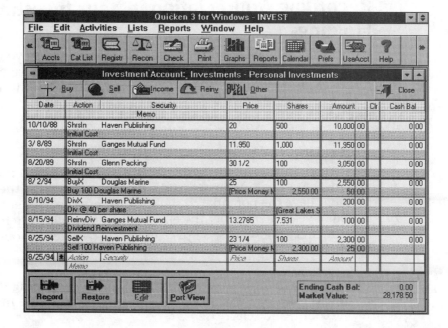

Investments register after the August 1994 transactions have been made

Figure 9-9.

9

8. Select Mort Int from the Category drop-down list box. Type **Interest Portion of Payment** in the Memo field, and press ⌈Tab⌉. Select OK.

   This step returns you to the account register.

9. Select Re̲cord, and Quicken records the transaction in the register.

As you can see, the balance in the account has been reduced by the amount of the payment. At the same time, Quicken has recorded the transaction in your Great Lakes Mtg account and reduced the obligation by the $25.00 principal portion of the payment.

How Transactions Affect Your Net Worth

Let's take a look at the effect of the previous transactions on your net worth. If you compare the report in Figure 9-10 to the previous Net Worth report, you'll see that your net worth has increased by $68.50 compared to the net worth shown in Figure 9-7. This difference is the net effect of the transactions you recorded during the month of August in your Investment, Cash, and Bank accounts.

Your net worth can grow if you either increase the value of your financial resources or decrease the amount of your obligations. In the following section, you will see how increases in the value of your investments are recorded and the effect they have on your net worth.

Recording Appreciation in Your Investment Holdings

In this section, you record the increased appreciation in your investments and residence occurring since the Net Worth report prepared on 8/1/94. Although the amounts may seem high, remember that this is an example. Also, remember that what you make in the stock market and housing market this year could be lost next year.

Appreciation of Your Investments

Quicken permits you to record increases and decreases in the value of your holdings. As noted in the net worth formula, changes in the value of your holdings have the potential to significantly affect your net worth over a period of years. Remember the effect of compounding interest on your investments. Follow these steps to enter the changes to your investments for the month of August:

1. Move to the Investments account register by opening the Accounts list. (Select the Acct icon from the Iconbar, highlight the Investments account, and select U̲se.)

2. Select Port View.
3. Select Price Update from the View drop-down list.
4. Press Ctrl-G, enter **8/31/94**, and select OK.

```
                        Net Worth Report
                     (Includes unrealized gains)
                          As of 8/31/94
  8/2/94                                                    Page 1
  INVEST-All Accounts

                                                     8/31/1994
                                    Acct               Balance
  -------------------------------------------     ----------------

  ASSETS
    Cash and Bank Accounts
      Great Lakes Chk                                     3,125.00
      Great Lakes Svg                                     2,700.00
      Price Money Mkt                                    14,750.00
                                                  ----------------
    Total Cash and Bank Accounts                         20,575.00

    Other Assets
      Residence                                         100,000.00
                                                  ----------------
    Total Other Assets                                  100,000.00

    Investments
      Investments                                        28,178.50
                                                  ----------------
    Total Investments                                    28,178.50

                                                  ----------------
  TOTAL ASSETS                                          148,753.50

  LIABILITIES
    Other Liabilities
      Great Lakes Mtg                                    84,975.00
                                                  ----------------
    Total Other Liabilities                              84,975.00

                                                  ----------------
  TOTAL LIABILITIES                                      84,975.00

                                                  ----------------
  OVERALL TOTAL                                          63,778.50
                                                  ================
```

Net Worth
report after
stock is
acquired and
a mortgage
payment is
made
Figure 9-10.

Notice the letter *e* next to the prices. An *e* tells you that Quicken is using an estimated value for the investment. For example, Quicken valued the Glenn Packing shares at $30 per share. Because you didn't buy or sell any shares of this stock during August, Quicken uses the 7/31/94 price shown in Figure 9-9 until you revalue the stock. The Ganges Mutual Fund stock is shown at its actual value on 8/15/94 because you recorded the dividend reinvestment transaction in your account on that date. Quicken automatically updates your market valuation each time you provide new price information when recording account transactions throughout the year.

5. Enter the new market prices for the stocks, as shown in Figure 9-4. Press ⬇ or ⬆ after you record each new price.

6. Select Register to return to the account register.

Appreciation of Your Residence

As your home increases in value, you will want to record this change in Quicken because it will affect your net worth. In this example, as a result of recent sales in your neighborhood, you feel that $105,000 would be a conservative estimate of the market value of your home. Follow these steps to value your home at $105,000:

1. From the Account List window, select the Residence account, and select Use.

   Quicken opens the register for this account and highlights the next blank transaction.

2. Select Update Balances from the Activities menu.

3. Select Update Cash Balance.

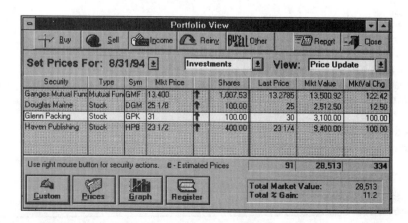

Portfolio View window after recording revaluations
Figure 9-11.

4. Type **105000**, and press ⌷Tab⌷.
5. Press ⌷Tab⌷ twice to decline to specify a category.
6. Type **8/31/94**, and select OK.

Your register should look like Figure 9-12.

Your Ending Net Worth Determination

Having prepared the adjustments to the various accounts in the INVEST file, you are now prepared to print your Net Worth report for the end of the period.

1. Select <u>H</u>ome from the <u>R</u>eports menu, and select <u>N</u>et Worth. The Create Report dialog box appears.
2. Press ⌷Tab⌷, type **8/31/94**, and select OK.

   The Net Worth report appears on your screen.
3. Press ⌷Ctrl⌷-⌷P⌷. The Print Report dialog box appears.
4. Complete the appropriate selections in the dialog box. When you select OK to leave the dialog box, your printer prints the report, which is shown in Figure 9-13.

An examination of Figures 9-7 and 9-13 reveals that your net worth increased by almost $6,000 during the time period. What were the reasons

9

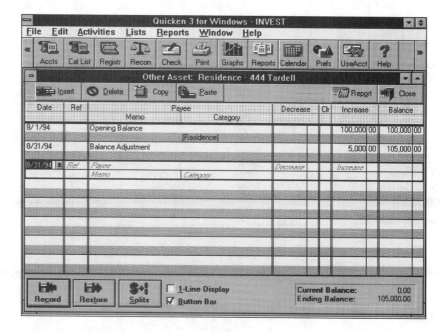

Residence register after a value increase is recorded
Figure 9-12.

```
                    Net  Worth  Report
                   (Includes unrealized gains)
                       As of 8/31/94

   8/2/94                                            Page 1
   INVEST-All Accounts

                                              8/31/1994
                        Acct                   Balance
   --------------------------------------   ----------------
   ASSETS
     Cash and Bank Accounts
       Great Lakes Chk                             3,125.00
       Great Lakes Svg                             2,700.00
       Price Money Mkt                            14,750.00
                                             ----------------
     Total Cash and Bank Accounts                 20,575.00

     Other Assets
       Residence                                 105,000.00
                                             ----------------
     Total Other Assets                          105,000.00

     Investments
       Investments                                28,513.42
                                             ----------------
     Total Investments                            28,513.42

                                             ----------------
   TOTAL ASSETS                                  154,088.42

   LIABILITIES
     Other Liabilities
       Great Lakes Mtg                            84,975.00
                                             ----------------
     Total Other Liabilities                      84,975.00

                                             ----------------
   TOTAL LIABILITIES                              84,975.00

                                             ----------------
   OVERALL TOTAL                                  69,113.42
                                             ================
```

Net Worth report for 8/31/94 after all transactions affecting the INVEST file are recorded **Figure 9-13.**

for these changes? For the most part, the increased values of your investments and residence explain the greater net worth.

The importance of monitoring your net worth has been stressed throughout this chapter. This book's focus is teaching you how to use Quicken to assist in your financial planning and monitoring activities. Once you have a good picture of your net worth from the Quicken reports, you can focus on additional planning. You might want to set your net worth goal for a future point or make plans to protect your existing holdings.

If you have not taken any actions regarding estate planning, this is another area you should address. Making a will is a very important part of the estate planning process and should not be delayed. Although the complexities of planning for the transfer of your estate are significant, the special section "The Need for a Will" highlights some problems that can be encountered when estate planning is not combined with financial planning activities. You may also be surprised to learn that a lawyer's fee for a simple will can be relatively low. You can also write a will with one of the new software packages specifically designed for that purpose.

The Need for a Will

A will is important to ensure that your heirs benefit from the net worth that you have accumulated and to make sure that your wishes control the distribution of your assets at your death. Without a will, the laws of your state and the rulings of a probate court decide what happens to your assets and award the custody of your minor children. The following may also occur:

✦ A probate court may appoint an administrator for your estate.

✦ State laws may distribute your assets differently than you would wish.

✦ Fees for probate lawyers may consume from 5 to 25 percent of your estate. The smaller your estate, the higher the percentage will be for the probate lawyer.

✦ If your estate is large enough to be affected by federal estate taxes ($600,000 or more), absence of a will and lack of other estate planning can increase the tax obligations on your estate.

9

Quicken's Investment Reports

Quicken offers five investment reports that provide information on your investments from different perspectives. You can use these reports to look at detailed investment transactions or to assess gains or losses in investment value over a period of time. The many options available provide different variations on each of the basic reports.

Portfolio Value Report

A Portfolio Value report gives you the values of all the investments in your portfolio at a given date based on price information stored in Quicken. The Portfolio Value report displays the number of shares, the current price, the cost basis of the shares, the gain or loss, and the current value of the shares. Follow these steps from the Investments account to create a Portfolio Value report:

1. Select Investment from the Reports menu.
2. Select Portfolio Value.
3. Enter **8/31/94** in the Report Value as of text box, and select Customize.
4. Clear the Cents in Amounts check box, and select OK.

   The report is displayed on your screen. (A printed copy of the report is shown in Figure 9-14.)

5. Select Close to close the report window.

Investment Performance Report

The Investment Performance report lets you look at your investments' gains or losses over time. The Investment Performance report indicates your return for

```
              Portfolio Value Report
                (Includes unrealized gains)
                     As of 8/31/94

   8/2/94                                               Page 2
   INVEST-Investments


   Security          Shares   Curr Price  Cost Basis  Gain/Loss   Balance
   ----------        -------- ----------- ----------- ----------- ---------
 Douglas Marine       100.00     25 1/8     2,550        -38        2,513
 Ganges Mutual Fund 1,007.53     13.400    12,050       1,451      13,501
 Glenn Packing        100.00     31.000     3,050         50        3,100
 Haven Publishing     400.00     23 1/2     8,000       1,400       9,400
                                           ----------- ----------- ---------
 Total Investments                          25,650       2,863      28,513
                                           =========== =========== =========
```

Portfolio
Value report
Figure 9-14.

```
                  Investment Performance Report
                      8/1/94 Through 8/31/94
    8/2/94                                                    Page 2
    INVEST-Investments

                                                            Avg. Annual
     Date    Action    Description      Investments  Returns  Tot. Return
     ------   --------  ------------     ------------ -------- ------------


              8/1/94 - 8/31/94


     7/31/1994            Beg Mkt Value       27,210
     8/2/1994   BuyX     100 Douglas Marine    2,550
     8/10/1994  DivX     Haven Publishing                200
     8/25/1994  SellX    100 Haven Publishing          2,300
     8/31/1994            End Mkt Value        28,513
                                          ------------ -------- ------------
            TOTAL 8/1/94 - 8/31/94          29,760    31,013      64.5%
```

Investment
Performance
report
Figure 9-15.

the period and projects an average annual return based on the results of the
period selected. Follow these steps to create an Investment Performance report:

1. Select Investment from the Reports menu, and select Investment
   Performance.
2. Enter **8/1/94** in the from text box.
3. Enter **8/31/94** in the to text box.
4. Select Customize.
5. Clear the Cents in Amounts check box, and select OK.

   A printed copy of the report showing an annualized return of 64.5
   percent is shown in Figure 9-15.
6. Select Close.

Capital Gains Report

The Capital Gains report is useful for tax purposes because it shows the gain
or loss on sales of investments. One Capital Gains report you can create
allows you to look at the difference between short- and long-term capital
gains. Follow these steps to create the report:

1. Select Investment from the Reports menu.
2. Select Capital Gains.

3. Enter **8/1/94** in the from text box.

4. Enter **8/31/94** in the to text box.

5. Select Customize.

6. Clear the Cents in Amounts check box, and select OK.

   Figure 9-16 shows a printout of this report.

7. Select Close to close the report window.

Investment Income Report

The Investment Income report shows the total income or expense from your investments. Dividends and both realized and unrealized gains and losses can be shown on this report. Follow these steps to create the report:

1. Select Investment from the Reports menu.

2. Select Investment Income.

3. Enter **8/1/94** in the from text box.

4. Enter **8/31/94** in the to text box.

5. Select Customize.

6. Clear the Cents in Amounts check box.

7. Select Show Rows.

8. Select Exclude All from the Transfers drop-down list.

9. Select OK to display the report on your screen.

   Your report will match the printout shown in Figure 9-17.

10. Select Close to close the report window.

```
                         Capital Gains Report
                         8/1/94 Through 8/31/94
      8/2/94                                                          Page 1
      INVEST-Investments


  Security       Shares      Bought      Sold    Sales Price  Cost Basis  Gain/Loss
  ----------   ----------  ----------  ---------  -----------  ----------  ---------
               LONG TERM


  Haven Pub...     100     10/10/1988  8/25/1994      2,300       2,000         300

                                                  -----------  ----------  ---------
               TOTAL LONG TERM                         2,300       2,000         300
                                                  ===========  ==========  =========
```

Capital Gains
report
Figure 9-16.

```
                    Investment  Income  Report
                      8/1/94 Through 8/31/94
    8/2/94                                                Page 1
    INVEST-Investments
                                              8/1/1994-
                  Category Description        8/31/1994
    ------------------------------------   -----------------
    INCOME/EXPENSE
       INCOME
         _DivInc                                  300
         _RlzdGain                                300
                                               ---------------
       TOTAL INCOME                               600


                                               ---------------
    TOTAL  INCOME/EXPENSE                         600
                                               ===============
```

Investment
Income report
Figure 9-17.

Investment Transactions Report

The Investment Transactions report is the most detailed of the five
investment reports Quicken offers. It reports on all investment transactions
during the selected period. Follow these steps to create the report:

1. Select Investment from the Reports menu.
2. Select Investment Transactions.
3. Enter **8/1/94** in the from text box.
4. Enter **8/31/94** in the to text box.
5. Select Customize.
6. Clear the Cents in Amounts check box.
7. Select Transactions, and mark the Include Unrealized Gains check box.
8. Select OK to display the report on your screen.

   Your report will match the printout shown in Figure 9-18.
9. Select Close to close the report window.

Using Quicken's Financial Planning Tools

Quicken for Windows has a number of financial planning tools. These tools
are designed to perform calculations that can help you plan and make
decisions about your financial goals. You used one financial tool, the Loan

```
                Investment Transactions Report
                     (Includes unrealized gains)
                        8/1/94 Through 8/31/94
      8/2/94                                                        Page 1
      INVEST-Investments


         Date        Action      Secur      Categ        Price       Shares
      ---------    ----------  ------------- ---------  ------------- ----------


            BALANCE 7/31/94


         8/2/1994                 Douglas M...  _Unr...       25.000

         8/2/1994    BuyX         Douglas M...  [Pri...       25.000         100

         8/10/1994   DivX         Haven Pub...  _DivInc
                                                [Gre...

         8/15/1994                Ganges Mu...  _Unr...       13.2785

         8/15/1994   ReinvDiv     Ganges Mu...  _DivInc      13.2785       7.531

         8/25/1994                Haven Pub...  _Unr...       23 1/4

         8/25/1994   SellX        Haven Pub...  [Pri...       23 1/4         100
                                                _Rlz...

         8/31/1994                Haven Pub...  _Unr...       23 1/2
         8/31/1994                Ganges Mu...  _Unr...       13.400
         8/31/1994                Glenn Packing _Unr...       31.000
         8/31/1994                Douglas M...  _Unr...       25 1/8


            TOTAL 8/1/94 - 8/31/94


            BALANCE 8/31/94
```

Investment
Transactions
report
including
unrealized
gains and
losses
Figure 9-18.

Planner, to calculate the split between mortgage principal reductions and interest in Chapter 8. In this section, you see how the Savings Planner, Retirement Planner, College Planner, and Refinance Planner are similar in that they provide the information you need to make a good decision and allow you to look at different scenarios. All the financial planning tools are accessed by selecting Financial Planners from the Activities menu.

```
                Investment Transactions Report
                       (Includes unrealized gains)
                        8/1/94 Through 8/31/94
      8/2/94                                               Page 2
      INVEST-Investments

                              Invest.    Cash +
      Commssn    Cash         Value      Invest.
      ---------- ---------- --------- ------------

                        0    27,210     27,210

                                -50        -50

         50    -2,550        2,550
                2,550                     2,550

                 200                       200
                -200                      -200

                               69          69

                -100          100
                 100                       100

                              300         300

         25     2,000       -2,000
               -2,300                    -2,300
                 300                       300

                              100         100
                              122         122
                              100         100
                               13          13

               ---------- --------- ------------
                        0     1,303      1,303

                        0    28,513     28,513
```

Investment Transactions report including unrealized gains and losses (*cont.*)
Figure 9-18.

NOTE:　All the financial planning tools require you to make assumptions about interest rates, yields, and so on. You should continue to monitor your assumptions over time and make corrections as the economy or other factors change.

9

Savings Planner

Early in this chapter, you saw a table illustrating the effects of investing $100 a month for 20 years. You can use the Savings Planner in Quicken to see how future value information is generated. The Savings Planner is so flexible that it also allows you to calculate other things such as current value. To access this planner, select Savings from the Financial Planners submenu of the Activities menu.

In order to complete the entries in the Investment Savings Planner dialog box, shown in Figure 9-19, you must tell Quicken that the opening balance is zero, because you are starting with no money in the account. The other entries are the annual yield of 8 percent, a period of 240 months, and the $100 monthly payment. The expected yield is an educated guess on your part. Quicken displays a future value of $26,501.63, which does not confirm the value shown in the table earlier in this chapter. Quicken is telling you that this is the value in today's dollars with an expected inflation rate of 4 percent over the 20-year period. This highlights the effect that inflation has on your future purchasing power. The actual dollar amount in your account will be $58,902.04. This can be shown by clearing the Ending Balance in Today's $ check box. If you select Schedule, Quicken presents a schedule of your payments and the accumulated savings during the 240 periods assumed in this illustration.

Although it was not done in the example, you can also have Quicken adjust your payments for inflation. If you want to have a value of $58,902 in today's dollars at the end of 20 years, you should select the Inflate Contributions check box and select Schedule. Quicken provides a payment schedule that is adjusted for the 4 percent annual inflation rate. Your first payment would still be $100, but your last payment would be $221.52. Your

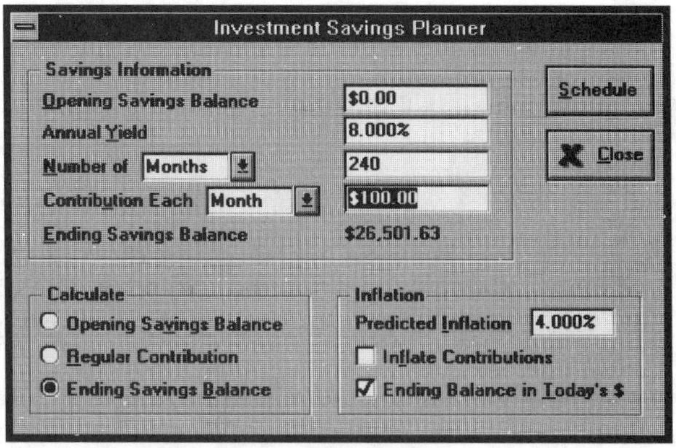

Investment
Savings
Planner dialog
box showing
the return for
the investment
example
Figure 9-19.

final account balance would be $81,126.62 if you maintain your 8 percent yield and adjust for inflation.

You can see how easy it is to enter a few numbers and get help from Quicken on your investment decisions. There are many changes that you can make as you select weekly, monthly, quarterly, or annual payment periods from the drop-down list boxes. You can adjust annual yield and inflation expectations. You can also select whether to calculate the regular contribution required to match a future value and whether to calculate the opening value necessary to reach a future value. For example, if you expect an 8 percent return and want to know how much money you need to deposit today to have $58,902 in the future, you would select Opening Savings Balance. Clear the Opening Savings Balance text box, select Years in the Number of drop-down list, press Tab, and enter **20**. Then select Years in the Contribution Each box, press Tab to clear the amount in this text box, and enter 58902 in the Ending Savings Balance text box. Quicken will compute a $12,637.32 deposit that you might want to make with a finance or insurance company.

Retirement Planning

You can also use Quicken to help project your expected income flows from your various retirement investments (for example, your SEP-IRA, Keogh plan, Individual IRA, 401(K), or retirement savings account). Figure 9-20

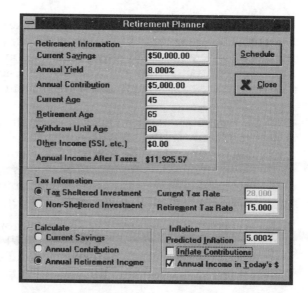

Retirement Planner dialog box with sample entries
Figure 9-20.

shows the Retirement Planner dialog box, which appears when you select Financial Planners from the Activities menu and then select Retirement.

To complete the dialog box, you must provide your best estimates for some of the information. You should review this information at least annually to see if modifications are needed and what effect the changes have on your expected retirement income. The following sections describe the type of information you must provide.

Current Savings Enter the current balance in your investment account. For example, if your IRA has a $50,000 balance at the beginning of the year, you would enter that balance here. Enter your current tax rate and your expected retirement tax rate, or accept the defaults.

Annual Yield Enter your estimate of the expected annual return on this investment. You could use past returns on this investment as a guide; however, you cannot rely solely on this source. Use a conservative but realistic estimate of your expected annual yield.

Annual Contribution Enter your best guess of the future annual contributions that will be made to this investment. Remember to include matching contributions from your employer in addition to your own contributions to the account.

Age Information Change Quicken's default ages to match your situation. If you are 45, wish to retire at 65, and wish to have income provided from this investment until you are 80, enter that information on your screen.

Tax Information Indicate whether or not the current account is tax sheltered. Enter your current tax rate and your expected retirement tax rate, or accept the defaults. Most retirement investments are tax sheltered; however, personal savings (CDs, mutual fund accounts, and so on) that you may plan to use to supplement your retirement plans are taxable.

Predicted Inflation Accept Quicken's default annual rate of 4 percent, or modify it to see what the potential impact of various rates would be. Select the Inflate Contribution check box if you would like Quicken to adjust your yearly payment schedule to reflect the increasing amount you will need to contribute to protect your investment against inflation. The default setting is for inflation adjustment to your yearly payments.

When you enter this information, Quicken provides you with retirement planning information, as shown in Figure 9-20. The Annual Income After Taxes amount shows what your expected future income in today's dollars will be. If Quicken shows that this investment will provide $10,000, that is the spending value of your investment in today's dollars. That is, Quicken has taken your future payments and adjusted them for inflation.

Quicken also allows you to enter expected payments from Social Security or other sources to give you a better picture of your total future retirement income. When you select Schedule, you can ask Quicken to print out your payment schedule for the retirement investment account. This process provides valuable information for retirement planning. As a result of this type of exercise, you might decide that you need to increase your retirement investment contributions or that you are on track for future financial security. This type of review should be an annual planning assessment. It is very important to protect your retirement quality of living, and this easy-to-use Quicken feature can be a valuable tool toward that end.

College Planning

The College Planner is shown in Figure 9-21. The assumptions for this college-planning scenario are

◆ Your child will attend a nationally known private university with a current tuition of $15,000 a year.

◆ It will be 18 years before your child enrolls in this university.

◆ Your child will pursue a major that requires five years of study to complete the degree requirements.

◆ Your annual yield will be 8 percent over the period.

◆ Predicted inflation for tuition is 6 percent.

9

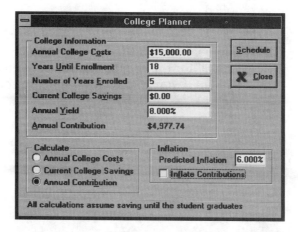

College Planner dialog box
Figure 9-21.

Figure 9-21 shows that you would need to make annual payments of $4,977.74 from 1994 to 2016. (Note that the calculations are based on your continuing payments during the five years that your child is in school.) When you select Schedule, you can see that tuition will rise to $42,815 for your child's freshman year if you assume a 6 percent annual increase. If you change the assumptions to have your child complete a major in an area requiring only four years of study, your annual payments would decrease to $4,086.16.

Refinance Planner

As interest rates fall, you can use the Refinance Planner to assess whether to approach your financial institution about refinancing your loan. You can use the information from the Loan Planner example in Chapter 8 for an example of an actual loan. In the example in Chapter 8, you had a $40,000 loan at 9.519 percent interest for 25 years with payments of $350 a month. If you were considering refinancing after 36 months, you could print out the payment schedule to see that you still had a balance of $38,642.29. The Refinance Planner will show you how much a lower interest rate will reduce your payments and how long it will take to recover the cost of refinancing. Follow these steps to provide the information you need:

1. Select Activities, select Financial Planners, and then select Refinance.

2. Type **350.00** in the Current payment text box, and press (Tab).

   In Chapter 8, the illustration did not provide for an escrow account (insurance, property taxes, and so on) held by the mortgage company. If escrow had been included, you would have entered the monthly escrow account as well. You can obtain your escrow information from the monthly statement that your mortgage company provides.

3. Type **38642.29** in the Principal amount text box, and press (Tab).

   This is the principal for the remaining mortgage after 36 $350 payments are applied.

4. Type **22** in the Years text box, and press (Tab).

   This number assumes that you want the house paid off within the 25-year goal for the original mortgage. You can negotiate a 15-year or a 30-year loan if you prefer, in which case you would change the Years information accordingly.

5. Type **8.375** in the Interest rate text box, and press (Tab).

   This is the interest rate quoted by your financial institution.

6. Type **900** in the Mortgage closing costs text box, and press (Tab).

Even when you refinance with your existing loan holder, you can expect to pay closing costs for the new loan. In this example, your lender has provided an estimate of $900.

7. Type **.25** in the Mortgage points text box, and press ⌧Tab. Your screen displays the Refinance Planner shown in Figure 9-22.

The .25 represents the 1/4 point that your lender will charge to give you the 8.375 percent interest rate on the 22-year loan.

Notice that if you refinance your home under these conditions, your monthly payments will be reduced to $320.84 (principal and interest), saving you $29.16 a month. Since you must pay out $900 in closing costs plus 1/4 point, the last line on the screen tells you that you must stay in the home another 34.18 months before your monthly savings will offset the closing costs and points. You can shop around for better terms with other institutions and use the Refinance Planner to pick the best deal.

Graphing Your Investments

Quicken gives you an opportunity to visually review your investment activities at specified points in time or over a period of time. Graphing options include an Investment Performance graph that shows your portfolio's value and average annual return over a selected time period. You can also use Quicken's QuickZoom feature to view your portfolio's composition, graph the price history for individual securities, and prepare a Price and Value History report for securities. From the Price and Value

9

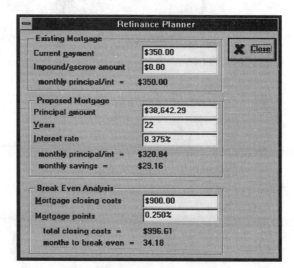

Refinance Planner dialog box
Figure 9-22.

History report, you can use QuickZoom to select individual security transactions from their origination transactions. Graphing activities begin from the Investments register.

1. Select Reports, select Graphs, and then select Investments.

    Quicken presents a Create Graphs dialog box with Investment Graph preselected. You can also open this dialog box by selecting the Graphs Icon from your buttonbar and then selecting Investment Graph. From this dialog box, you can select the Investment accounts you want to include in the graph and also whether you want to limit your selection of securities.

2. Type **7/94** in the From text box.

3. Type **8/94** in the To text box, and select Create.

    Quicken presents a graph similar to the one in Figure 9-23, showing the monthly portfolio value by security. As you specified in the previous steps, a two-month period is shown in this illustration. Quicken also presents a graph of your average annual total return for the portfolio, as well as the return for your individual securities.

4. Move the mouse pointer to the 8/94 bar on the Monthly Portfolio Value graph. The pointer changes to a magnifying glass with a *Z* inside. Double-click the left mouse button. You will see this graph:

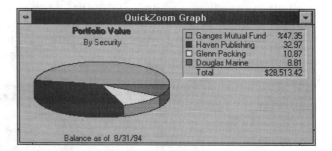

    QuickZoom prepares a pie chart that shows the composition of your portfolio by individual security. From the graph, you can see that Ganges Mutual Fund comprises 47 percent of your portfolio's total value, Haven Publishing 33 percent, Glenn Packing 11 percent, and Douglas Marine 9 percent.

5. If you want to print any graphs, you can select the print button on your screen.

For all the graphs you print with Quicken, the default is to include all your investment accounts in the graphing option. In Figure 9-23, only the

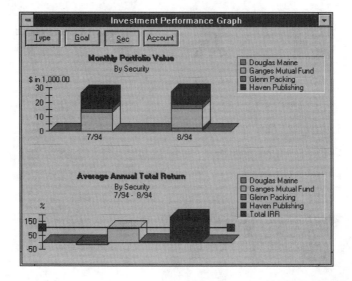

Investment
Performance
graph
Figure 9-23.

Investments account is included because you have only established one Investment account in this chapter. If you have several Investment accounts, you can select the Accounts option in the Create Graph dialog box to choose the accounts you want included in the graph. If you have an IRA, a 401(K), and a personal Investment account, you can choose to graph each account separately. If you do not make a selection, Quicken merges all three accounts into one graph.

There are several additional graphing features that you can use when viewing the Investment Performance Graph and the QuickZoom pie chart. You can use the QuickZoom feature to select any of your securities included in the Average Annual Total Return portion of the Investment Performance Graph to have Quicken prepare an Average Annual Total Return report for the security. You can then use the QuickZoom feature once again to trace individual transactions to their origination entry. In addition, from the QuickZoom pie chart you can QuickZoom on any security to have Quicken prepare a Price and Value History report for that security. Within this report, you can use QuickZoom once again to prepare a Price and Value History report for the security. Then QuickZoom again on an individual transaction to view its origination entry in the Sell, Buy, or other investment entry dialog box in which you created the entry.

9

CHAPTER

10

CREATING CUSTOM REPORTS

Periodically you'll want to step back from the detail in your Quicken register and look at the reports and graphs Quicken can create. You can view the reports onscreen, or you can print them to share with others. Graphs allow you to analyze your data in just a few minutes.

Quicken can prepare both standard and custom reports. Standard reports have a predefined format most Quicken users will find acceptable for their personal, business, and investment reporting needs.

However, as you become more familiar with Quicken, you may want to customize your reports to make them even more useful to you. Custom reports allow you to alter the report format to meet your specific requirements.

Quicken can create eight different standard reports for personal use: Cash Flow, Monthly Budget, Itemized Categories, Tax Summary, Net Worth, Tax Schedule, Missing Checks, and Comparison. You can create any of these reports by selecting Home from the Reports menu, as shown here:

```
Reports
  Home           Cash Flow...
  Investment     Monthly Budget...
  Business       Itemized Categories...
  Other          Tax Summary...
                 Net Worth...
  Memorized...   Tax Schedule...
  Graphs         Missing Checks...
  Reconciliation...   Comparison...
```

With Quicken, you can prepare 13 preset standard and custom reports.

You have seen several examples of standard reports in earlier chapters. Quicken allows you to customize any of the standard reports while you are creating them or after they are displayed on your screen. You can see from the Memorized option in the preceding menu that Quicken can access reports that you have memorized. (More information about memorized reports appears at the end of this chapter.)

Quicken also provides five custom report types that you access by selecting Other from the Reports menu: Transaction, Summary, Comparison, Budget, and Account Balances. Notice that you can access the Comparison report through either the Home or the Other selection in the Reports menu. Selecting any of the custom report types from the Reports menu causes a custom Create Report dialog box to be displayed, from which you can create many different report frameworks. Although the exact contents of the dialog box depend on the type of report you are creating, each of the custom Create Report dialog boxes allows you to enter information such as the accounts you want to use, directions for totaling and subtotaling the report, the type of cleared status you want to use for included transactions, and specific transactions you wish to include. You specify some of these options by making entries directly in the custom Create Report dialog box, and others require you to use the Customize selection in the custom Create Report dialog box to see additional customization options.

You used a custom option in Chapter 7, "Quicken as a Budgeting Tool," when you selected the current account item to customize the Monthly Budget report for Cardinal Bank. (This report is shown in Figure 7-5 in Chapter 7.) In this chapter, you look at additional custom report options and report filtering features as you build additional custom reports. After completing the exercises in this chapter, you will be able to create your own custom reports and memorize them for later use. Be sure to look at the special "Documenting Your Decisions" section to learn how to safeguard your time investment.

Documenting Your Decisions

As you work with Quicken's custom report features, you will probably try a number of custom report options before you decide on the exact set of reports that meets your needs. If you had an accountant prepare these reports for you, there might also be some trial and error before the exact format to use was determined. Once the decisions were made, the accountant would document them to ensure you received the exact reports you requested on a regular basis. You will benefit by following the same procedure and documenting the custom reports and options you select with Quicken. Follow these steps when putting together your documentation:

◆ Place all your report documentation in one folder.

◆ Include a copy of each report you want to produce on a regular basis.

◆ If you are using a Quicken report to obtain information for another form, such as an income tax form, include a copy of the form and note on it which line or lines in the Quicken report are used to obtain the information.

◆ Include the selections you used in the Customize Report dialog boxes. If you have a screen-capture utility, you can capture and print these screens when you create the report the first time. If not, make a note of the selections you used.

◆ If you are creating multiple copies of some reports, write down the information for creating the report on the extra copies and write down what must be done with the copies.

◆ Memorize each custom report to make it instantly available when you need it again.

10

In Chapter 7, you created graphs of your budget performance. Graphs are designed to give you a quick picture of your account information, without all the detail of reports, to help you spot trends and make analyses.

Customizing Report Options

By selecting Quicken's customizing option, you can modify any of the preset formats to meet your specific reporting needs.

You can create reports in many different formats. As noted earlier, the standard settings are sufficient for most reporting needs. However, as you become familiar with Quicken's customization options, you may want to modify some of the formats to meet your special needs. Once you customize a report the way you want, memorize it so that you can always access an updated report with just a few commands. Figure 10-1 shows the Customize Comparison Report dialog box. To open this dialog box, select Comparison from the Report menu, and then select Customize from the Create Report dialog box. The Customize Report dialog box varies slightly depending on the type of report you are preparing, but the vast majority of the selections are available when preparing all standard and custom reports.

In Figure 10-1, the customization features you can access when preparing your report appear in the left side of the dialog box. You can explore the options by using your mouse to select various customization options and then reviewing the default setting for each report. (Some of these options vary between reports.) Each time you select a customization option, Quicken presents a view that shows the current settings for each feature controlled by that option.

The first customization option shown for the Comparison report—Report Dates—allows you to modify your specified reporting dates. If you had a Comparison report on your screen and wanted to modify the reporting dates, you could just select this option and change the compared period. For all other reports, you make a change in the reporting dates by using the Report Layout option.

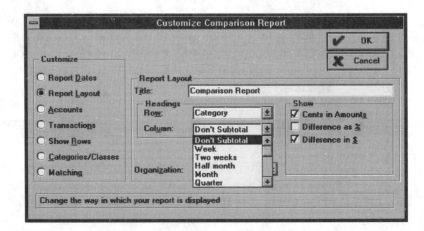

Customize Comparison Report dialog box
Figure 10-1.

The Report Layout option allows you to customize your report title and modify the settings for row and column heads. You can see in Figure 10-1 that you can change the setting in the Column drop-down list box from no subtotal to various time periods ranging from a week to a year. If you don't specify an interval, the default selection is the date identified in the Report Dates option. In this case, you may have defined your comparison dates as the years 1993 and 1994. In this example, if you request the report interval of Month, Quicken will prepare a Comparison report that shows monthly comparisons of inflows and outflows during 1993 and 1994. You can also use the Report Layout option to change the report organization to the cash flow or income and expense format. Finally, you can use the Report Layout option to have Quicken show cents in your report and to show the differences between the comparative periods in percentages or in dollar amounts. You change these setting by toggling the check boxes in the Show selection box. The check marks shown in Figure 10-1 are the default settings for the Comparison report.

The Accounts option allows you to select the accounts you want to include in the current report. Depending on the type of report being prepared, Quicken may select just one account, some accounts, or all your accounts by default. With this option, you can modify these preset selections to meet your needs.

You can filter your report to include transactions that contain a specific payee, category, class, or memo.

Selecting Transactions lets you modify several features. You can designate specific amounts to be included in your report. The default is all amounts, but you may want a report to include only amounts that are less than, equal to, or greater than a specified amount. You can also use this option to designate transaction types, specify whether to include unrealized gains and tax-related transactions, and designate the status of the transactions to include in your report. By toggling a check box, you can indicate whether you want blank, newly cleared, and reconciled transactions included in the report.

The Show Rows option allows you to designate if you want to show or hide all subcategories or display them reversed with their parent categories. You can also choose include all transfers, exclude all, or exclude only those to other accounts in the report. The Categories/Classes option allows you to select specific categories and classes to include in your report. The final customization feature, Matching, lets you filter your report to include only transactions that contain a specific payee, category, class, or memo.

Creating a Comparison Report

To create a Comparison report, select Home or Other from the Reports menu and then select Comparison. If you accept the default settings for this report,

Quicken provides a comparison of any two time periods you specify. For example, you might want to compare your checking account inflows and outflows for 1993 and 1994 to give you a feeling for how your spending habits have changed during the past year. You could also see whether you have been able to decrease expenditures or increase revenues to increase your savings during the past year.

For all the examples in this chapter, you use the PERSONAL file. To change to the PERSONAL file and open the Cardinal Bank account register, follow these steps:

1. Select Open from the File menu.
2. Select the PERSONAL file from the File Name list box, and select OK.
3. If necessary, press Ctrl-A or select the Accts icon from the Iconbar to open the Account list. Highlight the Cardinal Bank account, and select Use. Quicken opens the Cardinal Bank account register.

Follow these steps to produce a Comparison report.

A comparison report lets you review your financial activities during two time periods for comparative purposes.

1. Select Home from the Reports menu.

    Quicken displays the menu shown at the beginning of this chapter.
2. Select Comparison, and a Create Report window appears.

    If you wanted to accept the standard settings, you would enter your comparative dates and press OK. Then the standard report would appear.
3. Select Customize.

    Quicken displays the Customize Comparison Report dialog box with the Report Dates customization option selected. You now designate the time periods you want to use as your comparative periods. Remember that you can select reporting subperiods such as weekly or monthly by using the Report Layout option discussed earlier.
4. Enter **8/1/94** in the Compare from date text box.
5. Enter **8/31/94** in the Compare to date text box.
6. Enter **9/1/94** in the to from date text box.
7. Enter **9/30/94** in the to to date text box.
8. Select Report Layout.
9. Clear the Cents in Amounts check box.

    As discussed in the previous section, there are many additional customization options you can select while deciding on the final format that meets your reporting needs.
10. Select OK, and the Comparison report shown in Figure 10-2 appears on your screen.

```
                    Comparison Report
                    8/1/94 Through 9/30/94
  8/5/94                                                  Page 1
  PERSONAL-Bank,Cash,CC Accounts
                              9/1/94-       8/1/94-          $
       Category Description   9/30/94       8/31/94      Difference
  ---------------------------  -------------  -------------  ------------

  INFLOWS
    Salary                      2,000         2,000           0
                              -------------  -------------  ------------

  TOTAL INFLOWS                 2,000         2,000           0

  OUTFLOWS
    Auto:
      Fuel                      23            23              0
                              ---------     ---------      ---------

    Total Auto                    23            23              0
    Clothing                      50            50              0
    Dining                        60            60              0
    Entertain                     50            50              0
    Furniture                      0           217           -217
    Groceries                    180           218            -38
    Medical                      212           142             70
    Misc                          50            50              0
    Mort Int                     301           301           -301
    Mort Prin                     49            49              0
    Tax:
      Fed                      130           130              0
      Local                      9             9              0
      Medicare                  29            29              0
      Soc Sec                  124           124              0
      State                     80            80              0
                              ---------     ---------      ---------

    Total Tax                    372           372              0
    Telephone                     29            23              6
    Utilities:
      Electric                 44            31             13
      Gas                      19            19              0
                              ---------     ---------      ---------

    Total Utilities              63            50             13
                              -------------  -------------  ------------

  TOTAL OUTFLOWS                1,439         1,605          -166


                              -------------  -------------  ------------
  OVERALL TOTAL                 561           395            166
                              =============  =============  ============
```

Comparison
report
Figure 10-2.

In order to present a realistic Comparison report in this figure, the payroll and mortgage payment split transactions were added to the September transactions in the database. If you have not done this, these transactions will look different in your report, but the format will be exactly the same.

Creating a Custom Transaction Report

A custom transaction report lets you group transactions in many different ways for decision-making purposes.

You can print all the transactions in any Quicken account register by selecting Print Register from the File menu. Quicken prints a list of all the transactions in a given time frame. You can use this approach for printing a complete listing of register activity for backup purposes. However, that sort of listing doesn't provide much information for decision making. The custom Transaction report provides an alternative. When creating this report, you can subtotal transaction activity in many different ways, use all or only selected accounts, or show split transaction details to include the specific transaction details you need for better decision making. Let's take a look at some examples.

Showing Split Transaction Details

If a transaction is split among several categories, the word "SPLIT" appears in the Category field when the account register is printed. Suppose you want to prepare a custom report that captures all the details recorded in each split transaction within a selected time frame. Follow these steps:

1. Select Other from the Reports menu.
2. Select Transaction.

   Quicken displays the Create Report dialog box.
3. Select Customize.
4. Enter **8/1/94** in the from text box.
5. Enter **8/31/94** in the to text box.
6. Place a check mark in the Split Transaction Detail check box.

   Your screen looks like Figure 10-3.
7. Select OK, and the Transaction report appears on the screen.
8. Select the Print button.
9. Select the Printer option button, and then select Print to create the report. Figure 10-4 shows the first few transactions in this report.

   Notice that the report shows the details of the split transactions on 8/1 and 8/2, and a portion of the 8/3 Easy Credit Card split transaction.
10. Press (Esc) to clear the report from the screen.

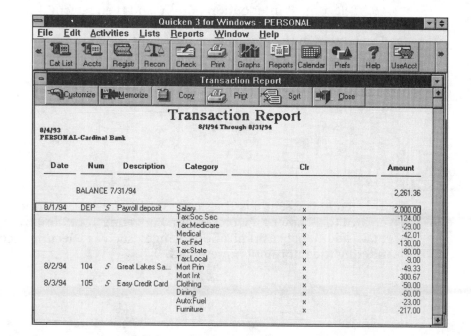

Customize
Transaction
Report dialog
box
Figure 10-3.

Adding Subtotals to the Transaction Report

When you produce a Transaction report without subtotals, the transactions
are simply listed in order by date, as shown in Figure 10-4. You can change
the Subtotal By drop-down list box setting to Week, Two Weeks, Half
Month, Month, Quarter, Half Year, or Year. The report still lists the
transactions by date, but it also provides a subtotal of the transactions each

Transaction
report with
split
transactions
printed
Figure 10-4.

10

time the selected interval occurs. For example, if you select Month, the report shows a subtotal for each month.

You can also change the Sort By setting to Category, Class, Payee, Account, Acct/Chk, or Date/Acct. Quicken orders the transactions by the field you select, and it prints a subtotal whenever the value in the selected field changes. For example, if you choose to sort 8/1 through 8/31 transactions by category, Quicken lists the transactions alphabetically by category and by date within each category, and it provides a subtotal for each category.

Follow these steps to create a Transaction report subtotaled by category for the Cardinal Bank account:

1. Select Other from the Reports menu.
2. Select Transaction, and the Create Report dialog box appears.
3. Select Customize.
4. Enter **8/1/94** in the from text box.
5. Enter **8/31/94** in the to text box.
6. Select Category in the Subtotal By drop-down list box.
7. Clear the Cents in Amounts check box, and select OK.

   The Transaction report appears on your screen.
8. Select the Print button to display the Print Report dialog box.
9. Select the Printer option button, and then select Print.

The bottom of the first page of the report shows three transactions for the Groceries category, as you can see in this partial report:

```
            Groceries
8/4/94     106   Maureks      Groceries      Groceries      -60
8/15/94    108   Meijer       Groceries      Groceries      -65
8/27/94    112   Meijer       Food           Groceries      -93
                                                          ------
           Total ...                                        -218
```

This report is essentially the same as the Itemized Categories report you created in Chapter 7, "Quicken as a Budgeting Tool," unless you choose to make additional customization changes, such as selecting accounts or filtering the information presented.

Creating a Summary Report

Summary reports can be based on categories, classes, payees, or accounts. You can use them to analyze spending patterns, prepare tax summaries, review major purchases, or look at the total charge card purchases for a given period.

Subtotaling a Summary Report by Month

Although you can choose any of the time intervals for the report subtotals, subtotaling by month is a common choice since many people budget expenses by month. This type of report shows a monthly summary of your financial transactions. Follow these steps to create a Summary Report subtotaled by month for the Cardinal Bank account register:

1. Select Other from the Reports menu.
2. Select Summary, and the Create Report dialog box appears.
3. Select Customize.
4. Enter **8/1/94** in the from text box.
5. Enter **10/31/94** in the to text box.
6. Select Month in the Column drop-down list box.
7. Clear the Cents in Amounts check box.
8. Select Cash flow basis in the Organization drop-down list box.

   This step instructs Quicken to prepare the report on a cash flow basis; it will be organized by cash inflows and outflows. This is the same basis used for the Monthly Budget reports prepared in Chapter 7. You will be able to compare this report to those prepared earlier to gain additional information for assessing your budget results.

9. Select OK, and the Summary report appears on your screen. Figure 10-5 shows a printout of this report.

   If you adjusted all your salary and mortgage payment transactions to agree with the August entries discussed in Chapter 8, "Using Quicken to Organize Tax Information," some of your entries will look different. Your totals will show 6000 for salary, 390 for federal tax, 87 for Medicare, 372 for Social Security tax, and 240 for state tax.

10. Select the Print button to display the Print Report dialog box.
11. Select the Printer option button, and select Print.

10

```
                    Summary Report by Month
                       8/1/94 Through 10/31/94

8/4/94                                                           Page 1
PERSONAL-Cardinal Bank

                                                            OVERALL
   Category Description     8/94       9/94       10/94      TOTAL
------------------------  ---------  ---------  ----------  ----------

INFLOWS
  Salary                    2,000      1,586      1,586      5,172
                          ---------  ---------  ----------  ----------

TOTAL INFLOWS               2,000      1,586      1,586      5,172

OUTFLOWS
  Auto:
    Fuel             23          23         37          83
                    --------    --------   ----------  -----------

  Total Auto                    23          23         37          83
  Clothing                      50          50         75         175
  Dining                        60          60         45         165
  Entertain                     50          50        100         200
  Furniture                    217           0        550         767
  Groceries                    218         180        250         648
  Medical                      142         170        100         412
  Misc                          50          50        150         250
  Mort Int                     301           0          0         301
  Mort Pay                       0         350        350         700
  Mort Prin                     49           0          0          49
  Tax:
    Fed             130           0          0        130
    Local             9           0          0          9
    Medicare         29           0          0         29
    Soc Sec         124           0          0        124
    State            80           0          0         80
                    --------    --------   ----------  ---------

  Total Tax                    372           0          0         372
  Telephone                     23          29         28          80
  Utilities:
    Electric         31          44         37        112
    Gas              19          19         17         55
                    --------    --------   ----------  -----------

  Total Utilities               50          63         54         167
  To Cardinal Saving           200         395        366         961
                          ---------  ---------  ----------  -----------

TOTAL OUTFLOWS              1,805      1,420      2,105      5,330


                          ---------  ---------  ----------  -----------
OVERALL TOTAL                195        166       -519        -158
                          =============  =============  ============  ===========
```

The report presents a cash inflow and outflow summary by month for the
period August through October. It provides additional cash flow information
about the Monthly Budget reports prepared in Chapter 7. Thus, this Summary
report supplements the previously prepared Monthly Budget reports.

Filtering to See Tax-Related Categories

You can filter Quicken reports to only include tax-related categories.

Filters allow you to select the information you want to include in a report. In Chapter 3, "Quicken Reports," you used a filter to look for a payee name containing "Small." Other possible selections include memo, category, or class matches. You can also choose specific categories or classes to include. You can specify tax-related items or transactions greater or less than a certain amount, and you can choose payments, deposits, unprinted checks, or all transactions. Checking the cleared status is another option; that is, you may wish to prepare a report using only transactions that have cleared the bank as part of your reconciliation process.

In the example that follows, you create a Summary report for tax-related items. Use the Cardinal Bank account in the PERSONAL file. Follow these steps:

1. Select Other from the Reports menu.
2. Select Summary. The Create Report dialog box appears on your screen.
3. Select Customize.
4. Enter **8/1/94** in the from text box.
5. Enter **10/31/94** in the to text box.
6. Clear the check mark in the Cents in Amounts check box.
7. Select Cash flow basis from the Organization drop-down list box.
8. Select Transactions.
9. Place a check mark in the Tax-related Transactions Only check box. Your Customize Summary Report dialog box looks like this:

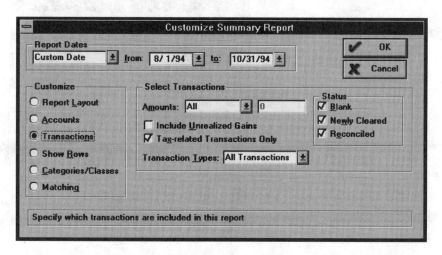

10

10. Select OK, and the Summary report appears onscreen.

11. Select the Pri<u>n</u>t button to display the Print Report dialog box.

12. Select the P<u>r</u>inter option button, and select <u>P</u>rint.

Don't clear the report from your screen since you'll use it in the next section.

Figure 10-6 shows the completed report with the information filtered for tax-related transactions only. (The report shown reflects the split salary and mortgage transactions for August only.) This type of report can be used to monitor your tax-related activities for any part of the tax year or for the year to date. You can use this information for tax planning as well as for tax preparation.

Memorizing Reports

Once you customize a report, use the memorize feature to always have the format available for future use.

You have already seen how you can gain productivity by using Quicken's memorized transactions. Quicken also allows you to memorize reports. Memorized reports store your custom report definitions so that you can produce a new report instantly. This means you can enter a title or filter once and use it again by recalling the memorized report definitions.

To memorize a report, you use the same (Ctrl)-(M) sequence used to memorize specific transactions. The only difference is that you must have a report displayed on the screen. Alternatively, you can select the <u>M</u>emorize button in the report window. The Memorize Report dialog box appears to allow you to enter a name for the report:

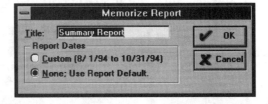

If you were memorizing the definition for the Summary report shown in Figure 10-5, you might enter the title "Tax Related Summary by Month." Although you can use the entire space for your report name, ensure that the first 29 characters of your entry uniquely define your report since this part of the entry will be displayed in the list of memorized reports.

You can choose to memorize the report with the currently assigned dates or without them. If you memorize the report without them, the default dates will be substituted when you use the memorized report again later. This

```
                        Summary Report
                     8/1/94 Through 10/31/94
    8/4/94                                                Page 1
    PERSONAL-Cardinal Bank
                                                8/1/94-
                    Category Description        10/31/94
                    ---------------------       ----------------

                    INFLOWS
                      Salary                          5,172
                                                   ---------
                    TOTAL INFLOWS                      5,172

                    OUTFLOWS
                      Medical                            412
                      Mort Int                           301
                      Tax:
                        Fed                   130
                        Local                   9
                        Medicare               29
                        Soc Sec               124
                        State                  80
                                             ------
                      Total Tax                          372
                                                   ---------
                    TOTAL OUTFLOWS                     1,085


                                                   ---------
                    OVERALL TOTAL                      4,087
                                                   =========
```

Filtered
Summary
report of
tax-related
transactions
Figure 10-6.

10

feature allows you to quickly create a periodic report, such as a monthly report used for reconciling your checking account.

To create a report from a memorized report definition, select Memorized from the Reports menu. A list of memorized reports appears that looks similar to this:

Highlight the desired report, and select Use. The report is displayed on the screen. If you select Edit, you can access the report definition and change it before displaying the report again.

Using Graphs for Additional Analyses

Graphs provide another way to help analyze your Quicken transactions.

The graphs that you created in Chapter 7 were related to your budget entries. If you activate the Graphs submenu of the Reports menu, you will see that Quicken for Windows offers many additional options for analyzing your data. Follow these steps to create a Net Worth graph:

1. Select Graphs from the Reports menu.

2. Select Net Worth Graph.

3. Type **8/94** in the From text box.

4. Type **10/94** in the To text box.

5. Select Create.

   The graph appears onscreen, as shown in Figure 10-7. The upper portion of the graph shows your assets for each of the periods designated. Your liabilities are shown in the bottom part of the graph as negative numbers. Your net worth is shown by the line connecting the assets for each of the periods. In this case your net worth is positive, as it hopefully always is.

6. Select Print from the buttonbar to print the graph to the default report printer.

7. Place your mouse pointer over one of the assets in the graph so that the mouse pointer becomes a magnifying glass, and double-click.

   Quicken displays a QuickZoom Graph of your asset composition, as shown here:

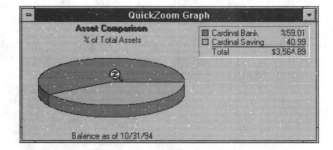

In this case, it shows the percentage composition of your two bank accounts to your total assets. You can do the same thing with your liabilities. You can also QuickZoom on the QuickZoom graph. If you click and hold down the mouse button when the magnifying glass is on

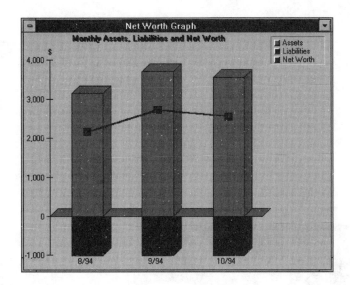

Net Worth
graph
Figure 10-7.

the Cardinal Bank portion of the QuickZoom pie chart, the dollar
amount of the account appears on your screen. When you release the
mouse button, the amount disappears.

10

T I P S

TAX AND ACCOUNTING TIPS

Your accounting records are the pulse of your business. They can tell you and your creditors how your business is doing. It is important that you maintain accurate records and follow good accounting practices to safeguard the assets of your firm. The tips that follow relate to maintaining your records as accurately as possible and maintaining good accounting controls. There are also some specific tax tips of interest to many small businesses.

1. As an employer, you can provide a per diem allowance to employees that is non-taxable as long as it is not in excess of the rate the federal government allows its own employees. This rate is to include lodging, meals, and incidentals. In 1993, the rate ranged from $67 to $174, with rates set individually for over 500 localities.

2. If your business receives cash, you must record the amount immediately. Encourage customers to report incorrect receipts by offering a free good or service if the receipt is not correct.

3. Consider hiring a shopping service to check on employees if you suspect that all sales are not being recorded.

4. Have an employee receiving goods verify that the shipment is complete before he or she authorizes a cash disbursement.

5. If you establish a petty cash fund for convenience, use a petty cash voucher for each disbursement, and require that a bill or receipt be submitted along with it.

6. Assets may be written down ahead of schedule if they have become obsolete and if you must replace them to remain competitive. Take the item's accumulated depreciation into account when determining the write-off value.

7. Determine the most economic order quantity for items purchased regularly, taking into account the amount of usage in a given time period, the quantity discount, storage costs, and order processing costs.

8. A sole proprietorship is not taxed as a business; instead, its profits appear on the owner's tax return.

9. An S corporation does not pay a corporate tax. It operates much like a partnership from a tax standpoint.

10. Accrual accounting methods are required for C Corporations and partnerships.

11. Tax laws are revised each year. To keep up with these changes, you are likely to need the services of a good accountant.

12. Your accountant can help you establish some quick ratios to monitor the liquidity of your business and look at other measures of risk or success.

13. Keep in mind that the cap amount and percentage for FICA and Medicare are not necessarily the same each year.

14. Involve employees in budget planning and performance monitoring.

15. Instituting a voucher system for disbursements and requiring several signatures can help control disbursements.

16. Reconcile all bank and credit card accounts monthly so that you will spot problems immediately.

17. Entertainment expenses for business that meet all qualifying rules are only 80% deductible.

18. A credit card purchase is treated as an expense on the date of purchase, not the date of payment, even if you maintain your business books on a cash basis.

19. If you keep accurate records of business mileage you can deduct .28 cents a mile. This is likely to be much better than accumulating gasoline and toll expenses, because the IRS includes vehicle depreciation in their rate.

20. In order to deduct business mileage, you must be able to provide a record showing the date and purpose of each business trip and the mileage traveled, as well as the total mileage for the vehicle during the year.

21. You may deduct business gifts to clients in full if their cost does not exceed $25 per recipient per year.

22. The following information is needed to substantiate a business gift: the recipient, the cost, the date given, the purpose of the gift, and a description of the gift.

23. IRS publication 463 will provide valuable information on travel, entertainment, and gifts. It is available by calling the IRS at (800) 829-3676.

24. Business startup expenses are those expenses incurred before the business is actually established and producing income. These costs can be amortized over a five-year period.

25. Advertising expenses are deductible as long as they promote your business products, services, or name.

26. A gift of tickets to an event must be treated as entertainment if you accompany the customer to the event, and is therefore subject to the 20% reduction rule. If you do not accompany the recipient, and the tickets are $25 or less, they can be treated as a gift.

27. Meal expenses incurred while traveling on business are subject to an 80% limitation.

28. Travel expense restrictions are stricter for foreign travel. If you spend extra days sightseeing, you will need to allocate your travel expense based on the number of business and personal days included on the trip.

29. If you convert personal assets to business assets, the cost basis for depreciation will be either the cost or the market value, depending on which is lower.

30. Requirements for qualifying for the home office deduction are stringent; they require that a part of your residence be used exclusively for your business, and as the main place where you conduct your business.

31. Tax rules let you take advantage of low Saturday night stayover airfares by allowing you to deduct the extra cost of your weekend hotel room for this period.

32. If you switch between calendar and fiscal year reporting, you must file a separate, special return for the period that is less than a full year long.

33. You are much more likely to deduct all the expenses you are entitled to if you record these expenses in Quicken as soon as they occur.

34. The cost of a company cafeteria and any meals and beverages made available to employees is deductible.

35. Both voluntary and involuntary business losses may be deductible.

36. If you recover a business debt that you have written off, you must increase your income by the amount of this recovery.

37. If you are uncertain whether to treat an individual as an employee or an independent contractor, submit FORM SS-8 to the IRS to get a ruling.

38. Inventory is typically valued either at cost, or at the lower of cost or market value.

39. If you own multiple businesses, it may be possible to use cash basis accounting for one business and accrual basis accounting for the other.

40. Unless all of your income comes from wages, you must keep accounting records that are acceptable to the IRS. All income and expenses are among the items that must be accurately documented.

41. In most cases, you can deduct the inventories donated to charity at their cost.

42. Accounts receivable, cash, securities, and equipment are not considered inventory.

43. Wages paid for overtime and bonus awards are subject to withholding.

44. If you want to find out more about business report requirements for the IRS, call (800) 829-3676 and ask for publication 937, "Business Reporting."

45. Income taxes withheld must be paid to a Federal Reserve Bank, and submitted with Form 8109 or your own personalized forms.

46. You must report the amount of tips your employees report to you on their W-2 forms.

47. You may have a Taxpayer Identification Number for personal use and an Employer Identification Number for business use.

48. If you obtain a filing extension, it does not grant you a tax payment extension.

49. A corporation conforming to a calendar year must file a return by March 15 of the following year.

50. Keep a log in your car to note business mileage right away. Otherwise, you are likely to forget to record some of it and not claim all of your allowable deduction.

51. If you purchase a few business items along with personal supplies, it is preferable to get two separate receipts. If all items are on one receipt, note immediately each item that you purchase for business.

52. Consider employer-paid parking a non-taxable fringe benefit.

53. Before writing off a bad debt, make sure you have documented collection efforts.

54. Utilize Quicken's budget features to put together a budget plan. A plan is essential to monitoring your progress.

55. Analyze budget results on a regular basis, and make decisions about bringing costs into line where necessary.

56. Engage in tax planning to control the timing of revenues and expenses, when possible.

57. Consult with your accountant to make decisions about your fiscal or calendar year, cash versus accrual accounting basis, and your inventory valuation method.

58. Carefully evaluate a business location as well as the business before buying. Your business can fail just by being in the wrong location.

59. Always keep your personal and business accounts separate.

60. Maintain records of your daily bank balances.

61. Take collection action on slow payers at least weekly.

62. Check to see how the profitability of your business compares with that of similar businesses.

63. Maintain all of your business receipts for a minimum of three years.

64. Currently, it is necessary to pay 90% of your tax liability in estimated taxes by the year's end to avoid a penalty. Congress is considering legislation that would allow you to base your estimated payments on last year's income. A return prepared according to this method would make it easier for those whose incomes fluctuate widely to pay the correct amount of estimated taxes.

65. Inspect shipments as they are received, and establish reorder points for inventory to avoid shortages.

66. Cross-train employees who handle critical financial functions. You can have periodic duty rotations to prevent fraudulent behavior and maintain some measure of protection if you lose one of your employees.

67. Start organizing your tax records early.

68. If you are on a fiscal-year reporting basis, schedule the end of your year during a slow time.

69. Try to have inventories at their lowest possible level at year's end to lower the cost of taking a physical inventory.

70. Never write checks with erasable ink.

71. The IRS has special tax publications for specific types of business, such as farms. Call (800) 829-3676 to see if they have anything specific to your needs.

72. Return damaged goods for credit immediately.

73. Use a copier key, and require employees to log the purpose of copy work. Also keep a log of all long distance calls.

74. Use different colored checks for different accounts.

75. Consider using a separate checking account for payroll; this will help you increase control over one of your major expenditures.

76. Consider writing payroll checks yourself to oversee this task closely.

77. If you do not have time to attend to payroll yourself, consider using a payroll service.

78. Deposit cash receipts daily.

79. Check with your accountant to see if any of your equipment purchases qualifies for a section 179 direct deduction.

80. Require that your personnel take annual vacations.

81. Use preprinted, prenumbered business forms for control purposes.

82. If you are operating a business from your home and qualify for a home office deduction, your can allocate heat and electric costs based on square footage.

83. Improve your controls by having one person write checks and another reconcile the checking account statement.

84. You must issue 1099s to all subcontractors whom you pay $600 or more.

85. Revenue earned from foreign sales is taxable in this country.

86. You must withhold federal and state tax, as well as FICA and Medicare, from part-time employees.

87. Interview several accountants before making your selection. You want to select one who not only has the right credentials, but with whom you feel you can communicate and work.

88. When selecting an accountant, check to ensure that he or she is a member of the state professional society and the American Accounting Institute. Members of these organizations have to comply with continuing education requirements.

89. Keep in mind that self-employed individuals must pay twice the Medicare and FICA on their earnings as an employee.

90. Be sure to discuss fees with your accountant up-front.

91. Enter your accounting transactions daily.

92. Prepare and distribute W-2s for all your employees by January 31.

93. Depreciate part of your home if you qualify for a home office deduction.

94. Check with your state and local authorities to see if you are required to collect sales tax on goods and services sold.

95. If you are planning to claim a car as a business expense, consult IRS publication 917, "Business Use of a Car."

96. If you are self-employed, remember that 50% of your Social Security payments in your own behalf are deductible on your tax return.

97. If you are confused about depreciation, call the IRS at (800) 829-3676 and order publications 534, "Depreciation," and 946, "How to Begin Depreciating Your Property."

98. There are some attractive retirement plan options for the self-employed. After 1993 the cap amount on these will change to a lower figure. Consult IRS publication 560, "Retirement Plans for the Self-Employed," for more information.

99. If you currently handle your business taxes yourself, research different tax software packages that might make your job easier. If you are a sole proprietor, you are likely to find that the TurboTax product will meet all of your needs, including Schedule C.

100. Obtain a vendor's license before attempting to sell merchandise.

101. Consult IRS publication 544 for help with the disposition of assets.

T
I
P
S

PART

3

BUSINESS
APPLICATIONS

CHAPTER

11

SETTING UP QUICKEN FOR YOUR BUSINESS

Many small business owners find that the Quicken system of record-keeping can improve the quality of financial information used in making business decisions. You can use Quicken to record business transactions in your check register while maintaining cost and depreciation records for assets in other registers. You can also use Quicken to budget your cash flow, track the cost of jobs in progress, monitor and record your payroll, and generate summary tax information to assist you in preparing your tax returns. If you are a building contractor, you can track the costs incurred on various jobs as they progress through construction. If you provide landscaping services, you can track the costs incurred for each job and prepare Summary reports to determine the profits generated by each job. If you are an author, you can use Quicken to monitor royalties by publisher and record the costs you incurred while writing.

Although Quicken improves your ability to record and monitor your business' financial transactions, it may not eliminate the need for accounting services. There are important tax issues that affect the business transactions you record. In addition, you may want your accountant to establish the hierarchy of categories you use to record transactions. This hierarchy, used to categorize all transactions, is called a *chart of accounts*. Your accountant should help establish the structure for your chart of accounts, which will ensure the information is organized to reduce the time required for other services, such as year-end tax preparation, that the accountant will continue to supply. This is particularly important if you will be recording business expenses in both your personal and business checking accounts.

The first section of this book introduced you to Quicken's basic features. If you completed the exercises in Chapters 6 through 10, you built upon the basic skills by recording split transactions, such as mortgage payments allocated between principal and interest, and by memorizing recurring transactions. In those chapters you also used Quicken to prepare and monitor budgets, collect tax-related transactions, and prepare custom reports. In the remaining chapters you look at some of these concepts again, from a business perspective. If you plan to use Quicken for both home and business use, you may find it beneficial to read through the earlier chapters, if you haven't done so, rather than moving directly to business transactions.

You will find many tips in the following chapters to help you avoid some of the problems encountered by small businesses. In addition, the special section "Ten Common Reasons for Business Failure" in this chapter identifies some of the pitfalls to tell you which ones Quicken can help you avoid.

This chapter is longer than the others since there are many decisions you need to make as you set up Quicken for your business. You also need to develop a number of basic skills to apply Quicken to all aspects of your business. The first step is to consider some alternatives. The next sections provide an overview of two important decisions that you must make before you use Quicken for your business. If you need additional guidance, consult with your accountant to be certain your information will be in the format you need for your entire business year.

Ten Common Reasons For Business Failure

Many of the new businesses that start each year fail. To improve your chances of success, you will want to look at some of the more common reasons for business failures and address these areas to prevent problems in your own business. Quicken can help you address of some of these common problems.

Insufficient Capital

Many businesses fail because the owners don't properly plan for the capital they will need to get the business started, and they don't seek outside financing, if needed, before starting. Quicken can help you put together a budget and plan your cash flow needs.

Pricing Doesn't Cover Costs

Many small business owners don't properly evaluate their costs, and they set prices too low to cover all thier costs. The need to pay a variety of taxes, cover depreciation expenses, and pay for expensive repairs are often overlooked when determining pricing for services. Many individuals considering self-employment don't realize that their FICA and Medicare payments will be double what they were when they were working for someone else. Quicken can help you get a handle on all your costs so you can price your services appropriately.

High Fixed Costs

Fixed costs must be paid even in months when sales are low, placing a strain on a small business. Quicken can help you take a look at your fixed costs for rent, car or truck payments, other loan obligations, telephone service, utilities, and fixed salary costs. With the information Quicken can provide, you are better equipped to make decisions to help you lower fixed costs.

Inadequate Accounting Information and Controls

Shoebox record keeping will not serve you well if you are trying to keep your business afloat. Quicken's organizational capabilities make it easy to see which jobs were profitable ventures. Quicken's graph features let you get a quick picture of this information. Quicken also offers some accounting controls such as password protection.

11

Employee Theft

Inadequate monitoring of employee activities and lack of controls can cause a business owner to inadvertently overlook theft until it is too late. Quicken provides reports and a framework for you to implement controls to help you protect your business assets.

Poor Location

There has to be a need for your product at the location you select. If buyers are unlikely to visit the area selected, your business can be doomed to failure from the beginning. The Small Business Administration and SCORE (Service Corps of Retired Executives) can provide some help in overcoming problems with site selection.

Lack of Owner Commitment

Many new business owners don't realize that they'll have to put in more time in their own business than they did when working for someone else. If family commitments and other responsibilities do not permit this, the business may be in trouble.

No Demand for Your Product

If there is no demand for your product or you can't generate the needed demand, you can't generate the revenue you need to succeed. To overcome this potential problem, you need to invest in adequate market research before starting your business. You must also realize that attempting to generate needed demand can be an expensive venture. Quicken can help you budget advertising and marketing costs.

Lack of Business Knowledge

Knowing the ropes of any business can be an important first step to success. Although you can succeed without it, your chances for success are enhanced with it. The Small Business Administration provides some low-cost seminars that can help you.

Poor Timing

Even the best conceived idea with adequate funding, a good location, and owner commitment and knowledge can fail due to bad timing. A strong economic decline just as you start your business can cause significant problems for the business. Unfortunately, this is not something which can necessarily be planned for.

You need to check one preference setting before beginning the activities in this chapter. To do so, select Preferences from the Edit menu, and then select QuickFill. Make sure that the Automatic Memorization of New Transactions check box is selected. Then select OK and Done. The effects of this feature are explained in the "Memorized Transactions" section later in this chapter.

Cash Versus Accrual Accounting

The first decision you need to make is the timing of recording financial transactions. You can record a transaction as soon as you know that it will occur, or you can wait until cash changes hands between the parties involved in the transaction. The former alternative is accrual-basis accounting, and the latter is cash-basis accounting. There is a third method, called modified-cash-basis accounting, that is discussed shortly. If your business is organized as a corporation, you must use the accrual method.

Most small businesses use the cash basis because it corresponds to their tax-reporting needs and because the financial reports prepared provide information summarizing the cash-related activities of the business. With *cash-basis* accounting, you report income when you receive cash from customers for services you provide. For example, if you are in the plumbing business, you recognize income when a customer makes a payment for services. You might provide the services in December and not receive the customer's check until January. In this case, you record the income in January, when you receive and deposit the customer's check. Similarly, you recognize your expenses when you write your checks for the costs you incur. Thus, if you order supplies in December but don't pay the bill until January, you deduct the cost in January when you write a check to the supplier. Briefly, with a purely cash-basis accounting system, you recognize income when you receive cash and recognize expenses when you pay for expenses incurred for business purposes.

With the *accrual-basis* approach, you record your revenues and expenses when you provide services to your customers, regardless of when the cash flow occurs. Using the plumbing example from the preceding paragraph, you recognize the income from the plumbing services in December, when you provide the services to the customer, even though the cash is not received until the next year. Likewise, if you purchase supplies in December and pay for them in January, the cost of the supplies is recorded in December, not in January when they are actually paid for. The same information is recorded under both methods.

11

The basic difference between cash-basis and accrual-basis accounting is what accountants call *timing differences*. When a cash basis is used, the receipt of cash determines when the transaction is recorded. When the accrual basis is used, the time the services are provided determines when the revenue and expenses are recorded.

A third method of reporting business revenues and expenses is the *modified-cash-basis* approach. This method uses the cash basis as described but modifies it to report depreciation on certain assets over a number of years. In this case, you must spread the cost of trucks, computer equipment, office furniture, and similar assets over the estimated number of years they will be used to generate income for your business. The Internal Revenue Service has rules for determining the life of an asset. In addition, the tax laws allow you to immediately deduct the first $10,000 of the acquisition cost of certain qualified assets each year without worrying about depreciation. Once again, these are areas where your accountant can be of assistance in setting up your Quicken accounts.

Whether you use the cash, accrual, or modified cash basis in recording your transactions is determined by a number of factors. Some of the considerations are listed in the special section "Cash Versus Accrual Methods" in this chapter.

Since many small businesses use the modified cash basis of recording revenues and expenses, this method is illustrated in all the examples in Chapters 11 through 15.

Establishing Your Chart of Accounts

You can use the basic set of categories that Quicken provides to categorize your business transactions, or you can create a new set. Each of the existing categories is named in a way similar to the categories in earlier chapters. For example, the category name Ads has the description Advertising. These organizational units are called categories in Quicken despite the fact that you may have been referring to them as accounts in your manual system.

If you do not have an existing chart of accounts, making a few modifications to Quicken's standard category options is the best approach. Quicken's category names are suitable for most businesses. Later in this chapter, you learn to add accounts of your own.

If you have an existing set of accounts, you will want to retain this structure for consistency. Many businesses assign a number to each category of income or expense—for example, a business might use 4001 as the account

Cash Versus Accrual Methods

✦ *Tax requirements* You must decide what your tax reporting obligations are and whether those requirements alone will dictate the methods you use for financial reporting. For most small businesses, tax requirements are the overriding factor to consider. For instance, if inventories are part of your business, you must use the accrual method for revenues and purchases. If inventories are not part of your business, you will probably find it best and easiest to use the cash basis of accounting.

✦ *Users of the financial reports* The people who use your financial reports can have a significant influence on your reporting decisions. For example, do you have external users such as banks and other creditors? If so, you may find that they require special reports and other financial information that will influence how you set up your accounting and reporting system.

✦ *Size and type of business activity* The kind of business you have influences the type of financial reports you need to prepare and the method of accounting you will adopt. Are you in a service, retail, or manufacturing business? Manufacturing concerns should use the accrual method since they have sales that are billed and collected over weeks or even months and they carry inventories of goods. Retail stores such as small groceries should also use the accrual method of accounting, at least for sales and purchases, since they have inventories that affect the financial reports they prepare. On the other hand, a small landscaping business should probably use the cash basis since it has no inventory and the majority of the costs associated with the business are payroll and other costs generally paid close to the time the services are performed. If this business uses one or more pieces of equipment which represent a significant investment, it should use the modified cash basis to record depreciation on the property.

11

number for book sales. The business might use the first two digits of the number to group asset, liability, income, and expense accounts together. If you use this type of structure, you need to invest a little more time initially to establish your chart of accounts. You can delete the entries in the existing list of categories and then add new categories, or you can edit the existing categories one by one. The category names in your Category List (chart of accounts) might be numbers, such as 4001 or 5010, and the corresponding descriptions, such as 4001—Book Sales, and 5010—Freight. When you are finished, each category will contain your account number and each description will contain both the account number and some text describing the income or expense recorded in the category. You should work through all the examples in this chapter before setting up your own categories.

A Quick Look at the Business Used in the Examples

An overview of the business used for the examples in Chapters 11 through 15 will help you understand some of the selections you will make in the exercises. The business is run by an individual and is organized as a sole proprietorship. The individual running the business is married and must file a Form 1040 showing both business income and the W-2 income earned by the individual's spouse. Income categories in addition to the standard categories Quicken provides are needed for the different types of income generated. Since the company in the example offers services rather than merchandise, the income categories are appropriate for a service-type business. You can also use Quicken for retail or wholesale businesses that sell goods, and you can use Quicken for any organization, including sole proprietorships, partnerships, and small corporations. Look at the special section "Business Organization Options" in this chapter for a definition of these three types of businesses.

The example business is based in the individual's home, which necessitates splitting some expenses, such as utilities and mortgage interest, between home and business categories. Other expenses, such as the purchase of office equipment, are business expenses. A number of expenses incurred by the business don't have appropriate entries in the Category List Quicken provides; you will have to add these categories.

The example business in this book is a little more complicated than a business run from outside the home that has no transactions split between business and personal expenses. If you have a clear separation, you can simply establish a file for all your business accounts and another file for your personal transactions. The example used here includes separate checking

Business Organization Options

You can choose from the following organization options when you set up your business:

◆ *Sole proprietorship* A sole proprietorship provides no separation between the owner and the business. The debts of the business are the personal liabilities of the owner. The profits of the business are included on the owner's tax return since the business does not pay taxes on profits directly. This form of business organization is the simplest.

◆ *Partnership* A partnership is a business defined as a relationship between two or more parties. Each person in the partnership is taxed as an individual for his or her share of the profits. A partnership agreement defines the contributions of each member and the distribution of the profits.

◆ *Corporation* A corporation is an independent business entity. The owners of the corporation are separate from the corporation and do not personally assume the debt of the corporation. This is referred to as *limited liability*. The corporation is taxed on its profits and can distribute the remaining profits to owners as dividends. The owners are taxed on these dividends, resulting in the so-called "double tax" that occurs with the corporate structure. Unlike sole proprietorship and partnership businesses, corporations pay salaries to the owners.

◆ *S Corporation* An S corporation is a special form of corporation that avoids the double tax problem of a regular corporation. A number of strict rules govern when an S corporation can be set up. Some of the limitations are that only one class of stock is permitted and that there is an upper limit of 35 shareholders.

11

accounts for business and personal records, but both accounts are placed in one file.

The use of separate accounts should be considered almost mandatory. All business income should be deposited into a separate account, and all expenses that are completely business related should be paid from this account. Anyone who has experienced an IRS audit can testify to the necessity of having solid documentation for business transactions. One part of that documentation is the maintenance of a business checking account and supporting receipts for your expenses and revenue. If you maintain a separate business account, your bank statement provides the supporting details for business transactions in a clear and concise manner that supports your other documentation of business activities. If your business is so small that it is not feasible to establish and maintain two checking accounts, you need to be particularly careful when recording entries in your Quicken register.

Quicken Files

When you began using Quicken, you created a file for your data. This file was named QDATA, and Quicken created four files on your hard disk to manage all the accounts and the information within them. You can use this file to record all your transactions if you decide to handle your business and personal financial transactions in a single file.

In the first five chapters, you worked with only one account in QDATA. If you completed Chapters 6 through 10, you learned that it was possible to create additional accounts such as a separate savings account and an Investment account. You can also create accounts for credit cards, cash, assets, and liabilities. You created the PERSONAL file in Chapter 6 to organize all the personal accounts, and you created the INVEST file in Chapter 9 to hold the example Investment account.

You could enter the transactions in this chapter in one of these files by setting up a new account. However, you want to set up new transactions in a separate file, so you should create a new file.

Adding a New File

If you completed Chapters 1 through 9, you already have the QDATA, PERSONAL, and INVEST files, which contain all the transactions entered in the first two sections of this book. If you skipped Chapters 6 through 10, you have only the QDATA file. In this section, you learn how to create a new file and create accounts within it. If you're running short on hard disk space, you might need to delete these files. You can delete them from within Quicken or you can use the Windows File Manager to delete them when you are finished creating the new file.

You will create a file called BUSINESS and initially set up a business checking account, a personal checking account, and an asset account. The asset account will be used to record information about equipment. Later in this chapter, you will establish other accounts for this file. Follow these steps to set up the new file and add the first three accounts to it:

1. Select New from the File menu.

   Quicken displays the dialog box for setting up a new file or account.

2. Select New File, and select OK.

   Quicken opens the dialog box for creating a new file.

3. Check the location of your data files, and make changes to reference a valid drive or directory, if a change is required, by using the Drives or Directories boxes.

4. Type **BUSINESS** in the File Name text box.

   Quicken creates four DOS files with four different filename extensions from the name you type in the File Name text box. You must provide a valid filename of no more than eight characters. The filename must not include spaces or special symbols.

5. Select both the Home and Business check boxes.

6. Select OK to create the new file.

Since this is a new file, there are no accounts in it. The Select Account Type dialog box shown in Figure 11-1 appears to allow you to set up a new account. Leave your screen as it is for a few minutes while you explore some new account options.

Adding Accounts to the New File

Quicken makes it easy to create multiple accounts. All the accounts here will be created in the same file so that you will be able to print one report for all

11

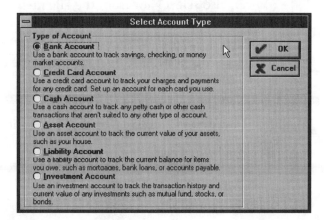

Selecting the type for the new account
Figure 11-1.

of them as well as print reports for individual accounts. Quicken sets up an account register for each account you create.

Savings accounts, Investment accounts, Cash accounts, Asset accounts, Liability accounts, and Credit Card accounts are all possible additions. Savings accounts and Investment accounts should definitely be kept separate from your checking account since you will be monitoring both the growth and balance in these accounts separately. As mentioned earlier, separate business and personal checking accounts are another good idea.

You can set up Quicken accounts to conform to the needs of your business. In this section you add the first few accounts. In later chapters, you establish additional accounts to monitor other business activities. From the Select Account Type dialog box, follow these steps to create a new account:

1. Select Bank Account for the account type, and select OK.

2. Type **ANB Business** in the Account Name text box.

    "ANB" represents the bank name, and "Business" indicates that this account is the business checking account. Although you could use Cardinal Bank again in this new file, ANB (for American National Bank) will be used to eliminate confusion with the earlier examples.

3. Type **4000** in the Balance text box.

4. Enter **1/1/94** in the as of text box by typing or using the drop-down calendar.

5. Type **Business Checking** in the Description text box, and select OK.

    The ANB Business account register appears in the Quicken window. Now you will establish an account for your personal checking. Using separate accounts is important to maintain accurate records.

6. Select Create New Account from the Activities menu.

    You can also select New from the File menu, select New Account and OK, and continue with the following steps.

7. Select Bank Account and OK.

8. Type **ANB Personal** in the Account Name text box.

9. Type **2500** in the Balance text box.

10. Enter **1/1/94** in the as of text box.

11. Type **Personal Checking** in the Description text box.

12. Select OK.

13. Select New from the File menu.

14. Select New Account and OK.

15. Select Asset Account and OK.

16. Type **Equipment** in the Account Name text box.

    This account is used to record financial transactions affecting the equipment you use in your business.

17. Type **0** in the Balance text box.

    You enter the value of these assets later in this chapter.

18. Enter **1/1/94** in the as of text box.

19. Type **Capital Equipment** in the Description text box.

20. Select OK.

You have now created a new file and three accounts for organizing personal and business transactions.

Changing the Active File

In the last exercise you created a new file. You can work in any file at any time, and can work with any account within a file. To change from the BUSINESS file to the QDATA file, follow these steps:

1. Select Open from the File menu.

2. Select QDATA.QDT from the File Name list box.

3. Select OK.

The QDATA file is now active. The windows that were displayed when you closed QDATA by opening a new file are displayed. If you go to the register or Write Checks screen, you'll find that the 1st U.S. Bank account is active. Change back to the BUSINESS file and open the account for ANB Business.

Backing Up a File

It may seem a little early to be discussing backups since you haven't even entered data in this new file. However, backing up your file is important, and you'll want to get into the habit of backing up your files immediately after you create them. You should regularly back up the data managed by the Quicken system. Regular backups allow you to recover all your entries in the event of a hard disk failure since you can use your copy to restore all the entries. You need a blank formatted disk to record the backup information the first time. Subsequent backups can be made on this disk without reformatting it.

Creating Backup Files

Quicken provides a Backup and Restore feature that allows you to safeguard the investment of time you have made in entering your data. You can back

11

up all your account files, or you can back up specific files by selecting the
Backup option from the File menu. Follow these steps to back up the current file:

1. Select Backup from the File menu.

2. Place your blank formatted disk in drive A, and then select OK.

   If you want to back up another Quicken file, select the Select from List
   option button before selecting OK. Then select the file you want to back
   up, and select OK again. If you want to back up your file to a drive other
   than A, select that drive from the Backup Drive drop-down list box.

3. When Quicken displays the successful backup message, select OK to
   acknowledge the completion of the backup.

4. Select the ANB Business register window, shown in Figure 11-2.

NOTE: If your hard disk ever fails, you can re-create your data by
selecting Restore from the File menu to copy your backup file to your
directory. You should schedule backups on a regular basis to minimize the
risk of data loss.

Customizing Categories

When you set up the new BUSINESS file, you selected both Home and
Business as category options. This selection provides access to the more than
60 category choices shown in Table 11-1. You can see from this table that
some categories are listed as expenses and others as income. Notice that
some of the expense categories have more detailed subcategories beneath
them. You learn how to create additional subcategories in the "Using

Register for
the new
account
Figure 11-2.

![Bank Account: ANB Business - Business Checking register window showing columns for Date, Num, Payee, Memo, Category, Payment, Clr, Deposit, Balance. Row 1/1/94 Opening Balance [ANB Business] x 4,000 00 4,000 00. Buttons: Insert, Delete, Copy, Paste, Report, Close, Record, Restore, Splits. 1-Line Display, Button Bar checkboxes. Current Balance: 0.00, Ending Balance: 4,000.00]

Subcategories" section later in this chapter. Note the column in the table that shows you which categories are tax related.

Category	Description	Tax Rel	Type
Bonus	Bonus Income	*	Inc
CPP	Canadian Pension	*	Inc
Div Income	Dividend Income	*	Inc
Gift Received	Gift Received	*	Inc
Int Inc	Interest Income	*	Inc
Invest Inc	Investment Income	*	Inc
Old Age Pension	Old Age Pension	*	Inc
Other Inc	Other Income	*	Inc
Rent Income	Rent Income	*	Inc
Salary	Salary Income	*	Inc
Ads	Advertising	*	Expns
Auto	Automobile Expenses	*	Expns
Fuel	Auto Fuel		Sub
Loan	Auto Loan Payment		Sub
Service	Auto Service		Sub
Bank Chrg	Bank Charge		Expns
Bus Insurance	Insurance (not health)	*	Expns
Bus Utilities	Water, Gas, Electric	*	Expns
Business Tax	Taxes & Licenses	*	Expns
Car	Car & Truck	*	Expns
Charity	Charitable Donations	*	Expns
Cash	Cash Contributions	*	Sub
Non-Cash	Non-Cash Contributions	*	Sub
Childcare	Childcare Expense		Expns
Christmas	Christmas Expenses		Expns
Clothing	Clothing		Expns

Home and Business Category Options
Table 11-1.

11

Category	Description	Tax Rel	Type
Commission	Commissions	*	Expns
Dining	Dining Out		Expns
Dues	Dues		Expns
Education	Education		Expns
Entertain	Entertainment		Expns
Freight	Freight	*	Expns
Gifts	Gift Expenses		Expns
Groceries	Groceries		Expns
GST	Goods and Services Tax	*	Expns
Home Rpair	Home Repair & Maint.		Expns
Household	Household Misc. Exp		Expns
Housing	Housing		Expns
Insurance	Insurance		Expns
Int Exp	Interest Expense	*	Expns
Int Paid	Interest Paid	*	Expns
Invest Exp	Investment Expense	*	Expns
L&P Fees	Legal & Prof. Fees	*	Expns
Meals & Entertn	Meals & Entertainment	*	Expns
Medical	Medical & Dental	*	Expns
Doctor	Doctor & Dental Visits	*	Sub
Medicine	Medicine & Drugs	*	Sub
Misc	Miscellaneous		Expns
Mort Int	Mortgage Interest Exp	*	Expns
Office	Office Expenses	*	Expns
Other Exp	Other Expense	*	Expns
Recreation	Recreation Expense		Expns
Rent on Equip	Rent-Vehicle,mach,equip	*	Expns
Rent Paid	Rent Paid	*	Expns

Home and
Business
Category
Options
(continued)
Table 11-1.

Category	Description	Tax Rel	Type
Repairs	Repairs	*	Expns
Returns	Returns & Allowances	*	Expns
RRSP	Reg Retirement Sav Plan		Expns
Subscriptions	Subscriptions	*	Expns
Supplies	Supplies	*	Expns
Supplies Bus	Supplies	*	Expns
Tax	Taxes	*	Expns
Fed	Federal Tax	*	Sub
Medicare	Medicare Tax	*	Sub
Other	Misc. Taxes	*	Sub
Prop	Property Tax	*	Sub
Soc Sec	Soc Sec Tax	*	Sub
State	State Tax	*	Sub
Tax Spouse	Spouse's Tax	*	Expns
Fed	Federal Tax	*	Sub
Medicare	Medicare Tax	*	Sub
Other	Misc. Taxes	*	Sub
Prop	Property Tax	*	Sub
Soc Sec	Soc Sec Tax	*	Sub
State	State Tax	*	Sub
Telephone	Telephone Expense		Expns
Travel	Travel Expense	*	Expns
UIC	Unemploy. Ins. Commission	*	Expns
Utilities	Water, Gas, Electric		Expns
Gas & Electric	Gas and Electricity		Sub
Water	Water		Sub
Wages	Wages & Job Credits	*	Expns

Home and
Business
Category
Options
(continued)
Table 11-1.

11

Editing the Existing Category List

You can change the name of any existing category, change its classification as income, expense, or subcategory, and change your assessment of its being tax related. To make a change to a category, follow these steps:

1. Select the Cat List icon from the Iconbar or choose Category and Transfer from the Lists menu to display the Category & Transfer List.
2. Move to the category you want to change.
3. Select Edit to edit the information for the category.
4. Change the settings you wish to alter.
5. Select OK to complete the changes.

If you change the name of the category, Quicken changes the category's name in any transactions that have already been assigned to the category.

If you need to totally restructure the categories before you begin using them, you may find it easier to delete the old categories and add new ones by following the instructions in the next section. To delete a category, follow these steps:

1. Select the Cat List icon or select Category and Transfer from the Lists menu to display the Category & Transfer List.
2. Move to the category you want to delete.
3. Select Del to delete the information in the category.

   You should not delete categories already assigned to transactions. If you do, you delete the category part of the transactions in your register. Delete categories before you start recording transactions.
4. Select OK to complete the changes.

Adding Categories

You can add categories to provide additional options specific to your needs. Each type of business will probably have some unique categories of income or expenses. For the example in this chapter, both income and expense category additions are needed.

The business in this example has three sources of income: consulting fees, royalties, and income earned for writing articles. It would be inappropriate to use the salary category for this income since that category should be reserved for income earned from a regular employer (reported on Form W-2 at the end of the year). You could use the Gross Sales category to record the various types of income for the business. Another solution would be to create new categories for each income source. For the examples in this chapter, you'll use three new income categories.

Many of the existing expense categories are suitable for recording business expenses, but for this example additional expense categories are needed. Equipment maintenance, computer supplies, and overnight mail service categories are needed. Although a category already exists for freight, a more specific postage category is also needed. New categories are not needed to record computer and office equipment and furniture purchases. These will be handled through an "other asset" type account, with the specific purchase listed in the Payee field of the transaction.

You can add a new category by entering it in the Category field when you record a transaction in a register or on the Write Checks screen. If you press Tab to move to the next field, Quicken indicates that the category does not exist in the current list. You are then given the choice of selecting a category already in the list or adding the new category to the list. You would choose to add it, just as you did with the category for auto loans in Chapter 4, "Reconciling Your Quicken Register."

If you have a number of categories to add, it is simpler to add them before starting data entry. To add the new categories needed for the exercises in this chapter, follow these steps:

1. Select Preferences from the Edit menu or select the Prefs icon, and then select General.

2. Check the Use Tax schedules with Categories check box to make sure it's selected. If it isn't, select it.

    You will assign the tax-related categories you create in this example to particular lines of tax forms. This allows you to easily create reports that will help you fill out your tax forms, as discussed in Chapter 14, "Organizing Tax Information and Other Year-End Needs."

3. Select OK and Done.

4. Select the Cat List icon, or select Category and Transfer from the Lists menu.

    The Category & Transfer List window opens.

5. Select New.

    Quicken opens the Set Up Category dialog box to allow you to enter a new category:

11

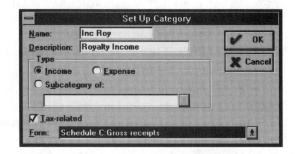

The dialog box shown here contains entries for a new royalty income category called Inc Roy. Note that the first part of the category name is Inc. If you begin all your income categories this way, you can later select all income categories by entering **Inc** in your report filter window. (See Chapter 3, "Quicken Reports.")

6. Type **Inc Roy** in the Name text box.

7. Type **Royalty Income** in the Description text box.

8. Select the Income option button.

9. Select the Tax-related check box.

10. Select Schedule C:Gross Receipts from the Form drop-down list box.

11. Select OK to have Quicken return you to the Category & Transfer List window.

12. Repeat steps 3 through 8 for each of the categories that follow; then return to the register window.

Name:	**Inc Cons**
Description:	**Consulting Income**
Type:	Income
Tax-related:	✓
Form:	Schedule C:Gross receipts

Name:	**Inc Art**
Description:	**Article Income**
Type:	Income
Tax-related:	✓
Form:	Schedule C:Gross receipts

Name:	**Equip Mnt**
Description:	**Equipment Maintenance**
Type:	Expense
Tax-related:	✓
Form:	Schedule C:Repairs and maintenance

Name:	**Supp Comp**
Description:	**Computer Supplies**
Type:	Expense
Tax-related:	✓
Form:	Schedule C:Supplies

Name:	**Postage**
Description:	**Postage Expense**
Type:	Expense
Tax-related:	✓
Form:	Schedule C:Other business expense

Name:	**Del Overngt**
Description:	**Overnight Delivery**
Type:	Expense
Tax-related:	✓
Form:	Schedule C:Other business expense

You should feel free to customize Quicken by adding any categories you need. However, be aware that the amount of available RAM (random-access memory) in your computer limits the number of categories you can create in each Category List.

Requiring Categories for All Transactions

By default, Quicken reminds you that a category should be entered for each transaction before it is recorded. If you attempt to record a transaction without a category when this option is active, Quicken won't complete the process until you confirm that you want the transaction added without a category.

If this option has been turned off and you want to require categories for all transactions, select Preferences from the Edit menu or select the Prefs icon, and then select General. Select the Warn Before Recording Uncategorized Transactions check box. Select OK and Done to finalize the setting change. The next time you attempt to record a transaction without a category, Quicken stops to confirm your choice before saving.

11

Using Classes

Classes are another tool for organizing transactions. They allow you to define the who, when, or why of a transaction. It is important to understand that although they, too, allow you to group data, classes are distinct from categories. You will continue to use categories to provide specific information about the transactions to which they are assigned. Categories tell you what kind of income or expense a specific transaction represents. You can tell at a glance which costs are for utilities and which are for entertainment. In Summary reports, you might show transactions totaled by category.

Classes provide another way to organize your data.

Classes allow you to slice the transaction pie in a different way. They provide a different perspective on your data. For example, you can continue to organize data in categories such as Utilities or Snow Removal yet also classify it by the property requiring the service. Classes were not needed in the earlier chapters of this book since categories provide all the organization you need for very basic transactions. But if you want to combine home and business transactions in one file, classes are essential for differentiating between the two types of transactions. Here, every transaction you enter will be classified as either personal or business. Business transactions will have a class entered after the category. By omitting the class entry from personal transactions, you classify them as personal. Class assignments can be used without category assignments, but in this chapter they are used in addition to categories.

Defining Classes

Quicken does not provide a standard list of classes. As with categories, you can set up what you need before you start making entries or you can add the classes you need as you enter transactions. To assign a class while entering a transaction, you type the class name in the Category field after the category name (if one is used). You must type a slash (/) before the class name.

In this example, you create the class you need before you enter transactions (except the opening balance transaction). Follow these steps from the ANB Business account register to add a class for business:

1. Select Class from the Lists menu to open the Class List window.

2. Select New. Quicken displays the Set Up Class dialog box, shown here:

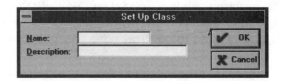

3. Type **B** in the Name text box.

   You can use a longer entry, such as Business, but Quicken has a limited amount of space to display categories, classes, and other organizational groupings, so you should keep it as short as possible.

4. Type **Business** in the Description text box, and select OK.

    Quicken adds the entry to the list in the Class List window. You could create a second class for personal transactions, but it isn't really necessary. You can consider any transactions that aren't designated class B to be personal.

5. Press (Esc) to return to the register window.

    Each new class is added to the Class List window.

REMEMBER: To create a class as you enter a transaction, simply type the category followed by a slash (/) and the class you want to use.

6. Highlight the opening balance transaction.
7. Tab to the Category field.
8. Type **/B**.
9. Select Record to record the changed entry.

Entering Transactions with Classes

You record the business transactions in the same manner you recorded earlier transactions. It is important that you remember to enter the class in the Category field. Follow these steps to begin entering business transactions:

1. Move to a blank transaction, and enter **1/2/94** in the Date field.
2. Type **Arlo, Inc.** in the Payee field.
3. Type **12500** in the Deposit field.
4. Type **Seminars conducted in 11/93** in the Memo field.
5. Type **Inc Cons/B**.

    The first part of this entry categorizes the transaction as consulting income. The slash (/) and the *B* classify the transaction as business related.

    When you start to record this category, Quicken uses its QuickFill feature to assist you in entering the transaction. In this case, Quicken supplies the category Inc Art. You can easily move to the desired category by pressing the ⬆ or ⬇ keys to move through the drop-down list of categories. If your category is not on the standard list, you need to add it as you did earlier in this chapter. You can always continue to type the entire category entry without using QuickFill's suggestions.

11

6. Select Re<u>c</u>ord to record the transaction. Your register looks like this:

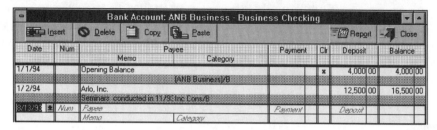

You can record an expense transaction in the ANB Business account in a similar fashion. Follow these instructions:

1. Enter **1/2/94** in the Date field.
2. Type **101** in the Num field.
3. Type **Office All** in the Payee field.
4. Type **65** in the Payment field.
5. Type **Cartridge for copier** in the Memo field.
6. Select Supplies from the drop-down list.

   As you can see, you can select the category from the list rather than typing it.
7. Type **/B**, and select Re<u>c</u>ord.

   The register window looks like Figure 11-3.

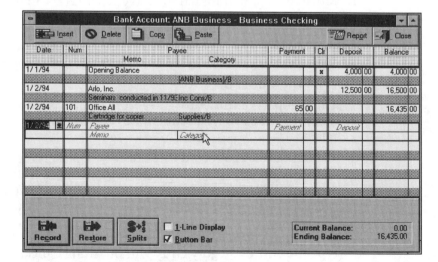

Recording business transactions in the register window

Figure 11-3.

The next transaction is for clothing. Since this is a personal expense paid with a personal check, it cannot be added to the current account. You must open the ANB Personal account for your entry. Follow these steps:

1. Select the Accts icon from the Iconbar, or select Accounts from the Lists menu.
2. Select ANB Personal.
3. Select Use.

    You can also double-click the account name in the Accounts window to open its register.

When you enter the transaction for clothing, you will not enter a class; this indicates that the clothing transaction is a personal expense. Although you could have created another class, called *P*, for personal transactions, the approach used here minimizes typing; only business transactions require the extra entry. Follow these steps to add the clothing transaction:

1. Enter **1/3/94** in the Date field.
2. Type **825** in the Num field.

    This check number is not sequential with check number 101, the last business check used, since this check is from your personal account.
3. Type **Discount Coats** in the Payee field.
4. Type **120** in the Payment field.
5. Type **New winter coat** in the Memo field.
6. Enter **Clothing** in the Category field.

    Notice that no slash (/) is used since a class is not being added for personal expenses.
7. Select Record to record the transaction. Your entries should match the ones shown here:

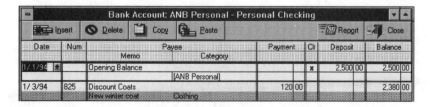

11

Splitting Transactions

Split transactions are transactions that affect more than one category or class. You decide how a transaction affects each of the categories or category/class combinations involved. If you split an expense transaction, you are saying that portions of the transaction should be considered as expenses in two different categories or classes. For example, a purchase at an office products store might include school supplies for your children and products for the office. You need to know exactly how much was spent for personal expenses and how much for business expenses in this transaction. Many expenses can be part business and part personal, especially if you operate a business from your home. Quicken allows you to allocate the amount of any transaction among different categories or classes by using the Splits dialog box. Before using the Split Transaction feature, you can define categories more precisely with the Subcategory feature, explained in the next section.

If you select Splits, Quicken displays the Splits dialog box for entries in the Category field. You can then enter different categories or classes for each part of the transaction. Even though the largest portion of the following expense was for business, it was paid with a personal check and so must be recorded in the ANB Personal account. Follow these steps to complete an entry in the ANB Personal register for a purchase at Campus Stationery, which includes both personal and office supply expenses:

1. Enter **1/3/94** in the Date field.
2. Enter **826** in the Num field.
3. Type **Campus Stationery** in the Payee field.
4. Type **82** in the Payment field.
5. Type **Calendar and computer paper** in the Memo field.
6. Select Splits to activate the Splits dialog box.
7. Enter **Supp Comp/B** in the Category field.
8. Type **Paper for laser printer** in the Memo field.

   Quicken displays the entire amount of the transaction in the Amount field.

9. Type **75.76** in the Amount field.

   Quicken subtracts this amount from $82.00 and displays the amount remaining in the Amount field for the second split.

10. Type **Misc** in the Category field.
11. Type **New calendar for kitchen** in the Memo field.

    This completes the entries since $6.24 is the cost of the calendar. Your screen should look like Figure 11-4.

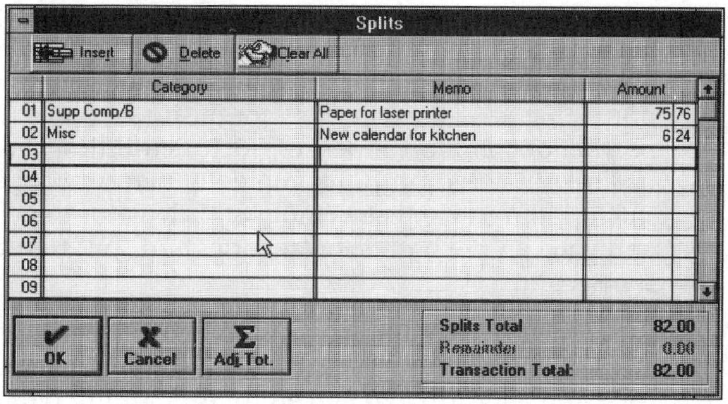

Splits dialog
box for the
Campus
Stationery
transaction
Figure 11-4.

If the total of your purchases did not equal the total you entered in the register, there would still be something left in the Remainder field. You could select Adj. Tot. to have Quicken insert the total of the splits in the register as the total amount of the transaction.

13. Select OK to close the Splits dialog box.

14. Select Record to record the transaction.

Using Subcategories

Since you are quickly becoming proficient at basic transaction entry, you will want to see some other options for recording transactions. One option is to create subcategories to further define a category. Unlike classes, subcategories provide a detailed breakdown of the category. For instance, you could continue to allocate all your utility bills to the Utilities category, but you could create subcategories that allow you to allocate expenses to electricity, water, or gas. You will still be able to classify these transactions as either business or personal expenses using the class you established.

You can add subcategories by modifying the Category List as you add new categories, or you can create them as you enter transactions and realize the existing category entries don't provide the breakdown you want.

11

Entering a New Subcategory

When you enter a subcategory for a transaction, you type the category name, a colon (:), and the subcategory name. It is important that the category be specified first and the subcategory second. If a transaction has a class assigned, the class name comes third in the sequence, separated from the category and subcategory by a slash (/).

The business used in this example is run from the home of the owner, which necessitates the splitting of certain expenses between business and personal. Tax guidelines state that the percentage of the total square footage in the home that is used exclusively for business can be used to determine the portion of common expenses, such as utilities, allocated to the business. The business in this example occupies 20 percent of the total square footage in the home. You can use Windows' Calculator to perform these computations, and you can use both subcategories and split transactions to record the first transactions.

Enter the utility bills in the new account. Follow these steps to complete the entries for the gas and electric bills, creating a subcategory under Utilities for each and allocating 20 percent of each utility bill to business by splitting the transactions between classes:

When you need to monitor expenses closely, subcategories can help by showing a breakdown of costs at a more detailed level.

1. With the next blank transaction in the ANB Personal register highlighted, enter **1/3/94** as the date for the transaction.
2. Enter **827** in the Num field.

   Instead of typing the check number, you can select Next Chk# from the drop-down list box to have Quicken enter the number of the next check for you.
3. Type **Consumer Power** in the Payee field.
4. Type **80.00** for the payment amount.
5. Type **Electric Bill** in the Memo field.
6. Select Splits to open the Splits dialog box.
7. Type **Utilities:Electric/B** in the Category field.

   Quicken prompts you with the Set Up Category dialog box.
8. Type **Electric Utilities** in the Description text box.

   Although the description is optional, it is a good idea to enter one so that your reports will be informative. Notice that the Subcategory option button is selected.
9. Select the Tax-related check box.
10. Select Schedule C:Utilities in the Form drop-down list box.

    The Set Up Category dialog box shown here should match the one on your screen:

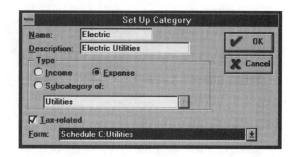

11. Select OK to close the dialog box, and move to the Memo field in the Splits dialog box.

12. Type **Business part of electric** in the Memo field.

13. Type **20%** in the Amount field, and move to the next line.

    Quicken calculates 20 percent of your total transaction amount and enters it in the Amount field when you move to another field. The 80 percent remaining is displayed in the Amount field of the next split.

14. Type **Utilities:Electric** in the Category field.

    Note that a class was not added to the entry; Quicken will consider the entry a personal expense.

15. Type **Home part of electric** in the Memo field.

    The Splits dialog box looks like this:

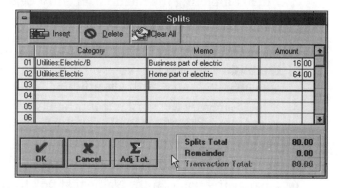

    Quicken has computed the difference between $80.00 and $16.00 and displayed it in the Amount field.

16. Select OK to close the Splits dialog box.

17. Select Record to record the transaction entry.

    The transaction is displayed in the register window, as shown here:

11

Date	Num	Payee		Payment	Clr	Deposit	Balance
		Memo	Category				
1/ 1/94		Opening Balance			x	2,500 00	2,500 00
			[ANB Personal]				
1/ 3/94	825	Discount Coats		120 00			2,380 00
		New winter coat	Clothing				
1/ 3/94	826	Campus Stationery		82 00			2,298 00
		Calendar and computer pap	--Splits--				
1/ 3/94	827	Consumer Power		80 00			2,218 00
		Electric Bill	--Splits--				

Bank Account: ANB Personal - Personal Checking
Insert   Delete   Copy   Paste   Report   Close

Completing the Utility Subcategories

You have one more utility bill to enter. The bill for gas utilities also requires a new subcategory. Complete the following steps to create a subcategory for the gas bill and complete the transaction entry.

1. Enter the following information in each of the fields shown:

Date:	**1/7/94**
Check:	**828**
Payee:	**Western Michigan Gas**
Payment:	**40.00**
Memo:	**Gas Bill**

2. After completing the Memo field entry, select Splits to open the Splits dialog box.

    Quicken's default categories include the subcategories Utilities:Gas & Electric and Utilities:Water. Since you already have a subcategory established for electric, you will want to modify the Gas & Electric subcategory for use with gas utilities.

3. Select Category & Transfer from the Lists menu or select the Cat List icon from the Iconbar to display the Category & Transfer List window.

4. Highlight Utilities: Gas & Electric.

5. Select Edit to edit the current category.

6. Change the name in the Name text box to Gas.

7. Type **Gas Utilities** in the Description text box.

8. Make sure the Subcategory option button is selected.

9. Select the Tax-related check box.

10. Select Schedule C:Utilities from the Form drop-down list box.

11. Select OK.

12. Select Use, and type **/B**.

13. Type **Business part of gas bill** in the Memo field.

14. Type **20%**, and move to the next line.

15. Enter **Utilities:Gas** in the Category field.

16. Type **Home part of gas bill** in the Memo field.

17. Select OK to close the Splits dialog box.

18. Select Re*c*ord to record the transaction entry.

    If you move to the top of the register, your entries will look like Figure 11-5.

Entering the Remaining Business Transactions

You are now acquainted with all the skills needed to enter transactions that affect a business or personal account. You should, however, complete the remaining transactions for January. Split transactions are shown in detail. The other transactions are shown in summary form; each field in which you need to enter data is shown with the entry for that field. Use these steps to complete the remaining entries:

1. Select *A*ccounts from the *L*ists menu or select the Accts icon to open the Account List.

2. Select ANB Business, and select *U*se.

3. Enter **1/8/94** in the Date field.

4. Enter **102** in the Num field.

5. Type **Computer Outlet** in the Payee field.

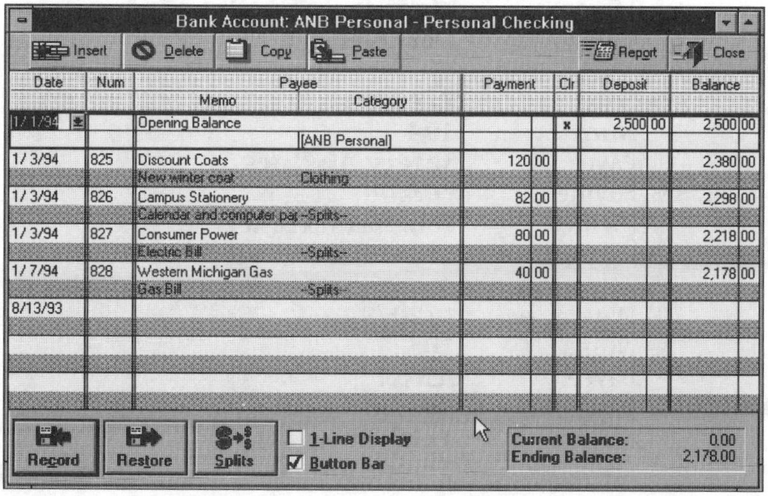

Register entries in the ANB Personal account
Figure 11-5.

6. Type **300** in the Payment field.

7. Type **Cartridges, ribbons, and disk** in the Memo field.

8. Select Splits to open the Splits dialog box.

   The same category and class will be used for each transaction entered in this dialog box. The transaction is split to provide additional documentation for purchases.

9. Complete the entries in the Splits dialog box as shown here:

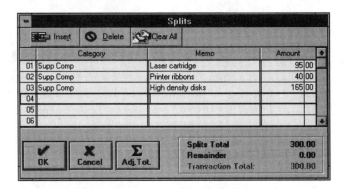

10. Select OK, and then select Record.

11. Enter the following transactions by completing the entries in the fields and selecting Record after each transaction:

Date:	**1/15/94**
Num:	**103**
Payee:	**Quick Delivery**
Payment:	**215.00**
Memo:	**Manuscript delivery**
Category:	**Del Overngt/B**

Date:	**1/15/94**
Num:	**104**
Payee:	**Safety Airlines**
Payment:	**905.00**
Memo:	**February Ticket**
Category:	**Travel/B**

Date:	**1/20/94**
Num:	**105**
Payee:	**Alltel**
Payment:	**305.00**
Memo:	**Telephone Bil.**
Category:	**Telephone/B**

12. Enter the beginning of the next transaction as follows:

Date: **1/20/94**
Num: **106**
Payee: **Postmaster**
Payment: **28.25**
Memo: **Postage for Mailing**

13. With the cursor in the Category field, select Splits.

14. Complete the following entries in the Splits dialog box:

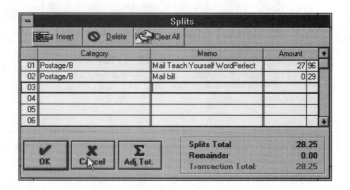

15. Select OK, and select Record.

16. Complete the next transaction to record a maintenance expense for existing equipment:

Date: **1/20/94**
Num: **107**
Payee: **Fix-It-All**
Payment: **1100.00**
Memo: **Equipment Contract**
Category: **Equip Mnt/B**

17. Select Record to record the transaction.

The entries in your register look like Figure 11-6.

The remaining transactions all relate to equipment. You will need to use the Equipment account you created earlier to handle these transactions.

Using the Asset Account

Earlier in this chapter you established an Asset account called Equipment. You'll use this account to track total equipment holdings and depreciation expenses. Purchase transactions for equipment will be recorded in your business checking account register as transfers to the Equipment account.

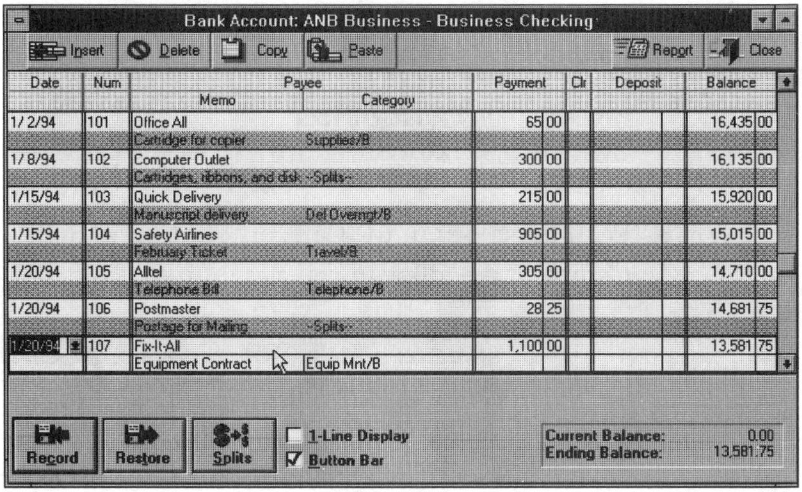

Register entries in the ANB Business account

Figure 11-6.

Other transactions, such as entering information about equipment purchased before you started using Quicken and a depreciation transaction, will be entered directly in the asset register. In the next section, you look at recording transactions for existing equipment and a new purchase. In Chapter 14, "Organizing Tax Information and Other Year-End Needs," you learn how to record depreciation expenses as the asset ages and declines in value.

Recording Transactions for Existing Equipment Holdings

When you record asset transactions you will notice that the register fields are a little different since you are increasing or decreasing the value of the account but are not writing a check or making a deposit.

The existing equipment cannot be recorded as a purchase since you don't want to affect the balance in the business checking account. You need to make the transaction entry directly in the Equipment account. The fields in an Asset account register are somewhat different than those in other account registers, as you can see in Figure 11-7. Follow these steps to record the equipment transactions:

1. Select <u>A</u>ccounts from the <u>L</u>ists menu, or select the Accts icon from the Iconbar.

2. Select the Equipment account, and select <u>U</u>se.

3. Enter **1/1/94** in the Date field.

4. Type **High Tech Computer** to enter the name of the asset in the Payee field.

   You can record an inventory number as part of this entry if one is assigned.

Other Asset: Equipment - Capital Equipment							

Insert | Delete | Copy | Paste | Loan | Report | Close

Date	Ref	Payee Memo Category	Decrease	Clr	Increase	Balance
1/1/94		Opening Balance [Equipment]				0 00
1/1/94		High Tech Computer Original cost of equip. [Equipment]/B			3,000 00	3,000 00
1/1/94		High Tech Computer Depreciation Expense [Equipment]/B	600 00			2,400 00
1/1/94	Ref	Payee Memo Category	Decrease		Increase	

Record | Restore | Splits

☐ 1-Line Display
☑ Button Bar

Current Balance: 0.00
Ending Balance: 2,400.00

Equipment
transactions
Figure 11-7.

5. Type **3000** to record the original purchase price in the Increase field.

6. Type **Original cost of equipment** in the Memo field.

7. Enter **Equipment/B** in the Category field, and select Re<u>c</u>ord.

Quicken displays the category as [Equipment] since the category is an account name and the transaction will increase the balance of that account. (The brackets are always added when an account name is placed in the Category field.)

To change the book value of the asset, another adjusting transaction is required. This transaction reduces the book value by the amount of the depreciation expense recognized last year. The transaction must be recorded against the Equipment account rather than as a depreciation expense, or the amount of the depreciation for last year will appear in this year's expense reports. You do not want to record the depreciation expense in your checking account register because you are not writing a check for this expense. Follow these steps to complete the second transaction entry:

1. Enter **1/1/94** in the Date field.

2. Type **High Tech Computer** in the Payee field.

11

NOTE: It is important to use the same name in all transactions relating to a given piece of equipment.

When you typed *H*, Quicken used its QuickFill feature to complete the Payee field with "High Tech Computer." Quicken reviews all the payees for the past three months and all the payees in the Memorized Transaction List to make the suggestion for the payee name to use in the transaction. You can use ⬆ and ⬇ to review other options beyond QuickFill's first suggestion. When you find the correct payee, press Enter. Quicken records the entire previous transaction for this payee. You must edit the copy of the original transaction if you want to make changes to the new entry. In this case, the following editing steps are needed:

3. Press Del to remove the value in the Increase field.

4. Type **600** in the Decrease field.

5. Press Del to remove the Memo field entry, and type **Depreciation Expense**.

6. Select Re̱cord, accepting [Equipment]/B as the category and finalizing the transaction.

Your register entries should match the ones in Figure 11-7.

Adding a New Equipment Purchase

Purchasing an asset reduces the balance in a checking account. When the asset is equipment, there must also be an entry in the Equipment account. If you list the Equipment account as the Category field in the transaction, Quicken will handle the transfer. Another difference in this transaction entry is that you use the name of the asset in the Payee field in the check register. Record the payee's name in the Memo field instead of the Payee field. Follow these steps to record the purchase of a laser printer:

1. Select A̱ccounts from the Ḻists menu, or select the Accts icon from the Iconbar.

2. Select ANB Business, and select U̱se.

3. Enter **1/25/94** in the Date field.

4. Select Next Check # in the Num drop-down list to enter 108 as the check number.

5. Type **Laser 1** in the Payee field.

6. Type **1500** in the Payment field.

7. Type **Printer from Fran's Computer** in the Memo field.

8. Enter **Equipment/B** in the Category field.

9. Select Re̱cord to record the transaction.

Your transaction looks like this:

1/25/94	108	Laser 1		1,500	00					12,081	75
		Printer from Fran's Computer [Equipment]/B									

10. Select <u>A</u>ccounts from the <u>L</u>ists menu, or select the Acct List icon from the Iconbar.

11. Select Equipment, and then select <u>U</u>se.

Figure 11-8 shows the transactions in the Equipment account after the transfer transaction is recorded.

Memorized Transactions

Many of your financial transactions are likely to repeat; you pay your utility bills each month, for instance. Likewise, overnight delivery charges, phone bills, payroll, and other bills are paid at about the same time each month. Cash inflows for some businesses are daily, weekly, or monthly. Other payments, such as supply purchases, also repeat, but perhaps not on the same dates each month.

As discussed in Chapter 6, "Expanding the Scope of Financial Entries," Quicken memorizes transactions entered in the register or the Write Checks window once you change the default Preferences setting. Once memorized, these transactions can be used to generate identical transactions. Although amounts and dates may change, you can edit these fields and not have to reenter payee, memo, and category information.

Register entries in the Equipment account after the printer purchase
Figure 11-8.

11

NOTE: By default, transactions are not memorized. To have them memorized, you need to select Preferences from the Edit menu and then select QuickFill. Select the Automatic Memorization of New Transactions check box, select OK, and select Done. If this option has not been selected, you cannot follow the steps in the rest of this chapter.

Editing and Deleting Memorized Transactions

To change a memorized transaction, begin by opening the Memorized Transactions List by selecting Memorized Transactions from the Lists menu. Select the transaction you want to edit from the list, and select Edit. The Edit Memorized Transaction dialog box appears, as shown here:

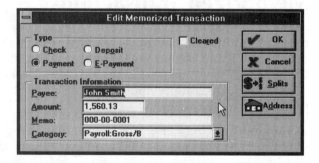

You can change the desired settings in this dialog box.

To delete a memorized transaction, open the Memorized Transaction List. Highlight the transaction you want to delete, and then select Del. A warning message appears, asking you to confirm the deletion. When you select OK, the transaction is no longer memorized. You can delete one-time transactions that are not likely to be often repeated. Follow these steps to delete a memorized transaction:

1. Select Memorized Transactions from the Lists menu to open the Memorized Transaction List window.

2. Highlight the Arlo Inc. transaction.

   This is a payment for a one-time service rather than an ongoing series of payments, so there is no real need to maintain this particular transaction.

3. Select Del.

4. When Quicken prompts you to confirm the deletion, select OK.

5. Repeat steps 1 through 4 for this series of transactions:

Campus Stationery
High Tech Computer
Laser I

Using Memorized Transactions

To recall a memorized transaction and place it in the register, move to the next blank transaction record. If you recall a memorized transaction while a previously recorded transaction is highlighted, the existing transaction is replaced by the memorized transaction. Open the Memorized Transaction List window by selecting Memorized Transactions from the Lists menu. Select the transaction you want to add to the register, and then select Use. If you type the first few letters of the payee name after you open the Memorized Transaction List, Quicken takes you to the correct area of the list since it is in alphabetical order by payee. When the selected transaction is added, it appears with the date of the preceding transaction in the register, not the date on which the selected transaction was last recorded. Edit the transaction in the register, and select Record when you are ready to record the entry.

Follow these steps to record a payment to Quick Delivery for later in the month:

1. Move to the end of the ANB Business register entries.

2. Select Memorized Transactions from the Lists menu.

3. Highlight the Quick Delivery transaction, and select Use.

   Quicken adds the transaction to the register.

4. Enter **1/30/94** in the Date field.

5. Enter **109** in the Num field.

6. Type **55.00** in the Payment field, and select Record to record the transaction.

   The transaction looks like this:

| 1/30/94 | 109 | Quick Delivery | | 55 | 00 | | | 12,026 | 75 |
| | | Manuscript delivery | Del Overngt/B | | | | | | |

Memorizing a Check

The procedure for memorizing transactions while writing checks is identical to the procedure for memorizing register transactions. You must be in the Write Checks window when you begin, but otherwise the steps are the same. Check and register transactions for the same file will appear in the same Memorized Transaction List and can be edited, deleted, or recalled from either the Write Checks window or the account register window.

11

Working with Scheduled Transactions

Although you can recall memorized transactions individually as a way to reenter similar transactions, a better method can be to have Quicken automatically schedule and enter transactions for you. Quicken 3 for Windows can schedule individual transactions or groups of transactions. If you want to schedule groups of transactions, the transactions must be memorized first. You use the Financial Calendar to schedule individual transactions and transaction groups.

You can use Quicken's Financial Calendar to either prompt you to enter scheduled transactions or to enter the transactions for you at the scheduled time. You can create scheduled transaction groups, which are groups of transactions scheduled to occur together, using the Scheduled Transaction List.

Scheduling with the Financial Calendar

The Financial Calendar provides the easiest method for quickly scheduling repeated transactions. There are other uses for the Financial Calendar. It shows when each of the transactions entered in your register occurred, and it can be used for tracking your future obligations.

Scheduling Transactions

You can schedule any transaction you have entered in the Financial Calendar, whether or not it is memorized. You can schedule a transaction that will occur only a specified number of times, or you can set the transaction to recur indefinitely.

You can display the Financial Calendar by selecting Financial Calendar from the Activities menu or by selecting the Calendar icon from the Iconbar. Your Financial Calendar should look like Figure 11-9.

NOTE: The Financial Calendar initially shows the current month. Since it is unlikely that you are using this book during the dates that are given for the sample transactions, you will probably have to change the month displayed by selecting the Prev or Next button at the top of the calendar to move to January 1994 to see the transactions which are entered in this file.

At the right side of the Financial Calendar window, Quicken displays a list of the transactions you have entered. You can quickly schedule a transaction by using the mouse to drag one of these transactions to a day on the calendar. When you release the mouse button, Quicken displays the Set Up Scheduled Transaction dialog box. To schedule the regular payments for equipment mainte nce, follow these steps:

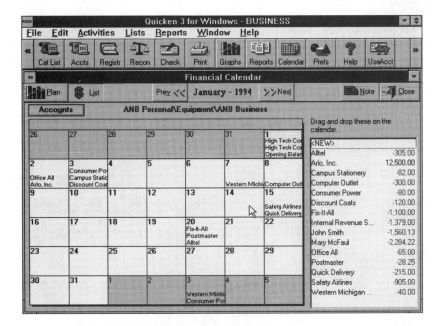

Financial
Calendar for
January 1994
Figure 11-9.

1. Display the Financial Calendar by selecting Financial Calendar from the
    Activities menu or by selecting the Calendar icon from the Iconbar.

2. Select Prev or Next to display the calendar for April 1994.

3. Drag the Fix-It-All transaction from the list box on the right side of the
    window to April 30, at the bottom of the calendar. The Set Up
    Scheduled Transaction dialog box appears:

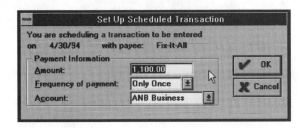

4. Enter Quarter in the Frequency of Payment text box, using QuickFill or
    the drop-down list.

5. Select OK.

Quicken will prompt to enter the scheduled transaction the first time you
start Quicken 3 for Windows after the scheduled date for the transaction.

Editing Scheduled Transactions

You can easily edit your scheduled transactions. For example, you can edit
the transaction you just scheduled so that Quicken will enter the transaction
without prompting you first. To edit the scheduled transaction, follow these
steps:

1. Double-click on the day the transaction is currently entered on—in this
   case, 4/30/94. Quicken displays the dialog box shown here:

2. Select Edit. The Edit Scheduled Transaction dialog box opens, as shown
   here:

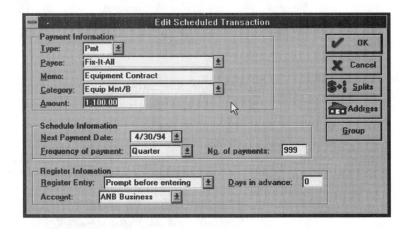

3. Select Enter w/o prompting in the Register Entry drop-down list box.
   Now Quicken will enter your payroll deposit without prompting you
   about it.

4. Select OK.

You may edit your transaction again when your contract changes, or if you
decide you want it entered in the register a few days before it will actually be
there. This is useful as a reminder about bills you need to pay.

Paying a Scheduled Transaction Early

You may want to register a transaction as being paid early, either because
you are going out of town or because you decided to pay the bill before the
due date. To do this, click on the day containing the scheduled transaction,

and then select Pay Now. Quicken prompts you to review the details of the transaction. When you select OK, the transaction is entered in the register.

Working with Scheduled Transaction Groups

Quicken 3 for Windows can schedule both individual transactions, as just described, or groups of transactions. If you have several memorized transactions that occur at the same time, a scheduled transaction group lets you focus on other tasks while Quicken remembers to enter the transactions you need. Quicken will record the entire group for you with or without prompting you about its entries, depending on how you define the scheduled transaction group.

Defining a Scheduled Transaction Group

Quicken allows you to set up many scheduled transaction groups. Defining a group is easy. First you memorize all the transactions that will be placed in the group. Then you select the number of transactions in the group you want to define, and you describe the group. Finally, you assign specific memorized transactions to the group. Although expense transactions are frequently used to create groups, you can also include an entry for a direct deposit payroll check that is deposited at the same time each month.

For your first transaction group, which you will title Utilities, you will group the gas and electric transactions that occur near the end of each month. Follow these steps to open the ANB Personal account and create the transaction group:

1. Select Accounts from the Lists menu or select the Accts icon from the Iconbar to open the Account list.
2. Highlight ANB Personal, and select Use.
3. Select Scheduled Transactions from the Lists menu.

   Quicken displays the Scheduled Transaction List window:

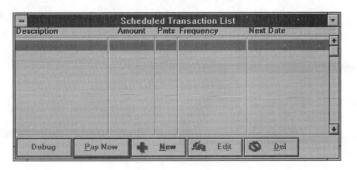

11

4. Select <u>N</u>ew.

Quicken displays a dialog box so that you can define the group.
The following dialog box contains the entries you will make in the
next steps:

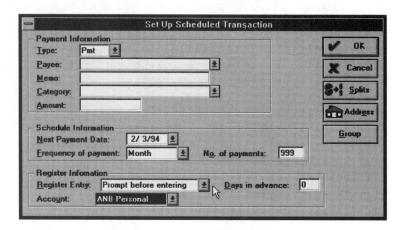

5. Type **2/3/94** in the <u>N</u>ext Payment Date text box. Remember that you
    can use the drop-down calendar to select this date.

    Quicken will remind you three days in advance of this date. You can
    change this by changing the Billminder Preferences. Quicken displays a
    dialog box listing transactions you can assign to Group 1. Only
    memorized transactions are present in this list. They are listed in
    alphabetical order by payee to make it easy to locate the desired
    transactions.

6. Select **Month** from the <u>F</u>requency of payment drop-down list box.

    If you don't want to be reminded weekly, every two weeks, twice a
    month, every four weeks, monthly, quarterly, twice a year, or annually,
    you can choose None.

7. Make sure that the N<u>o</u>. of Payments box is still set to 999, which causes
    Quicken to continue entering these transactions indefinitely.

8. Make sure that the <u>R</u>egister Entry text box still shows "Prompt before
    entering" so that Quicken prompts you about the transactions before
    entering them into your account register.

9. Select ANB Personal from the Acc<u>o</u>unt drop-down list box to indicate
    the account these transactions should be entered in.

10. Select <u>G</u>roup. If prompted for the category, simply select <u>Y</u>es.

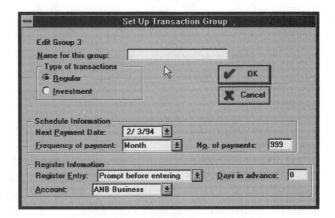

Set Up
Transaction
Group dialog
box
Figure 11-10.

The Set Up Transaction Group dialog box, shown in Figure 11-10, is displayed. Many of the entries you made in the previous dialog box could have been made here. However, you must specify the account being used before you can select Group.

11. Type **Utilities** in the Name for this Group text box.

12. Select OK.

13. In the Assign Transactions to Group dialog box, double-click the Consumer Power transaction, or highlight it with the arrow keys and select Mark, to assign the transaction to the Utilities group.

    Note the 1 in the Grp column, which indicates that the transaction is now part of the Utilities group.

14. Select the Western Michigan Gas transaction by double-clicking it, or by highlighting it and selecting Mark.

    Quicken also marks this transaction as part of the Utilities transaction group, as shown here:

11

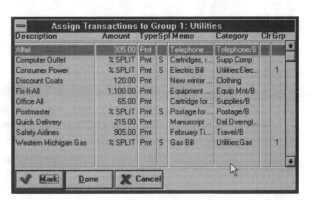

15. Select Done to indicate that you have finished selecting transactions.

You may want to define other transaction groups to include payroll, loan payments, and anything else that you might pay at the beginning of the month. You don't need to define additional groups to complete the remaining exercises in this section.

You can also create transaction groups that generate checks for you. These groups contain transactions that are memorized from the Write Checks window. The procedure is the same as that just described. You can identify these transactions in the Assign Transactions dialog box by the Chk entry in the Type field. Remember that a Pmt entry in the Type field indicates an account register transaction.

Changing a Transaction Group

You can add to a transaction group at any time by opening the Scheduled Transaction List window, highlighting the group, and selecting Edit. As you proceed through the normal group definition procedure, you can select additional transactions for inclusion in the group.

To make a change to the description or frequency of the reminder, use the same procedure, and make the necessary changes in the Describe Group dialog box.

To delete a transaction group, open the Scheduled Transactions list. Highlight the group you want to delete, and select Delete. Quicken eliminates the group but does not delete the memorized transactions that are part of it. Deleting a transaction group does not affect any transactions recorded in the register by earlier executions of the transaction group.

If you want to alter a transaction that is part of a transaction group, you need to alter the memorized transaction. This means that you have to make your changes and memorize the edited transaction. Follow the procedures in the "Changing and Deleting Memorized Transactions" section earlier in this chapter.

Recording a Transaction Group

Once you have defined a transaction group, you do not need to wait for the reminder to record the group in your register or the Write Checks window. Since you can memorize entries for both the register and the Write Checks window, make sure you have the group correctly defined for your current needs. A group type of Chk is created in the Write Checks window and can be recorded in either the account register or the Write Checks window. Payment (Pmt) groups are recorded in the account register and can only be used to record account register entries.

To execute a transaction group from the account register, follow these steps:

1. Select Scheduled Transactions from the Lists menu.

    Quicken displays a Scheduled Transaction List window like the one shown here:

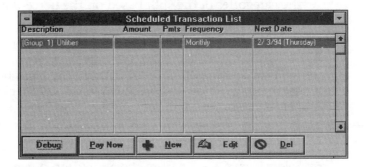

2. Highlight the Utilities group.

3. Select Pay Now.

    Quicken displays the Enter Scheduled Transaction dialog box, as shown here:

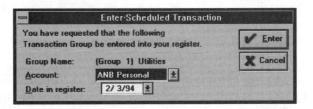

    If you were actually planning to pay these bills early, you would enter the current date in the Date in register text box so that the register showed the date you actually recorded the transaction. In this case, you aren't going to do this.

4. Select OK to enter the transactions in the register.

    The new transactions are entered with the date 2/3/94, as shown here:

2/ 3/94	Sched	Consumer Power		72	00				2,106	00	
		Electric Bill -Splits-									
2/ 3/94	Sched	Western Michigan Gas		45	00				2,061	00	
		Gas Bill -Splits-									

    The check numbers and amounts need to be altered for the new utility bills. You don't need to open the Splits dialog box for each transaction and distribute the new amounts because you entered the amounts as

11

percentages. When you enter the new amounts, Quicken automatically distributes the amounts according to those percentages. If you enter a single memorized or scheduled transaction with splits defined as percentages, instead of a scheduled transaction group with split transactions, Quicken prompts you for the total amount of the new transaction before inserting it into the register, and divides it between the categories of the split based on the percentages.

TIP: When you use a transaction group to enter a transaction, ensure that you are on a blank transaction form. If you are not, the first newly inserted transaction will have an entry in the Num field that is already used for another transaction, and you will have two checks with the same number. If this occurs, Quicken displays a message to that effect.

5. Highlight the Consumer Power entry for 2/3/94.
6. Select Next Check # from the Num drop-down list to assign a check number to this transaction.
7. Type **72.00** in the Payment field.
8. Select OK, and select Record.
9. Select Next Check # in the Num field for the West Michigan Gas transaction.
10. Type **45.00** in the Payment field of the West Michigan Gas transaction.
11. Select OK, and select Record.

Having Quicken Remind You to Record Transactions

Quicken will remind you to enter upcoming transaction group transactions. The reminder will occur either when you boot your system, when you start Windows, or when you start Quicken. You can control when Quicken's Billminder feature reminds you to enter upcoming transaction group transactions by the selections you make when you install Quicken. If you change the way you use the computer and you need to change the Billminder settings, use Edit Preferences to make a change.

Important Customizing Options As You Set Up Your Files

Quicken provides a number of options for customizing the software to meet your needs. These include options for the addition of passwords for accessing files, options already discussed such as requiring category entries, and other options that affect the display of information on your screen and in reports.

Once you know how to access these settings, you will find that most are self-explanatory.

Adding Passwords

To add a password, select P̲assword from the F̲ile menu. Quicken presents a submenu that allows you to decide if you want to protect a file using F̲ile or protect existing transactions with T̲ransaction. Although you can add protection with a password at both levels, you will need to select each individually.

If you select F̲ile, Quicken asks you to enter a password. Once you do so and select OK, the password is added to the active file and anyone wishing to work with the file must supply the password. T̲ransaction is used to prevent unauthorized changes to existing transactions entered before a specified date. If you choose T̲ransaction, you are presented with a dialog box that requires you to enter both a password and a date.

If you want to change or remove a password, you must be able to provide the password. Quicken then displays a Change Password dialog box for the entry of the old and new passwords. After you complete the entries and select OK, the new password is in effect.

11

C H A P T E R

12

QUICKEN'S PAYROLL ASSISTANCE

For a small-business owner under the day-to-day pressure of running a business, preparing the payroll can be a time-consuming and frustrating task. Besides withholding forms and tables to complete, there are annual earnings limits that affect the amount you withhold in social security taxes from employees' earnings. In addition to these weekly considerations, there are monthly, quarterly, and year-end reports that may need to be filed for the federal, state, or local government.

In this chapter, you will see how Quicken can help to reduce the effort it takes to prepare your payroll. Although you must still invest some time, you'll find that an early investment of time will substantially reduce your payroll activities once the system is running. With Quicken, you can easily prepare the payroll entry for each employee and maintain information for the Internal Revenue Service (IRS) about federal income tax withholdings, Federal Insurance Contribution Act (FICA) withholdings, and employer FICA payments. You can also maintain accounts for any state and local withholding taxes or insurance payments that must be periodically deposited. In addition to this information, you can accumulate data to be used in the preparation of W-2 forms for your employees at the end of the year. See the special "Payroll Forms" section in this chapter for a list of some of the standard payroll-related payment and tax forms that Quicken can assist you in preparing.

Payroll Forms

If you are thinking of hiring employees, you need to be prepared for your paperwork to increase. You must complete forms at the federal, state, and local level regarding payroll information.

Federal Payroll Forms

The following list provides an overview of the payroll-related tax forms that employers need to file with the Internal Revenue Service. You can obtain copies of the federal forms you need by calling the IRS toll-free number (800) 829-3676. If this number is not valid in your locale, check your telephone directory for the correct number. You will probably need to file the following forms:

✦ *SS-4, Application for Federal Employer Identification Number* The federal employer identification number is used to identify your business on all business-related tax forms.

✦ *Form 46-190, Federal Tax Deposit Receipt* This is your record of the deposits of withholding and payroll taxes you make to a Federal Reserve bank or an authorized commercial bank.

✦ *Form 940, Employer's Annual Federal Unemployment (FUTA) Tax Return* This is a return filed annually with the IRS summarizing your federal unemployment tax liability and deposits.

✦ *Form 941, Employer's Quarterly Federal Tax Return* This return summarizes your quarterly FICA taxes and federal income tax withholding liability and the amounts of the deposits your business has made during the quarter.

✦ *Form 943, Employer's Annual Tax Return for Agricultural Employees* This is a special form completed annually for FICA taxes and federal income tax withholding liability for agricultural employees.

✦ *Form 1099-MISC, Statement for Recipients of Miscellaneous Income* This must be filed for all nonemployees paid $600.00 or more in the current tax year.

✦ *Form W-2, Wage and Tax Statement* This is a six-part form (an original and five duplicates) summarizing an employee's gross earnings and tax deductions for the year. The form must be prepared annually for each employee by January 31.

✦ *Form W-3, Transmittal of Income and Tax Statements* This form summarizes your business' annual payroll, related FICA taxes, and federal income tax withheld during the year. You send it with the Social Security Administration's copy of W-2 forms by February 28th of the following year.

✦ *Form W-4, Employee's Withholding Allowance Certificate* This form is completed annually by employees and is used to declare the number of withholding exemptions they claim.

State and Local Government Payroll Information

These forms vary by state. The following list provides an indication of some of the forms you are likely to need to file.

✦ Unemployment insurance tax payments

✦ Workers' compensation tax payments

✦ State income tax withholding payments

✦ Local income tax withholding payments

✦ Form W-2, Wage and Tax Statement (one copy of federal form)

12

Intuit offers a separate package, QuickPay, that contains built-in payroll tables to provide additional payroll help.

The Quicken Payroll System

Payroll entries are processed along with your other business-related payments in your Quicken account register. To set up your system to process payroll entries, you need to establish some new categories and subcategories specifically related to payroll. You can create some or all of the categories and subcategories needed to record your payroll transactions. The payroll subcategories are shown here:

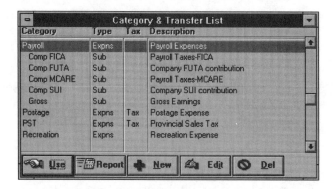

Payroll:Gross keeps track of the total wages earned by employees, and Payroll:Comp FICA keeps track of matching FICA contributions. The other payroll subcategories are used to record federal unemployment tax contributions, Medicare contributions, state unemployment tax contributions, and state disability insurance contributions.

In addition, you need to establish several *liability accounts* to maintain records of taxes withheld and employee-authorized payroll deductions for medical insurance, charitable contributions, and so on. These accounts are called liability accounts because you are holding the withheld funds for payment to a third party. Some examples of these are as follows:

Payroll-FUTA	Federal unemployment taxes owed by employer
Payroll-FICA	FICA owed by employer
Payroll-FWH	Federal income tax withheld from employees' earnings
Payroll-MCARE	Medicare tax withheld from employees' earnings
Payroll-SWH	State income tax withheld from employees' earnings
Payroll-SUI	State unemployment tax owed by employer

As an
employer, you
are responsible
for making
payments to
the federal,
state, and
local
governments
for employee
withholding
and payroll
taxes.

Notice that all of these account names begin with "Payroll." This allows Quicken to prepare the Payroll report by finding all transactions that have a category title that begins with "Payroll." All the categories listed in this section start with "Payroll" and have a subcategory added—for example, Payroll:Gross. When you prepare the Payroll report in this chapter, you will see the relationship between the category designation and the preparation of the report.

Another point to note is that although employees must pay federal taxes as well as any state and local taxes, the employer is responsible for the actual withholding and payment of these funds to the appropriate agencies. In addition, there are certain payroll taxes that the employer must pay, such as unemployment, workers' compensation, and matching FICA. The amount of these taxes is not withheld from the employee's pay since the responsibility for these payments rests with the employer. With Quicken, you can monitor your liability for these payments. This is important since you will be assessed penalties and late fees for failing to file these payments on time. Quicken's ability to memorize payment formats and remind you of dates for periodic payments can be most helpful.

Recording Payroll Activity

To record your payroll entries in this chapter, you will use the file BUSINESS, which was established in Chapter 11, "Setting Up Quicken for Your Business." As noted in the previous section, you need to expand your category list and accounts in order to accumulate the payroll information. Once you have completed the example for processing payroll that is included in this chapter, you will be able to customize your own accounts to handle your payroll needs. For example, you might withhold medical and life insurance premiums from your employees' checks. These amounts can be recorded in another liability account established just for that purpose.

For the example in this chapter, it is assumed that your work force consists of salaried workers paid monthly. This means that their pay and deductions will be the same month after month. John Smith is paid $2000.00 a month, and Mary McFaul is paid $3000.00 a month. If your employees are paid hourly and if they have a varying number of hours in each pay period, you will need to recompute their pay and deductions each period. Otherwise, the procedures shown in this chapter apply. In this example, you draw payroll checks on the last day of the month.

12

Establishing Payroll Liability Accounts and New Payroll Categories

The first step in recording payroll in the Quicken system is to establish the payroll liability accounts you will use throughout the year. These accounts allow you to keep track of the amounts you withhold from employees' earnings so that you can make periodic payments to various governmental agencies, health insurance companies, and pension plans. When a payment is due, you can open the liability account to determine its balance. This tells you the amount of the payment you must make.

Make sure you are in the ANB Business Account in the BUSINESS file. Then follow these steps to establish the payroll liability accounts you will use in this chapter:

1. Select Create New Account from the Activities menu.

2. Select the Liability Account option to set up a liability account, and select OK.

3. Type **Payroll-FICA** in the Account Name text box.

   This identifies the new account as a payroll liability account in the BUSINESS file. You will accumulate all employee FICA withholdings in this account.

4. Type **0** as the opening balance.

   The opening balance is 0.00 in this example since this is the first pay period for the business illustrated. When you set up your own account, you should enter the amount you have at the time you begin to use Quicken. If you were in business the previous year, you will probably have outstanding tax liabilities that would not be paid until January or February. The amount of these liabilities would be entered as the balance for each account.

5. Type **1/1/94** as the opening date.

6. Type **FICA Withholding** in the Description text box.

7. Select OK.

8. Select Cancel when Quicken shows a Set Up Amortized Loan dialog box.

   Whenever you establish a liability account, Quicken prompts you about setting up an amortized loan to associate with the account.

NOTE: Set up an amortization loan when creating liability accounts for loans you are paying so that you can track the money spent on interest and principal.

Repeat steps 1 through 7 to establish the liability accounts for the information that follows:

Account Type: **Liability**
Account Name: **Payroll-MCARE**
Balance: **0**
Date: **1/1/94**
Description: **Medicare Withholding**

In this account, you keep track of all employee Medicare withholdings during the year.

Account Type: **Liability**
Account Name: **Payroll-FWH**
Balance: **0**
Date: **1/1/94**
Description: **Federal Withholding**

You use this account to keep track of all employee federal income tax withholdings during the year.

Account Type: **Liability**
Account Name: **Payroll-SWH**
Balance: **0**
Date: **1/1/94**
Description: **State Withholding**

In this account, you keep track of all employee state income taxes withheld during the year.

Account Type: **Liability**
Account Name: **Payroll-FICA-Co**
Balance: **0**
Date: **1/1/94**
Description: **FICA Matching**

You use this account to keep track of the amount of your FICA matching payment each pay period.

Account Type: **Liability**
Account Name: **Payroll-MCARECo**

12

Balance: **0**

Date: **1/1/94**

Description: **Medicare Matching**

In this account, you keep track of the amount of your Medicare matching payment each pay period.

Close these register windows when you have finished creating them to clean up your Quicken window. After adding these liability accounts, your account list will look like this:

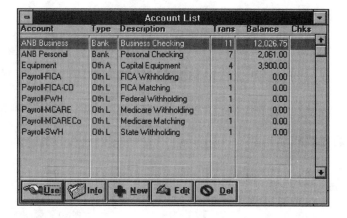

Open the ANB Business account register to continue.

Establishing New Payroll Categories

Several new categories are needed to record the payroll information. Follow these steps to establish Payroll and Gross Earnings as categories, with Gross and Co (for company) as subcategories, under Payroll. You don't need to establish new categories for FICA, MCARE, and the other types of withholdings you keep track of because you can simply select the account names from the Category & Transfer List.

1. Select the Cat List icon, or select _C_ategory & Transfer from the _L_ists menu. The Category & Transfer List window opens.
2. Select _N_ew.
3. Type **Payroll** as the category name.
4. Type **Payroll Expenses** as the category description.
5. Select the _E_xpense option button, and select OK.

Repeat steps 2 through 5 to create these other new categories:

Name:	**Gross**
Description:	**Gross Earnings**
Type:	Subcategory of Payroll

Name:	**Comp FICA**
Description:	**Payroll Taxes-FICA**
Type:	Subcategory of Payroll

Name:	**Comp MCARE**
Description:	**Payroll Taxes-MCARE**
Type:	Subcategory of Payroll

Name:	**Comp FUTA**
Description:	**Company FUTA contribution**
Type:	Subcategory of Payroll

Name:	**Comp SUI**
Description:	**Company SUI contribution**
Type:	Subcategory of Payroll

Monthly Payroll Entries

In this section, you record paycheck entries for John Smith and Mary McFaul on January 31. Many steps are required to complete the entire entry for an individual. After you record basic information, such as the check number and the employee's name, amounts must be determined. You establish each of the withholding amounts and subtract the total withholding amount from the gross pay to compute the net pay. For hourly workers, a computation is needed to determine the gross pay as well. Tax tables are used to determine the correct withholding for federal, state, and local taxes. For figures such as FICA and net pay, you can use Windows' Calculator to compute the amount.

Once you have determined withholding amounts and net pay, you need to enter this information. Each of the withholding amounts, such as federal income tax, FICA, and state withholdings, is entered in a Splits dialog box. Use the following steps to record the transactions.

12

1. Move to the next blank transaction in the ANB Business account register.
2. Type **1/31/94** in the Date field.
3. Type **110** as the check number.
4. Type **John Smith** in the Payee field.
5. Type **1560.13** in the Payment field.

   This amount is equal to John's gross pay of $2000.00 less federal income tax, state income tax, FICA, and Medicare withholdings.
6. Type **000-00-0001** in the Memo field.

   This is the employee's social security number. You may find this field useful in filtering payroll reports.
7. Select <u>S</u>plits, and the Splits dialog box appears on your screen.

   This is what the Splits dialog box looks like after you complete the next series of steps:

8. Enter **Payroll:Gross/B** in the Category field.

   You can use QuickFill for the entries throughout this chapter even though they include subcategories and classes. When you type a *P*, Quicken displays "Payroll." Type **:** to accept "Payroll" and display the first subcategory. Type the first letter of the subcategory. When the subcategory appears, type **/B** to accept the subcategory and mark the transaction with the Business class.
9. Type **Gross Earnings** in the Memo field.
10. Type **2000.00** as the amount.
11. Enter **Payroll-FICA/B** in the category field.

    Quicken adds brackets around the Payroll-FICA category, as you can see in the previous Splits dialog box, when the transaction involves a transfer between two Quicken accounts. Here, Quicken records the liability account name in the Category field. This indicates that you are keeping track of the amount of your employee withholding in this account until you make your payment to the IRS.

12. Type **FICA Withholding** in the Memo field.

13. Type **–124.00** as the amount.

This is the amount of FICA tax withheld from John's paycheck. The negative amount indicates that this is a deduction from the $2000.00 gross earnings entered on the previous line. For 1993, the rate for FICA with-holdings is .062 on the first $57,600.00 of earnings per employee. You can calculate this amount with the Windows Calculator before starting the transaction. Although the $57,600.00 earnings limit does not affect the employees in this example, Quicken can be used to help monitor employees' gross earnings to determine when the limit is reached.

14. Enter **Payroll-FWH/B** in the Category field.

15. Type **Federal Withholding** in the Memo field.

16. Type **–232.00** as the amount.

This is the amount of federal income tax withheld from John's paycheck. Remember that you must manually determine the amounts from with-holding tables before beginning the payroll transaction entry since you need these amounts to compute net pay.

17. Enter **Payroll-SWH/B** as the category.

18. Type **State Withholding** in the Memo field.

19. Type **–54.87** as the amount.

Once again, you use the appropriate state withholding tables to determine the amount of the deduction from John's paycheck. If you live in an area where local taxes are also withheld, you need to add another liability account to accumulate your liability to that government agency.

20. Enter **Payroll-MCARE/B** in the next Category field.

21. Type **Medicare Withholding** in the Memo field.

Notice that the Remainder field at the bottom-right of the Splits dialog box now contains 0. This indicates that the balance of the transactions entered in the Split Transaction window now equals the amount you entered in the Payment field of the transaction.

12

22. Type **–29.00** in the Amount field.

For 1993, the Medicare withholding rate is .0145 on the first $135,000 earned by each employee.

At this point, you have recorded John Smith's gross earnings and the amounts withheld from his check. In the next series of steps, you record your employer payroll expenses. After you complete these steps, the Splits dialog box will look like this:

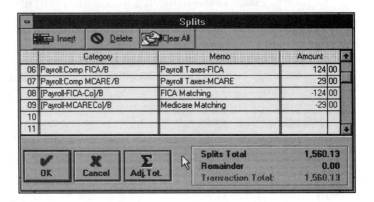

23. Enter **Payroll:Comp FICA/B** in the Category field.

    As an employer, you have to match your employees' FICA contributions. This is an expense of doing business and must be recorded in your category list.

24. Type **Payroll Taxes-FICA** in the Memo field.

25. Type **124.00** in the Amount field.

    This records the amount of your matching FICA payroll expense. Notice that it is a positive amount because this is a business expense that Quicken will record in the account register.

26. Enter **Payroll:Comp MCARE/B** in the Category field.

27. Type **Payroll Taxes-MCARE** in the Memo field.

28. Type **29.00** in the Amount field.

29. Enter **Payroll-FICA-Co/B** in the Category field.

30. Type **FICA Matching** in the Memo field.

31. Type **–124.00** in the Amount field.

32. Enter **Payroll-MCARECo/B** in the Category field.

33. Type **Medicare Matching** in the Memo field.

34. Type **–29.00** as the amount.

35. Select OK.

36. Select Record to record the transaction in the current register.

You have now completed the payroll entry for John Smith for the month of January. You must now complete the recording process for Mary McFaul. Follow these steps to record the transaction in the ANB Business account register:

1. Enter **1/31/94** in the Date field.
2. Enter **111** in the Num field.
3. Type **Mary McFaul** in the Payee field.
4. Type **2284.22** in the Payment field.
5. Type **000-00-0002** in the Memo field.
6. Select Splits, and the Splits dialog box appears on your screen.
7. Enter **Payroll:Gross/B** in the Category field.
8. Type **Gross Earnings** in the Memo field.
9. Type **3000.00** in the Amount field.
10. Enter **Payroll-FICA/B** in the Category field.
11. Type **FICA Withholding** in the Memo field.
12. Type **–186.00** in the Amount field.
13. Enter **Payroll-FWH/B** in the Category field.
14. Type **Federal Withholding** in the Memo field.
15. Type **–382.00** in the Amount field.
16. Enter **Payroll-SWH/B** in the Category field.
17. Type **State Withholding** in the Memo field.
18. Type **–104.28** in the Amount field.
19. Enter **Payroll-MCARE/B** in the Category field.
20. Type **Medicare Withholding** in the Memo field.
21. Type **–43.50** in the Amount field.
22. Enter **Payroll:Comp FICA/B** in the Category field.
23. Type **Payroll Taxes-FICA** in the Memo field.
24. Type **186.00** in the Amount field.
25. Enter **Payroll:Comp MCARE/B** in the Category field.
26. Type **Payroll Taxes-MCARE** in the Memo field.
27. Type **43.50** in the Amount field.
28. Enter **Payroll-FICA-Co/B** in the Category field.
29. Type **FICA Matching** in the Memo field.

12

30. Type **–186.00** in the Amount field.
31. Enter **Payroll-MCARECo/B** in the Category field.
32. Type **Medicare Matching** in the Memo field.
33. Type **–43.50** in the Amount field.
34. Select OK.
35. Select Record to record the transaction for Mary McFaul in the account register.

The paycheck transactions recorded in this section show the basic expenses and liabilities associated with the payment of wages. Your payroll entries will be more complex if you withhold medical insurance, pension contributions, and other amounts such as contributions to charities or deposits to savings accounts from employee checks. The basic format of the split transaction remains the same; you simply expand the number of categories in the split transaction and add liability accounts to cover your obligation to make payments to the parties involved. Regardless of the number of withholding categories, the procedures you just performed can be used to expand your withholding categories and liabilities.

Recording Periodic Deposits for the Internal Revenue Service

The Internal Revenue Service provides guidelines for making periodic payments for employee withholding and employer payroll taxes.

You must periodically make deposits to the Internal Revenue Service for FICA and federal income tax withheld from employees' paychecks, as well as for your matching FICA contribution. You make your deposits to authorized banks within the Federal Reserve System. You should check with your bank to be sure it can provide this service. If it can't, you must take cash or a bank check, along with the appropriate forms, to an authorized bank and make your deposit. When you record the withholding deposit in Quicken, you designate the Internal Revenue Service as the payee.

Specific guidelines govern the timing of the payments. At the time this book is being written, the fictitious company used in this example would be required to make a withholding deposit for the January paychecks under the IRS's Rule 1 discussed in the "IRS Deposit Rules" section of this chapter. The rule states that you must make a deposit for social security taxes and withheld federal income tax by the fifteenth of the following month if your total tax liability for last year was $50,000 or less. In this example, your total tax liability for the month is $1379.00. You should consult your accountant or read IRS Form 941 for a full explanation of the deposit rules. Depending on the size of your payroll, you may have to make periodic payments throughout the month in order to comply with the regulations.

IRS Deposit Rules

How often you must make deposits of social security and federal income taxes is dependent on the amount of your liability. Effective January 1, 1993, the IRS has simplified the rules that affect when you must make these deposits. Each November, the IRS will tell you which rule you should use throughout the upcoming year. If you are not notified, you should use the following rules to make a determination. New employers should use Rule 1. Since the penalties for noncompliance can be steep, it is important to follow the rules strictly. Notice 931 describes the new rules in detail, but a quick summary is provided here:

Rule 1	If your tax liability for the previous four quarters was $50,000 or less, file monthly.
Rule 2	If your tax liability for the previous four quarters was greater than $50,000, file every two weeks.
Rule 3	If your cumulative tax liability is $100,000 or more, you must make daily deposits.

Through the end of 1993, you can continue to use the old rules. Follow the instructions that come with Form 941 for the transition. The old rules are summarized here:

Rule 1	If your tax liability for the quarter is less than $500, no deposit is required.
Rule 2	If your tax liability for the month is less than $500, carry it forward to the next month.
Rule 3	If your tax liability for the month is between $500 and $3000, you must make a deposit within 15 days after the end of the month.
Rule 4	If your tax liability at the end of any of the eight monthly periods (the 3rd, 7th, 11th, 15th, 19th, 22nd, 25th, and the last day) of a month is greater than $3000 and less than $100,000, you must make a deposit within three banking days.
Rule 5	If your tax liability at the end of any of the eight monthly periods is greater than $100,000, you must make a deposit by the end of the next banking day.

12

The following example demonstrates how you would record a payment for your business' liabilities for social security taxes, Medicare, and federal withholding taxes. You would record the transaction in the ANB Business account register when you paid the federal government the amount of the liabilities for FICA, Medicare, and federal income tax withholdings for the two paycheck entries recorded in the previous section.

From the ANB Business account register, record the following transaction for the required deposit:

1. Move to the Date field in the blank transaction form.
2. Enter **2/1/94** in the Date field.
3. Enter **112** in the Num field.
4. Type **Internal Revenue Service** as the payee.
5. Type **1379.00** in the Payment field.
6. Type **Form 941 Withholding Payment** in the Memo field.
7. Select Splits to open the Splits dialog box. After you complete the following steps, your Splits dialog box looks like this:

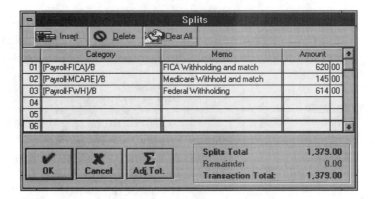

8. Enter **Payroll-FICA/B** in the Category field.
9. Type **FICA Withholding and match** in the Memo field.
10. Type **620.00** in the Amount field.
11. Enter **Payroll-MCARE/B** in the Category field.
12. Type **Medicare Withhold and match** in the Memo field.
13. Type **145.00** in the Amount field.
14. Enter **Payroll-FWH/B** in the Category field.
15. Type **Federal Withholding** in the Memo field.

16. Select OK to record the split.
17. Select Record to record the transaction in the account register.

You follow these same steps to record the payment of your state withholding tax liability when the payment date arrives.

Notice that no expense category was charged in the previous Splits dialog box. This is because the deposit reduces the liability account balances that were established when payroll checks were written on 1/31/94. If you look at those transactions in your register, you can see that the gross earnings were charged to the Payroll:Gross category and that your matching FICA contribution was charged to the Payroll:Comp FICA category. Both of these categories are classified as expenses and will be shown on your business Profit and Loss statement. The amounts withheld for payroll taxes, on the other hand, were charged to liability accounts that will be paid at a future date. Thus, when you pay these liabilities, as you just did, you are meeting your financial obligation to the government, not incurring additional expenses.

Other Liability Accounts

Let's look at the impact of recording the paychecks and the IRS payment on the other liability accounts. Specifically, you will see the effects of these transactions on the Payroll-FWH liability account. Follow these steps to enter the Payroll-FWH account from the ANB Business account register:

1. Select Account from the Lists menu, or select the Accts icon from the Iconbar. The Account List window appears.
2. Select the Payroll-FWH account, and then select Use. The register shown in Figure 12-1 appears.

   Notice that the account has accumulated $614.00 as the FWH withholding liability from the January paychecks. Also notice that when you made your deposit on 2/1/94, the balance was reduced to zero. This will occur each month when you record your deposit to the IRS.
3. Select Accounts from the Lists menu, or select the Accts icon from the Iconbar again. Then highlight ANB Business, and select Use. You are now back in the ANB Business account register.

12

Memorized Monthly Paycheck and Withholding Deposit Entries

Since you will be paying your employees on a regular basis and making monthly withholding deposits, you will want to memorize these entries to simplify recording future transactions. Since the employees in this example

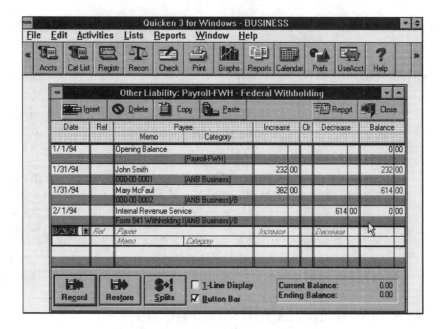

Activating the
Payroll-FWH
account
Figure 12-1.

are all salaried, the only changes needed each month are new dates and
check numbers on each transaction. All the split transaction details will be
accurate. For hourly employees or employees making more than the FICA
cap amount, some pay periods will require changes to the entries in the split
transaction details.

Completing the Payroll Entries

In this section, you expand your payroll transactions by adding some entries
to the ANB Business account register. You add these transactions so that the
examples will contain enough pay periods to generate realistic reports. You
won't record check numbers for most of the remaining example transactions
in this chapter, but this won't affect the reports.

Establishing Scheduled Transaction Groups

In Chapter 11, "Setting Up Quicken for Your Business," you established a
transaction group for utilities payments. The object of transaction grouping is
to batch together similar transactions that occur around the same time each
month so that Quicken can automatically record them for you the next time
they need to be made. Remember that only memorized transactions can be
batched into transaction groups. From the ANB Business account register,
perform the following steps to establish a transaction group for the payroll:

1. Select Scheduled Transaction from the Lists menu. The Scheduled Transaction List window appears.
2. Select New. The Set Up Scheduled Transaction dialog box appears.
3. Enter **ANB Business** in the Account field. Remember that you can type the entry or select it from the drop-down list box.
4. Select Group, and the Set Up Transaction Group window appears.
5. Type **Payroll** in the Name for this group text box.
6. Enter **2/28/94** in the Next Payment Date text box.
7. Select Enter w/o prompting from the Register Entry drop-down list box.
8. Type **2** in the Days in advance text box to have Quicken enter the transactions two days before the payment date.
9. Select OK, and the Assign Transactions to Group dialog box appears.
10. Select Month from the Frequency of payment drop-down list box.
11. To include the transaction with John Smith as the payee, double-click this transaction or highlight it and select Mark. Note the 2 in the Grp column, indicating that the transaction is now part of Group 2.
12. Mark the transaction with Mary McFaul as the payee to include it in the group. This transaction also becomes a part of Group 2.
13. Select Done to indicate that you are finished selecting transactions.

Recording February Transactions

In this section, you add the remaining transactions to the account register to complete the payroll entries for the month of February. You should be in the ANB Business account register.

1. Move to the next blank transaction form.
2. Select Scheduled Transaction from the Lists menu.

   Quicken displays a list of transaction groups.
3. Move to the Payroll group, and select Pay Now.

   Quicken displays the target account—ANB Business—and the date of the next scheduled entry for the group—2/28/94.
4. Select Enter to confirm that this information is valid and to enter and record the group of payroll transactions in the ANB Business account register.

   If the date was not the last date of the month for payroll purposes, you could have typed the correct date in the Transaction date text box and then selected OK. In this example, you don't modify the payroll amounts since they are the same from month to month. If you have employees who work on an hourly basis, you would need to select each

12

new transaction, open the Splits dialog box, and make the necessary modifications to the dollar amounts recorded.

Quicken has entered the scheduled transaction for the monthly payroll for February. It looks like this in the account register:

2/28/94	Sched	John Smith		1,560 13			5,243 27
		000-00-0001	--Splits--				
2/28/94	Sched	Mary McFaul		2,284 22			2,959 05
		000-00-0002	--Splits--				

Notice that Quicken displays Sched in the Num field. When you write your payroll checks, you can enter the check number in this field. If you want to search your register to see if Sched still appears for any transactions, you can choose Find from the Edit menu and place "Sched" in the Num field.

The payroll entries are the only February transactions that are being added to the account register at this time. Figure 12-2 shows a printout of the account register, including the two payroll entries recorded on 2/28/94 and the remaining transactions that will be entered in this chapter.

Recording March Transactions

The March entries can be divided into three groups. The first entry is a deposit for federal social security, Medicare, and income tax withholdings in February. The second and third entries record income earned during the month from consulting and royalties. The last two entries record the payroll transactions for March.

The February Withholdings Entry

To record the deposit for taxes withheld during February, you use a memorized transaction and QuickFill. From a blank transaction form in the ANB Business account register, perform the following steps:

1. Type **3/1/94** in the Date field.

2. Type **I** in the Payee field, and press Tab.

   QuickFill finds only one memorized transaction with a Payee that starts with *I* and provides "Internal Revenue Service" to finish the field. When you press Tab, QuickFill fills in the remainder of the fields for the transaction. QuickFill doesn't fill in the other fields if you use the mouse instead of Tab to move to another field.

3. Select Record to record this transaction.

```
                      Check Register
ANB Business                                          Page 1
07/29/1994
Date  Num        Transaction        Payment  C  Deposit   Balance
02/28 Sched John Smith             1,560.13           5,243.27
/1994 SPLIT 000-00-0001
      cat:  Payroll:Gross/B        2,000.00
            Gross Earnings
            [Payroll-FICA]/B                 124.00
            FICA Withholding
            [Payroll-FWH]/B                  232.00
            Federal Withholding
            [Payroll-SWH]/B                   54.87
            State  Withholding
            [Payroll-MCARE]/B                 29.00
            Medicare Withholding
            Payroll:Comp FICA/B     124.00
            Payroll Taxes-FICA
            Payroll:Comp MCARE/B     29.00
            Payroll Taxes-MCARE
            [Payroll-FICA-Co]/B              124.00
            FICA Matching
            [Payroll-MCARECo]/B               29.00
            Medicare Matching
02/28 Sched Mary McFaul            2,284.22           2,959.05
/1994 SPLIT 000-00-0002
      cat:  Payroll:Gross/B        3,000.00
            Gross Earnings
            [Payroll-FICA]/B                 186.00
            FICA Withholding
            [Payroll-FWH]/B                  382.00
            Federal Withholding
            [Payroll-SWH]/B                  104.28
            State Withholding
            [Payroll-MCARE]/B                 43.50
            Medicare Withholding
            Payroll:Comp FICA/B     186.00
            Payroll Taxes-FICA
            Payroll:Comp MCARE/B     43.50
            Payroll Taxes-MCARE
            [Payroll-FICA-Co]/B              186.00
            FICA Matching
            [Payroll-MCARECo]/B               43.50
            Medicare Matching
```

12

Account register showing additional transactions **Figure 12-2.**

```
                    Check Register
ANB Business                                          Page 2
07/29/1994
Date   Num            Transaction       Payment   C   Deposit    Balance
03/01          Internal Revenue Service  1,379.00           1,580.05
/1994 SPLIT Form 941 Withholding Payment
       cat:  [Payroll-FICA]/B             620.00
             FICA Withholding and match
             [Payroll-MCARE]/B            145.00
             Medicare Withhold and match
             [Payroll-FWH]/B              614.00
             Federal Withholding
03/01          Tyler Corp.                       25,000.00  26,580.05
/1994 memo: Seminars conducted Jan. 94
       cat:  Inc Cons/B


03/31          Big Books                         10,000.00  36,580.05
/1994 memo: Royalties
       cat:  Inc Roy/B
03/31 Sched John Smith               1,560.13              35,019.92
/1994 SPLIT 000-00-0001
       cat:  Payroll:Gross/B          2,000.00
             Gross Earnings
             [Payroll-FICA]/B                      124.00
             FICA Withholding
             [Payroll-FWH]/B                        232.00
             Federal Withholding
             [Payroll-SWH]/B                         54.87
             State  Withholding
             [Payroll-MCARE]/B                       29.00
             Medicare Withholding
             Payroll:Comp FICA/B       124.00
             Payroll Taxes-FICA
             Payroll:Comp MCARE/B       29.00
             Payroll Taxes-MCARE
             [Payroll-FICA-Co]/B                    124.00
             FICA Matching
             [Payroll-MCARECo]/B                     29.00
             Medicare Matching
```

Account
register
showing
additional
transactions
(*continued*)
Figure 12-2.

```
                        Check Register
ANB Business                                               Page 3
07/29/1994
Date   Num            Transaction        Payment  C  Deposit   Balance
03/31 Sched  Mary McFaul                 2,284.22            32,735.70
/1994 SPLIT  000-00-0002
      cat:   Payroll:Gross/B             3,000.00
             Gross Earnings
             [Payroll-FICA]/B                       186.00
             FICA Withholding
             [Payroll-FWH]/B                         382.00
             Federal Withholding
             [Payroll-SWH]/B                         104.28
             State Withholding
             [Payroll-MCARE]/B                        43.50
             Medicare Withholding
             Payroll:Comp FICA/B          186.00
             Payroll Taxes-FICA
             Payroll:Comp MCARE/B          43.50
             Payroll Taxes-MCARE
             [Payroll-FICA-Co]/B                     186.00
             FICA Matching
             [Payroll-MCARECo]/B                      43.50
             Medicare Matching
04/01        Internal Revenue Service    1,379.00            31,356.70
/1994 SPLIT  Form 941 Withholding Payment
      cat:   [Payroll-FICA]/B             620.00
             FICA Withholding and match
             [Payroll-MCARE]/B            145.00
             Medicare Withhold and match
             [Payroll-FWH]/B              614.00
             Federal Withholding
04/15        Internal Revenue Service     104.00            31,252.70
/1994 memo:  FUTA
      cat:   Payroll:Comp FUTA/B

04/15        Bureau of Employment Ser...  520.00            30,732.70
/1994 memo:  SUTA
      cat:   Payroll:Comp SUI/B
```

Account
register
showing
additional
transactions
(*continued*)
Figure 12-2.

12

Consulting and Royalty Income Entries

In the ANB Business account register, enter the following information for the two deposit entries shown in Figure 12-2:

1. Enter **3/1/94** in the Date field.
2. Type **Tyler Corp.** in the Payee field.
3. Type **25000** in the Deposit field.
4. Type **Seminars conducted Jan. 94** in the Memo field.
5. Enter **Inc Cons/B** in the Category field.
6. Select Record. This records the Tyler Corp. revenue transaction.
7. Enter **3/31/94** in the Date field.
8. Type **Big Books** in the Payee field.
9. Type **10000** in the Deposit field.
10. Type **Royalties** in the Memo field.
11. Enter **Inc Roy/B** in the Category field.
12. Select Record.

You have now recorded both income transactions for March.

March Payroll Entries

In this section, you add the remaining transactions to the account register to complete the payroll entries for the month of March:

1. Select Scheduled Transaction from the Lists menu.
2. Highlight the Payroll group, and select Pay Now. Quicken displays the date of the next scheduled entry for the group—3/28/94—and the target account—ANB Business.
3. Enter **3/31/94** in the Date in register text box, and select Enter.

   This changes the date to the last day in March and enters the group of payroll transactions in the account register.
4. Press Esc or click on the control menu box to close the Scheduled Transactions List window.

Recording April Transactions

The only transactions you will record for April are the Internal Revenue Service deposit for the March payroll and the Federal Unemployment Tax Act (FUTA) and State Unemployment Tax Act (SUTA) payments.

Complete the following steps to record the IRS transaction in the ANB Business account register. (This transaction will help you prepare several reports for the Internal Revenue Service. These reports are discussed later in this chapter.)

1. Move to the end of the register.
2. Select Memorized Transactions from the Lists menu.
3. Highlight the Internal Revenue Service transaction, and select Use.
4. Enter **4/1/94** in the Date field.
5. Select Record.

In addition to your withholding tax liabilities, employers must pay unemployment taxes. This program is mandated by the federal government but administered by the individual state governments. Because of this method of administration, you must make payments to both the state and the federal government. At the time this book is being written, you must contribute .008 percent to the federal government to cover its administrative costs and up to .054 percent to the state agency that administers the program. These percentages apply to the first $7000.00 of earnings for each employee. In some states, the salary cap on earnings may be higher; however, the example in this chapter uses a $7000.00 limit for both federal and state employer payroll tax contributions.

You must make deposits to the federal government whenever your contribution liability reaches $100.00. You make these deposits in the same way you make the FICA, Medicare, and federal income tax withholding payments discussed earlier in this chapter.

Your actual contributions to the state agency are based on historical rates for your business and industry classification. You may qualify for a percentage rate lower than the maximum rate allowed by law. The contribution rate for the business in this example is .04 percent.

Generally, payments to the state agency that administers the program are made quarterly. Each quarter, you are required to complete an Employer's Report of Wages form, summarizing your employees' total earnings during the quarter and the amount of your FUTA and SUTA liabilities.

From the ANB Business account register, follow these steps to make the payments for federal and state unemployment payroll taxes during the month of April:

1. Make certain you are at the next available form for recording a transaction.
2. Enter **4/15/94** in the Date field.

12

3. Enter **Internal Revenue Service** in the Payee field, and press `Tab`.

   The QuickFill feature automatically fills in the remaining fields. If you move to the Payment field by using the mouse instead of by pressing `Tab`, these fields are not filled in, and you can ignore steps 4, 5, and 6.

4. Select Splits to open the Splits dialog box.

5. Select Clear All to delete the first line of the split transaction, select Yes, and then select OK.

6. When Quicken asks you how you want to reconcile the fact that the entered payment amount and the split transaction window don't agree, simply select OK.

7. Type **104** in the Payment field.

   In the "Payroll Reports" section of this chapter, you will see that Smith received $6000.00 and McFaul received $9000.00 in gross pay. McFaul has reached the salary limit for employer unemployment contributions for the year. The amount entered here was determined by multiplying the first $7000.00 of McFaul's salary and all $6000.00 of Smith's by the FUTA rate of .008.

8. Type **FUTA** in the Memo field.

9. Enter **Payroll:Comp FUTA/B** in the Category field, and select Record.

   You have now completed the recording of the FUTA payroll tax deposit.

10. Type **Bureau of Employment Services** in the Memo field for the next transaction.

11. Type **520** in the Payment field.

12. Type **SUTA** in the Memo field.

    The payment amount of 520 was determined by multiplying 13,000.00 ($7000.00+$6000.00) by .04.

13. Enter **Payroll:Comp SUI/B**, and select Record.

Now you have completed all the transactions that will be added to the account register in this chapter.

Payroll Reports

Through the use of filters and customization features, you can obtain a substantial amount of the payroll-related information you need to prepare federal, state, and local payroll tax and withholding forms. However, as you will see in the following sections, you must perform some functions manually, such as totaling amounts from several Quicken reports to determine the numbers to place on some lines of tax forms.

In this section, you practice preparing some of the reports you may find useful for your business filing requirements. Although it is impossible to provide illustrations of all the variations, preparing the reports that follow will help you become familiar with the possibilities. You can then begin to explore modifications that suit your payroll and withholding reporting needs.

From the transactions you entered for January through April, you can gather information that will assist you in preparing your quarterly reports: the FUTA form, SUTA form, workers' compensation report, and federal, state, and local withholding tax reports. Although you have not entered a full year's worth of transactions, you will see that Quicken can also help you prepare year-end W-2s, W-3s, 1099s, annual forms for federal, state, and local tax withholdings, and other annual tax forms required for unemployment and workers' compensation purposes.

Payroll Report Overview

Quicken's Payroll report summarizes all your payroll activities in any period for which you need information—that is, you can prepare the report for weekly, monthly, quarterly, or yearly payroll summary information. You can gather the information for all your employees in one report, or you can limit the report to information about one employee at a time.

Keep in mind that Quicken's Payroll report is preset to interface with only the Payroll category. All payroll-related charges are charged against the main Payroll category. Earlier in the chapter, you established subcategories such as Payroll:Gross and Payroll:Comp FICA to keep track of specific types of payroll charges. If you don't use this format, you need to select Summary from the Custom submenu of the Reports menu and customize your reports to gather the information necessary for tax-reporting purposes. For all the reports in this section, you will use the Payroll command in the Business submenu of the Reports menu.

Employer's Quarterly Federal Tax Return

In the previous sections of this chapter, you prepared entries that accumulated FICA and Medicare withholdings, the matching employer's contribution, and the federal income tax withheld from each employee's paycheck. You also recorded the required payments to the IRS, which are made to a local bank authorized to receive these funds.

12

Let's now examine how you can use Quicken to assist you in preparing Form 941 (shown in Figure 12-3) to meet your quarterly filing requirements. Consult the special "Dates for Filing Federal Payroll Tax Returns" section in this chapter for the deadlines for filing quarterly Form 941 and annual Form

Form **941**
(Rev. January 1993)
Department of the Treasury
Internal Revenue Service

4141

Employer's Quarterly Federal Tax Return
► See separate instructions for information on completing this form.
Please type or print.

OMB No. 1545-0029
Expires 1-31-96

Enter state code for state in which deposits made . ► (see page 2 of instructions).

Name (as distinguished from trade name)

Trade name, if any

Address (number and street)

Date quarter ended

Employer identification number

City, state, and ZIP code

T
FF
FD
FP
I
T

If address is different from prior return, check here ►

IRS Use

1 1 1 1 1 1 1 1 1 1 2 3 3 3 3 3 3 4 4 4
5 5 5 7 8 8 8 8 8 9 9 10 10 10 10 10 10 10 10 10

If you do not have to file returns in the future, check here . ► ☐   Date final wages paid . . . ► _____
If you are a seasonal employer, see **Seasonal employers** on page 1 and check here ► ☐
1   Number of employees (except household) employed in the pay period that includes March 12th ►

2 Total wages and tips subject to withholding, plus other compensation	**2**
3 Total income tax withheld from wages, tips, pensions, annuities, sick pay, gambling, etc.	**3**
4 Adjustment of withheld income tax for preceding quarters of calendar year (see instructions) . .	**4**
5 Adjusted total of income tax withheld (line 3 as adjusted by line 4—see instructions) . . .	**5**
6a Taxable social security wages . . . . . $ × 12.4% (.124) =	**6a**
b Taxable social security tips . . . . . . $ × 12.4% (.124) =	**6b**
7 Taxable Medicare wages and tips . . . $ × 2.9% (.029) =	**7**
8 Total social security and Medicare taxes (add lines 6a, 6b, and 7)	**8**
9 Adjustment of social security and Medicare taxes (see instructions for required explanation) .	**9**
10 Adjusted total of social security and Medicare taxes (line 8 as adjusted by line 9—see instructions)	**10**
11 Backup withholding (see instructions)	**11**
12 Adjustment of backup withholding tax for preceding quarters of calendar year	**12**
13 Adjusted total of backup withholding (line 11 as adjusted by line 12)	**13**
14 **Total taxes** (add lines 5, 10, and 13)	**14**
15 Advance earned income credit (EIC) payments made to employees, if any	**15**
16 Net taxes (subtract line 15 from line 14). **This should equal line 20, col. (d), below or line D of Schedule B** (plus line D of Schedule A if you treated backup withholding as a separate liability)	**16**
17 Total deposits for quarter, including overpayment applied from a prior quarter, from your records	**17**
18 Balance due (subtract line 17 from line 16). This should be less than $500. Pay to the Internal Revenue Service	**18**

19 **Overpayment,** if line 17 is more than line 16, enter excess here ► $ _____ and check if to be:
☐ Applied to next return   **OR**   ☐ Refunded.

20 **Monthly Summary of Federal Tax Liability. If line 16 is less than $500, you need not complete line 20.** If you are a monthly depositor, summarize your monthly tax liability below. If you are a semiweekly depositor or have accumulated a tax liability of $100,000 or more on any day, attach Schedule B (Form 941) and check here (see instructions) . . . . . . ► ☐

	(a) First month	(b) Second month	(c) Third month	(d) Total for quarter
Liability for month				

Sign Here

Under penalties of perjury, I declare that I have examined this return, including accompanying schedules and statements, and to the best of my knowledge and belief, it is true, correct, and complete.

Signature ►

Print Your Name and Title ►

Date ►

For Paperwork Reduction Act Notice, see page 1 of separate instructions.   Cat. No. 17001Z   Form **941** (Rev. 1-93)

☆ U.S. GOVERNMENT PRINTING OFFICE: 1993 339-478

IRS Form 941
Figure 12-3.

943. Starting from your ANB Business account register, complete the following steps:

1. Select Business from the Reports menu, or select the Reports icon from the Iconbar and then select the Business option button.
2. Select Payroll from the menu or dialog box.
3. Type **1/1/94** in the from text box.
4. Type **4/1/94** in the to text box.
5. Select OK, and the Payroll report appears on your screen.

   Although the report is for the quarter that ends on 3/31/94, you need to include the March FICA, Medicare, and income tax withholding payment entered in the register on 4/1/94.

   This is a wide screen report; it will be printed on several pages.
6. Select Print, and the Print Report window appears.
7. Select Print to print the report.

If you select a small font or landscape mode, you can capture more of the report on each page.

Dates for Filing Federal Payroll Tax Returns

Form 941, Employer's Quarterly Federal Tax Return

First Quarter (January - March)

If deposit is required with filing	April 30
If you deposited all taxes when due	May 10

Second Quarter (April - June)

If deposit is required with filing	July 31
If you deposited all taxes when due	August 10

Third Quarter (July - September)

If deposit is required with filing	October 31
If you deposited all taxes when due	November 10

12

Dates for Filing Federal Payroll Tax Returns (*continued*)

Fourth Quarter (October - December)	
If deposit is required with filing	January 31
If you deposited all taxes when due	February 10

Form 943, Employer's Annual Tax Return for Agricultural Employees	
Calendar year filing	
If deposit is required with filing	January 31
If you deposited all taxes when due	February 10

Using the Payroll Report to Complete Form 941

The Payroll report is shown in Figure 12-4. (Unless you use a wide-carriage printer or a very small font, the Payroll report will print on several pages instead of just one.) Let's take a look at the information gathered and discuss how you can use it to complete the appropriate lines of the Employer's Quarterly Federal Tax Return form, shown in Figure 12-3. Look at the following lines on the Employer's Quarterly Federal Tax Return form:

✦ *Line 2* This line is for the total wages subject to federal withholding. On the Payroll report, under EXPENSES, the Gross line shows that a total of $15,000.00 was earned by Smith and McFaul during the quarter.

✦ *Line 3* This line is for the total amount of income tax withheld from employee wages. On the Payroll report, under TRANSFERS, the TO Payroll-FWH line shows that the total federal income tax withheld from employees was $1842.00. If you look at the FROM Payroll-FWH line, you can see that $696.00 was paid by Smith and $1146.00 was paid by McFaul.

✦ *Line 6a* This line is for the amount of social security taxes accumulated during the quarter. If you look at the Payroll report under TRANSFERS, you can see in the TO Payroll-FICA line that the total amount is $1860.00. The totals in the FROM Payroll-FICA and the FROM Payroll-FICA-Co lines are combined to obtain this amount.

Payroll Report
1/1/94 Through 4/1/94

7/30/93
BUSINESS-All Accounts

Category Description	Internal Revenue Service	John Smith	Mary McFaul	Opening Balance	OVERALL TOTAL
INCOME/EXPENSE					
EXPENSES					
Payroll:					
Comp FICA	0.00	372.00	558.00	0.00	930.00
Comp MCARE	0.00	87.00	130.50	0.00	217.50
Gross	0.00	6,000.00	9,000.00	0.00	15,000.00
Total Payroll	0.00	6,459.00	9,688.50	0.00	16,147.50
TOTAL EXPENSES	0.00	6,459.00	9,688.50	0.00	16,147.50
TOTAL INCOME/EXPENSE	0.00	-6,459.00	-9,688.50	0.00	-16,147.50
TRANSFERS					
TO Payroll-FICA	-1,860.00	0.00	0.00	0.00	-1,860.00
TO Payroll-FWH	-1,842.00	0.00	0.00	0.00	-1,842.00
TO Payroll-MCARE	-435.00	0.00	0.00	0.00	-435.00
FROM Payroll-FICA	0.00	372.00	558.00	0.00	930.00
FROM Payroll-FICA-CO	0.00	372.00	558.00	0.00	930.00
FROM Payroll-FWH	0.00	696.00	1,146.00	0.00	1,842.00
FROM Payroll-MCARE	0.00	87.00	130.50	0.00	217.50
FROM Payroll-MCARECo	0.00	87.00	130.50	0.00	217.50
FROM Payroll-SWH	0.00	164.61	312.84	0.00	477.45
TOTAL TRANSFERS	-4,137.00	1,778.61	2,835.84	0.00	477.45
Balance Forward					
Payroll-FICA	0.00	0.00	0.00	0.00	0.00
Payroll-FICA-CO	0.00	0.00	0.00	0.00	0.00
Payroll-FWH	0.00	0.00	0.00	0.00	0.00
Payroll-MCARE	0.00	0.00	0.00	0.00	0.00
Payroll-MCARECo	0.00	0.00	0.00	0.00	0.00
Payroll-SWH	0.00	0.00	0.00	0.00	0.00
Total Balance Forward	0.00	0.00	0.00	0.00	0.00
OVERALL TOTAL	-4,137.00	-4,680.39	-6,852.66	0.00	-15,670.05

Payroll report
Figure 12-4.

12

To verify the FICA tax owed, multiply the amount on line 2 of the form ($15,000.00) by .124. This should equal the total calculated in the preceding paragraph ($1860.00), which it does. You record this amount on line 6a.

✦ *Line 7*   This line is for the amount of Medicare taxes accumulated during the quarter. On the Payroll report, you get the total from the TO Payroll-MCARE line; the total is $435.00. This total comes from adding the amounts in the FROM Payroll-MCARE and FROM Payroll-MCARECo rows of the report.

To verify the Medicare taxes owed, multiply the amount on line 2 of the form ($15,000) by .029 to get the amount on line 7.

✦ *Line 17*   This line is for the total deposits made to the IRS during the quarter. This amount can be obtained from the Internal Revenue Service column in the Payroll report. The OVERALL TOTAL row shows that $4137.00 was deposited with the Internal Revenue Service during the quarter. Note that this amount includes the 4/1/94 payment. When you complete your IRS deposit slip, you designate the quarter for which the payment applies. In this case, the payment was made for the first quarter and would thus be included in this report.

The bottom portion of Form 941 requires you to calculate your tax liabilities at specified time intervals during the deposit periods. Since you made your payments in a timely fashion during the quarter, you do not need to complete this portion. If you did need to complete this portion of the form for the example in this chapter, you could use Quicken to gather information for you. Figure 12-5 shows the Federal Tax Liability report, which would capture the information for the first quarter to help you to complete the lines at the bottom of Form 941. If you pay your employees weekly, you could produce this same report for weekly periods during the quarter. If you want to reproduce Figure 12-5 with your account register, complete the following steps from the ANB Business account register:

1. Select Business from the Reports menu, or select the Reports icon and the Business option button.
2. Select Payroll from the menu or dialog box.
3. Type **1/1/94** in the from text box.
4. Type **3/31/94** in the to text box.
5. Select Customize. The Customize Report dialog box appears on the screen.
6. Type **Federal Tax Liability By Month** in the Title text box.
7. Select Payee from the Row drop-down list box.
8. Select Month from the Columns drop-down list box.

```
                Federal Tax Liability By Month
                       1/1/94 Through 3/31/94
        7/30/94                                              Page 1
        BUSINESS-Selected Accounts

                                                       OVERALL
             Payee         1/1        2/1        3/1    TOTAL
        ------------------ ---------- ---------- ---------- ----------


        John Smith            538.00     538.00     538.00   1,614.00
        Mary McFaul           841.00     841.00     841.00   2,523.00
        Opening Balance         0.00       0.00       0.00       0.00
                           ---------- ---------- ---------- ----------


        OVERALL TOTAL       1,379.00   1,379.00   1,379.00   4,137.00
                           ========== ========== ========== ==========
```

Tax report for employee federal tax withholding **Figure 12-5.**

9. Select the Matching option button.

   The Matching dialog box elements appear. A tilde (~) is used in the Payee matches row to tell Quicken to exclude transactions with this payee from the report.

10. Type ~**Internal Revenue Service** in the Payee contains text box.

11. Enter **[Payroll..** in the Category contains text box.

    This text box contains "Payroll.." by default, telling Quicken to include only transactions with a Payroll category. Adding the square bracket tells Quicken to include only transfers to Payroll liability accounts.

12. Select the Categories/Classes option button.

13. Unmark the liability account Payroll-SWH, as shown here:

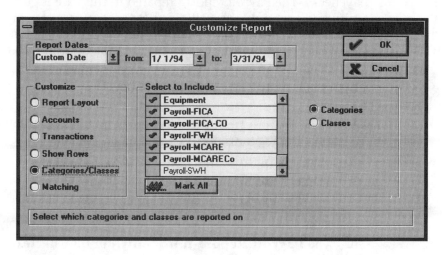

12

14. Select OK.

15. Select Pri<u>n</u>t, and the Print Report dialog box appears.

16. Select <u>P</u>rint to print the Federal Tax Liability report shown in Figure 12-5.

Preparing Other Tax Forms

In addition to the Employer's Quarterly Federal Tax Return, you will need to complete several other quarterly tax returns and reports, depending on the state where your business is located. These additional reports and tax forms may include state (SWH) and local (LWH) withholding tax reports and state unemployment tax (SUTA) reports. The Payroll report shown in Figure 12-4 provides the information needed to prepare some of these reports. For example, under TRANSFERS, the FROM Payroll-SWH line shows that $477.45 was withheld from employee wages for state taxes. You have not recorded this entry in your register; however, when the check is sent to the state taxing unit, the payment would be handled in the same manner as the payments to the IRS. You will also need to monitor individual employees' gross earnings to complete several of the other forms. Determining the total earnings for an employee for a given time period and determining your FUTA and SUTA contributions are discussed in the section "Other Annual Tax Forms and Reports" later in this chapter.

Preparing W-2 Forms

At the end of the year, you must give each employee who worked for you during the year a W-2 form. In the example developed here, assume that John Smith left your business at the end of March and received no further paychecks. The Payroll report prepared in this case is customized for John Smith and uses only the ANB Business account register since this is the account from which you write your payroll checks. All the information concerning John Smith's earnings are included in this account.

Starting from the ANB Business account register, complete the following steps to gather the information needed to complete John Smith's W-2 form:

1. Select <u>B</u>usiness from the <u>R</u>eports menu, or select the Reports icon and select the <u>B</u>usiness option button.

2. Select <u>P</u>ayroll from the menu or dialog box.

3. Type **1/1/94** in the <u>f</u>rom text box.

4. Type **12/31/94** in the <u>t</u>o text box.

5. Select <u>C</u>ustomize to open the Customize Report dialog box.

6. Type **Payroll Report-John Smith** in the T<u>i</u>tle text box.

7. Select Matching.

   The Category Contains text box contains "Payroll" by default, which causes Quicken to limit the report to Payroll category transactions. As mentioned earlier, this feature of Quicken requires you to record all payroll activity in the Payroll category. Otherwise, Quicken's Payroll report will not gather your payroll transactions correctly. In that case, you would need to prepare your reports by using the Summary Report option.

8. Type **John Smith** in the Payee Contains text box, and select OK. You have filtered the report so that it will include only the payroll information for John Smith.

9. Select Print, and the Print Report dialog box appears.

10. Select the Printer option button, and select Print.

The Payroll report shown in Figure 12-6 provides the payroll history for John Smith in 1994. Although you have not entered the entire year's payroll transactions for Mary McFaul, the same steps would generate her W-2 information.

Using the Payroll Report to Complete a W-2
The payroll report can be used to complete John Smith's W-2 Wage and Tax Statement:

✦ Under EXPENSES, the Gross line shows the total earnings reported ($6000).

✦ Under TRANSFERS, the FROM Payroll-FWH line shows the total federal withholding amount ($696.00).

✦ The FICA withholding amount ($372.00) is found in the FROM Payroll-FICA line. Notice this amount is equal to the company's FICA matching contribution since the company matches employee FICA contributions dollar for dollar up to $57,600 of gross earnings.

✦ The Medicare withholding amount ($87.00) is shown in the FROM Payroll-MCARE line. Notice that this amount is equal to the company's Medicare matching contribution since the company matches employee Medicare contributions dollar for dollar up to the first $135,000 of gross earnings.

✦ The state withholding amount ($164.61) is shown in the FROM Payroll-SWH line of the report.

12

No local taxes were withheld in this example. If you do business in an area where local income taxes are withheld, you need to add the appropriate liability accounts to accumulate this information.

```
                    Payroll Report-John Smith
                     1/1/94 Through 12/31/94
     7/30/94                                                   Page 1
     BUSINESS-All Accounts


             Category Description              John Smith
     --------------------------------     ------------------------
     INCOME/EXPENSE
       EXPENSES
         Payroll:
           Comp FICA                  372.00
           Comp MCARE                  87.00
           Gross                    6,000.00
                                    ----------
          Total Payroll                            6,459.00
                                                 -----------
         TOTAL EXPENSES                            6,459.00

                                                 -----------
       TOTAL INCOME/EXPENSE                       -6,459.00

     TRANSFERS
       FROM Payroll-FICA                           372.00
       FROM Payroll-FICA-Co                        372.00
       FROM Payroll-FWH                            696.00
       FROM Payroll-MCARE                           87.00
       FROM Payroll-MCARECo                         87.00
       FROM Payroll-SWH                            164.61
                                                 -----------
       TOTAL TRANSFERS                            1,778.61


                                                 -----------
       OVERALL TOTAL                             -4,680.39
                                                 ===========
```

Annual
Payroll report
for John Smith
Figure 12-6.

Other Annual Tax Forms and Reports

The information provided in the preceding reports can also be used to prepare other year-end tax reports. For example, Payroll reports for the full year, similar to those shown in Figures 12-4 and 12-6, can be used to complete sections of the following reports:

✦ Form W-3, Transmittal of Income and Tax Statements

✦ Form 940, Employer's Annual Federal Unemployment (FUTA) Tax Return

✦ Various state and local withholding and state unemployment tax (SUTA) reports

FUTA and SUTA Contributions

In the "Recording April Transactions" section of this chapter, you recorded entries on 4/15/94 for your FUTA and SUTA contributions. When completing your quarterly and annual reports, you can use Quicken's Filter option to prepare a report showing the total FUTA and SUTA contributions paid during the quarter or the year. To do this, you prepare a Payroll report using Quicken's Customize Report window, and you make the category match Payroll:Comp FUTA. Then you prepare a second report in which the category matches Payroll:Comp SUI. Figures 12-7 and 12-8 show reports prepared from your account register that have been filtered in this way. The reports show FUTA payments of $104.00 and SUTA payments of $520.00.

You can also prepare filtered reports to determine the total federal and state payments for unemployment taxes during the entire year. You can then use that information when completing your Form 940 and the corresponding state SUTA form.

Form 1099

The last payroll-related statement discussed here is Form 1099. You must provide a Form 1099 to all individuals who are not regular employees and to whom you have paid more than $600.00 during the tax year. The easiest way to record transactions for payments of this nature is to type **1099** in the

```
                          FUTA Payments
                     1/1/94 Through 4/15/94
   7/30/94                                              Page 1
   BUSINESS-All Accounts


            Category Description        Internal Revenue Service
   ---------------------------        ----------------------------

   INCOME/EXPENSE
     EXPENSES
       Payroll:
         Comp FUTA                     104.00
                                       ---------

       Total Payroll                               104.00
                                                   ---------
     TOTAL EXPENSES                                104.00


                                                   ---------
   TOTAL INCOME/EXPENSE                            -104.00
                                                   =========
```

Report showing FUTA payments **Figure 12-7.**

12

```
                              SUTA Payments
                          1/1/94 Through 4/15/94
        7/30/94                                                    Page 1
        BUSINESS-All Accounts


                   Category Description      Bureau of Employment Services
         ------------------------------     -------------------------------
         INCOME/EXPENSE
            EXPENSES
               Payroll:
                  Comp SUI                   520.00
                                             ---------

               Total Payroll                         520.00
                                                     ---------
            TOTAL EXPENSES                            520.00


                                                     ---------
            TOTAL INCOME/EXPENSE                     -520.00
                                                     =========
```

Report
showing
SUTA
payments
Figure 12-8.

Memo field when you record the transactions in your business account
register during the year. You can then prepare a Transaction report for the
year filtered by Payee and Memo field matches to gather the information
needed to prepare 1099s for each payee. If you are not certain of all the
payees to whom you have paid miscellaneous income, you may want to
filter the Memo field for 1099 first and print all these transactions. You can
then use that information to group your 1099 information by Payee
matches. You could also assign all 1099 payments to a category (for example,
Consult-1099) and filter a Summary or Transaction report by payee and
category to accumulate the necessary 1099 information.

CHAPTER

13

PREPARING BUDGET REPORTS AND CASH FLOW STATEMENTS

Operating a successful business involves more than just having a good product or service to sell to customers or clients; you also need to develop a sound financial management program that will allow your business to grow and develop. Financial management is more than just being able to prepare the basic reports your banker or other creditors request; it includes a plan of action that will show your creditors you are prepared to manage your business in a changing environment. This means you need to start considering developing a program to manage the finances of your business. Your program would consist of the following:

✦ A business plan

✦ The development of strong business relations with your banker or other creditors

✦ The use of budgets and cash flow statements to help in managing your financial resources

In order to develop a financial management program, you need a sound accounting system that will provide the financial information you need to make better management decisions. Quicken can help you generate this type of information for your business.

Developing a Financial Management Program

Developing a sound financial management program is an important aspect of managing your business.

If you look closely at the parts of the financial management program just listed, you will notice that two of the three parts do not directly involve the accounting system. Let's take a more in-depth look at the program components.

A business plan is a well-developed concept of where your business has been and where it is going. The special box entitled "Preparing a Business Plan" highlights the key points that a business plan should cover. You can see that nonfinancial considerations play a major role in your business plan—that is, you need to know your product and potential market before you can begin to budget sales and costs for your business. The budget process you follow in this chapter demonstrates how budgeting and cash flow statements are prepared. More importantly, you will see that the decisions you make in estimating budget income and expenses come from nonfinancial considerations. In short, developing a business plan forces you to think through your business, both financially and operationally. In the long run, the plan makes it easier for you to estimate the expected sales and related costs.

The importance of developing strong relations with your banker and creditors cannot be underestimated. However, a word of caution: Don't expect a bank to finance a new business for you. A good banker is going to expect you to provide a significant part of the capital needed. You might think that you would not need the banker if you had the money to finance your ideas. But from the banker's perspective, it is not good business to risk the bank's money if you are not willing to invest your own capital. The box entitled "Sources of Funding" shows some alternative ways to obtain financing for your business if a bank is not a realistic source of cash.

Preparing a Business Plan

If you have never prepared a business plan, determining what to include can be difficult. Your goal is to create a concise document that presents a realistic picture of your company, including its needs, assets, and products. Outside lenders will be especially interested in the financial history and resources of the firm and your sales projections. Be sure to include the following as you prepare your plan:

✦ A brief overview of your firm, its products, and its financing requirements. It is important to keep this short and simple.

✦ A brief history of the firm, including product successes and copyrights or patents held. Include a résumé of the firm's owners or partners.

✦ A short description of your product(s). Include information on the competition, production plans, and prices.

✦ A description of the market for the product(s) and your distribution plans.

✦ Sales and cost projections showing current capital and financing requirements.

When you choose a banker, it's important to maintain a strong relationship for the long term. One way of doing this is to obtain a modest bank loan when your business is prospering, even though you may not need the loan now. This will help strengthen your banking relationship. Then, when you really need a loan, your banker will already be familiar with you and your business activities. This might make the difference between loan approval or rejection.

The final part of the financial management program is budgeting and the regular monitoring of your cash flow. A budget is a plan in which you estimate the income and expenses of your business for a period of time: a week, a month, a quarter, a year, or longer. Creating a budget report requires some advance work, since you enter projected amounts for each category in the budget. Quicken guides you through the budget development process to minimize the work required. Then, you can enter your income and expenses and check the status of your actual and budgeted amounts whenever you wish. You can also use your budget figures to project the future cash flow of your business. This type of information is valuable in forecasting loans you may need and demonstrates to your banker that you are anticipating your financial needs. This is a sign of sound business and financial planning.

13

Sources of Funding

Securing financing for a new business can be difficult even if you have a good product. Banks are often wary of lending money for a new venture, unless you are willing to take the high-risk position of offering your home or other assets as collateral. Here are some other financing options to consider:

✦ A commercial bank loan under the Small Business Administration Loan Guarantee Program.

✦ Borrowing against your life insurance policy.

✦ Short-term borrowing through supplier credit extensions.

✦ Finance companies.

✦ Venture capitalists—you must normally give up a part of the ownership of your business with this option.

✦ Small business investment enterprises—you can find these by contacting your local governments about agencies and programs for small business development.

✦ For economically disadvantaged groups and minority businesses, there may be other options for public or private funding which you can locate through your local government or minority organizations.

A cash flow report is related to your budget and allows you to look at the inflow and outflow of cash for your business. This report is valuable. It can enable you to identify problems stemming from a lack of available cash, even though your business may be highly profitable at the current time.

In this chapter, you learn how to use Quicken in the preparation of a business budget. Remember the concepts discussed here as you go through the example; you are learning more than just the procedures involved. Budgeting and cash flow statement analysis can give you and your creditors important information. Quicken provides the necessary ingredients to help you prepare a financial management program that will make you a better business manager.

In the chapter example, you prepare budget entries for several months. Transaction groups from Chapters 11 and 12 are used to speed the entry process while providing enough transactions to get a sense of what Quicken can do. After making your entries, you will see how Quicken's standard Budget and Cash Flow reports can help you keep expenses in line with your budget.

Quicken's Budgeting Process

Quicken allows you to enter projected income and expense levels for any category or subcategory. You can enter the same projection for each month of the year or choose to change the amount allocated by month. For the business in this example, it is essential to be able to enter different budget amounts each month, especially for the projected income figures. Royalties are received at the end of each quarter, which causes some months to show a zero income in this category. Also, some other income-generating activities are seasonal and vary widely between months.

Quicken can help you manage your business finances.

Once you have entered the budget amounts, Quicken matches your planned expenses with the actual expense entries and displays the results in a Budget report. Although there is only one entry point for budget information, Quicken can collect the actual entries from all of your bank, cash, and credit card accounts in the current file. Therefore, if you have not paid any business expenses from your personal checking account, you may want to exclude this account from the Budget report. You can do this by selecting the accounts to use with the report. However, since in this example you have paid both personal and business expenses from the ANB Personal account, you cannot exclude it here. Instead, you will use the class code of B to select all business transactions when preparing reports in this chapter. You can also choose whether or not transfers between accounts should be shown in the budget. You can change whether transfers are shown by selecting Layout from the buttonbar, then selecting or clearing the Show Transfers check box.

Although Quicken can take much of the work out of entering and managing your budget, it cannot prepare a budget without your projections. Once you have put together a plan, it is time to record your decisions in Quicken. You can enter Quicken's budgeting process through the Activities menu of an account register. Quicken's budgeting process will be presented in the following stages: retrieving the Set Up Budgets window, specifying revenue amounts, moving around the Set Up Budgets window, entering expense projections, and printing the report.

Setting Up the Budget

The Set Up Budgets window is the starting place for Quicken's budget process. You can access this window in any account register. From the ANB Business account register, follow these steps to start the budget procedure:

13

1. Select <u>A</u>ctivities.

2. Select <u>S</u>et Up Budgets.

   Figure 13-1 shows the top portion of the Set Up Budgets window. The category descriptions are listed down the left side of the screen and the months of the year across the top. The layout of the information is similar to a spreadsheet; if you have ever used a package such as Lotus 1-2-3 or Quattro Pro, you will feel instantly familiar with the format.

Only a few category descriptions appear on the screen at any time. Quicken displays the total budget inflows and outflows at the bottom of the window and the total for the categories at the right and updates these totals as you make changes. The instant updating allows you to make changes to a budget amount and immediately assess the effect on budget differences.

You can budget periods of months, quarters, or years from the Layout option on the buttonbar.

3. Select Layout from the buttonbar to display the Layout Budgets dialog box.

4. Select Quarter for Columns then select OK to review the data in the Set Up Budgets window.

5. Repeat step 3 but select Year for Columns and select OK again to see the change in the Set Up Budgets window.

6. Repeat step 3 but select Month for Columns and select OK to change the time period back to the original display.

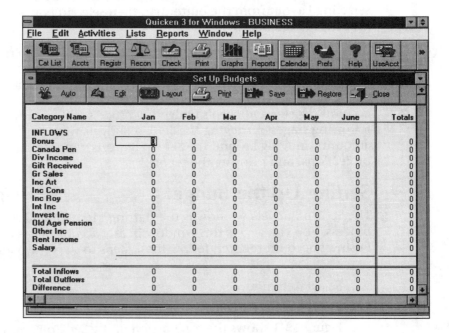

Portion of Set Up Budgets window
Figure 13-1.

Other Budget Buttonbar Options

Quicken will use last year's transaction to create a budget for you.

You can select options from the buttonbar at the top of the window with either the mouse or the keyboard by either clicking the button or by pressing (Alt) and the underlined letter. Although you will look at many of the budget buttonbar options in more detail in the exercises that follow, a quick overview will help you feel comfortable with this new Quicken window.

Select A̲uto to automatically create a budget from this year's transactions. You can select the period for the transactions or the categories that you want to use when creating the budget. You can select Use Monthly D̲etail or Use A̲verage for Period. You can also choose R̲ound Values to Nearest with options for $1, $10, or $100.

Select E̲dit to alter the existing budget display. Selecting 2-W̲eek lets you create a budget for an individual category or subcategory for a two-week time period. Cop̲y to Clipboard copies the budget to the Windows clipboard. Clear R̲ow lets you clear all the budgeted amounts in a specific category. Clear A̲ll Budgets lets you clear all budget amounts. Fill R̲ow Right lets you fill in the same amount for a specific category in all remaining budget periods. Fill C̲olumns allows you to fill all columns with the amounts recorded in the current column.

In the previous example, you looked at changing Layout options to specify the period for the budget. Other Lay̲out options allow you to enter whether subcategories (Show S̲ubcats) and transfers (Show T̲ransfrs) are shown on the budget layout. The H̲ide Zero Budget Categories option hides all the budgeted category amounts that are zero.

The Prin̲t button displays the Print Report dialog box so you can print your budget report. The Sa̲ve button saves a copy of your budget.

The Res̲tore button lets you restore a previous Set Up Budget window if you have saved it.

The C̲lose button closes the Set Up Budget window and saves the current budget.

Entering Revenue Projections

Entering budget projections is easy. If you want the same numbers in January through December, you will be able to enter a number for January and copy the number across to the other months. You can copy the last number entered across the row or you can copy an entire column across. After completing the copy, you can always customize entries for some of the months by typing a new number.

13

To set up the budget amounts for revenues, follow these steps:

1. Move to the Jan field for Inc Art category.

2. Type **50** and press ⬚→.

   You can move to the next field in this current row by pressing ⬚Tab or ⬚→. You can also use the mouse, but it is usually quicker to use the keyboard, since you are already typing. When you move to another field, Quicken records 50 as the January amount and then waits for you to enter an amount for February.

Entering and changing budgeted amounts is an easy task.

3. Repeat step 2 twice more to record 50 for February and March, and then position the highlight for an April entry.

4. Type **3575** and press ⬚→.

5. Repeat step 4 to enter the same amount for May.

6. Type **2000** and press ⬚→.

7. Type **3575** and press ⬚→.

8. Type **2000** and select E_dit, then Fill _Row Right.

   You will want to select the button before finalizing the 2000 entry, or the highlight will move to another row or column.

9. Select _Yes to confirm the action.

   Quicken enters 2000 for the remaining months of the current category.

10. Move the highlight until it is on the Inc Cons field for January.

11. Type **10000**, select E_dit then Fill _Row Right, and select _Yes.

12. Move to the far right of the screen; you see the 10,000 for Inc Cons in December.

    You can use the mouse, or you can press ⬚End twice.

13. Return to the January column with the mouse or by pressing ⬚Home twice.

14. Move to the July column for Inc Cons, and type **12000**.

15. Move to the March column for Inc Roy, and type **10000**.

16. Repeat step 15 for the months of June, September, and December.

Moving Around the Budget Set Up Window

Before entering additional budget data, you will want to practice moving around within the budget window and using the keyboard, since the keyboard is usually much more convenient than the mouse while in this window. After you complete the entries in the previous section, the highlight should be on the 10,000 in the Inc Roy December column. Follow these steps from that location:

1. Press [Home] twice and [Ctrl]-[Home] once.

   The highlight appears at the top of the window.

2. Press [End] twice to move to the top cell in the December column.

3. Press [Ctrl]-[End] to move to the bottom of the December column.

4. Press [Pg Up] to move up one window.

5. Repeat step 1 to move to the top left of the budget window.

Entering Expense Projections

To complete your budget picture, you need to enter projections for your expense categories. Using the information provided, complete the Set Up Budgets window for the categories. Follow these steps:

1. Enter the following amounts for the categories shown, after selecting Layout from the buttonbar and ensuring that the Show Subcats option is selected to display the subcategories:

Category	Budget Amount
Del Overngt (Overnight Delivery)	200
Dues	25
Equip Mnt (Equipment Maintenance)	100
Freight	20
Insurance	50
Misc (Miscellaneous)	25
Office (Office Expenses)	80
Payroll:	
Gross	5,000
Comp FICA	310
Comp MCARE	73
Postage	10
Supp Comp (Computer Supplies)	210
Supplies	50
Telephone	120
Travel	300
Utilities:	
Electric	30
Gas	30

13

2. Select E_dit, then Fill _Row Right and _Yes after making each entry to copy the January entries to all columns to the right.

3. Select _Close and then _Yes to close the Set Up Budget window and save the budget. Return to the ANB Business account register.

Printing the Budget Report

After entering your budget data, you can print your budget report by following these steps:

1. Select _Other on the _Reports menu, or select the Reports icon and select the Othe_r option button.

2. Select _Budget from the menu or dialog box.

3. Select _Customize.

The Customize Budget Report dialog box as you will complete it is shown here:

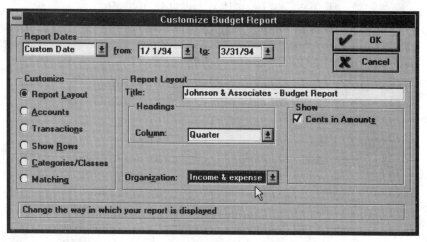

4. Enter **1/1/94** in the _from text box.

5. Enter **3/31/94** in the _to text box.

6. Type **Johnson & Associates - Budget Report** in the Ti_tle text box. You are limited to 39 characters for a customized title.

7. Select Quarter from the Col_umn drop-down list box.

8. Clear the Cents in Amount_s check box.

9. Select the Acc_ounts option button.

10. Select _Mark All, if all accounts are not already marked to be included in the report.

11. Select the Matching option button and enter **B** in the Class Contains text box and your window looks like this:

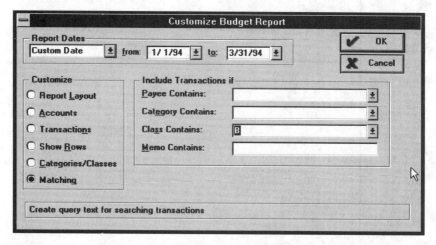

12. Select OK to display the budget report in a window.

13. Select the Print button from the report window buttonbar, then select Print. The report prints as shown in Figure 13-2.

You can also use the Customize Report dialog box to tell Quicken which categories you want displayed on your screen. Select the Show Rows option button, and then select from the Categories drop-down list box. If you select "Include All" Quicken will show the entire category list even if many of the categories were not used for budgeting purposes (for example, Canadian Pension). You could also select "Non-Zero Actual/Budgeted" or "Budgeted only" to be displayed. The default option is "Budgeted Only" where Quicken only displays the accounts for which budget information was entered.

If you need to change printer settings, refer to Chapter 3. You might want to use smaller fonts when printing reports to capture more of your report on each page. For example, your monthly report will be printed across two pages unless you use a font smaller than the default.

Report Discussion

Let's take a look at the report shown in Figure 13-2. The report compares the actual expenditures made during the quarter with those you budgeted. An analysis of the income section shows you received more income than you budgeted during the period. This was due to receiving more in consulting income than anticipated, although you received no income from articles. You would want to examine whether these differences were caused by your failing to project all the consulting activities you were involved in during the quarter or perhaps by a client paying you earlier than you had anticipated.

13

Johnson & Associates - Budget Report
1/1/94 Through 3/31/94

8/1/94   Page 1
BUSINESS-All Accounts

Category Description	1/1/94 Actual	– Budget	3/31/94 Diff
INCOME/EXPENSE			
INCOME			
Inc Art	0	150	-150
Inc Cons	37,500	30,000	7,500
Inc Roy	10,000	10,000	0
TOTAL INCOME	47,500	40,150	7,350
EXPENSES			
Del Overngt	270	600	-330
Dues	0	75	-75
Equip Mnt	1,100	300	800
Freight	0	60	-60
Insurance	0	150	-150
Misc	0	75	-75
Office	0	240	-240
Payroll:			
Comp FICA	930	930	0
Comp MCARE	218	219	-2
Gross	15,000	15,000	0
Total Payroll	16,148	16,149	-2
Postage	28	30	-2
Supp Comp	376	630	-254
Supplies	65	150	-85
Telephone	305	360	-55
Travel	905	900	5
Utilities:			
Electric	30	90	-60
Gas	17	90	-73
Total Utilities	47	180	-133
TOTAL EXPENSES	19,244	19,899	-655
TOTAL INCOME/EXPENSE	28,256	20,251	8,005

Budget report
for the first
quarter
of 1994
Figure 13-2.

Comparing budgeted revenues and expenses with actual amounts is an important aspect of managing your business finances.

The expense portion of the report shows the actual and budgeted expenses for the period. An analysis of individual categories is not worthwhile since the data you entered did not include expense entries for all the months in the report. However, you can see that the report compares budgeted with actual expenses during the period and shows the differences in the Diff column. In general, you are concerned with all the differences shown in this report, but you will probably only want to spend your time investigating the large dollar differences between budgeted and actual amounts. For example, you might decide to investigate in detail only those budget differences that exceed $300.00. For these categories, you might want to examine the underlying transactions in more depth.

The essence of budgeting is to determine where potential problems exist in your business and detect them early. Quicken's budget reporting capabilities can help you in making these business decisions.

Modifying the Budget Report

In the early stages of budgeting, it generally takes several months to develop sound estimates for all your expense categories. You can change your projections at any time by selecting Set Up Budgets from the Activities menu. You can also modify the report you just created to show different time periods or a selected group of accounts. Follow these steps to look at a monthly budget report for the same time period:

1. From the ANB account register, select the Reports menu or icon. Select Other, then select Budget.
2. Select Customize.
3. Enter **1/1/94** in the from text box and **3/31/94** in the to text box.
4. Type **Johnson & Associates - Budget Report** in the Title text box.
5. Select Month from the Column drop-down list box, telling Quicken you want a monthly report prepared.
6. Clear the Cents in Amounts check box.
7. Select Matching.
8. Type **B** in the Class Contains text box.
9. Select OK.
10. Select Print, and the Print Report dialog box opens. Select Printer and select Print, and the report is printed. Since this report is too wide for one page, Figure 13-3 is split over four pages.

13

Budget Report By Month

1/1/94 Through 3/31/94

8/1/94   Page 1

BUSINESS-All Accounts

	1/1/94	-	1/31/94
Category Description	Actual	Budget	Diff
INCOME/EXPENSE			
INCOME			
Inc Art	0	50	-50
Inc Cons	12,500	10,000	2,500
Inc Roy	0	0	0
TOTAL INCOME	12,500	10,050	2,450
EXPENSES			
Del Overngt	270	200	70
Dues	0	25	-25
Equip Mnt	1,100	100	1,000
Freight	0	20	-20
Insurance	0	50	-50
Misc	0	25	-25
Office	0	80	-80
Payroll:			
Comp FICA	310	310	0
Comp MCARE	73	73	-1
Gross	5,000	5,000	0
Total Payroll	5,383	5,383	-1
Postage	28	10	18
Supp Comp	376	210	166
Supplies	65	50	15
Telephone	305	120	185
Travel	905	300	605
Utilities:			
Electric	16	30	-14
Gas	8	30	-22
Total Utilities	24	60	-36
TOTAL EXPENSES	8,456	6,633	1,823
TOTAL INCOME/EXPENSE	4,044	3,417	627

Budget Report by Month for the first quarter of 1994
Figure 13-3.

```
                  Budget Report By Month
                    1/1/94 Through 3/31/94
8/1/94                                                      Page 2
BUSINESS-All Accounts
                              2/1/1994        -        2/28/1994
         Category Description    Actual      Budget      Diff
-----------------------------  ------------  ----------  ----------

INCOME/EXPENSE
   INCOME
      Inc Art                      0            50          -50
      Inc Cons                     0        10,000      -10,000
      Inc Roy                      0             0            0
-----------------------------  ------------  ----------  ----------

   TOTAL INCOME                    0        10,050      -10,050

   EXPENSES
      Del Overngt                  0           200         -200
      Dues                         0            25          -25
      Equip Mnt                    0           100         -100
      Freight                      0            20          -20
      Insurance                    0            50          -50
      Misc                         0            25          -25
      Office                       0            80          -80
      Payroll:
         Comp FICA               310           310            0
         Comp MCARE               73            73           -1
         Gross                 5,000         5,000            0
-----------------------------  ------------  ----------  ----------

      Total Payroll            5,383         5,383           -1
      Postage                      0            10          -10
      Supp Comp                    0           210         -210
      Supplies                     0            50          -50
      Telephone                    0           120         -120
      Travel                       0           300         -300
      Utilities:
         Electric                 14            30          -16
         Gas                        9            30          -21
-----------------------------  ------------  ----------  ----------

      Total Utilities            23            60          -37
-----------------------------  ------------  ----------  ----------

   TOTAL EXPENSES             5,406         6,633       -1,227
-----------------------------  ------------  ----------  ----------

TOTAL INCOME/EXPENSE         -5,406         3,417       -8,823
=============================  ============  ==========  ==========
```

Budget Report by Month for the first quarter of 1994 (*cont.*)
Figure 13-3.

13

```
                Budget Report By Month
                  1/1/94 Through 3/31/94
8/1/94                                                    Page 3
BUSINESS-All Accounts

                              3/1/1994       -        3/31/1994
      Category Description     Actual      Budget       Diff
------------------------------ ----------- ----------- -----------
INCOME/EXPENSE
  INCOME
    Inc Art                        0          50          -50
    Inc Cons                   25,000      10,000       15,000
    Inc Roy                    10,000      10,000            0
------------------------------ ----------- ----------- -----------
  TOTAL INCOME                 35,000      20,050       14,950


  EXPENSES
    Del Overngt                     0         200         -200
    Dues                            0          25          -25
    Equip Mnt                       0         100         -100
    Freight                         0          20          -20
    Insurance                       0          50          -50
    Misc                            0          25          -25
    Office                          0          80          -80
    Payroll:
      Comp FICA                   310         310            0
      Comp MCARE                   73          73           -1
      Gross                     5,000       5,000            0
------------------------------ ----------- ----------- -----------
    Total Payroll              5,383       5,383           -1
    Postage                         0          10          -10
    Supp Comp                       0         210         -210
    Supplies                        0          50          -50
    Telephone                       0         120         -120
    Travel                          0         300         -300
    Utilities:
      Electric                      0          30          -30
      Gas                           0          30          -30
------------------------------ ----------- ----------- -----------
    Total Utilities                 0          60          -60
------------------------------ ----------- ----------- -----------
  TOTAL EXPENSES               5,383       6,633       -1,251


------------------------------ ----------- ----------- -----------
TOTAL INCOME/EXPENSE          29,618      13,417       16,201
============================== =========== =========== ===========
```

Budget Report by Month for the first quarter of 1994 (*cont.*)
Figure 13-3.

```
              Budget  Report  By  Month
                   1/1/94 Through 3/31/94
  8/1/94                                            Page 4
  BUSINESS-All Accounts
                         1/1/1994        -        3/31/1994
          Category Description   Actual      Budget       Diff
  ------------------------------  ----------------  --------------  -------------

  INCOME/EXPENSE
    INCOME
      Inc Art                         0         150         -150
      Inc Cons                   37,500      30,000        7,500
      Inc Roy                    10,000      10,000            0
  ------------------------------  ----------------  --------------  -------------

    TOTAL INCOME                 47,500      40,150        7,350


    EXPENSES
      Del Overngt                   270         600         -330
      Dues                            0          75          -75
      Equip Mnt                   1,100         300          800
      Freight                         0          60          -60
      Insurance                       0         150         -150
      Misc                            0          75          -75
      Office                          0         240         -240
      Payroll:
        Comp FICA                   930         930            0
        Comp MCARE                  218         219           -2
        Gross                    15,000      15,000            0
  ------------------------------  ----------------  --------------  -------------
        Total Payroll            16,148      16,149           -2
      Postage                        28          30           -2
      Supp Comp                     376         630         -254
      Supplies                       65         150          -85
      Telephone                     305         360          -55
      Travel                        905         900            5
      Utilities:
        Electric                     30          90          -60
        Gas                          17          90          -73
  ------------------------------  ----------------  --------------  -------------
        Total Utilities              47         180         -133
  ------------------------------  ----------------  --------------  -------------
    TOTAL EXPENSES               19,244      19,899         -655


  ------------------------------  ----------------  --------------  -------------
  TOTAL INCOME/EXPENSE           28,256      20,251        8,005
  ==============================  ================  ==============  =============
```

Budget Report
by Month for
the first
quarter of
1994 (*cont.*)
Figure 13-3.

13

Budget Report Extension

The reports prepared so far in this chapter give you an overview of the budget report preparation process by comparing budget to actual expenditures for the first quarter of 1994. For your own situation, you need to extend the budget over a longer period. It is impractical to enter transactions for all of the included categories at this time, but you can still look at a report for a year, with budget and actual amounts shown monthly. To try working with a larger report, follow these steps:

1. From the ANB account register, select the Reports menu or icon and select Other then select Budget.
2. Select Customize.
3. Enter **1/1/94** in the from text box.
4. Enter **12/31/94** in the to text box.
5. Select Month from the Column drop-down list box.
6. Select Matching.
7. Enter **B** in the Class Contains text box.
8. Select OK.

   The Budget Report by Month appears. Although there are no actual figures beyond the first few months, the instructions in the next section will show you how to look at a wide report like this on screen.

Wide-Screen Reports

You can use shortcuts to move around wide-screen reports.

The Monthly Budget report just generated spreads across more than one Quicken window, since it is wider than the widest window. This might be difficult to comprehend until you realize how it is structured. In this section, you explore the wide-screen report and become more familiar with Quicken results. The following discussion will help you become familiar with the Monthly Budget report generated from the additional data you entered. Remember, you can use the mouse to scroll by using the scroll bars. The instructions given here are for using the keyboard, which is less intuitive than using the mouse.

Use [Tab], [Shift]-[Tab], [Pg Up], [Pg Dn], [Home], and [End] to navigate through the report and become familiar with the appearance of the wide screen for the budget report. Notice how easy it is to move around the report. Pressing [Home] twice returns you to the left side of the wide-screen report; pressing [End] twice takes you to the right side of the report. [Tab] moves you right one column, and (Shift)-(Tab) moves you left one column. (Pg Up) moves you up, and (Pg Dn) down, one screen. (Ctrl)-(Home) moves you to the first category in the same column, and (Ctrl)-(End) moves you to the last category in the same column. (Ctrl)-(←) moves you one screen to the left and (Ctrl)-(→) moves you one screen to the right.

It is recommended you use a small font to print wide reports. This significantly increases the amount of material you can print on a page. When you print wide-screen reports, Quicken numbers the pages of the report so you can more easily follow on hard copy.

Preparing a Cash Flow Report

*Budget
Reports can
be combined
with a Cash
Flow report
to project
your future
cash needs.*

Quicken's Cash Flow report organizes your account information by cash inflow and outflow. In this example, the results presented will be the same as the amounts in the budget. Chapter 14 introduces you to depreciation expense, which would be shown on the budget report but not on the Cash Flow report. This is because this expense does not require a cash outlay in the current year. Prepare a Cash Flow report for the first quarter by following these steps:

1. Open the Reports menu or select the Reports icon.
2. Select Business, then Cash Flow from the menu or dialog box.
3. Select Customize.
4. Enter **1/1/94** in the from text box.
5. Enter **3/31/94** in the to text box.
6. Clear the Cents in Amounts check box.

   Notice that Cash Flow Basis is selected for the Report Organization drop-down list box and that Exclude internal is selected in the Transfers drop-down list box that you see after selecting Show Rows to include only transfers to accounts outside this report. Quicken selected these options by default when you selected the Cash Flow report.

7. Select Matching.
8. Enter **B** in the Class Contains text box to restrict the report to business transactions.

   This step is essential; you will need to include both ANB Personal and ANB Business in this report because business expenses were paid from both accounts. If you did not restrict the class to business, all of the personal expenses included in ANB Personal would appear on the report as well.

9. Select the Accounts option button.

13

10. Unmark the Equipment account by highlighting it and pressing (Spacebar) or by clicking it, so the list box looks like the one shown here:

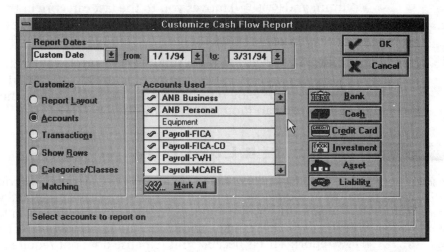

Equipment is excluded because Quicken does not show transfers between accounts included in the Cash Flow report. However, since the purchase of equipment involved the use of cash funds, that amount should be shown as a cash outflow. Quicken will show this as an outflow to the Equipment account on this report.

11. Select OK to create the Cash Flow report. Quicken displays the report shown in Figure 13-4.

Notice that this report shows the entire amount of payroll ($15,000) as a cash outflow, even though you have not paid the entire amount of federal and state withholding to the governmental agencies at the end of the period. This is caused by Quicken's assumption that transfers between accounts included in the report are cash outflows. If you want to eliminate these amounts from the report, you can re-create the report with only the ANB Personal and ANB Business accounts included. However, since the liability exists for the withheld amounts, the Cash Flow report shown in Figure 13-4 is a conservative approach to presenting the cash flow.

Creating a Budget Variance Graph

Graphs can provide a much better overview of your data than a report that displays all the numbers. Quicken provides a budget variance graph that lets you visually compare budgeted versus actual numbers in a bar graph format.

```
                    Cash  Flow  Report
                    1/1/94 Through 3/31/94
  8/1/94                                                Page 1
  BUSINESS-Selected Accounts

                                           1/1/1994-
            Category Description           3/31/1994
  ------------------------------- --------------------
  INFLOWS
      Inc Cons                             37,500
      Inc Roy                              10,000
                                           ------
  TOTAL INFLOWS                            47,500

  OUTFLOWS
      Del Overngt                             270
      Equip Mnt                              1100
      Payroll:
          Comp FICA               930
          Comp MCARE              218
          Gross                15,000
                                ------
      Total Payroll                        16,148
      Postage                                  28
      Supp Comp                               376
      Supplies                                 65
      Telephone                               305
      Travel                                  905
      Utilities:
          Electric                30
          Gas                     17
                                ------
      Total Utilities                          47
      TO Equipment                          1500
                                           ------
  TOTAL OUTFLOWS                           20,744

                                           ------
  OVERALL TOTAL                            26,756
                                           ======
```

Cash Flow
report for the
first quarter of
1994
Figure 13-4.

13

You can zoom in for a closer look at any part of the graph. In the example
that follows, the graph is created for a quarter. Then a bar in the graph is
selected for a closer look, and a graph showing a breakdown by month is

displayed with the QuickZoom feature. A bar in the QuickZoom graph is selected and the data is displayed in a report. To look at a budget variance graph for 1/94 through 3/94 follow these steps:

1. Open the Reports menu.
2. Select Graphs.
3. Select Budget Variance.

    You can also click Graphs in the Iconbar and select Budget Variance Graph in place of steps 1 through 3.

4. Type **1/94** in the from text box.
5. Type **3/94** in the to text box.
6. Select Create to display the graph.
7. Select Next 5 three times to display additional data.
8. Click Print in the Iconbar to print the graph as shown in Figure 13-5.

To use the QuickZoom feature, move the mouse to the object on the graph you wish to view in more detail, such as the Utilities bars shown in Figure 13-5. When you do, the mouse pointer displays as a magnifying glass with a *Z* for zoom inside it. Double-click the mouse, and you will see a close-up display such as that shown here:

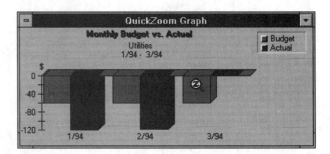

If you need to look even closer, you can double-click one of the QuickZoom graph bars and see the actual transactions in a report format. You can continue to explore graph options on your own or take a look at another graph option in Chapter 15.

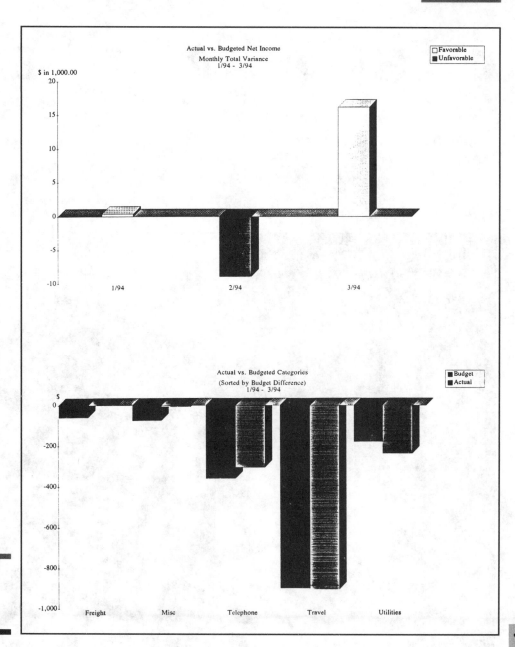

Actual versus budgeted graph
Figure 13-5.

CHAPTER

14

ORGANIZING TAX INFORMATION AND OTHER YEAR-END NEEDS

For the small-business owner, it seems as though tax time is always just around the corner. If it is not time to file one of the payroll tax forms, it is time to file quarterly tax estimates or year-end tax returns. Just as Quicken lent assistance with payroll tax forms in Chapter 12, it can save a significant amount of time and effort when you are preparing income tax returns.

Although Quicken can provide all the information you will need to complete your tax returns you might want to spend a little time learning more about the tax requirements, unless you have a CPA do everything for you. The box titled "Free Tax Information" provides a list of some of the free forms that you can get from the U.S. Government relating to tax requirements.

Free Tax Information

Tax regulations can be complex. To help you determine filing options, due dates, payment methods, and estimated tax, the Department of the Treasury provides a number of free tax publications to provide the information you need to fill out the necessary returns. You can order these publications by calling the IRS toll-free number (800) 829-3676.

Publication Number	Publication Name
334	Tax Guide for Small Business
463	Travel, Entertainment, and Gift Expenses
510	Excise Taxes
515	Withholding of Tax on Non-Resident Aliens
533	Self-Employment Tax
534	Depreciation
535	Business Expenses
538	Accounting Periods and Methods
541	Tax Information on Partnerships
542	Tax Information on Corporations
544	Sales and Other Dispositions of Assets
551	Basis of Assets
560	Retirement Plans for the Self-Employed
587	Business Use of Your Home
589	Tax Information for S Corporations
686	Certification for Reduced Tax Rates in Tax Treaty Countries
911	Tax Information for Direct Sellers
917	Business Use of a Car
937	Business Reporting
946	How to Begin Depreciating Your Property

In this chapter, you see how Quicken can be used to gather information to complete the tax forms for your business-related activities. You are introduced to the concept of depreciation and how it affects business profits. You learn how to use Quicken to prepare your Schedule C, Profit or Loss from Business statements, shown in Figure 14-1. You can also use Quicken features to help you prepare for recording the following year's transactions.

Depreciation

*Depreciation
expense is not
a cash
expenditure
in the
current year.*

Depreciation is an expense recorded at the end of the tax year (or any accounting period). The concept of depreciation can be confusing, since it does not follow the same rules as other expenses. Depreciation does not require a cash expenditure in the current year; you are recognizing a part of a cash outflow that occurred in a prior year when you record depreciation expense. Tax rules do not allow you to recognize the full cost as an expense in the earlier tax year because the resource is used in business for many tax years. For example, resources such as a truck or piece of machinery are not expensed in the year purchased since they benefit the business over a number of years. Purchases such as paper, on the other hand, would be consumed in the year purchased and their entire cost would be recognized in that tax year.

A basic definition of depreciation is that it is a portion of the original cost of an asset charged as an expense to a tax period. For the example developed in this section, suppose you purchased computer hardware that is used in your business. This is an asset of your business that will help generate revenues in the current and future tax years. You may think the cost of the equipment you purchased should be charged to your business in the year you paid for it, just as other cash expenses apply to the year paid. This seems fair since the purchase involved a significant cash outflow for the year. Unfortunately, from an accounting or tax perspective, the purchase of a piece of equipment is an acquisition that will affect your business operations over a number of years and thus cannot be expensed or deducted from revenues only in the year of purchase. The cost of the asset must be expensed over the years that it is expected to generate business revenues. For this reason, accountants and the Internal Revenue Service require that you apply the concept of depreciation when you prepare your Schedule C, Profit or Loss from Business statements. However, in the "Section 179 Property" section later in this chapter, you will find out about one important exception to the requirement that you depreciate your long-lived assets.

You can depreciate only assets that lose their productivity as you use them in your business activity. For example, you cannot record depreciation on the land where your building stands. Even though you may feel your land has lost value in recent years, you cannot recognize this decline until you

14

SCHEDULE C (Form 1040)	Profit or Loss From Business (Sole Proprietorship)	OMB No. 1545-0074 **1992**	
Department of the Treasury Internal Revenue Service (0)	▶ Partnerships, joint ventures, etc., must file Form 1065. ▶ Attach to Form 1040 or Form 1041. ▶ See Instructions for Schedule C (Form 1040).	Attachment Sequence No. 09	

Name of proprietor | Social security number (SSN)

A Principal business or profession, including product or service (see page C-1) | **B** Enter principal business code (from page 2) ▶

C Business name | **D** Employer ID number (Not SSN)

E Business address (including suite or room no.) ▶ ....
City, town or post office, state, and ZIP code

F Accounting method: (1) ☐ Cash (2) ☐ Accrual (3) ☐ Other (specify) ▶ ....

G Method(s) used to value closing inventory: (1) ☐ Cost (2) ☐ Lower of cost or market (3) ☐ Other (attach explanation) (4) ☐ Does not apply (if checked, skip line H) | Yes | No

H Was there any change in determining quantities, costs, or valuations between opening and closing inventory? If "Yes," attach explanation

I Did you "materially participate" in the operation of this business during 1992? If "No," see page C-2 for limitations on losses

J Was this business in operation at the end of 1992?

K How many months was this business in operation during 1992? ▶

L If this is the first Schedule C filed for this business, check here ▶ ☐

Part I Income

1	Gross receipts or sales. Caution: *If this income was reported to you on Form W-2 and the "Statutory employee" box on that form was checked, see page C-2 and check here* ▶ ☐	1	47,500 00
2	Returns and allowances	2	
3	Subtract line 2 from line 1	3	47,500 00
4	Cost of goods sold (from line 40 on page 2)	4	
5	Gross profit. Subtract line 4 from line 3	5	47,500 00
6	Other income, including Federal and state gasoline or fuel tax credit or refund (see page C-2)	6	
7	Gross income. Add lines 5 and 6 ▶	7	47,500 00

Part II Expenses (Caution: *Do not enter expenses for business use of your home on lines 8–27. Instead, see line 30.*)

8	Advertising	8		21 Repairs and maintenance	21	1,100	00
9	Bad debts from sales or services (see page C-3)	9		22 Supplies (not included in Part III)	22	440	76
10	Car and truck expenses (see page C-3—also attach Form 4562)	10		23 Taxes and licenses	23	1,147	50
11	Commissions and fees	11		24 Travel, meals, and entertainment:			
12	Depletion	12		a Travel	24a	905	00
13	Depreciation and section 179 expense deduction (not included in Part III) (see page C-3)	13	275 00	b Meals and entertainment			
				c Enter 20% of line 24b subject to limitations (see page C-4)			
14	Employee benefit programs (other than on line 19)	14		d Subtract line 24c from line 24b	24d		
15	Insurance (other than health)	15		25 Utilities	25	352	40
16	Interest:			26 Wages (less jobs credit)	26	15,000	00
a	Mortgage (paid to banks, etc.)	16a		27a Other expenses (list type and amount):			
b	Other	16b		*Misc. Expense 298.25*			
17	Legal and professional services	17					
18	Office expense	18					
19	Pension and profit-sharing plans	19					
20	Rent or lease (see page C-4):						
a	Vehicles, machinery, and equipment	20a					
b	Other business property	20b		27b Total other expenses	27b	298	25
28	Total expenses before expenses for business use of home. Add lines 8 through 27b in columns ▶				28	19,518	91
29	Tentative profit (loss). Subtract line 28 from line 7				29	27,981	09
30	Expenses for business use of your home. Attach Form 8829				30		
31	Net profit or (loss). Subtract line 30 from line 29. If a profit, enter here and on Form 1040, line 12. Also, enter the net profit on Schedule SE, line 2 (statutory employees, see page C-5). If a loss, you MUST go on to line 32 (fiduciaries, see page C-5)				31	27,981	09
32	If you have a loss, you MUST check the box that describes your investment in this activity (see page C-5)				32a ☐ All investment is at risk. 32b ☐ Some investment is not at risk.		
	If you checked 32a, enter the loss on Form 1040, line 12, and Schedule SE, line 2 (statutory employees, see page C-5). If you checked 32b, you MUST attach Form 6198.						

For Paperwork Reduction Act Notice, see Form 1040 instructions. | Cat. No. 11334P | Schedule C (Form 1040) 1992

Schedule C
Figure 14-1.

sell the land. On the other hand, a *depreciable asset* is an asset that has a life longer than one year and benefits business operations in several accounting periods. Equipment is a depreciable asset; land is not.

Depreciation Terminology

Several terms pertaining to depreciation need to be discussed in more depth. You must always depreciate the original cost of an asset. *Original cost* is the total cost of the asset. For example, if you purchased a piece of machinery and paid shipping charges and sales tax, these additional costs are considered to be associated with getting the asset into an income-producing condition and are therefore part of the original cost. The screen in Figure 14-2 shows the Equipment account register after recording the transactions in Chapter 11. The first transaction recorded in the register shows the original cost of the High Tech computer, $3000.00. The printer purchase on 1/25/94 is recorded at its original cost of $1500.00.

In Chapter 9, you learned to revalue personal assets to market value. You cannot do this with business assets. If your asset increases in value, you cannot recognize this increase in your Quicken system. You must always carry (show on your business accounting records) your business assets at their original cost.

Another important term is *accumulated depreciation*. This is the amount of depreciation you have recorded for an asset in all previous years. Your assets will always be shown on the balance sheet at original cost minus

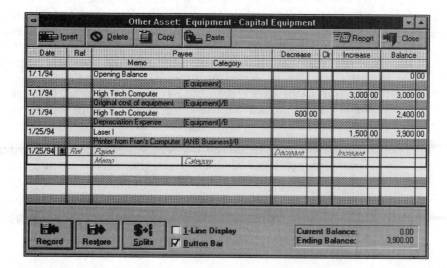

Equipment
Account
Register
window
Figure 14-2.

14

accumulated depreciation. For example, for the $3000.00 High Tech Computer asset, you recorded depreciation expense of $600.00 in the previous year. You have an accumulated depreciation of $600.00 from the previous year so your asset carrying value is $2400.00 before recording this year's depreciation.

Establishing Accounts for Assets

You probably will establish another asset account for each major type of depreciable asset used in your business. You would follow the same procedures used in Chapter 11 to set up the Equipment account. If you have equipment, office furniture, and buildings that you use in your business, including the portion of your home used exclusively for business purposes, you will depreciate the original cost of each of the assets. On the other hand, you may decide to establish a separate account for each asset if you have few depreciable assets. Quicken's default limit on the number of accounts in the system is 64. In the example, you learn how to depreciate more than one asset in an account.

NOTE: Quicken provides a shortcut for switching between accounts that you use frequently. You can assign an account to a UseAcct icon on the Iconbar. When you select that icon in the future, that account register appears. You will learn to edit the Iconbar in Appendix D.

Depreciation Methods

The straight-line method of depreciation described in the next section is appropriate for income tax purposes. However, for the most part, you will probably use the modified accelerated cost recovery system (MACRS) and the accelerated cost recovery system (ACRS) methods of determining your depreciation amounts. Generally speaking, MACRS covers tangible assets put into business use after December 31, 1986, and ACRS covers tangible assets put into place after December 31, 1980. *Tangible assets* are property that can be felt and touched. All the assets mentioned in our discussion (equipment, office furniture, and buildings) would fit this description.

The reason most taxpayers use MACRS is that the method builds in a higher level of depreciation deductions in the early years of an asset's life than would be calculated using the straight-line method of depreciation. Consult IRS Publication 534 before computing your depreciation on tangible assets.

Straight-Line Depreciation Method

In this example, you use the straight-line method to record depreciation on an asset. *Straight-line depreciation* expenses the cost of the asset evenly over the life of the asset. For example, the High Tech Computer has a useful life of five years, and you recorded depreciation expense at $600.00 in 1993. Since this method does not attempt to recognize more depreciation in the early years of an asset's life, it is always acceptable to the IRS. Many other depreciation methods can be used and may be more favorable since they recognize greater depreciation in the early years of the asset's life. IRS Publication 534 lists the many rules that apply to the selection of a depreciation method. One of the considerations that determines the depreciation method chosen is the year in which you placed the asset in service. A rule that applies to all types of depreciation is that once you select a method of depreciation for an asset, you cannot change to another depreciation method. Table 14-1 lists some of the other depreciation methods. You will need to check with your accountant or check IRS Publication 534 for specific rulings on which methods you can use.

The Internal Revenue Service has established guidelines for depreciation assets. Consult IRS publication 534 for details.

When using the straight-line method of depreciating an asset, use the following formula:

$$\frac{\text{original cost–salvage value}}{\text{useful life of asset}}$$

The original cost of depreciable assets has already been discussed; however, "salvage value" is a new term. Salvage value is the amount of cash you expect to recover when you dispose of your depreciable asset. This is, obviously, always an estimate and in the case of a computer not easily estimated due to rapid changes in the computer field. For this reason, many accountants assign a salvage value of zero to this type of asset, stating in effect that it will have no value at the end of its estimated life. This is also the assumption made in the entries recorded here. When you record salvage values for your assets, you can use the history of similar assets when estimating depreciation. If equipment that is five years old typically sells for 20 percent of its original cost, that would be a good estimate for the salvage value of a piece of equipment with an estimated life of five years bought today.

14

Method	Description
ACRS	The Accelerated Cost Recovery System is an accelerated depreciation method that can be used for assets placed in service after December 31, 1980, and before December 31, 1986.
Declining-balance	This method allows the deduction of depreciation expense at a faster rate than straight-line. There are several different percentages used in computing this type of depreciation. One acceptable option is 150 percent of straight-line depreciation.
MACRS	The Modified Accelerated Cost Recovery System is an accelerated depreciation method used for assets placed in service after December 31, 1986.
Straight-line	This method is the easiest to compute since the cost of the asset is depreciated evenly over the life of the asset. It is also the least advantageous to the business owner since it does not accelerate depreciation expense in the early years of the asset's life.

Depreciation
Methods
Table 14-1.

Depreciation Calculation

The amounts used in the depreciation entries in this chapter were determined by the calculations shown here:

High Tech Computer:

$$\frac{\$3000.00 \text{ (original cost)} - 0 \text{ (salvage value)}}{5 \text{ years (useful life)}} = \$600.00 \text{ depreciation per year}$$

Laser Printer:

$$\frac{\$1500.00 \text{ (original cost)} - 0 \text{ (salvage value)}}{3 \text{ years (useful life)}} = \$500.00 \text{ depreciation per year}$$

Depreciation is generally recorded only once, at the end of the year, unless you need financial statements prepared for a bank or other third party during the year. The amounts calculated in this example are the annual depreciation expenses for the computer and printer—the amounts you would use to record depreciation for the year ending 12/31/94. (Note that even though the printer was acquired at the end of January, it is acceptable to record a full year's depreciation on the asset since the difference between

11 and 12 months' worth of depreciation is so small that it would not be considered to have a material effect.)

In the examples developed in Chapters 11 and 13, the account register transactions have been limited to the first quarter of the year. (In Chapter 12, you completed several April 1994 entries in order to see the complete process of payroll accounting.) Since there is not a full year of expense entries, you can compute the depreciation on the computer and printer for just the first quarter of 1994. This is accomplished by dividing both annual amounts of depreciation by four. Thus, here are the first quarter's depreciation charges that you will record:

High Tech Computer:
$$\frac{\$600.00 \text{ (annual depreciation)}}{4 \text{ (quarters)}} = \$150.00 \text{ depreciation for first quarter, 1994}$$

Laser Printer:
$$\frac{\$500.00 \text{ (annual depreciation)}}{4 \text{ (quarters)}} = \$125.00 \text{ depreciation for first quarter, 1994}$$

Now that you are familiar with the method used to record depreciation in the example and how the amounts you will record were determined, you are ready to begin recording the depreciation entry in your account register.

Establishing Depreciation Categories

Before recording the depreciation entries in this chapter, you establish a Depreciation category with Computer and Printer subcategories in your category list. Select the Equipment account in the BUSINESS file, open the account register, and follow these steps:

1. Select the Cat List icon to open the Category & Transfer List window.
2. Select New to open the Set Up Category dialog box.
3. Type **Depreciation** in the Name field.
4. Type **Depreciation Expense** in the Description field.
5. Select the Expense option button.
6. Select the Tax-related check box.

   Remember to assign tax schedules you need to set your preferences by selecting Edit, then Preferences, then General, and check the Use Tax Schedules with Categories box.

As you establish new tax-related accounts, Quicken lets you assign them to the appropriate tax forms. This helps in preparing your year-end tax returns.

7. Select Schedule C:Other business expense.

8. Select OK.

9. Select New.

10. Type **Computer** in the Name field.

11. Type **Depreciation-Computer** in the Description field.

12. Select the Subcategory of option button.

13. Select Depreciation from the drop-down list box.

14. Select the Tax-related check box.

15. Select Schedule C:Other business expense.

16. Select OK.

17. Select New.

18. Type **Printer** in the Name field.

19. Type **Depreciation-Printer** in the Description field.

20. Select the Subcategory of option button.

21. Select Depreciation from the drop-down list box.

22. Select the Tax-related check box.

23. Select Schedule C:Other business expense.

24. Select OK.

25. Press (Esc) to return to the register.

    You can now begin recording your depreciation expense transactions.

Depreciation Expense Transactions

Let's record the depreciation on the assets in your Quicken account. Starting from the next blank transaction form in the Equipment account register (Figure 14-2) in the BUSINESS file:

1. Enter **3/31/94** in the Date field.

   Notice that no check numbers are recorded in this register since all checks are written against the business checking account.

2. Type **High Tech Computer** in the Payee field.

3. Type **150** in the Decrease field.

4. Type **Depreciation-1994** in the Memo field.

5. Type **Depreciation:Computer/B** in the Category field and select Record.

You have just recorded the depreciation expense on the computer for the months January through March of 1994. The remaining steps record depreciation on the laser printer you acquired in January.

6. Enter **3/31/94** in the Date field.
7. Type **Laser 1** in the Payee field.
8. Type **125** in the Decrease field.
9. Type **Depreciation-1994** in the Memo field.
10. Type **Depreciation:Printer/B** in the Category field and select Record.

These register entries show how your depreciation transactions will appear after you record both of them:

3/31/94	High Tech Computer		150	00			3,750	00
	Depreciation-1994	Depreciation:Computer/B						
3/31/94	Laser I		125	00			3,625	00
	Depreciation-1994	Depreciation:Printer/B						

This completes the depreciation transaction entry for the first quarter of 1994. Remember, depreciation is normally recorded only at the year's end. However, for purposes of this example, we have prepared the entries at the end of the first quarter.

Customized Equipment Report

After recording the depreciation transactions in the Equipment account, you will want to look at a customized Equipment report. This report, which you will prepare shortly, summarizes all the activity in the account. Figure 14-3 shows the Equipment report for your business since 1/1/94. Notice that the report shows the depreciation expense taken during the first quarter for both the computer and the printer, as well as the total for the category. You can also see that there was a transfer of $1500.00 from business checking for the purchase of the printer in January.

Finally, you can see that the balance forward amount of $2400.00 is the $3000.00 original cost of the asset minus the $600.00 accumulated depreciation taken in the prior year. Thus, when you prepare a balance sheet in Chapter 15, the equipment asset will total $3625.00.

If you want to produce the Equipment report, follow these steps starting from the Equipment account register:

1. Select Other from the Reports menu.
2. Select Summary, and the Create Report window appears.
3. Select Customize and the Customize Report window appears.

14

4. Select Custom Date.
5. Enter **1/1/94** in the from field.
6. Enter **3/31/94** in the to field.
7. Type **Equipment Report** in the Title field and select OK.
8. Select Print, and the Print Report dialog box appears.
9. Select Printer and then Print.

```
                        Equipment Report
                      1/1/94 Through 3/31/94
     8/1/94                                                    Page 1
     BUSINESS-Equipment

                                                   1/1/94-
            Category Description                    3/31/94
     --------------------------------------- -----------------------

     INCOME/EXPENSE
       EXPENSES
         Depreciation:
            Computer                           150.00
            Printer                            125.00
                                              ----------

         Total Depreciation                            275.00
                                                      ---------
       TOTAL EXPENSES                                  275.00


                                                      ---------
       TOTAL INCOME/EXPENSE                            -275.00

       TRANSFERS
         FROM ANB Business                           1,500.00
                                                      ---------
       TOTAL TRANSFERS                               1,500.00

       Balance Forward
         Equipment                                   2,400.00
     ------------------------------------------- ---------
       Total Balance Forward                         2,400.00
                                                      ---------
       OVERALL TOTAL                                  3,625.00
                                                      =========
```

Equipment
report
Figure 14-3.

Depreciation and the IRS

The transactions in this chapter record depreciation using the straight-line method to determine the amounts for the entries. This method was demonstrated to cover the recording process without going into too much detail about IRS rules for determining depreciation expense for tax purposes. However, we need to briefly discuss one additional aspect of deducting the cost of long-lived assets for IRS purposes, section 179 property. Be sure to obtain IRS Publication 534 (free upon request) before making decisions concerning the amount of depreciation you will charge against income on your tax return.

Section 179 Property

At the time of this writing, Congress is planning to increase the deductible limit. Consult your accountant or the IRS for final details.

Many small businesses will be interested in the type of property called *section 179 property*. Here, certain capital expenditures are treated as deductions in the current year rather than depreciating the cost of the asset over its life. Buildings, air conditioning units, and structural components of a building do not qualify as section 179 property. For a complete list of qualified property and the specific rules that apply, consult IRS Publication 534.

Under section 179 of the Internal Revenue Service code, you can deduct up to $10,000.00 of the cost of property in the current tax year at the time of this writing. In this chapter, you would have been able to deduct the entire cost of the laser printer this year against your business income and not depreciate the asset in future years.

Schedule C, Profit or Loss from Business

Schedule C is the tax form sole proprietorships use when reporting business income and expenses during the year. Quicken can be used to provide the information you need to complete your form. If you examine Schedule C (Figure 14-1), you see that it is a business profit and loss statement. This statement can be prepared from the Quicken Reports menu.

Starting from the ANB Business account register in the BUSINESS account group, complete the following steps:

1. Select Business from the Reports menu.
2. Select P&L Statement.
3. Select Customize, and the Create Report dialog box appears.
4. Select Custom Date.
5. Enter **1/1/94** in the from field.
6. Enter **3/31/94** in the to field.

14

7. Select Matching.

8. Select B in the Class Contains field.

9. Select OK, and the Profit and Loss Statement window appears.

10. Select Pri<u>n</u>t and the Print Report dialog box appears.

11. Select <u>P</u>rinter and then <u>P</u>rint.

   The printed Profit and Loss statement is shown in Figure 14-4.

Completing Schedule C

Profit or loss
from a sole
proprietorship
is shown on an
individual's
Form 1040.

With Quicken's Profit and Loss statement, you can now complete the appropriate lines of the federal tax form Schedule C. Because Schedule C is basically just a profit and loss statement, many of the entries can be obtained directly from your Quicken report. The following is a list of line numbers and how you can complete them in Schedule C.

✦ *Line 1*   This line shows gross sales. The total income ($47,500.00) shown on your report would be placed on this line.

✦ *Line 13*   This section shows depreciation and section 179 deduction from Form 4562, Depreciation and Amortization. The Total Depreciation Expense ($275.00) would be entered here.

✦ *Line 21*   This line shows repairs. The amount you show for Equip Mnt ($1100.00) would be entered here.

✦ *Line 22*   This line shows the total of all your business supplies. You would add the amounts shown for Computer Supplies ($375.76) and Supplies ($65.00) by using the Calculator and enter the total ($440.76) here.

✦ *Line 23*   This line shows taxes. The amounts that are shown as Payroll:Comp FICA and Payroll:Comp MCARE ($1147.50) would be entered here.

✦ *Line 24*   This line shows the total amount of your business travel. The amount of Travel Expense ($905.00) would be entered here. This assumes that all these expenses are associated with travel and not meals or entertainment. You can establish separate categories for these items in your Quicken Category and Transfer list.

✦ *Line 25*   The total for utilities and telephone is placed on this line. You would use the calculator to add the amounts shown for Telephone Expense ($305.00) and Total Utilities ($47.40) and record the total expense as $352.40.

✦ *Line 26*   This line shows the total wages paid. You would enter the amount shown as Payroll:Gross ($15,000.00).

```
                     Profit & Loss Statement
                      1/1/94 Through 3/31/94
   8/1/94                                                   Page 1
   BUSINESS-All Accounts

                                              1/1/94-
              Category Description            3/31/94
   ------------------------------------  --------------------------
     INCOME/EXPENSE
      INCOME
        Inc Cons                                  37,500.00
        Inc Roy                                   10,000.00
                                                 -----------
      TOTAL INCOME                                47,500.00

      EXPENSES
        Del Overngt                                  270.00
        Depreciation:
          Computer                      150.00
          Printer                       125.00
                                       ----------
        Total Depreciation                           275.00
        Equip Mnt                                  1,100.00
        Payroll:
          Comp FICA                     930.00
          Comp MCARE                    217.50
          Gross                      15,000.00
                                       ----------
        Total Payroll                             16,147.50
        Postage                                       28.25
        Supp Comp                                    375.76
        Supplies                                      65.00
        Telephone                                    305.00
        Travel                                       905.00
        Utilities:
          Electric                       30.40
          Gas                            17.00
                                       ----------
        Total Utilities                               47.40
                                                   ----------
      TOTAL EXPENSES                               19,518.91


                                                   ----------
     TOTAL INCOME/EXPENSE                          27,981.09
                                                   ==========
```

Profit and Loss
statement
Figure 14-4.

14

+ *Line 27a* This line shows your other business expenses. You would add the amounts shown for Postage ($28.25) and Del Overngt ($270.00) and show the total ($298.25) as Misc Exp in this section.

+ *Line 28* This line shows your total deductions. This is the amount of Total Expense ($19,518.91).

+ *Line 29* This line shows your net profit (or loss). This is the amount of net profit ($27,981.09).

NOTE: You can round the cents to the nearest dollar when completing your tax forms.

After completing this exercise, you can see there are many alternatives for establishing classes to help in gathering your tax information. Remember, one of the constraints faced in this example was that you were recording business expenses in both personal and business checking accounts. However, this example could be modified to use subclasses to designate lines on the different tax forms when recording your entries. This would allow you to capture the information by form and line number.

Other Business-Related Tax Forms

When you completed line 13, Depreciation, you used the Total Depreciation Expense amount from your Profit and Loss statement. This information must be included on Form 4562, Depreciation and Amortization. After reading through Publication 534, you would have entered the appropriate amounts for section 179 property and ACRS or MACRS depreciation. This results in a total of $275.00, shown on line 20 of Form 4562 and transferred to line 13 on Schedule C.

As a sole proprietor, you also need to complete Schedule SE, Social Security Self-Employment Tax. The net profit from your Schedule C, $27,981.09, would be carried to line 2 of that form, and the rest of the form can be easily completed. See the special "Year-End Business Tax Forms" box for a list of important tax forms for the small-business owner.

Year-End Business Tax Forms

Form	Title
Sole Proprietorship	
Schedule C (Form 1040)	Profit or Loss from Business
Form 4562	Depreciation and Amortization
Schedule SE (Form 1040)	Social Security Self-Employment Tax
Form 1040ES	Estimated Tax for Individuals
Partnership	
Form 1065	U.S. Partnership Return of Income
Schedule D (Form 1065)	Capital Gains and Losses
Schedule K-1 (Form 1065)	Partner's Share of Income, Credits, Deductions, Etc.
Corporation	
Form 1120-A	U.S. Corporation Short-Form
Form 1120	U.S. Corporation Income Tax Return
Form 1120S	U.S. Income Tax Return for an S Corporation
Schedule K-1 (Form 1120S)	Credits, Deductions, Etc.

Year-End Activities

You are not required to take any special actions at the end of the year to continue to use Quicken. The package allows you to select transactions by date if you want to purge some of the older transactions from your file. Unless you need the disk space or begin to notice sluggish response time from your system, you should plan on keeping at least three years of historical information in your file. You may find it convenient to be able to print historical reports for comparison with this year's results.

To copy accounts, categories, classes, and other information to a new file, you need to use the Copy command from the File Operations submenu of the File menu. You can then decide how far back to go in copying

14

transactions to the new file. You can also remove uncleared transactions from an earlier date from this file.

The following steps explain how to copy the BUSINESS file you have been using since Chapter 11. Complete these steps:

1. Open the File menu.

2. Choose File Operations.

3. Select Copy, and the Copy File dialog box, shown here, appears.

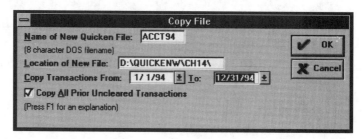

4. Type **Acct94** in the Name of New Quicken File field. This is the name of the new file.

5. Type a new directory location or press Tab to accept the existing location.

6. Type **1/1/94** in the Copy Transactions From field.

7. Type **12/31/94** in the To field.

   You have now defined all the transactions between 1/1/94 and 12/31/94 as those you want to transfer to the new file.

8. Select the Copy All Prior Uncleared Transactions check box and select OK.

   This command tells Quicken to copy all uncleared transactions from the period prior to 1/1/94. This means that any checks that clear your bank after the year-end will be included in your account register for reconciliation purposes.

9. Select the Reload original file option button and select OK.

   If you were really ready to begin recording transactions in the next accounting period in the ACCT94 file, you would select Load new copy instead to use the new file.

CHAPTER

15

MONITORING FINANCIAL CONDITIONS

You have already seen that you can prepare financial statements with Quicken's report features. In previous chapters, you created a Profit and Loss statement, a Cash Flow report, and an Equipment report. You can use these reports to monitor the financial condition of your firm and to see how your business has performed over a period of time. These reports not only help you assess the success you've had in managing the business, but they can also be used by outsiders for the same purpose. Bankers and other creditors review your financial statements to determine whether to make loans to your business. Quicken can prove a valuable tool in preparing loan applications or, as you saw in earlier chapters, in providing information to others who use financial statements, such as the Internal Revenue Service.

This chapter presents a final major financial statement: the Balance Sheet. The Balance Sheet provides a snapshot of the financial resources and obligations of your business. Although the Profit and Loss statement, the Cash Flow report, and the Balance Sheet have been introduced separately, they are interrelated. Bankers and other readers will review these statements as a package when assessing the past and projecting the future success of your business.

The Balance Sheet

The Profit and Loss Statement helps explain the changes that occur between two Balance Sheets.

The Balance Sheet shows your business assets, liabilities, and equity or investment at a specific date. Remember that *assets* are things of value that are used in your business to generate revenue. Cash, for example, is an asset that is used to acquire other assets, such as supplies and labor, which are then used to generate revenue.

Liabilities are the obligations incurred as part of your business operations. Borrowing from the bank is a financial obligation. This obligation is shown as a liability on your Balance Sheet.

Owner's equity is the amount of personal resources you have invested in the business. In the example you've been working on in the preceding chapters, you opened your business checking account with a $4,000.00 deposit and put $2,400.00 of equipment in the Equipment account ($3,000.00 original cost – $600.00 of accumulated depreciation). This $6,400.00 is the amount of your personal assets invested in the business and is your owner's equity at the beginning of the year. Bankers and other creditors are interested in your equity in the business. If you are asking for a loan, they will want to know how much of your own financial resources you are risking. This is measured by your equity in your business, as well as by any other personal assets you may be willing to offer as collateral.

Before you prepare a Balance Sheet, it's important to know two concepts. First, the Balance Sheet is prepared at a specific date. Quicken asks you to define the time period you want to use in preparing your Balance Sheet. For example, you define the period 1/1/94 to 3/31/94 in this chapter; you are telling Quicken to prepare the Balance Sheet using transactions in that time period. The resulting printed Balance Sheet will show the balances in your business accounts on 3/31/94.

The second important concept is that the Profit and Loss statement and the Balance Sheet are related. The Balance Sheet shows your assets, liabilities, and equity at a specific date, and the Profit and Loss statement details the changes in your assets, liabilities, and equity between two Balance Sheets. Remember these two concepts as you prepare the Balance Sheets in this chapter: the Balance Sheet is prepared at a specific date, and the Profit and Loss statement helps explain how assets, liabilities, and equity changed between two Balance Sheets. In the examples that follow, you see how the Profit and Loss statement demonstrates how changes in owner's equity occurred between 1/1/94 and 3/31/94.

Creating a Balance Sheet

The Balance Sheet is prepared as of a specific date. Each transaction you enter in Quicken will change your Balance Sheet amounts.

In this section, you prepare a Balance Sheet as of 3/31/94 from the transactions you entered in the BUSINESS file in previous chapters. This report shows the assets, liabilities, and owner's equity of the business at the end of the quarter. Starting from the ANB Business account register in the BUSINESS file, follow these steps:

1. Select Business from the Reports menu.
2. Select Balance Sheet.
3. Select Customize to open the Customize Balance Sheet dialog box.
4. Enter **1/1/94** in the from text box.
5. Enter **3/31/94** in the to text box.
6. Select Matching.
7. Select B from the Class Contains drop-down list box, and select OK.
8. Select Print, and the Print Report dialog box appears.
9. Select Printer, and select Print. Your Balance Sheet looks like Figure 15-1.

Using the Balance Sheet

You can see from the Balance Sheet that the total of the Cash and Bank accounts is $32,612.54. This is the amount shown in your ANB Business checking account on 3/31/94 ($32,735.70) less $123.16. The deduction is the cash used from your personal checking account to cover business expenses. (Remember that you wrote several personal checks and charged a portion of the cost to business by using the /B class entry.) These amounts were included in the Profit and Loss statement prepared in the previous chapter and in the Cash Flow report prepared in Chapter 13, "Preparing Budget Reports and Cash Flow Statements." Thus, Quicken is adjusting your business assets by the amount of expenses paid from your personal accounts. The importance of this adjustment is discussed shortly.

```
                        Balance Sheet
                         As of 3/31/94
7/31/94                                                   Page 1

BUSINESS-All Accounts

                                                         3/31/94


                            Acct              Balance
         ------------------------------------   --------------

ASSETS

    Cash and Bank Accounts
      ANB Business                              32,735.70
      ANB Personal                                -123.16
                                                ----------
    Total Cash and Bank Accounts                32,612.54


    Other Assets
      Equipment                                  3,625.00
                                                ---------
    Total Other Assets                           3,625.00


                                                ---------
TOTAL ASSETS                                    36,237.54
                                                =========

LIABILITIES & EQUITY

    LIABILITIES
      Other Liabilities
        Payroll-FICA                              -310.00
        Payroll-FICA-Co                            930.00
        Payroll-FWH                                614.00
        Payroll-MCARE                             -72.50
        Payroll-MCARECo                           217.50
        Payroll-SWH                               477.45
                                                ---------
      Total Other Liabilities                    1,856.45


                                                ---------
    TOTAL LIABILITIES                            1,856.45

    EQUITY                                       34,381.09
                                                ----------
    TOTAL LIABILITIES & EQUITY                   36,237.54
                                                ==========
```

Balance Sheet
as of 3/31/94
Figure 15-1.

15

You can also see that the equipment is carried at a balance of $3,625.00. The carrying value of depreciable assets is discussed in Chapter 14, "Organizing Tax Information and Other Year-End Needs." The Equipment report produced there shows the underlying transactions that explain the carrying value on the Balance Sheet.

Your total assets are the resources available to your business on the date of the report. These resources are used to generate future income.

The amounts you withhold from employee wages are liabilities of your business.

The liabilities shown are all related to the payroll prepared on 3/31/94. You owe the federal and state governments $1,856.45 for withholding and social security tax payments. On 4/1/94, you made a deposit with your bank for all the federal government payroll liabilities. However, this doesn't affect the Balance Sheet prepared on 3/31/94. The payroll taxes were liabilities on the date the statement was prepared, even though the deposit on 4/1/94 reduces your total liabilities by $1,379. Likewise, the state withholding liability will remain on the Balance Sheet until you make a deposit to the state.

The difference between the total assets of the business and its total liabilities is the owner's equity in the business. In this case you have $34,381.09 of your equity invested in the business. Thus, the Balance Sheet shows that most of the business's assets were contributed by you, with only $1,856.45 outstanding to creditors.

Creating a Comparative Balance Sheet

In this section, you see how Quicken's Profit and Loss statement helps explain the changes that occur between two Balance Sheets. First, you prepare a comparative Balance Sheet; then the Balance Sheet's relationship with the Profit and Loss statement is discussed. Starting from the ANB Business account register in the BUSINESS file, follow these steps:

1. Select Business from the Reports menu.
2. Select Balance Sheet.
3. Select Customize to open the Customize Balance Sheet dialog box.
4. Enter **1/1/94** in the from text box.
5. Enter **3/31/94** in the to text box.
6. Select Quarter for the Headings Interval. This entry causes Quicken to create a comparative Balance Sheet, with account balances shown at the beginning and the end of the quarter.
7. Select Matching.
8. Select B from the Class Contains drop-down list box, and select OK.
9. Select Print, and the Print Report dialog box appears.
10. Select Printer, and select Print. Your report will look like Figure 15-2.

```
                    Balance Sheet by Quarter
                         As of 3/31/94
   7/31/94                                            Page 1

   BUSINESS-All Accounts

                                         1/1/94      3/31/94
                         Acct            Balance     Balance
   -------------------------------------  ----------  ----------

   ASSETS

     Cash and Bank Accounts
       ANB Business                       4,000.00   32,735.70
       ANB Personal                           0.00     -123.16
                                         ----------  ----------
     Total Cash and Bank Accounts         4,000.00   32,612.54

     Other Assets
      Equipment                           2,400.00    3,625.00
                                         ----------  ----------
     Total Other Assets                   2,400.00    3,625.00


                                         ----------  ----------
   TOTAL ASSETS                           6,400.00   36,237.54
                                         ==========  ==========

   LIABILITIES & EQUITY

     LIABILITIES
      Other Liabilities
        Payroll-FICA                          0.00     -310.00
        Payroll-FICA-Co                        0.00      930.00
        Payroll-FWH                           0.00      614.00
        Payroll-MCARE                         0.00      -72.50
        Payroll-MCARECo                       0.00      217.50
        Payroll-SWH                           0.00      477.45
                                         ----------  ----------
      Total Other Liabilities                 0.00    1,856.45


                                         ----------  ----------
      TOTAL LIABILITIES                       0.00    1,856.45

     EQUITY                               6,400.00   34,381.09
                                         ----------  ----------
   TOTAL LIABILITIES & EQUITY            6,400.00   36,237.54
                                         ==========  ==========
```

Comparative
Balance Sheet
as of 3/31/94
Figure 15-2.

Using the Comparative Balance Sheet

The comparative Balance Sheet prepared in this section shows the balances of the business on 1/1/94 and 3/31/94 side by side. You can see that the assets of the business on 1/1/94 consisted of the $4,000.00 initial deposit made to the business checking account and the $2,400.00 carrying value ($3,000.00 – $600.00) of the High Tech computer recorded in the Equipment account on 1/1/94. Thus, the total assets were $6,400.00. There were no liabilities at that time, so the owner's equity is the $6,400.00 shown as the overall total.

The question you should be asking now is, "What caused the changes in assets, liabilities, and equity between these two Balance Sheet dates?"

The change in assets was caused by the increase in cash, which is explained in the Cash Flow report. In Chapter 13, you prepared a Cash Flow report (see Figure 13-7) for which you selected all accounts except Equipment. This was a conservative approach to the preparation of the report since your federal and state withholdings were included as a cash transfer, even though the deposit for these liabilities was not made until 4/1/94. For your Cash Flow report to accurately reflect cash transactions for the period 1/1/94 through 3/31/94, you would need to re-create the report using only the ANB Personal and ANB Business accounts. Figure 15-3 shows the new report.

Understanding the underlying reasons for changes between two Balance Sheets will help you better manage your business.

This report is important since it shows the connection between the amounts in the Cash and Bank Accounts sections of the comparative Balance Sheet shown in Figure 15-2. There is a change of $28,612.54 in your total cash balance between 1/1/94 and 3/31/94, which equals the overall total, or the net cash flow, shown in Figure 15-3. If you were presenting your financial reports to a banker, you would want to present the Cash Flow report prepared in this chapter. If you were using the report for internal purposes, the report prepared in Chapter 13 would be satisfactory and is the more conservative of the two.

You can examine the Equipment report prepared in Chapter 14 to explain the increase in the Equipment account. You can see from the comparative Balance Sheet that the changes in your liabilities are clearly related to the payroll withholdings you owe on 3/31/94.

The owner's equity (investment) in a business is the difference between the total assets and total liabilities of the business. As just noted, the owner's equity on 1/1/94 was $6,400.00, whereas the owner's equity on 3/31/94 is $34,381.09. Let's look at the $27,981.09 change in the owner's equity. This change can be explained by examining the Profit and Loss statement prepared in Chapter 14, which is shown in Figure 15-4.

A Profit and Loss statement covers a specific time period—in this example, the first quarter of 1994. You can see that the net profit (total income – total

```
                        Cash Flow Report
                      1/1/94 Through 3/31/94
       7/31/94                                              Page 1


       BUSINESS-Bank,Cash,CC Accounts

                                                   1/1/94-
                 Category Description              3/31/94
       ----------------------------------    -----------------


         INFLOWS
           Inc Cons                                37,500.00
           Inc Roy                                 10,000.00
           FROM Payroll-FICA                          930.00
           FROM Payroll-FICA-Co                       930.00
           FROM Payroll-FWH                         1,842.00
           FROM Payroll-MCARE                         217.50
           FROM Payroll-MCARECo                       217.50
           FROM Payroll-SWH                           477.45
                                                  -----------
         TOTAL INFLOWS                             52,114.45

         OUTFLOWS
           Del Overngt                                270.00
           Equip Mnt                                1,100.00
           Payroll:
             Comp FICA              930.00
             Comp MCARE             217.50
             Gross              15,000.00
                                ----------
           Total Payroll                           16,147.50
           Postage                                     28.25
           Supp Comp                                  375.76
           Supplies                                    65.00
           Telephone                                  305.00
           Travel                                     905.00
           Utilities:
             Electric               30.40
             Gas                    17.00
                                ----------
           Total Utilities                            47.40
           TO Equipment                             1,500.00
           TO Payroll-FICA                          1,240.00
           TO Payroll-FWH                           1,228.00
           TO Payroll-MCARE                           290.00
                                                  ----------
         TOTAL OUTFLOWS                             23,501.91


                                                  ----------
         OVERALL TOTAL                              28,612.54
                                                  ==========
```

Cash Flow
report
Figure 15-3.

```
                    Profit & Loss Statement
                     1/1/94 Through 3/31/94
   7/31/94                                              Page 1

   BUSINESS-All Accounts
                                                    1/1/94-
             Category Description                   3/31/94
   ----------------------------------------   ------------------


   INCOME/EXPENSE
     INCOME
        Inc Cons                                   37,500.00
        Inc Roy                                    10,000.00
                                                ----------------

     TOTAL INCOME                                  47,500.00


     EXPENSES
        Del Overngt                                   270.00
        Depreciation:
          Computer                     150.00
          Printer                      125.00
                                     ----------

        Total Depreciation                            275.00
        Equip Mnt                                    1,100.00
        Payroll:
          Comp FICA                    930.00
          Comp MCARE                   217.50
          Gross                     15,000.00
                                     ----------

        Total Payroll                              16,147.50
        Postage                                        28.25
        Supp Comp                                     375.76
        Supplies                                       65.00
        Telephone                                     305.00
        Travel                                        905.00
        Utilities:
          Electric                      30.40
          Gas                           17.00
                                     ----------

        Total Utilities                                47.40

     TOTAL EXPENSES                                 19,518.91

                                                 ----------
     TOTAL INCOME/EXPENSE                          27,981.09
                                                 ==========
```

Profit and Loss
statement for
the period
ending 3/31/94
Figure 15-4.

expenses) is $27,981.09. This amount is equal to the change in the owner's equity between the two Balance Sheet dates. Thus, the net profit or loss of a business helps explain changes that occur between Balance Sheets from the beginning and from the end of the profit and loss period.

One final point to note about the Balance Sheet is that the amount –123.16 shown on the 3/31/94 Balance Sheet appears because you entered business expense transactions in your personal checking account. Although this is not recommended, it is not uncommon for small-business owners to make this sort of transaction using cash. You must remember that the $123.16 is included in the Profit and Loss statement as a business expense; thus, the reported net profit is reduced by that amount. Since you used cash for the payment, Quicken is telling you that using your personal funds has reduced your total business assets. Problems like this are more likely to occur when you are running a very small business in which office supplies and personal supplies may be purchased at the same time and with the same payment.

NOTE: Although Quicken can handle the payment of business expenses out of both business and personal checking accounts, it is better to limit business expense payments to your business checking account. If the nature of your business necessitates the payment of expenses with cash rather than with a check, you will probably find it useful to establish a Quicken Cash account for your business and use it in combination with your business checking account to record business expenses paid with personal cash.

Sole Proprietor Withdrawals from the Business

Withdrawals made by sole proprietors are not business expenses. They are reductions in owner equity.

So far in the example developed in this book, you have not spent any of the cash generated from your business for personal use. In accounting, it is called a *withdrawal,* or simply *draw,* when sole proprietors take cash or other assets out of their businesses for personal use. Obviously, these are not business expenses, so the Profit and Loss statement is not affected. On the other hand, you are reducing the assets of your business when you transfer cash from your business to your personal checking account.

In this section you see how owner withdrawals affect the Balance Sheet of a business. Starting from the ANB Business account register, follow these steps to record your withdrawal of cash from the business checking account:

1. Move to the Date field at the end of the account register.

2. Enter **3/31/94** in the Date field.

   The cash withdrawal is being handled as a transfer between your business and personal checking accounts. Just as it is not good practice to pay business expenses from a personal checking account, neither should you use business checks to pay for personal expenditures.

3. Type **Mr. Johnson** in the Payee field.

   Since the transaction is a withdrawal, the payee name matches the name of the business owner.

4. Type **5000** in the Payment field.

5. Type **Transfer - Withdraw** in the Memo field.

6. Select [ANB Personal] from the drop-down list box in the Category field.

7. Type **/B** after [ANB Personal] in the Category field, and select Record.

   The class designation indicates to Quicken that this transaction will affect the business checking account balance. This transaction now appears in your ANB Business account register, as shown here:

3/31/94	Mr. Johnson		5,000 00			27,735 70
	Transfer - Withdraw	[ANB Personal]/B				

8. Highlight the transaction you just entered, and press Ctrl-X to view the transaction in the ANB Personal register.

9. Move to the Memo field.

10. Type **Withdraw from business**, and select Record.

    This is an important step in recording the transaction. This memo is used to describe all withdrawals from the business, so the memo can later be used as a filter when preparing the Balance Sheet. Here is how this transaction appears in your ANB Personal account register:

3/31/94	Mr. Johnson			5,000 00	7,061 00
	Withdraw from business	[ANB Business]/B			

11. With this transaction highlighted, press Ctrl-X to return to the ANB Business register.

The Balance Sheet After an Owner's Withdrawal of Capital

Now that you have recorded your owner's withdrawal, let's take a look at the business' Balance Sheet. Follow these steps from the main menu of the ANB Business account:

1. Open the Reports menu.

2. Select Business.

3. Select Balance Sheet.

4. Select Customize to open the Customize Balance Sheet dialog box.

5. Enter **1/1/94** in the from text box.

6. Enter **3/31/94** in the to text box.

7. Select Quarter for the Headings Interval. This causes Quicken to create a comparative Balance Sheet that shows balances for the beginning and the end of the quarter.

8. Select Matching.

9. Type ~**Withdraw..** in the Memo Contains text box.

10. Select B from the Class Contains drop-down list box. The Customize Balance Sheet by Quarter dialog box looks now looks like this:

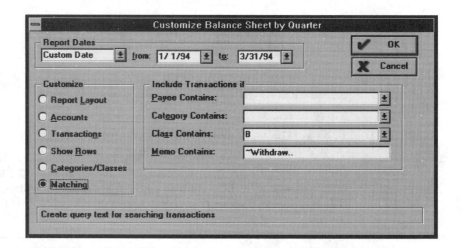

11. Select OK.

12. Select Print, and the Print Report dialog box appears.

13. Select Printer, and then select Print. Your Balance Sheet looks like Figure 15-5.

Effects of the Owner's Withdrawal

The Balance Sheet now shows your total equity as $29,381.09, which is $5000 less than the equity shown on the previous Balance Sheet. You can see that the owner's equity in a business is affected not only by net profits and losses, but also by owner withdrawals of equity. You also know that an investment of additional cash or assets in a business increases the owner's equity. This occurred on 1/1/94 when you invested cash and equipment to set up the business. Thus, you account for the owner's equity change

```
                    Balance Sheet by Quarter
                        As of 3/31/94
    7/31/94                                              Page 1


    BUSINESS-All Accounts
                                             1/1/94      3/31/94
                          Acct              Balance      Balance
    ------------------------------------    ----------   --------


    ASSETS

      Cash and Bank Accounts
        ANB Business                        4,000.00    27,735.70
        ANB Personal                            0.00      -123.16
                                            ----------   ---------
        Total Cash and Bank Accounts        4,000.00    27,612.54

      Other Assets
        Equipment                           2,400.00     3,625.00
                                            ----------   ---------
        Total Other Assets                  2,400.00     3,625.00


                                            ----------   ---------
    TOTAL ASSETS                            6,400.00    31,237.54
                                            ==========   =========
    LIABILITIES & EQUITY

      LIABILITIES
        Other Liabilities
          Payroll-FICA                          0.00      -310.00
          Payroll-FICA-Co                        0.00       930.00
          Payroll-FWH                            0.00       614.00
          Payroll-MCARE                          0.00       -72.50
          Payroll-MCARECo                        0.00       217.50
          Payroll-SWH                            0.00       477.45
        Total Other Liabilities                  0.00     1,856.45


                                            ----------   ---------
      TOTAL LIABILITIES                         0.00     1,856.45
                                            ----------   ---------
      EQUITY                                6,400.00    29,381.09
                                            ----------   ---------
    TOTAL LIABILITIES & EQUITY             6,400.00    31,237.54
                                            =========    =========
```

Comparative
Balance Sheet
after recording
owner's
withdrawal
Figure 15-5.

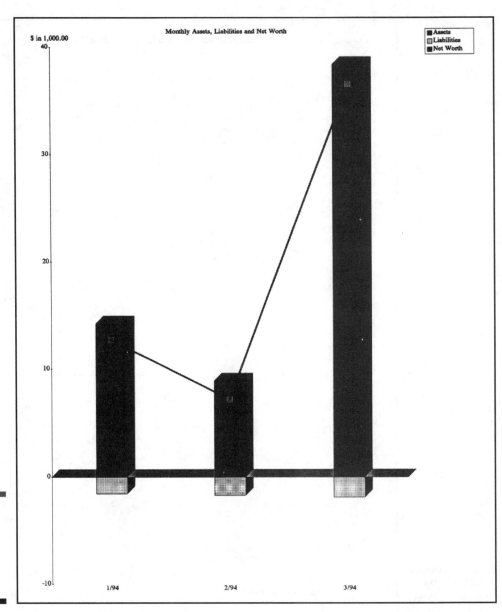

Monthly Assets, Liabilities and Net Worth

$ in 1,000.00

Monthly
Assets,
Liabilities and
Net Worth
graph
Figure 15-6.

between the two Balance Sheets by adding the net profits for the period to the beginning owner's equity and then reducing it by withdrawals ($6,400.00 + $27,981.09 − $5,000.00 = $29,381.09).

Quicken Graphs

15

Now that you have prepared reports for your business data, you might want to learn how to graph this data. Quicken can display graphs of your income and expenses, budget variances, net worth, and investments. In this section you prepare an Asset Comparison pie graph. Follow these steps:

1. Select Graphs from the Reports menu.
2. Select Net Worth.
3. Type **1/94**, and press (Tab); then type **3/94**, and press (Tab).

   Notice the check boxes that allow you to filter the data used in the graph.
4. Select Create, and Quicken displays the Monthly Assets, Liabilities and Net Worth graph shown in Figure 15-6.
5. Double-click on the column indicating assets for 3/94.

   When you point at the graph column, your mouse pointer becomes the QuickZoom magnifying glass pointer. When you double-click, you display a graph that provides more detailed information about the data represented by the graph column. In this case, you display the Asset Comparison graph shown here:

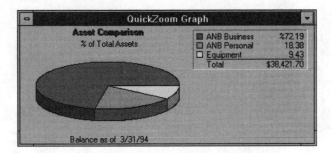

   This graph shows that your business bank account constitutes approximately 72 percent of your total assets, your personal bank account 18 percent, and your business equipment 9 percent.
6. Select the Print buttonbar to print the graph to the default report printer.

TIPS

101 COST-SAVING IDEAS FOR SMALL BUSINESSES

Whether you are a one-person operation or have a number of employees, you want to spend money on your business where it will count. You want to be certain not to cut costs too much where customers are concerned or you will lose business. You also want to be certain that you have adequate profit after covering your expenses to reward good employee performance. The list of ideas which follows can get you started with some cost-saving ideas of your own. You will want to ask your employees for their ideas as well—some of the best ideas in this list were contributed by ours.

1. If you use a laser printer, look for a reliable source for refilling laser cartridges.

2. Keep a stack of used paper and use the blank side for drafts. Also, when using preprinted forms, print a test run to insure that costly print stock will not be wasted.

3. Set your printer to print draft copies lighter to conserve toner. Some programs also have an option that allows you to make the change from your program rather than setting the printer.

4. Consider self insurance for equipment rather than maintenance agreements which can add up quickly.

5. See if switching your business and personal insurance to one company will result in a discount.

6. Always close the copier top when copying to avoid wasting toner at the edges of the copy.

7. Change temperature settings on nights and weekends to cut heating and cooling costs.

8. Buy supplies in bulk at warehouse clubs and other outlets.

9. Consider used office furniture and equipment.

10. Use cheap labor for some tasks. A high school student might enjoy the opportunity to work in your office several afternoons a week and will probably be willing to work for minimum wage.

11. Use free government information such as tax publications.

12. Consider an intern from one of the local colleges for the summer. They might even work part-time during the school year. Students today are very anxious for experience and if you can offer them a learning experience that they can add to their resume, they may even accept volunteer-type opportunities.

13. Use temps rather than adding a new position until you are sure you will need the position permanently.

14. Contract out for services that you need only occasionally.

15. Check phone discount options from all of the carriers.

16. Fax nonconfidential local mailings rather than use postage since there is no charge for the local phone call.

17. Fax nonlocal mailings after midnight when rates are low.

18. Use a file compression utility to shrink files and therefore increase the life of your existing hard disks. It is a good idea to compress files that you will be transmitting via modem to cut transmission time.

19. Consider making some equipment repairs yourself. We have replaced disk drives, changed keyboards, and added memory.

20. Buy mail order to save money but use C.O.D. for your protection. That way you will not pay until you have the merchandise.

21. Don't spend too much time saving pennies when you can focus on dollar-saving or dollar-making efforts.

22. Look for noncomputer products that can substitute for more expensive computer products. A travel case for your notebook computer and disk mailers are two examples where good substitutes might be much cheaper.

23. Arrange to trade current business periodicals with business associates rather than subscribe to all of them yourself.

24. Consider videotape training or books rather than off-site classes.

25. Look at local training opportunities at community colleges etc., for reasonably priced employee training.

26. Attend local computer club meetings. You can obtain information for free.

27. Consider purchasing generic paper towels and other products for office use.

28. Combine fans with air conditioning to achieve a comfortable temperature with lower energy costs.

29. Schedule business travel to include a Saturday night stay to obtain the lowest possible rate.

30. Join professional organizations in your field. You are bound to learn many tips from individuals faced with problems similar to yours.

31. Establish a per diem for employee meals and miscellaneous expenses when traveling.

32. Ask for the lowest possible hotel rate and inquire about special packages that might include breakfast. Sometimes there are better rates available than corporate rates. Also, sometimes it is better to book two separate reservations to take advantage of special rates on certain days of the week.

33. Plan your travel as far in advance as possible. Lower-cost options are normally not available close to the travel date.

34. Look in local papers when traveling for business to take advantage of special meal discounts.

T
I
P
S

35. Use coupons and other discounts when performing maintenance on company vehicles.

36. Close office blinds when the sun is beating against the windows in summer to cut cooling costs.

37. Leave the printer off until the first time you need it each day.

38. Have a potluck office function when you want to have a party on a low budget.

39. Look at renting community facilities for an office function rather than a more expensive banquet facility.

40. On extended business trips, try to rent a room with an efficiency where you can eat carry-out meals.

41. Create preprinted forms with your word processor.

42. If you have a long-term relationship with a bank, speak to the manager about free services such as traveler's checks, credit cards or ATM cards, or shop around for a better deal.

43. Consider services such as MCI Mail as a cheap and convenient way for sales personnel to stay in touch with the office while on the road.

44. Look at reducing the amount of work you send to an outside printing company by creating flyers and special brochures with your word processor.

45. Consider major medical insurance options rather than full coverage plans.

46. Where there is no prepayment penalty, increase monthly principal payments on business loans to cut interest costs.

47. Consider comp time rather than overtime pay for employees, if this is an option for your business.

48. Shop around for a business credit card that charges no fee and offers free points.

49. Keep a record of the discounts available through memberships such as AAA and other associations and use them.

50. Consider buying entertainment books and other discount offers for cities you visit on business frequently.

51. Make sure you take advantage of frequent flyer miles by flying on one airline as much as possible.

52. Look for other promotions that allow you to increase your frequent flyer miles such as car rentals, hotel stays, and so on.

53. Watch the dates for payroll deposits closely, as the fees for late payments can be very high.

54. Be sure to pay your invoices within the discount period.

55. Consider HMO coverage for employee health insurance.

56. Ask your insurance agent what you can do to reduce costs—safety training programs, and so on.

57. Utilize high school business programs where available for envelope stuffing.

58. Consider the retired work pool.

59. Consider renting or leasing special equipment rather than purchasing.

60. Consider UPS and the U.S. Postal Service's next day rates over the other air couriers.

61. Buy a switch box to share expensive equipment such as a laser printer.

62. Look for a bank that bases checking account charges on an average monthly balance rather than minimum monthly balance.

63. Have alcohol-free employee functions.

64. Prohibit smoking in the workplace.

65. Buy check stock from suppliers such as Currents to save money.

66. Turn off most lights at the end of the day to save money.

67. Utilize all mailings for multiple purposes. If you are mailing a bill, enclose a flyer on new goods and services or send a special promotional notice of an upcoming sale.

68. Send mailings bulk rate where information is not time critical.

69. Reuse shipping materials such as styrofoam peanuts.

70. Use free services such as SCORE before using paid consultants.

71. Utilize the reference librarians at your local library for business information that you need.

72. If you do not need canceled checks see if you can get a discount at your bank with a statement-only account.

73. Plan your business calls to utilize rate savings. If you are on EST, wait until evening to call California; they will still have several working hours left.

74. Reward employees for cost-saving suggestions.

75. Utilize employee recommendations to fill new positions. You can give them a small cash bonus for employees hired that stay at least six months. They are more likely than a head hunter to choose an employee that fits with the corporate culture.

76. Have a policy where employees pay for their own phone calls and copies rather than absorb these costs.

77. Look at buying repossessed or rental company cars for business use.

78. Provide clear instructions to employees as to the types of shipping companies to use for different priority materials. Many companies routinely send materials overnight or second-day delivery when a slower option would suffice.

79. When funds do not allow for adding costly employee benefits, look for free options such as flex-time or dress-down days.

80. Barter for services with other professionals to cut cash outlays.

81. Be creative about the location for a company outing. A baseball game or community event can offer a new activity at a much lower cost than a dinner dance or other formal affair.

82. Accept all the free help you can get from children, parents, and your spouse. It is often possible to make a fun project out of a repetitive task.

83. Avoid blackout periods when scheduling company travel as airfares will be the highest.

84. Be creative when spending your advertising dollars. Sponsoring a local marathon or other community event might get you the same exposure as other more expensive options.

85. Keep a list of office supplies needed in order to get everything on regularly scheduled trips.

86. Shop at thrift stores and garages sales for items like extra tables, file cabinets, and lamps needed for the office.

87. Use clear mailing labels rather than typing envelopes. Although the labels are more costly, the time savings will more than offset the cost.

88. Build a database or merge file for the names and addresses you mail to frequently. You will be able to create labels and letters with almost no use of time when you need them again.

89. Look at the efficiency of your operation—wasted steps and unnecessary checks are all costly activities.

90. Have employees verify as much output as possible onscreen before printing to avoid the waste of paper and toner or ribbon.

91. Consider overtime for a period rather than hiring a new employee since it avoids all the overhead costs and allows you to be certain that your business has grown enough to require permanent extra help.

92. Base raises strictly on performance. There is no need to reward mediocre results with even a small raise.

93. Implement profit-sharing plans that let employees share in increased profits and cost savings they help to achieve.

94. Retain good employees. It is much less expensive than training new ones.

95. Sell used equipment before it is totally obsolete.

96. Don't let key employees get so overworked and stressed out that they get sick. If necessary, enroll employees in stress management programs if the work environment is hectic.

97. Enroll in a time management class or read a good book on time management. Since time is definitely money you should quickly recoup what you have spent.

98. Utilize books about letters and forms rather than trying to create everything yourself.

99. Check into postal costs for different-sized mailings to make sure that the size you choose qualifies for the type of mailing you want to do.

100. Make sure that the packing materials you are using are not adding to the weight of the package. New featherweight options offer protection and reduced mailing costs.

101. Don't ignore problem employees. If you do not take action, the morale and productivity of all employees will be adversely affected.

T
I
P
S

P A R T

4

APPENDIXES

APPENDIX

SPECIAL QUICKEN AND WINDOWS TASKS

Quicken is easy to install with the right equipment. The package handles most of the installation work for you.

For the Windows version of the software discussed in this book, you need an IBM 286 or higher or a 100% compatible machine. You must have at least 2MB of RAM in the machine, a monitor with a graphics card, and a hard disk with 5MB of available disk space. You need Windows 3.1 or later to be able to install and run Quicken 3 for Windows.

Installing Quicken

Quicken is very easy to install. All you need to do is put the correct disks in drive A, select Run from the Program Manager's File menu, type **A:INSTALL** and select OK. Quicken offers four methods of customizing the installation procedure and will prompt for the other disks. Quicken's installation program copies all the files to the hard disk, and installs the program in a new program group in Windows.

Starting Quicken

To start the Quicken program, open the program group containing the Quicken program item and highlight it. Then double-click on the program item or press Enter. Alternatively, you can select Run from the Program Manager's File menu, type **c:\quickenw\qw**, and select OK. Quicken will help you set up your first file and account as described in Chapter 2.

Upgrading from an Earlier Release

You can use any files created with Quicken 1 or 2 for Windows with Quicken 3 for Windows without complications. If you have been using Quicken 5, 6, or 7 for DOS, Quicken 3 for Windows can read your files. You can use all the new features with your existing data immediately. You can even go back to your older Quicken release and still read the files after working with them in Quicken 3 for Windows.

If you are upgrading from Quicken 3 or 4 for DOS, Quicken 3 for Windows will convert the files the first time you open them but you will no longer be able to read them with the earlier release of Quicken. You might want to create a backup copy of the files before opening them in Quicken 3 for Windows in case you ever need to use them with the older release.

Working with Windows in Quicken

If you are new to the Windows operating environment, you will find that there are many differences from working with DOS. One of the differences that can be very confusing is that everything appears within a window. Your Quicken data appears in document windows within the bigger Quicken window. You can have any number of document windows open. You may soon find that your Quicken desktop is as crowded as a messy desk, showing your investment forms, a report, category or account lists, a register or two, just as you might keep paper copies of all of these documents on your desktop. You can see in Figure A-1 just how confusing this can be.

Remember, you can close windows you are not using by pressing Esc, or by double-clicking your mouse on the control menu box, which appears in the

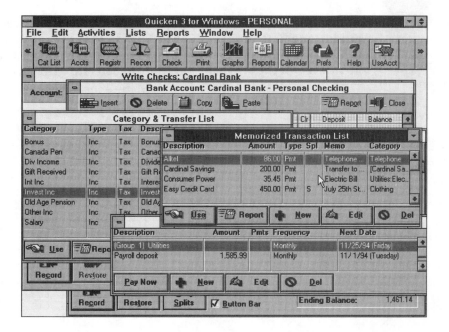

A messy
Quicken
desktop makes
it hard to work
Figure A-1.

upper-left corner of the window next to the title bar. You can also size and move windows.

The easiest way to size or move windows is to use your mouse. To move a window, point your mouse at the title bar of a window, press the mouse button, drag the window to a new location, and release the mouse button. To size a window using your mouse, move the mouse pointer to one of the window's borders. The mouse pointer will change to a double-headed arrow. Drag the border in or out to change the size of the window. An easier way is to click on one of the buttons in the upper-right corner of the window, next to the title bar. Click on an up arrow button to make the window as large as possible. Click on a down arrow button to make the window into a small icon, which reduces the window to a graphic image. Click the button with two arrows in a maximized window to restore the window to its previous size.

Moving and sizing windows with the keyboard is a little more complicated. First, you need to open the control menu box by pressing Alt-- (hyphen or minus sign). Select Move from this menu, then use the arrow keys to position the window. When you press Enter, the window moves to the location you specified. To size the window, open the control menu again, and select Size. Use the arrow keys again. The first arrow key you press determines which side of the window you are moving, and the rest move it. You can maximize the size of the window by selecting Maximize, or reduce it to an icon by selecting Minimize from this menu.

You can use Quicken to arrange the windows. Select Cascade from the Window menu to arrange the windows so that they are stacked on top of each other, with only the title bar of each showing. You will be able to click the title bar of the window you want to activate with this arrangement.

APPENDIX

B

GLOSSARY

There are various financial terms that are important to know in order to understand how Quicken supports your financial activities. A brief definition of terms used throughout this book is included here for your convenience.

Accelerated Depreciation   A method of depreciation in which more expense is recognized in the early years of an asset's life.

Account   Quicken document where personal and/or business transactions are recorded that increase or decrease the amount of money in the account. Examples include bank, cash, credit card, other assets, and other liabilities accounts.

Account Balance   The amount of money in an account.

Accounts Payable   Money owed to suppliers for goods or services.

Accounts Receivable   Money owed to you by customers or clients.

Accrual Basis   An accounting method in which income is recorded when services are provided rather than when cash is received. Expenses are treated similarly.

Accumulated Depreciation   The total amount of depreciation expense taken on an asset since the time it was placed in service.

ASCII (American Standard Code for Information Interchange)   This is a standard set of codes used for storing information. When you write information to disk with Quicken, the data is stored in ASCII format. This makes it easy to transfer the data to a word processing package or any other package that reads ASCII data.

Asset   Any item of value that a business or individual owns.

Average Annual Total Return   The average annual percent return on your investment. Interest, dividends, capital gains distributions, and unrealized gains/losses are used in computing this return on your investment.

Average Cost   The total cost of all shares divided by the total number of shares.

Balance Sheet   A financial statement that summarizes a business's assets, liabilities, and owner's equity at a specific time.

Book Value   The cost of an asset less the amount of depreciation expensed to date.

Brokerage Account   An account with a firm that buys and sells shares of stocks and other investments on your behalf.

Budget   A plan indicating projected income and expenses. Budget also refers to a comparison between the projections and actual amounts for each income or expense category.

Cash   Money or currency.

Cash Basis   A method of accounting used for business or tax purposes. Income is recorded when cash is received, and expenses are charged when cash is paid.

Cash Flows   The inflow and outflow of cash during a specific time period.

Category   Identifies the exact nature of income and expenses, such as salary income, dividend income, interest income, or wage expense. Categories are distinct from classes.

Chart of Accounts   A list of the categories used to classify transactions.

Class   Allows you to define the time period, location, or type of activity for a transaction. Classes are distinct from categories.

Cleared Item   An item that has been processed by the bank.

Control Codes   Special codes that can request a specific feature or function from your printer, such as compressed printing. Each manufacturer has its own unique set of codes for each printer model manufactured.

Corporation   A form of business organization that limits the liability of the shareholders.

Cost Basis   Total cost of stock bought or sold plus commission.

Current Balance   The present balance in an account. This does not include postdated items.

Deductions   Amounts that reduce the gross pay to cover taxes and other commitments, such as health insurance premiums.

Deposit   An amount of funds added to an account. A deposit is sometimes referred to as a "credit" to the account.

Depreciable Base   The cost of an asset that will be expensed over its useful life.

Depreciation   The portion of the cost of an asset that is expensed each year on a profit and loss statement.

Dividends   Cash payments made to the shareholders of a corporation from current or past earnings.

Double Entry System   An accounting method that requires two accounts to be used when recording a transaction. For example, when supplies are purchased, both the cash and supplies accounts are affected.

Equity   The amount of the owner's investment in the business. For individuals, this is the money invested in a property or other asset.

Expense   The cost of an item or service purchased or consumed.

FICA   Social security tax paid by employers and employees.

File   A group of related accounts, such as a personal checking account, a savings account, and an asset account for your home.

Financial Obligations   Commitments to pay cash or other assets in return for receiving something of value—for example, a bank loan for equipment or an automobile.

Financial Resources   Objects or property of value owned by a person or business that are expected to increase future earnings.

Financial Statements   Periodic reports prepared by businesses to show the financial condition of the firm. Major financial statements include balance sheets, profit and loss statements (income statements), and cash flow reports.

FUTA   Federal unemployment tax.

Future value   An expected value at some future point, given that today's investments appreciate at the expected rate.

FWH   Federal income tax withheld from employees' earnings.

Gross Earnings   Total earnings of an employee before deductions are subtracted.

Income   The money earned by an individual or business. On a cash basis, it is the amount of cash received for goods or services provided. On an accrual basis, it is the amount of income recognized and recorded during the year for services provided.

Income Statement   A summary of the income and expenses of a business.

IRA   Individual Retirement Account. Depending upon your income level, you may experience tax benefits from setting up an IRA.

Job/Project Report   A method of reporting revenues and expenses on a job or project basis.

Liability   The money you owe to a vendor, creditor, or any other party.

Life of an Asset   The number of years that the asset is expected to last.

Liquidity   A measure of how easy it is to convert an asset to cash.

Memorized Transaction   A transaction that you have asked Quicken to remember and recall at a later time.

Menu   A related list of commands, called "items," presented for selection. A menu is frequently used in software packages as a means of offering features to choose from.

Money Market Account   An account held with a bank or other institution used to preserve capital. Most provide limited checking account privileges.

Mutual Fund   An investment vehicle that allows you to purchase shares in the fund; the proceeds are used by the fund to buy shares in a variety of stocks or bonds.

Net Pay   The amount of pay received after deductions.

Net Worth   An amount determined by subtracting the value of financial obligations from financial resources.

P & L Statement   An abbreviation for profit and loss statement; it shows the profit or loss generated during a period.

Partnership   A form of business organization where two or more individuals share in the profits and losses of the business.

Payment   The amount paid to a vendor, creditor, or other party.

Payroll SDI   State disability insurance payments often referred to as Workers' Compensation.

Payroll Taxes   The taxes a business pays on employee earnings—for example, matching FICA contributions, federal and state unemployment taxes, and workers' compensation payments.

B

Point in Time   A specific time when some activity is occurring.

Postdated Transaction   A check dated after the current date.

Present value   A value in today's dollars for a sum that will not be received until a later time.

Reconciliation   The process of comparing a copy of the bank's records for your account with your own records. Any differences should be explained in this process.

Revenue   The money or income generated.

Salvage   The worth of an asset at the end of its useful life.

Security   An investment such as a stock, bond, or mutual fund.

Service Charge   A fee the bank adds for maintaining your account. This fee can be part of the difference in reconciling a bank statement.

Single Entry System   An accounting method in which one account is used to record a transaction. When supplies are purchased, only the cash (or checking) account is affected.

Sole Proprietorship   The simplest form of small-business organization. There is no separation between the owner and the company.

Straight-line Depreciation   A method of expensing the cost of an asset evenly over its life.

SUTA   State unemployment tax. (Also known as SUI.)

SWH   State income taxes withheld from employee gross earnings.

Transaction Group   A group of memorized transactions that can be scheduled whenever you need them.

Transfer   A transaction that affects the balance in two accounts at the same time by moving funds between them.

Unrealized Gain/Loss   A gain or loss estimated on the basis of current market value.

Valuation   The current value of an asset.

APPENDIX

ADVANCED OPTIONS

You have had enough practice with the examples in this book to feel comfortable with basic transaction entry and report creation. You might want to think about using Quicken for some more sophisticated tasks, such as managing your accounts payable and receivable or setting up job order costing. Although these sophisticated tasks can be handled with the same basic Quicken transactions that you have already mastered, the tips in this section will provide the secrets to setting them up quickly.

Accounts Receivable

You can use Quicken to track invoicing and to record the collection of cash. To set up this accounts receivable monitoring, you need to create a new account. Name this account to indicate that it contains accounts receivable information and set it up as an asset account with a zero balance. When you open the account, mark the opening balance as cleared with an X in the Cleared column to prevent its inclusion in reports. You should also set up a new Income category named Sales.

As you invoice customers, you will create a transaction for each invoice in the Accounts Receivable account. The Ref field can be used for the invoice number and can be incremented with a + for each new invoice. The amount of the invoice is entered in the Increase field, since it is a credit invoice. The invoice date can be placed in the Memo field.

As customer payments are received, you should match them with the invoices that they cover. Highlight the matching invoice transaction and click the Splits button or press Ctrl-S. Next, enter your business checking account for the second category, type - and the amount of the payment in the amount field and recalculate the split transaction so it shows a zero total.

You can use the A/R by Customer business report to prepare an accounts receivable aging. This report will allow you to track unpaid invoices and attempt collection.

Accounts Payable

Quicken can help you manage your accounts payable by tracking amounts owed and dates due. If you buy from vendors who give a discount for timely payment, you can ensure that you pay within this time period.

You will not need a separate account for accounts payable; you can enter the transaction directly into your checking account. You will record these payables when you receive the supplier's invoice but use the due date in the Date field. The other secret is using an * in the Num field and the invoice number in the Memo field.

Since you are recording the payable transaction before the check is written, Quicken handles it as a postdated check. The current balance will not show the effect of the entry although the ending balance will.

Use Quicken's Transaction report with headings by week to see which invoices will come due each week. When you make the payment, record the check number in the Num field and finalize the transaction.

 # Job Order Costing

The objective of a job order costing system is to record the income and costs of jobs over the time services are performed. The secret to getting it set up correctly is to create a class for each job that you must track. When you incur expenses that must be allocated to several jobs, use the split transaction to allocate the costs among the jobs and use the classes that you created within the split transaction. Likewise, income is recorded with the classes you created for each job.

You can use Quicken's Job/Project business report to summarize income and expense by job. The date range for the report should begin with the current date and encompass the due date range that you want to review. You will want to use a filter with ~Opening.. in the Payee field to exclude the opening balance from the report.

C

APPENDIX

CUSTOMIZING QUICKEN

Quicken allows you to customize many features, changing settings to affect the way that Quicken works and how it appears. By customizing Quicken to suit how you use the application, you will make your work with Quicken more productive.

To use Quicken's customization features, select Preferences from the Edit menu, opening the Preferences dialog box. You can select any of the twelve buttons in this dialog box to open dialog boxes in which you can set different preference options.

The twelve buttons found in this dialog box are: General, Checks, Reports, QuickFill, Billminder, Modem, Iconbar, Graphs, Qcards, Desktop, Fonts, and Colors. In this appendix, an explanation of the Preferences options is presented. Details for how to change the Iconbar are also given.

General Preferences

These preferences let you change how Quicken works in some general ways.

✦ Request Confirmation

When this check box is selected, Quicken prompts for confirmation before recording a changed transaction.

✦ Use Quicken's Custom Colors

When this check box is selected, Quicken uses a gray background in all windows, regardless of the color setting in Windows.

✦ Color Shading in Register

When this check box is selected, Quicken uses colors in the register to make each transaction visually separate.

✦ Enter Key Moves Between Fields in Register and Write Checks

When this check box is selected, pressing [Enter] moves the cursor between fields, instead of recording the transaction.

✦ Confirm Investment Transactions from Forms

When this check box is selected, Quicken prompts you to confirm transactions entered in an investment form before recording them in the register.

✦ Save Price History in DOS Quicken Form

When this check box is selected, Quicken saves price histories for securities in the format used for Quicken for DOS.

✦ Beep When Recording and Memorizing

When this check box is selected, Quicken beeps when you record a transaction or memorize a transaction or report.

✦ Warn Before Recording Uncategorized Transactions

When this check box is selected, Quicken warns you when you attempt to record a transaction which is not assigned a category.

✦ Use Tax Schedules with Categories

When this check box is selected, you can assign categories to lines of tax schedules, so that you can easily create reports that will be helpful when filling those forms out.

◆ Date Style

You can select either the <u>M</u>M/DD/YY or <u>D</u>D/MM/YY option buttons to determine the format used for dates in Quicken. The first is standard in the United States, while the second is standard in Canada and European countries.

Check Preferences

These preferences let you change the appearance of the checks you create in Quicken.

◆ Printed Date Style

Select one of the four date style buttons to choose how dates will be printed on your checks.

◆ Allow <u>E</u>ntry of Extra Messages on Checks

When this check box is selected, an extra field appears on checks in which you can enter short messages.

◆ <u>P</u>rint Categories on Voucher Checks

When this check box is selected, categories assigned to the transaction are printed on voucher checks.

◆ <u>W</u>arn if a Check Number is Re-used

When this check box is selected, Quicken warns you when you attempt to print a check with the same number as one printed previously.

◆ <u>C</u>hange Date of Checks to Date When Printed

When this check box is selected, checks are printed with the date they are printed, not the date you originally entered the check into Quicken.

Reports Preferences

These preferences let you change the appearance of your reports and set defaults to make report creation faster.

◆ Account Display

Select one of the three option buttons to set how account names are displayed in reports. You can display the account name, the account description, or both.

D

✦ Category Display

Select one of the three option buttons to set how categories are displayed in reports. You can display the category name, the category description, or both.

✦ Report Date Range

Set the default time period used for your reports by selecting a time period from this drop-down list box, or by entering specific dates in the two text boxes.

✦ Comparison Report Date Range

Set the default second time period used in comparison reports by selecting a time period from this drop-down list box, or by entering specific dates in the two text boxes.

✦ Skip Create Report Prompt

Select this check box to have Quicken create reports without first displaying the Create Report dialog box.

✦ QuickZoom to Investment Forms

Select this check box to have Quicken display an investment form rather than a transaction in an investment register when you use QuickZoom in an investment report.

✦ Use Color in Report

When this check box is selected, Quicken displays negative amounts and report headings in color on the screen.

QuickFill Preferences

These preferences let you change how the QuickFill feature works.

✦ Automatic Memorization of New Transactions

When this check box is selected, Quicken automatically adds all newly recorded transactions to the Memorized Transactions list.

✦ Automatic Completion as You Type an Entry

When this check box is selected, Quicken automatically completes entries as you type based on the QuickFill information.

✦ Automatic Recall When Tabbing Out of Payee Field

When this check box is selected, Quicken automatically fills in the remaining fields in a transaction when you use Tab to leave the payee field, and your payee field entry has a match in QuickFill.

D

✦ <u>D</u>rop Down Lists Automatically

When this check box is selected, Quicken automatically displays the drop-down list in a QuickFill field when you move the cursor to the field.

✦ <u>B</u>uttons in QuickFill Fields

When this check box is selected, Quicken displays arrows for activating drop-down lists in fields that can be filled using QuickFill.

Billminder Preferences

These preferences let you change how Quicken reminds you of upcoming transactions.

✦ <u>T</u>urn on Billminder

Select this check box to activate the Billminder feature.

✦ Days in advance

When you want an advance reminder of upcoming transactions, enter in this text box the number of days in advance you want the reminder to first appear.

✦ <u>R</u>eminder Messages on Startup

When this check box is selected, Quicken displays a special reminder box for upcoming transactions when you first start Windows.

Modem Preferences

These preferences let you set up Quicken for use with your modem.

✦ Dial Type

Select the option button for the type of phone you will use, <u>T</u>one or <u>P</u>ulse.

✦ P<u>o</u>rt

Select the port your modem is connected to in this drop-down list box.

✦ <u>S</u>peed

Select the speed at which your modem can exchange information from this drop-down list box.

✦ <u>C</u>ompuServe Local Access Number

Enter the local number for accessing CompuServe in this text box. You can use CompuServe for accessing the CheckFree and IntelliCharge services.

✦ <u>I</u>nitialization String

Enter any initialization string required by your modem in this text box.

Iconbar Preferences

The Iconbar provides shortcuts for carrying out various Quicken activities. You can either use the default Quicken Iconbar or you can customize the Iconbar to suit yourself. You can change the appearance of the current Iconbar, add new icons, or delete or edit existing ones. The Iconbar stays the same as you open or close files.

Changing the Iconbar's Appearance

Each icon that appears on the Iconbar has two visual elements. One is the picture that represents the action, and the second is the word that appears below this icon. You can customize the Iconbar so that it displays both the graphic image and the text, only the text, only the graphic image, or neither of them. To change the appearance of the Iconbar, follow these steps:

1. Select the Iconbar icon or select <u>P</u>references from the <u>E</u>dit menu, then select <u>I</u>conbar, opening the Customize Iconbar dialog box, shown here:

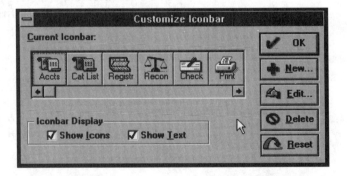

2. Select the Show <u>I</u>cons check box to display the graphic images, or clear it to remove them. The change in the Iconbar will appear as soon as you select or clear this check box, before you select OK to exit the dialog box.

3. Select the Show <u>T</u>ext check box to display the text, or clear it to remove the text. Again, the change in the Iconbar appears immediately.

4. Select OK to exit the dialog box.

Deleting an Icon

You can remove icons from the Iconbar, either to make room for icons more useful to you, or to trim the Iconbar down to those icons you use consistently. Follow these steps to delete an icon from the Iconbar:

1. Select the Iconbar icon or select <u>P</u>references from the <u>E</u>dit menu, then select <u>I</u>conbar, opening the Customize Iconbar dialog box.
2. Highlight the icon in the <u>C</u>urrent Iconbar list box of icons.
3. Select <u>D</u>elete.
4. Select OK to confirm that you want to delete the icon.

Adding or Editing an Icon

D

When you add a new icon, you can select the activity that the icon represents, the graphic image and the text that appear on the icon, and a speed key combination that selects the icon from the keyboard. When you edit an icon, you can change any of these properties of the icon.

To add or edit an icon, follow these steps:

1. Select the Iconbar icon or select <u>P</u>references from the <u>E</u>dit menu, then select <u>I</u>conbar, opening the Customize Iconbar dialog box.
2. Select <u>N</u>ew to add an icon or <u>E</u>dit to edit the one currently highlighted in the <u>C</u>urrent Iconbar list box of icons.
3. Select the action you want the icon to carry out in the Icon <u>A</u>ction list box.

   When you select an action, the icon that appears in the lower-right corner of the dialog box will change to match the action you have selected.
4. To change the appearance of the icon or to assign a speed key, select Chang<u>e</u>, opening the Change Iconbar Item dialog box.
5. Select a graphic image in the <u>G</u>raphic list box of images.
6. Type the text to use with the icon in the <u>I</u>con Text text box.
7. Enter a key such as **a** or **d** in the <u>S</u>peed Key text box if you want to be able to activate the icon with a key combination. You will press (Alt), (Shift), and the key you enter together to activate the icon. For example, if you used **a**, you would press (Alt)-(Shift)-(A).
8. When you have finished making these changes, select OK twice to return to the Customize Iconbar dialog box. Then select OK to close this dialog box.

When you assign some actions to an icon, you do not provide all the information that icon needs to have in order to work. The first time you select that button, another dialog box will appear, requiring further information, such as the account to use.

Graph Preferences

These preferences let you change how graphs are displayed and printed in Quicken.

✦ Display Patterns on Screen

When this check box is selected, Quicken uses patterns of black and white instead of solid colors in the graphs displayed on your screen.

✦ Create All Graphs in Separate Windows

When this check box is selected, each graph appears in a separate window, instead of sharing a window with another graph.

✦ Draw in 2D

When this check box is selected, graphs are displayed and printed without using the three-dimensional enhancements.

Qcard Preferences

These preferences let you turn on or off the Qcards which can guide you through some Quicken tasks.

✦ Qcards Off

Selecting this button turns all Qcards off, so they do not appear.

✦ Qcards On

Selecting this button turns all Qcards on, so they do appear.

Saving the Desktop Arrangement

These preferences let you save the arrangement of windows so you can return to the same place each time you start Quicken.

✦ Save Current

Select this button to save the current desktop arrangement to a file.

◆ Save Desktop on Exit

> Select this check box to have Quicken save the arrangement of all open windows each time you exit, so that the exact same display is shown when you restart Quicken.

Choosing the Register Font

You can use these preferences to select how your register entries are displayed on the screen.

D

◆ Font

> Select the typeface for the register font from this list box.

◆ Size

> Select the size of the register font from this list box.

◆ Bold

> Select this check box to have the register font boldfaced.

◆ Default

> Select this button to return to the default font for the register.

Choosing the Register Colors

You can use these preferences to select the colors used in the transactions in your registers' screen displays.

◆ Account Type

> Select the type of account you want to change the colors for in this list box.

◆ Color

> Select the color you want to use with the selected account type from this list box.

◆ Default

> Select this button to have all register colors return to the default.

APPENDIX

E

TRANSFERRING DATA TO AND FROM QUICKEN FOR WINDOWS

Once you enter data into any program, you will want the flexibility to use it wherever you need it. You may want to use your Quicken data with other programs or in a different way within Quicken. You may be especially interested in using your Quicken data with other programs since it represents a complete personal or business financial history. You have already seen some ways that you can interchange data between Quicken and other programs. In Chapter 5, you learned how you can transfer data to and from the CheckFree electronic payment service once you install the electronic payment option for Quicken. In Chapter 9, you learned how to download stock prices from the Prodigy Service to update your portfolio prices in Quicken investment accounts. There are other data transfer opportunities. You can use the Windows Clipboard to transfer Quicken data to other applications. You can also transfer data from a Quicken report to another program if you write the report to an ASCII file rather than sending it to a printer. You can use Quicken's data export feature to write data in a proprietary .QIF format. This special format allows you to create Quicken transactions and lists from data in any program that can write a .QIF file. The .QIF format also allows you to export Quicken data in one file to another Quicken file.

This appendix also includes a short discussion of QuickPay in the event that you are using Quicken for business and want to use the QuickPay product to save you time with your payroll.

Transferring Data from Quicken to Other Programs

There are three basic ways to transfer data to other programs: copying report data to the Windows Clipboard and from there to another application, writing a report to an ASCII file, and exporting Quicken data to a file in a proprietary Intuit format. The Windows Clipboard transfers all of the data in your report but not the report headings. It is an easy option to use since you can quickly paste the Clipboard data into other Windows applications such as Quattro Pro for Windows, Excel, or WordPerfect for Windows. You can use an ASCII format when you have the category, class list, or securities list displayed to write it to a disk rather than print it on your printer. Using the ASCII option with a report retains the heading information in the report but requires you to retrieve the ASCII file from the other program. The fact that the data is written to a file gives you a permanent copy of it on disk if you want to transfer it to several locations. Exporting data to the .QIF file allows you to transfer Quicken data to use in another Quicken file. In addition to transactions, you can export class lists and memorized transactions to a file like this. The .QIF file option permits you to transfer more of the detail than the other two options. Quicken's import feature will accept this format. You can obtain a precise specification of the .QIF format from Intuit if you want to write a program to place data stored in another program into this format so you can import it into Quicken. Since the Windows Clipboard, the .QIF format, and the standard ASCII options are useful under different circumstances, you will want to know how to use each of them. Let's take a look at the options for using the Windows Clipboard first. Then you can examine ASCII files and the many variations possible. The last part of this discussion will cover a special option for writing ASCII data to a .TXF file if you want to transfer data to TurboTax.

Using the Windows Clipboard to Transfer Report Data

If you have been using Windows for a while, you have probably already mastered the use of the Clipboard. If you haven't, trying it with Quicken will convince you how easy it is to work with. You can copy the data for any Quicken report to this Clipboard using the Copy button in the report buttonbar. Since the Clipboard does not display automatically, you will have to trust that it is there and switch to your other program. You can then use the Edit Paste option in the other program to paste the data into your other application. Once you have a report on your screen, the exact steps you need to follow to copy the report data to Windows Write (a word processor distributed with Windows) follow:

1. With a report displayed like the one as shown in Figure E-1, select the Copy button.

2. Activate the other program.

3. Move to the location in your document where you want to place the Quicken data.

   You can be in a spreadsheet, a word processing document, or a note field in a database.

4. Choose Paste from the Edit menu.

   The data is added to the document just as the data shown in Figure E-1 was added to the Write document in Figure E-2.

Printing Reports or Lists to an ASCII File

Any report that you create from Quicken can be printed to an ASCII file on disk rather than sent to a printer. If you are not familiar with the term ASCII, there is really no cause for concern. An *ASCII file* is nothing more than the text that appears on your reports without any of the printer codes that tell your printer how to display the data on the printed page. The ASCII format is accepted by almost all programs, making this data format almost universally acceptable as a way to transfer data on Quicken reports to other programs. You can transfer ASCII data to a word processor, then enhance it

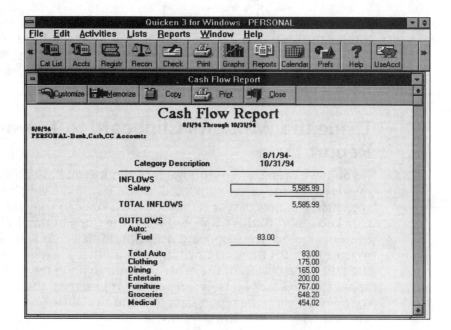

Report data to
be copied via
the Windows
Clipboard
Figure E-1.

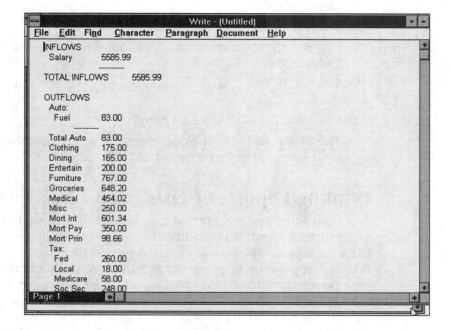

Pasting the
data that you
copied to a
manuscript file
Figure E-2.

with additional formatting options such as font changes or type style options such as boldface or underlining. You can even add your own logo or other graphic images to these reports, then print them from your word processor with the enhancements added. You may also want to transfer ASCII data to a spreadsheet package such as 1-2-3 or Quattro Pro to conduct additional data analysis. Since these other packages all support macros, once you work out the procedure for bringing Quicken data in, you can save it as a macro and run the macro whenever you want. The advantages of ASCII over the Clipboard are that it works with lists such as the class list, creates a permanent record on disk, and retains the report heading information.

Creating an ASCII File from Reports and Lists

To create an ASCII file for any report, you must first create the report that you want with any customizing changes. Next, you will select the Print button from the buttonbar. When the Print Report dialog box appears, select ASCII Disk File and select the Print button. The Create Disk File dialog box displays to allow you to enter the filename in the File Name text box. When you select OK, the file is written to disk.

Lists such as classes and securities can be printed to an ASCII file. After displaying the list, choose Print List from the File menu. Just as when you printed a report to a disk file, you need to specify that you want to use an ASCII file, then complete the filename in the second dialog box that displays. You can use lists to reference entries you have in your custom Quicken lists or transfer them to another program.

Using the ASCII File with a Word Processing Program

Most of the latest word processing programs have all kinds of desktop publishing features built into them. Depending on your word processing program and printer, you can use many options to dress up one of the financial reports or lists created with Quicken to a quality that could be used in any annual report. Figure E-3 shows a report that was shown earlier in the book in Chapter 9. In the earlier version a simple net worth report was created without changes. A few simple changes were made to this report with WordPerfect for Windows by altering the font (character style) and adding other enhancements such as the Money Bags graphic image as a watermark behind the text. Although you can change the font from within Quicken, WordPerfect has desktop publishing features beyond font changes that give you more flexibility in report appearance. Most popular word processors have graphic images included in their package. You can also buy other images in clip art collections. The image shown was obtained from a clip art library marketed by Presentation Task Force.

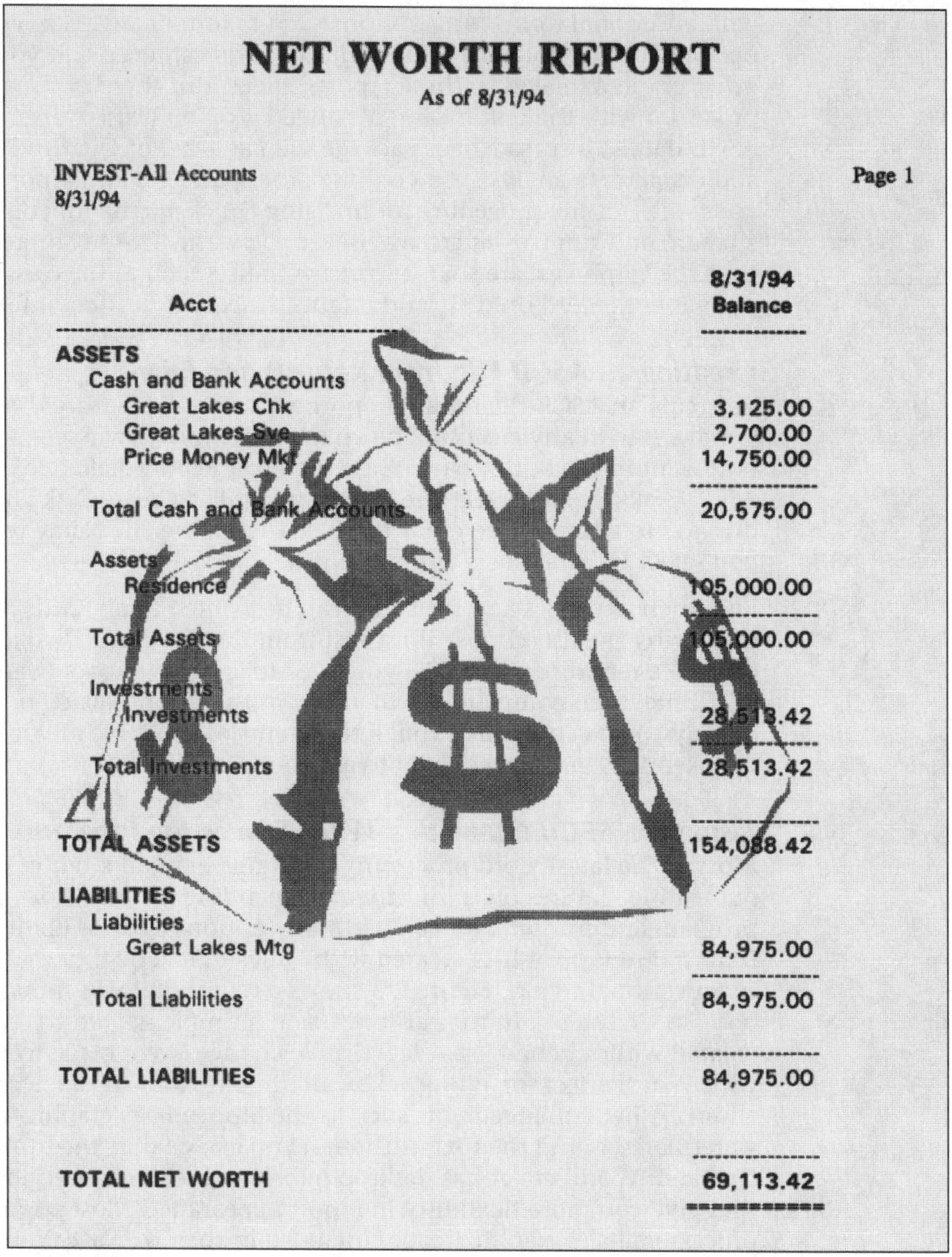

NET WORTH REPORT

As of 8/31/94

INVEST-All Accounts
8/31/94

Page 1

Acct	8/31/94 Balance
ASSETS	
Cash and Bank Accounts	
Great Lakes Chk	3,125.00
Great Lakes Sve	2,700.00
Price Money Mkt	14,750.00
Total Cash and Bank Accounts	20,575.00
Assets	
Residence	105,000.00
Total Assets	105,000.00
Investments	
Investments	28,513.42
Total Investments	28,513.42
TOTAL ASSETS	154,088.42
LIABILITIES	
Liabilities	
Great Lakes Mtg	84,975.00
Total Liabilities	84,975.00
TOTAL LIABILITIES	84,975.00
TOTAL NET WORTH	69,113.42

Quicken report enhanced with a word processing program
Figure E-3.

CAUTION: Data in these ASCII files have spaces separating them. You might want to stay with a monospace font rather than a proportional font when you take your data into a word processor. If you use a proportional font, you will need to remove spaces and insert tabs to get the numbers in columns to line up properly.

The exact method for bringing an ASCII file into a word processing program varies from product to product. Your word processing package might require you to take a special action to retrieve an ASCII file, or it might use the same procedure that works with a regular document file in the package.

Using an ASCII File with a Spreadsheet Program

You might want to bring Quicken data into a spreadsheet package in order to perform additional computations such as ratio analysis. Computations such as current ratio and other common financial ratios can be made if you are using Quicken with your business data. Another reason for using a spreadsheet might be to spruce up a report if you are more familiar with the desktop publishing features in your spreadsheet than you are with those in your word processing package.

All of the popular spreadsheet programs like Quattro Pro and 1-2-3 can accept ASCII data. With most of these programs ASCII data is accepted into the package with each line of the file placed in a single spreadsheet cell. You would need to use the parsing features of the package to split the one long label entry into component parts so that each field in the line is placed in a cell. You will need to start the parsing at the first line of data, or the parsing will follow the pattern established for the report or row headings and record the numbers as labels.

NOTE: In addition to the ASCII format you can choose to write your report to a 1-2-3 .PRN file. You may find that this format is easier to import into your spreadsheet program. Remember, if you prefer you can always use the copy and paste option that the Windows Clipboard provides.

Transferring Quicken Data to TurboTax

TurboTax is one of the leading tax programs available. Although the version that will support the preparation of your 1993 returns was not available at the time this book was printed, Quicken for Windows has an option that

E

will automate the preparation of the needed file for you. Before you create this file it is important that you have the appropriate categories (that you want Quicken to use when preparing the file) assigned as tax related with tax schedules specified. This is due to the fact that Quicken uses its Tax Schedule reports when it prepares the TurboTax .TXF file for you. To create the file all you really need to do is create a tax schedule or capital gains report. Next, select the Export button from the buttonbar. Then, you will need to complete the Create Tax Export File dialog box. You are asked to specify a filename which should be provided without a filename extension since a .TXF extension is automatically added. As with other filenames you are limited to any one-to-eight character filename acceptable to DOS.

Bringing Data from Other Programs into Quicken

Quicken will only accept data in an ASCII .QIF format file. The *.QIF format* was developed by Intuit and stores less data in each line of the file than when a report is printed to an ASCII file. Since Quicken can only read a .QIF format, other programs must write their data in Quicken's .QIF format or Quicken must have a special menu option for converting the data. Quicken is specifically designed to handle IntelliCharge, and Prodigy data through menu selections. The procedures for using data from these sources are discussed in the chapters where these features are covered.

The .QIF format adds a unique letter at the beginning of the data for each field to tell Quicken what data the field is for. Special headers are used to indicate the account for the transactions that follow, as well as other identifying information.

NOTE: Quicken does not support importing and exporting securities data, except the prices that you can update through Prodigy or the Quicken Companion option discussed in Appendix F.

Transferring Quicken Data from One Quicken File or Account to Another

There may be times when you accidentally enter Quicken data in the wrong account. You may want to transfer data to another Quicken file so that you can reuse your category and class list with new data. You may also want to change the account type after entering data and find that there is no menu option to do this. Whatever your reason for wanting to transfer data from one Quicken location to another, you will want to select Export from the File menu. You will need to choose Import from the File menu to bring the data into a Quicken file. Quicken uses the ASCII .QIF format when exporting or importing data. The only data that you cannot use in this way is your securities data. If you are working from the budget window you can save budget numbers and reload them into the same or a different file. You cannot save anything other than the budget amounts since budget categories cannot be changed in this way.

Export and Import Options

You have quite a bit of control over the type and amount of data that Quicken exports when you select Export from the File menu. After selecting the command and specifying the filename, you need to choose the dates for the transactions to be exported and which account's data to export. Next, you can decide whether or not to export transactions at all since in some instances you might just want to transfer categories from one file to another. You can select whether or not to export categories and classes. When you choose whether or not to export memorized transactions, the determination as to whether investment or non-investment transactions are exported is dictated by the account that is currently open. All of the selections for the type of data to export are made by selecting the appropriate check boxes to mark them.

When you are ready to import your data into a different account or file, that account or file should be open. If you are just trying to change the type of account, you would create a new account of the desired type and import the data from the other account which you already exported. After choosing Import from the File menu, the first step will be to specify the filename. If you are importing CheckFree data, the filename can be the name of a directory. If you are importing data formerly exported from a number of accounts, you will need to protect yourself against duplicates. In either situation make sure the check box for Special handling for transfers is checked. Before importing the data, you also need to select whether or not to import categories and classes, accounts, and memorized transactions. Each of these options is specified with a check box.

Budget Save and Reload

If you have created a budget that you want to save for use with another file, or would like to save your work in order to explore what-if options and then be able to restore your current projections, you can click Save in the buttonbar. When you are ready to restore numbers from the saved file, you will need to select Restore from the buttonbar.

You can also transfer your budget data to a spreadsheet if you like via the Windows Clipboard. Doing so, you can then use your budget as the basis for various what-if type analyses, letting you use the sophisticated spreadsheet features to help you determine the best way to spend your money.

NOTE: Once you build up a transaction base, the easiest way to put together accurate budget projections is to base the budget on historical data. Quicken can actually build budget projections for you on this basis.

Using Quicken with QuickPay

QuickPay is another program marketed by Intuit that can provide just the solution you are looking for if you are doing payroll with Quicken. The program integrates seamlessly with Quicken, making data transfer unnecessary. Also, the needed tax information is automatically provided for you for the federal, state, and local taxes, as well as other deductions and contributions such as Medicare and FICA. QuickPay has many additional features that provide a full range of options for payroll deductions.

NOTE: If you have been using Quicken to do your payroll without QuickPay, you will want to check to be certain that you are using the correct account names for all of the payroll accounts.

APPENDIX

F

USING QUICKEN COMPANION 2 FOR WINDOWS

Quicken Companion 2 for Windows is an auxiliary product that extends the features of Quicken 3 for Windows. It is marketed by Intuit, the developers of Quicken, and integrates seamlessly with the product.

Quicken Companion provides a home inventory feature, a stock quote retrieval capability (using a hotline number or your CompuServe account), and a tax estimator. Each of the features are accessible from the Quicken Activities menu once you have installed Quicken Companion.

New Features in Quicken Companion for Windows

Although the first version of Quicken Companion provided some stock price retrieval capabilities, as well as a tax estimator, the home inventory module is new to the latest release. The new home inventory module allows you to keep track of all of your possessions with a minimal investment of time. These records can be invaluable in the event of an insurance claim and are also needed as an attachment to your will.

The Quicken Tax Estimator module of the Companion has been updated for 1993-94. Because of the many pending changes in the tax law, you will have access to a tax hotline for dealing with changes as they occur. You can also use your Quicken data to create your estimates or annualize the Quicken numbers to simulate a full year of data.

The Quicken Quotes module has been updated to support mutual funds and options as well as stocks. It is also possible to get additional information on stocks such as high/low prices, trading volume, and the change since the last closing price. Multiple ticker symbol lists can also be maintained to allow you to update some stocks monthly and others on a weekly basis.

Installing Quicken Companion

Installing Quicken Companion is easy if you have the program and 2MB of free space on your hard disk. All you need to do is start Windows, put the Companion disk in your drive and choose Run from the Program Manager's File menu. Type **A:INSTALL** in the command line and click OK. You can change any of the Install settings, then click OK again.

Once the installation is complete, icons for each module of the Companion are added to the Quicken program group. You can click these icons to start a module or start Quicken and select any of the options from the Quicken 3 for Windows Activities menu, shown in Figure F-1.

Quicken Companion's Home Inventory

The Home Inventory module in Quicken Companion can be used to create and maintain a complete home or business inventory with a minimal investment of time. Even users who maintain adequate financial records frequently fail to inventory their possessions. These records can be important to make certain that you have adequate insurance coverage since

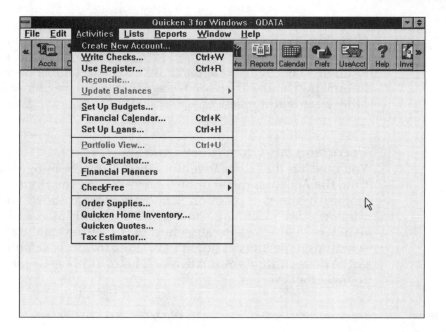

Activities
menu after
installing
Quicken
Companion 2
for Windows
Figure F-1.

many people are not fully aware of the total value of their possessions.
Inventory records are also useful in making insurance claims in the event of
loss due to theft, fire, or flood. A property inventory is also useful as an
attachment to your will.

Although you can maintain manual records, the total property inventory
numbers would not be included in your net worth computations with
Quicken. If you use Quicken Companion to record this information, you will
be able to automatically include it on the net worth reports that you create
with Quicken. Using Quicken to record your inventory is also much easier
than recording it manually. You can select common items and locations
from Quicken and minimize typing. Once entered, it is easy to sort your
inventory as well as to update the replacement cost or resale value of any item.

Entering a Basic Inventory

Although it has always been possible to enter inventory information in
Quicken through the use of asset accounts, the process is too time
consuming to interest many people. Also, there is no easy way to record
replacement cost and resale value for property items. All of these options can
be handled easily with Quicken Companion for Windows. As you record
each inventory item or possession, Quicken Companion can do much of the
work for you. Many of the needed entries can be made via simple list

selections. It is also easy to select the level of detail that you are interested in recording. As an example, you might want to record a quick list of each possession then go back later and record additional details to fill in the location where items were purchased, a serial number or other identifying information, and warranty coverage that you have on camera equipment or other electronic appliances.

Recording Basic Inventory Data

You can start the Home Inventory module by choosing Home Inventory from the Activities menu or by double-clicking the Home Inventory icon. A Home Inventory Application window appears as shown in Figure F-2. This window already contains some entries for furnishings and electronics in the living room location. Because most of the entries can be made with list selections or defaults, it doesn't take long to complete an inventory of an entire house. Intuit's estimate is one hour, although it took me a little longer to inventory everything.

NOTE: If you want to create an inventory for your business you will need to customize the locations and categories as discussed in "Customizing the Inventory Module," later in this section.

Quicken
Companion
Home
Inventory
window
Figure F-2.

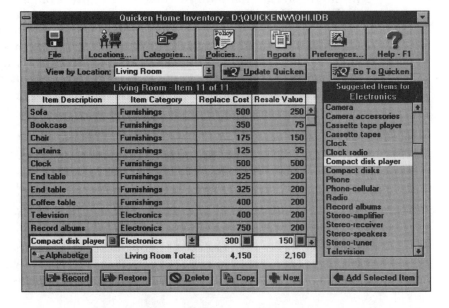

You will want to enter your inventory by location (building or room) and category (type of item) to speed up the entry process. Follow these steps to add an inventory item:

1. Select a location to inventory.

   Quicken Companion provides options for attic, basement, two baths, living room, dining room, clothes closets, garage, office/study, three bedrooms, and other locations.

2. Select a category.

   Some of your options are furnishings, clothing, appliances, electronics, hobbies and crafts, vehicles, linens, jewelry and valuables, and office equipment.

3. Select an item from the suggestions list for the category or type your own description, then add or change the replacement and resale values.

4. Repeat step 3 until you have entered all the items for the location.

   You might need to use several different categories to make it easy to complete the inventory for the location.

5. Choose a new location and continue entering items until you have completed your inventory.

6. Print a report and check to see if you have missed any items.

Adding More Detail to Selected Items

You can provide additional detail for any inventory item. You can add the location where the item was purchased, its original cost, a make and model number, a serial number, the insurance policy that covers the item, the purchase date, and notes. Once you activate the detail display you can use the Next Item and Prev Item buttons in the detail display to page through the detail for all inventory items. The detail display can be activated by selecting an inventory item and clicking the detail button to the right of the item. Your screen might look something like Figure F-3 after you have made a few entries in the detail display.

Creating Inventory Reports

Once you enter your inventory data, creating reports is easy. The appearance of the reports will depend on how much detail you have entered for inventory items. To create a report click the Reports button then select the desired report. Figure F-4 shows an Inventory Value Report to provide a quick look at the first entries for the living room. You can see from the Inventory Detail Report in Figure F-5 that you can look at much more detail if you need it.

F

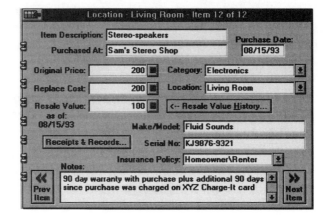

NOTE: You can create a custom Inventory Detail Report or Insurance Claim Report. You can select the items you want to appear in the report after clicking Select Items. After you select Done, the report is created with the selected items.

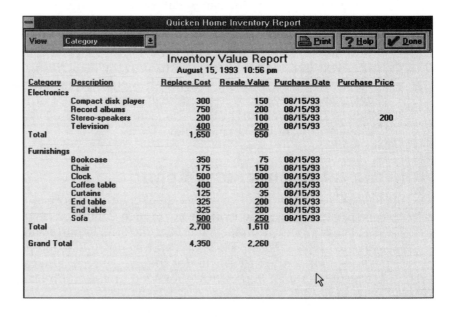

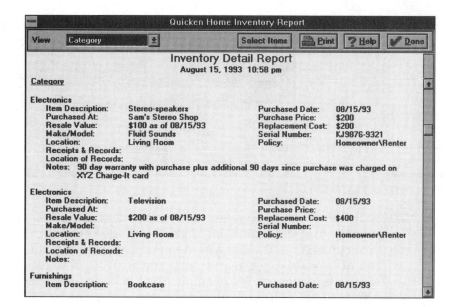

Customizing the Inventory Module

F

You will want to look at the customizing options for Quicken Companion. There may be changes that you can make so that the program better meets your needs. You can customize the entries in categories and lists as well as the preference settings.

Customizing Entries in Locations and Categories

You can add or edit locations to tailor the inventory module for your home or business use. You can also change the names of categories, although you cannot change the preset list of items within a category. This means that you will need to type the name of each inventory item as you enter it rather than being able to select the items from a list. This is appropriate when you need to add a category such as antiques since each item will probably be unique anyway. If you are attempting to use the inventory module for business, these changes may be adequate if you are a service business without a significant amount of specialized equipment.

To add or edit a location, click the Location button. When the Location dialog box displays, you can click New and complete a new location name, then select OK. To change an existing location, highlight the name, then click the Edit button. You might want to use this feature to change bedroom 1 to master bedroom and bedroom 2 to Johnny's Room.

To add or edit a category name, click the Categories button. When the Categories dialog box displays, as shown in Figure F-6, click New to add a

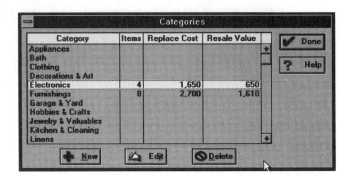

Categories
dialog box
Figure F-6.

new category and complete a name before clicking OK. To change an existing category name, highlight it and then click the Edit button. Make your changes to the category name and then click OK. Changes to category names may be especially useful if you are using the features to record your business inventory. For example, the Kitchen and Cleaning category may be changed to Catering Equipment if you are running a catering business.

Customizing Preference Settings

There are three types of preferences that you can specify. These options affect values assigned to new inventory items, the display and warnings provided, and general preferences that affect all aspects of the product's use. To set any of the preferences, click the Preferences button on your screen to display the dialog box shown in Figure F-7.

Setting Suggested Item List Preferences

There are two different list preferences that you can set:

✦ *Use suggested values for new inventory items* With this option activated, once you select an inventory item from the list, Quicken Companion displays its replacement cost and resale values automatically. If you find that these values are not the ones you typically want to use, you can clear this option.

NOTE: Some of the same protection features that you find in Quicken are built into the inventory module. You can assign a password to your files to protect them from unauthorized access. You can also use the backup features of the product to create a backup copy and store it off-site in the event that you need it for an insurance claim.

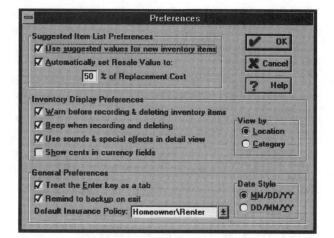

Inventory
Preferences
dialog box
Figure F-7.

✦ *Automatically set Resale Value to* This option allows you to have the replacement cost computed as a percentage of the cost. The default setting is to have this option selected with the percentage set at 50%. If you clear this option, replacement cost will not be computed for you.

Setting Inventory Display Preferences

These preferences might be called "sound and display" preferences since many of them control the sounds that the inventory module can produce. The options are

✦ *Warn before recording and deleting inventory items* This option displays a prompt before recoding and deleting inventory items.

✦ *Beep when recording and deleting* An audible tone is sounded when an item is recorded or deleted.

✦ *Use sounds and special effects in detail view* A sound is heard when you turn a detail page.

✦ *Show cents in currency fields* This option determines whether cents are shown for the amount displayed. If you have an inventory of coins, you might want cents displayed, but if you are only concerned with furnishings, this extra detail is not likely to add meaningful information.

✦ *View by Location or Category* This option determines whether inventory items are displayed by category or location.

Setting General Preferences

The general preference settings affect prompt messages and the action of specific keyboard keys. The general preference options are

+ *Treat the Enter key as tab*   Selecting this option causes the [Enter] key to act like the [Tab] key, moving you from field to field.

+ *Remind to backup on exit*   This option provides a prompt to remind you to back up your files each time you exit.

+ *Default Insurance Policy*   This option allows you to select the default insurance policy for each new inventory item.

+ *Date Style*   You can select from MM/DD/YY or DD/MM/YY.

Using Quicken Quotes

The Quotes module in Quicken Companion makes it easy to update your Quicken stock prices. You do not need to worry about typing in updated stock prices from the *Wall Street Journal*. If you have this package, you can download prices for stocks in your portfolio from CompuServe at one dollar for each minute of connect time. You can start Quicken Quotes from Quicken's Activities menu or from the desktop.

In addition to Quicken Companion you need a modem. You will want to have the highest speed possible, as a 9600-baud modem can receive thirty-two times as many prices in a minute as a 300-baud modem, and the price for connect time is the same with both. The baud rate measures the speed with which data is transmitted and received and higher numbers always represent faster transmission.

You will have a bit of setup work to do before you start. You will need a Quicken investment account that contains information for each of the stocks that you want to track.

Setting Up Your Quicken Investments

If you haven't already established your Quicken investment account you will want to read the section on Investments in Chapter 9. After establishing your investment account, create a securities list that contains each stock that you want to monitor. You will need to use the *ticker symbol* for the stock, which is the abbreviation that appears in the *Wall Street Journal* or *Investor's Daily*. You can list stocks, mutual funds, and options, but it is important that the ticker symbol be correct since this is what the service uses to extract the prices that you want. Quicken Quotes supports stock price updates from the New York and American Stock Exchanges as well as the over-the-counter NASDAQ Exchange.

NOTE: If you download stock prices several times a week you may find it more cost effective to establish your own CompuServe account. The procedure will still be the same except you will use your own CompuServe number rather than the Quicken Quotes 900 Hotline number.

When you start Quicken Quotes, a Quicken Quotes window similar to the one shown in Figure F-8 appears. You can activate this window from the Quicken Activities menu. You can select Get Symbols from Quicken to update the window with your Quicken ticker symbols.

Setting Up Your Modem

You need to establish modem and login entries before you can use Quicken Quotes the first time. When you select the Modem Settings button, the dialog box shown in Figure F-9 will display. You will need to know which port on your system is used for the modem. COM1 is the standard choice, but you may need to check with your computer vendor if you try this and it does not work. You will also need to specify your modem speed, and whether or not you have tone or pulse (rotary) phone service.

Retrieving Quotes

If you create more than one symbol set, make certain you select the one you want to update before retrieving prices (the current symbol set determines which prices are selected). Once you are ready, you can click the Retrieve

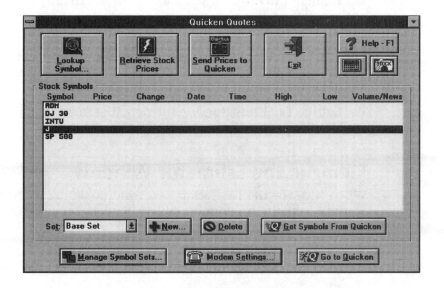

Quicken
Quotes
window
Figure F-8.

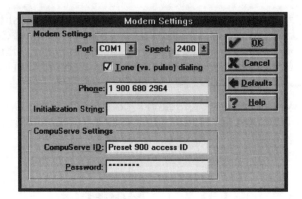

Modem
Settings dialog
box
Figure F-9.

Stock Prices button. You will be able to see the update occur in your Quotes window once the connection is made.

If you start Quotes from Quicken, your Quicken Portfolio updates are automatic. If you start Quotes from the desktop, Quicken is minimized to an icon. You can select Go to Quicken to see your updates there.

Using the Quicken Tax Estimator

In recent years, penalties for underpayment of taxes has increased. The Tax Estimator module can help you prevent underpayments. This is especially valuable if your income fluctuates throughout the year. Also, you can use the Tax Estimator to monitor your tax situation carefully to insure that you are not overpaying. It is also useful since many tax changes are expected in the current year that may be retroactive to the beginning of the year.

The Tax Estimator allows you to explore the tax implications of filing jointly versus separately, or buying a house. This type of tax planning can help you minimize the amount of taxes that you owe.

To start the Tax Estimator, use the Activities menu in Quicken or double-click the Tax Estimator icon on the desktop.

Filling in the Estimator Window

When you start the Tax Estimator a window similar to the one in Figure F-10 appears. Initially this window will be blank but the one shown already has some of the entries completed.

You can fill in the Tax Estimator window on your own using dialog boxes to complete the detail behind many of the entries. The following shows the

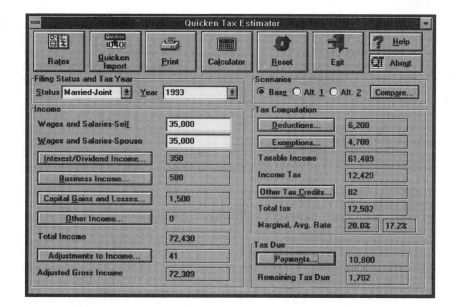

Quicken
Companion
Tax Estimator
window
Figure F-10.

Interest/Dividend Income - Schedule B dialog box that is displayed when the
Interest/Dividend Income button is selected:

Each of the buttons that you see on the Tax Estimator window in Figure F-10
will display another dialog box for more detail. Two additional dialog boxes
for a Schedule C Business Income/Loss and Other Income or Losses are
shown in Figures F-11 and F-12, respectively. All you need to do is fill in the
dialog box blanks and the Tax Estimator will complete the total and place
the correct number in the Tax Estimator window.

Getting and Annualizing Tax Information from Quicken

The Tax Estimator can import data from Quicken 3 for Windows. You can
select the Quicken Import button to bring in your Quicken data. You can

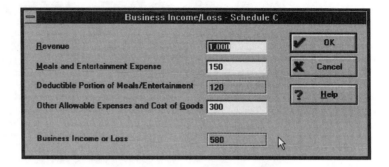

Business
Income/Loss -
Schedule C
dialog box
Figure F-11.

choose to annualize the data if you are not bringing in a full year of data.
The Preview Import button allows you to view the detail data imported from
Quicken. It shows the tax schedule and the Quicken amounts as well as the
Tax Estimator file the data will be used in. This allows you to pinpoint
misclassifications of data in Quicken, if you were to see unusually large
amounts in a field such as medicine and drugs when you had minimal
expenses in this category. When you are finished looking at these numbers
you can click OK to complete your estimate.

NOTE: If you want to project 1994 taxes with 1993 data, set the Year on
the Tax Estimator window to 1993 to do your import, then change it to
1994 to do your estimates.

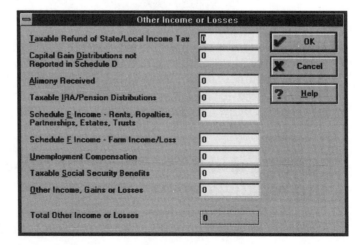

Other Income
or Losses
dialog box
Figure F-12.

Taking Action on Your Findings

Given the data in the estimator window, the results on the Tax Estimator screen tell you if you owe taxes or are due a refund. You can use this information to increase or decrease your withholding. If you need to file estimated tax payments, the Tax Estimator can help you determine the correct amount. You may also want to obtain a copy of IRS publication 505 Estimated Tax Payments for Individuals for more information on when to file these payments.

You can print your tax estimates if you click the Print button. The default Windows printer will be used.

F

INDEX

G

H

I

J

K

L

M